The Complete Histamine I & MCAS Diet Guide

A Science-Based Approach to Managing Symptoms Through Diet, Lifestyle, and Strategic Supplementation with 160+ Healing Recipes

Yvonne Cindy Searle

Table of Contents

ISBN: 978-1-7645190-1-4

First Edition, 2026

MEDICAL DISCLAIMER

The information contained in this book is for educational and informational purposes only and is not intended as medical advice, diagnosis, or treatment. The content represents general information about histamine intolerance and mast cell activation syndrome and should not replace consultation with qualified healthcare professionals. Readers should consult physicians, allergists, immunologists, registered dietitians, or other appropriate healthcare providers before implementing any dietary changes, supplement protocols, lifestyle modifications, or treatment strategies described herein.

Individual responses to dietary interventions, supplements, and medications vary substantially. The protocols, recipes, and recommendations presented reflect current scientific understanding and clinical practice but may not be appropriate for all individuals. Some people may experience adverse reactions to foods, supplements, or strategies described as generally safe. Case studies presented use pseudonyms and represent composite examples drawn from clinical practice patterns rather than specific individuals. Any resemblance to actual persons, living or deceased, or actual events is purely coincidental.

The author and publisher specifically disclaim all responsibility for any liability, loss, or risk, personal or otherwise, incurred as a consequence, directly or indirectly, of the use and application of any contents of this book. Statements regarding dietary supplements, natural products, and alternative therapies have not been evaluated by the Food and Drug Administration and are not intended to diagnose, treat, cure, or prevent any disease. Nutritional and supplement information reflects research available at time of publication and may change as new evidence emerges.

Readers taking prescription medications should not discontinue or modify medication regimens without physician supervision. Some supplements and dietary changes may interact with medications, requiring medical monitoring. Pregnant breastfeeding women should consult healthcare providers before implementing protocols described herein. Children with suspected histamine intolerance or MCAS require pediatric specialist evaluation and should not follow adult protoc without appropriate medical supervision.

This book does not establish a doctor-patient, nutritionist-client, or therapeutic relationship between the author and readers. Emergency medical situations including anaphylaxis, severe allergic reactions, difficulty breathing, or other ac symptoms require immediate emergency medical care through 911 or emergenc services. The emergency protocols described are for informational purposes and not replace emergency medical treatment.

Part 1: The Foundation

Chapter 1.0: Histamine Intolerance and MCAS Fundamentals

Maria had always considered herself healthy. At 42, she exercised regularly, ate what she thought was a nutritious diet, and managed stress reasonably well. But over six months, her body seemed to betray her. Meals that once nourished her now triggered unpredictable reactions. Fresh strawberries caused flushing and heart palpitations. A glass of wine at dinner brought crushing migraines. Leftover chicken from yesterday's meal resulted in digestive distress and brain fog. Her doctor ran standard allergy tests, which came back negative. "Maybe it's stress," he suggested. But Maria knew something deeper was wrong. What she didn't know was that her symptoms pointed to histamine intolerance, a condition affecting approximately 1-3% of the population that remains widely misunderstood and underdiagnosed (Maintz & Novak, 2007).

This chapter establishes the foundational knowledge you need to understand histamine intolerance and Mast Cell Activation Syndrome (MCAS). You will learn what histamine is and why it matters, how the body normally regulates histamine through the DAO enzyme system, what happens when this system fails, and how MCAS overlaps with histamine intolerance. We will explore diagnostic criteria, prevalence data, risk factors, and the mechanisms underlying these interconnected conditions. This foundation makes everything else in this book possible.

1.1 Histamine's Essential Biological Functions

Histamine is a biogenic amine that serves as a critical signaling molecule throughout the human body. This small but powerful compound participates in numerous physiological processes essential for survival and health (Maintz & Novak, 2007). Understanding histamine's normal functions illuminates why excess histamine creates such widespread, multi-system symptoms.

The body produces histamine from the amino acid histidine through the action of the enzyme histidine decarboxylase. Once formed, histamine is stored primarily in mast cells and basophils, two types of immune cells distributed throughout body tissues (Comas-Basté et al., 2020). When these cells receive appropriate signals, they release histamine to perform specific functions.

In the immune system, histamine acts as a first responder to threats. When tissues sustain injury or encounter pathogens, mast cells release histamine to initiate the inflammatory response (Theoharides et al., 2012). This histamine increases blood vessel permeability, allowing immune cells and antibodies to reach affected areas more easily. It also causes blood vessels to dilate, increasing blood flow to bring additional immune resources. These actions explain why inflammation produces redness, warmth, and swelling.

Within the digestive system, histamine plays an indispensable role in stomach acid production. Specialized cells in the stomach lining release histamine, which binds to H2 receptors on parietal cells, triggering hydrochloric acid secretion (Schubert, 2009). This acid breaks down food proteins and creates an inhospitable environment for many pathogens. Without adequate histamine signaling, digestion becomes impaired.

The nervous system relies on histamine as a neurotransmitter. Neurons in the brain's hypothalamus synthesize and release histamine, which regulates the sleep-wake cycle, appetite, body temperature, and various cognitive functions including attention and learning (Haas et al., 2008). This explains why antihistamine medications often cause drowsiness. They block histamine's action in the brain, reducing wakefulness.

Histamine also participates in cardiovascular regulation by affecting blood vessel tone and heart rate. It influences reproductive functions through effects on uterine contractions. The compound even modulates pain perception through interactions with sensory neurons (Leurs et al., 2002).

These diverse functions occur through histamine binding to four distinct receptor types, designated H1 through H4. Each receptor type localizes to different tissues and mediates different effects (Tiligada et al., 2011). H1 receptors predominate in smooth muscle and endothelial cells, mediating allergic responses and inflammation. H2 receptors concentrate in gastric parietal cells and cardiac tissue, controlling acid secretion and heart rate. H3 receptors function primarily in the central nervous system as presynaptic autoreceptors, regulating neurotransmitter release. H4 receptors appear mainly on immune cells, modulating inflammatory responses (Leurs et al., 2009).

This receptor diversity explains histamine's wide-ranging effects and why histamine-related disorders produce such varied symptoms. A problem with histamine regulation does not cause just one type of symptom. Instead, it potentially affects every system where histamine normally functions.

1.2 Understanding Histamine Intolerance Mechanisms

Histamine intolerance represents a state where the body cannot adequately break down and eliminate histamine, leading to accumulation and subsequent symptoms.

This condition differs fundamentally from true allergies, though symptoms may overlap (Comas-Basté et al., 2020).

The primary enzyme responsible for degrading dietary histamine is diamine oxidase (DAO), produced mainly in the small intestinal mucosa (Maintz & Novak, 2007). When functioning properly, DAO breaks down histamine in the gut before it enters systemic circulation. A secondary pathway involves histamine N-methyltransferase (HNMT), which metabolizes histamine primarily within cells throughout the body (Schwelberger, 2010).

Histamine intolerance develops when DAO activity becomes insufficient relative to histamine load. This creates an imbalance. Histamine from food, gut bacteria, and endogenous production exceeds the body's degradative capacity (Comas-Basté et al., 2020). The accumulated histamine then triggers receptor activation throughout the body, producing diverse symptoms.

Several factors reduce DAO activity. Genetic polymorphisms in the DAO gene (AOC1) can decrease enzyme production or function (García-Martín et al., 2007). Intestinal inflammation from conditions like inflammatory bowel disease, celiac disease, or small intestinal bacterial overgrowth (SIBO) damages the intestinal cells that produce DAO (Raithel et al., 2010). Certain medications inhibit DAO activity, including some antibiotics, pain medications, and cardiovascular drugs (Maintz & Novak, 2007).

Increased histamine load also contributes. Gut bacteria can produce substantial histamine from dietary histidine, particularly when dysbiosis allows histamine-producing species to predominate (Sánchez-Pérez et al., 2018). Foods naturally contain varying histamine levels, with aged, fermented, and processed foods generally containing the most (Bodmer et al., 1999). Histamine-liberating foods trigger endogenous histamine release from mast cells even without containing high histamine themselves (Maintz & Novak, 2007).

The threshold concept proves critical for understanding histamine intolerance. Each person has a unique tolerance threshold determined by their DAO capacity, HNMT activity, receptor sensitivity, and total histamine burden (Kohn, 2014). When histamine levels remain below this threshold, no symptoms occur. Once the threshold is exceeded, symptoms appear. This explains why someone might tolerate a food on one occasion but react to it on another. The total histamine load from all sources determines whether the threshold gets crossed.

Research indicates that approximately 1% of the general population experiences histamine intolerance, with prevalence reaching approximately 80% among patients with chronic gastrointestinal complaints (Maintz & Novak, 2007). Women represent approximately 80% of cases, possibly due to hormonal influences on DAO activity (Kohn, 2014). Estrogen appears to inhibit DAO, which may explain why symptoms often worsen during menstruation, pregnancy, or when using hormonal contraceptives (Sattler et al., 1988).

1.3 Mast Cell Activation Syndrome Explained

Mast Cell Activation Syndrome represents a distinct but related condition where mast cells inappropriately activate and release excessive amounts of mediators including histamine, tryptase, prostaglandins, leukotrienes, and other inflammatory compounds (Afrin et al., 2016). Unlike histamine intolerance, which primarily involves impaired histamine breakdown, MCAS centers on excessive histamine and mediator production.

Mast cells are immune cells that normally respond to allergens, pathogens, and tissue damage by releasing stored mediators. In MCAS, these cells become hyperreactive, releasing mediators in response to normally benign triggers or even without apparent provocation (Akin et al., 2010). This inappropriate activation creates widespread symptoms across multiple organ systems.

MCAS differs from systemic mastocytosis, another mast cell disorder. In mastocytosis, genetic mutations cause abnormal mast cell proliferation, resulting in excessive mast cell numbers in tissues (Valent et al., 2012). Bone marrow or tissue biopsies reveal characteristic mast cell infiltration. In contrast, MCAS involves normal mast cell numbers but abnormal activation patterns (Afrin et al., 2016). This distinction matters for diagnosis and treatment approaches.

The diagnostic criteria for MCAS require three elements (Valent et al., 2012). First, patients must exhibit episodic symptoms consistent with mast cell mediator release affecting two or more organ systems. These symptoms include flushing, hives, abdominal pain, diarrhea, nausea, throat swelling, hypotension, tachycardia, wheezing, headache, and neurological symptoms like brain fog.

Second, laboratory evidence must document elevated levels of mast cell mediators during symptomatic episodes. The preferred marker is serum tryptase, measured during symptoms and compared to baseline values (Valent et al., 2012). Tryptase levels should exceed baseline by at least 20% plus 2 ng/mL during reactions. Alternative markers include 24-hour urine histamine metabolites (N-methylhistamine), prostaglandin D2 metabolites, or serum chromogranin A (Afrin et al., 2016).

Third, patients must show symptomatic improvement with antimediator therapy such as H1 and H2 antihistamines, mast cell stabilizers, or leukotriene receptor antagonists (Akin et al., 2010). This therapeutic response requirement distinguishes MCAS from conditions with similar presentations but different underlying mechanisms.

Research indicates MCAS may affect approximately 17% of the general population when using broader diagnostic criteria, though prevalence estimates vary widely depending on diagnostic stringency (Afrin et al., 2016). The condition appears to affect all age groups and shows no clear gender predominance, though some studies suggest slightly higher prevalence in women (Molderings et al., 2011).

1.4 Case Study: Connecting Symptoms to Mechanisms

Background

Apollonia, a 38-year-old accountant, experienced escalating health problems over three years. Initially, she noticed occasional flushing after wine with dinner. Gradually, symptoms expanded to include unpredictable digestive distress, persistent fatigue, and episodes of rapid heartbeat. Multiple medical evaluations found no abnormalities in standard testing. Her primary care physician suggested anxiety, prescribing an SSRI that worsened her symptoms.

Presentation

During specialist evaluation, Apollonia described daily symptoms affecting multiple systems. Gastrointestinal symptoms included postprandial abdominal pain, alternating diarrhea and constipation, and significant bloating. Dermatological manifestations consisted of facial flushing, particularly after meals, periodic hives on her trunk, and generalized itching without visible rash. Cardiovascular symptoms encompassed palpitations, episodes of tachycardia reaching 120-130 bpm at rest, and occasional hypotensive episodes causing dizziness. Neurologically, she experienced frequent headaches, difficulty concentrating, anxiety, and disrupted sleep despite exhaustion.

Food triggers proved difficult to identify. Apollonia reacted to aged cheeses, wine, fermented foods, and leftovers stored more than 24 hours. Fresh foods sometimes caused reactions if combined with other triggers like stress or premenstrual timing. She had eliminated numerous foods but continued experiencing symptoms several times weekly.

Analysis

Apollonia's presentation illustrates the overlap between histamine intolerance and MCAS discussed in sections 1.2 and 1.3. Her multi-system symptoms affecting gastrointestinal, cardiovascular, dermatological, and neurological systems align with excessive histamine effects across all four histamine receptor types. The H1 receptor activation explains her flushing, hives, and itching (Leurs et al., 2002). H2 receptor effects account for gastrointestinal symptoms and some cardiovascular manifestations (Tiligada et al., 2011). H3 receptor involvement correlates with neurological symptoms including brain fog and sleep disturbance (Haas et al., 2008).

The pattern of food triggers suggests both dietary histamine overload and possible mast cell activation. Reactions to high-histamine foods (aged cheese, wine, fermented foods) indicate impaired histamine breakdown consistent with DAO deficiency (Maintz & Novak, 2007). However, reactions to fresh foods and the influence of hormonal and stress factors suggest mast cell hyperreactivity characteristic of MCAS (Afrin et al., 2016).

The temporal variability in Apollonia's reactions demonstrates the threshold concept from section 1.2. On days when hormonal factors, stress, environmental triggers, and dietary histamine converged, her total histamine load exceeded her degradative capacity, triggering symptoms. On better days, she remained below threshold despite some histamine exposure.

Intervention

A comprehensive approach addressed both histamine intolerance and potential MCAS. Apollonia began a strict low-histamine elimination diet, removing all high-histamine foods, histamine liberators, and DAO blockers. She implemented food preparation strategies to minimize histamine formation, including immediate freezing of cooked foods and consuming only freshly prepared proteins.

Medical management included H1 antihistamine (cetirizine 10 mg daily) and H2 blocker (famotidine 20 mg twice daily) to reduce histamine receptor activation. DAO enzyme supplementation before meals supported dietary histamine breakdown. Quercetin 500 mg twice daily and vitamin C 1000 mg daily provided natural mast cell stabilization (Weng et al., 2012). Stress management techniques addressed triggers for mast cell activation.

Outcome

Over 12 weeks, Apollonia experienced significant improvement. Gastrointestinal symptoms decreased in frequency from daily to 2-3 times weekly, with reduced severity. Flushing and hives became rare. Palpitations resolved except during premenstrual periods. Cognitive function improved notably, with better concentration and restored sleep quality. She successfully reintroduced some moderate-histamine foods in small quantities without reactions.

Teaching Points

- Histamine intolerance and MCAS frequently coexist, creating additive symptom burden from both impaired histamine breakdown and excessive mast cell mediator release
- Multi-system symptoms affecting gastrointestinal, cardiovascular, dermatological, and neurological systems strongly suggest histamine-related disorders requiring comprehensive evaluation
- Successful management requires addressing multiple intervention points including dietary histamine reduction, receptor blockade, enzyme supplementation, and mast cell stabilization

1.5 The Critical MCAS and Histamine Intolerance Overlap

The relationship between MCAS and histamine intolerance extends beyond simple coexistence. These conditions interact synergistically, with each potentially triggering or exacerbating the other (Afrin et al., 2016).

Patients with MCAS experience chronic mast cell mediator release, including substantial histamine production. This endogenously produced histamine adds to dietary histamine, increasing total body burden (Molderings et al., 2011). When mast cells chronically release histamine, even patients with normal DAO function may exceed their degradative capacity. The enzyme system becomes overwhelmed by the sheer volume of histamine requiring breakdown.

Conversely, elevated histamine levels from impaired DAO activity can trigger mast cell degranulation. Histamine itself acts as a mast cell activator through positive feedback mechanisms (Maintz & Novak, 2007). When histamine accumulates from poor breakdown, it stimulates further mast cell mediator release, creating a self-perpetuating cycle. This explains why histamine intolerance alone can evolve into a MCAS-like presentation over time.

Intestinal inflammation provides another connection point. MCAS frequently involves gastrointestinal mast cell activation, releasing mediators that damage the intestinal lining (Afrin et al., 2016). This damage impairs the mucosal cells that produce DAO, reducing histamine degradative capacity (Raithel et al., 2010). The resulting histamine accumulation further activates mast cells, worsening intestinal inflammation. This vicious cycle makes distinguishing primary from secondary pathology difficult.

Research indicates that approximately 44% of patients diagnosed with histamine intolerance meet criteria for MCAS when thoroughly evaluated (Molderings et al., 2011). This substantial overlap suggests that many cases diagnosed as histamine intolerance alone actually represent combined pathology requiring broader treatment approaches.

The clinical implication proves significant. Treating histamine intolerance through diet alone may provide incomplete relief if underlying MCAS remains unaddressed. Similarly, treating MCAS without considering dietary histamine load leaves a major trigger unmanaged. Optimal outcomes require recognizing and addressing both conditions simultaneously (Afrin et al., 2016).

1.6 Diagnostic Challenges and Criteria

Diagnosing histamine intolerance and MCAS presents substantial challenges due to lack of standardized, widely available diagnostic tests and symptom overlap with numerous other conditions (Comas-Basté et al., 2020).

For histamine intolerance, no single definitive diagnostic test exists. Serum DAO measurement shows promise but lacks established reference ranges and demonstrates significant variability (Mušič et al., 2013). Some patients with low DAO levels remain asymptomatic, while others with normal levels experience symptoms, suggesting additional factors beyond DAO alone influence histamine tolerance (Kofler et al., 2011).

Plasma histamine measurement proves unreliable due to rapid metabolism and technical challenges in sample handling (Maintz & Novak, 2007). Histamine metabolite measurement in 24-hour urine collections provides better stability but requires careful dietary control before testing and shows substantial individual variability (Schwelberger, 2010).

The most practical diagnostic approach combines clinical assessment, elimination diet trial, and reintroduction challenge (Kohn, 2014). Patients eliminate high-histamine foods for 4 weeks while monitoring symptoms. Significant improvement suggests histamine intolerance. Systematic reintroduction of histamine-containing foods should trigger symptom recurrence if histamine intolerance underlies the presentation. This functional approach provides diagnostic information while initiating treatment.

MCAS diagnosis requires meeting the three criteria described in section 1.3, yet executing these criteria proves challenging in practice (Valent et al., 2012). Obtaining tryptase measurements during acute symptoms requires patient education about timing and access to immediate laboratory services. Many patients experience symptoms unpredictably, making acute measurements difficult to capture.

Baseline tryptase measurement shows more feasibility but demonstrates limitations. Persistently elevated baseline tryptase (>20 ng/mL) suggests mastocytosis rather than MCAS (Akin et al., 2010). Normal baseline tryptase does not exclude MCAS, as many patients maintain normal levels between reactions. The diagnostic criteria require demonstrating elevation during symptoms compared to personal baseline, necessitating at least two measurements.

Alternative mediator measurements include 24-hour urine collection for N-methylhistamine, prostaglandin D2 metabolites (11-beta-PGF2α), or leukotriene E4 (Afrin et al., 2016). These tests provide broader mediator assessment but face similar timing challenges and limited laboratory availability.

The therapeutic trial criterion provides practical diagnostic information. Patients receiving H1 and H2 antihistamines should experience symptom improvement if histamine-mediated mechanisms contribute to their presentation (Valent et al., 2012). Mast cell stabilizers like cromolyn sodium or quercetin may provide additional benefit in MCAS. Response to these interventions supports the diagnosis while providing symptomatic relief.

1.7 Risk Factors and Genetic Considerations

Multiple factors influence susceptibility to histamine intolerance and MCAS, with genetic, acquired, and environmental elements contributing (Comas-Basté et al., 2020).

Genetic polymorphisms in the DAO gene (AOC1) significantly affect enzyme activity. The most studied variants include rs10156191, rs1049742, and rs2268999 (García-Martín et al., 2007). Individuals carrying certain allele combinations show reduced DAO activity, predisposing them to histamine accumulation. These polymorphisms appear more common in Caucasian populations, potentially explaining some ethnic variation in histamine intolerance prevalence (Maintz & Novak, 2007).

HNMT genetic variants also influence histamine metabolism. The Thr105Ile polymorphism reduces HNMT enzyme activity by approximately 40%, impairing intracellular histamine breakdown (Preuss et al., 1998). Combined DAO and HNMT polymorphisms create particularly high risk for histamine-related symptoms.

Female sex represents a clear risk factor, with women comprising 80% of histamine intolerance cases (Kohn, 2014). Hormonal influences explain this gender disparity. Estrogen inhibits DAO activity while progesterone appears neutral or slightly enhancing (Sattler et al., 1988). During high-estrogen states including menstruation, pregnancy, and hormonal contraceptive use, women experience reduced histamine degradation, lowering their tolerance threshold.

Age-related changes affect histamine metabolism. DAO activity generally increases with age in women, possibly explaining why some women experience symptom improvement after menopause (Maintz & Novak, 2007). However, this pattern shows substantial individual variation.

Intestinal health strongly influences DAO production. Conditions causing intestinal inflammation or damage reduce DAO-producing enterocytes (Raithel et al., 2010). Inflammatory bowel disease, celiac disease, and SIBO all correlate with reduced DAO activity and histamine intolerance symptoms. Even temporary intestinal insults like gastroenteritis may trigger histamine intolerance that persists after the acute infection resolves.

For MCAS, genetic factors remain less well characterized. Certain HLA types may increase susceptibility, though research continues (Molderings et al., 2011). Family clustering suggests genetic components, yet specific causative mutations remain largely unknown except in rare familial cases (Akin et al., 2010).

Environmental triggers activate or worsen MCAS. Viral infections can trigger mast cell dysregulation that persists long after viral clearance (Afrin et al., 2016). This phenomenon gained particular recognition with post-acute COVID-19 syndrome, where approximately 17-30% of patients develop MCAS-like presentations (Weinstock et al., 2021). Mold exposure, chronic stress, and toxic exposures also correlate with MCAS development in susceptible individuals.

1.8 Case Study: Genetic and Hormonal Influences

Background

Berenice, a 29-year-old graduate student, developed symptoms after a severe bout of food poisoning during international travel. Before this illness, she tolerated all foods without issue. Post-illness, she experienced progressively worsening reactions to foods she had previously eaten regularly. Her mother mentioned experiencing similar "food sensitivities" that began in her thirties and improved after menopause.

Presentation

Berenice's symptoms showed clear hormonal patterns. During the follicular phase of her menstrual cycle (days 1-14), she tolerated moderate-histamine foods with minimal symptoms. During the luteal phase (days 15-28), even low-histamine foods triggered reactions. Symptoms worsened dramatically in the 3-5 days before menstruation, when she experienced severe migraines, flushing, digestive distress, and anxiety.

The food poisoning incident had required hospitalization and antibiotics. Following recovery, Berenice noticed new sensitivities to aged cheeses, wine, and processed meats. Over six months, the list of reactive foods expanded to include spinach, tomatoes, and leftover proteins. She also developed new sensitivities to fragrances and temperature extremes.

Analysis

Berenice's presentation illustrates multiple risk factors discussed in section 1.7. The maternal history suggests genetic predisposition, possibly involving DAO or HNMT polymorphisms that run in families (García-Martín et al., 2007). Her mother's pattern of symptom onset in her thirties with perimenopausal improvement aligns with estrogen's inhibitory effect on DAO activity (Sattler et al., 1988).

The clear menstrual cycle pattern demonstrates hormonal influence on histamine tolerance. During the follicular phase, lower estrogen levels permitted better DAO function and higher histamine tolerance (Maintz & Novak, 2007). Rising estrogen and progesterone in the luteal phase, particularly premenstrually, reduced DAO activity and lowered her threshold. The same food containing the same histamine amount exceeded her threshold during high-hormone phases but remained tolerable during low-hormone phases.

The triggering gastrointestinal infection exemplifies how acute intestinal damage can precipitate chronic histamine intolerance (Raithel et al., 2010). Severe gastroenteritis damages intestinal mucosa, reducing DAO-producing enterocytes. Antibiotic use may have worsened the situation by altering gut microbiota composition, potentially increasing populations of histamine-producing bacteria (Sánchez-Pérez et al., 2018).

The progressive symptom expansion from high-histamine foods to moderate and low-histamine foods, plus development of non-food triggers, suggests evolution toward MCAS. Initial histamine intolerance from reduced DAO may have triggered mast cell sensitization through chronic histamine elevation, creating the positive feedback loop described in section 1.5.

Intervention

Treatment addressed multiple factors. Berenice began strict low-histamine diet during luteal phase, with some relaxation during follicular phase when tolerance proved higher. She took DAO enzyme supplements before all meals. During premenstrual weeks, she added H1 antihistamine (loratadine 10 mg daily) and H2 blocker (famotidine 20 mg twice daily).

Gut healing protocol included L-glutamine, zinc carnosine, and multi-strain probiotic containing histamine-degrading species. She avoided hormonal contraceptives that had been prescribed for menstrual regulation. Magnesium glycinate 400 mg daily provided menstrual symptom support and mast cell stabilization.

Outcome

After four months, Berenice experienced substantial improvement. Premenstrual symptoms decreased from severe to mild. She tolerated moderate-histamine foods during follicular phase without reactions. Luteal phase tolerance improved sufficiently to permit small amounts of previously reactive foods. Non-food triggers became less problematic. She successfully completed her graduate studies and reported feeling "almost back to normal" most of the time.

Teaching Points

- Genetic predisposition to histamine intolerance often manifests following intestinal insults that reduce DAO production in individuals carrying susceptible polymorphisms
- Hormonal cycles significantly affect histamine tolerance in women, requiring phase-specific dietary and medical management approaches
- Acute gastrointestinal infections can trigger chronic histamine intolerance through intestinal damage and microbiota disruption, necessitating comprehensive gut healing protocols alongside dietary management

1.9 Essential Concepts Summary

This chapter established foundational understanding of histamine intolerance and MCAS. Histamine serves essential physiological functions in immunity, digestion, and neurotransmission through four distinct receptor types distributed throughout the body. This normal role becomes problematic when production exceeds degradation capacity or when mast cells release excessive mediators inappropriately.

Histamine intolerance develops primarily from reduced DAO enzyme activity, creating imbalance between histamine load and breakdown capacity. Multiple factors reduce DAO including genetic polymorphisms, intestinal inflammation, medications, and hormonal influences. The threshold concept explains variable reactions to the same foods under different conditions.

MCAS represents inappropriate mast cell activation releasing excessive histamine and other mediators. Diagnosis requires multi-system symptoms, elevated mediator levels during reactions, and response to antimediator therapy. These conditions frequently coexist, with each potentially triggering or exacerbating the other through positive feedback mechanisms.

Risk factors include female sex, genetic variants affecting DAO and HNMT, intestinal disorders, hormonal states, and environmental triggers including infections. Understanding these mechanisms and risk factors enables recognition of these conditions and informs comprehensive management approaches developed in subsequent chapters.

Chapter 2.0: Recognizing Your Symptoms

When Dorothea first consulted her physician about her symptoms, she brought a detailed list spanning two pages. Chronic digestive problems. Unexplained skin reactions. Frequent headaches. Heart palpitations. Anxiety attacks. Crushing fatigue. Her doctor reviewed the list, ran standard tests, and found nothing abnormal. "It's probably stress," he concluded, recommending cognitive behavioral therapy. Dorothea felt dismissed and confused. She knew these symptoms were real, not psychological. What she didn't realize was that all her seemingly unrelated complaints shared a common root: excessive histamine affecting multiple body systems simultaneously. Her diverse symptom presentation, far from being psychiatric, actually provided the diagnostic clue that eventually led to proper recognition and treatment of her histamine intolerance and MCAS.

This chapter teaches you to recognize the diverse manifestations of histamine intolerance and MCAS across all major body systems. You will learn the "histamine bucket" concept for understanding individual tolerance thresholds, identify characteristic symptom patterns in gastrointestinal, dermatological, neurological, cardiovascular, and respiratory systems, distinguish immediate from delayed reactions, and understand connections to Long COVID and common comorbidities. This symptom recognition enables you to identify these conditions in yourself or others and communicate effectively with healthcare providers.

2.1 The Histamine Bucket Concept

Understanding histamine intolerance and MCAS requires grasping the **histamine bucket** or **histamine threshold** model, a conceptual framework that explains why symptoms appear inconsistently and why the same trigger produces reactions on some occasions but not others (Kohn, 2014).

Imagine a bucket representing your body's total histamine capacity. This bucket continuously fills from multiple sources: dietary histamine from food and beverages, endogenous histamine produced by mast cells and other body cells, histamine generated by gut bacteria, histamine liberated by certain foods and medications, and histamine from environmental triggers like stress, temperature changes, or fragrances (Maintz & Novak, 2007).

Simultaneously, the bucket drains through two primary enzymatic pathways. DAO enzyme degrades histamine primarily in the gut and extracellular spaces (Comas-Basté et al., 2020). HNMT metabolizes histamine intracellularly throughout the body (Schwelberger, 2010). Together, these systems determine your drainage rate.

The bucket has a maximum capacity, your personal histamine threshold. When total histamine load remains below this threshold, no symptoms occur. Your enzymatic systems successfully manage the histamine burden. Once the bucket fills past threshold level, it overflows. This overflow manifests as symptoms (Kohn, 2014).

Several factors determine bucket capacity and drainage rate. Genetic factors influence DAO and HNMT enzyme production and activity (García-Martín et al., 2007). Gut health affects DAO production since intestinal cells manufacture this enzyme (Raithel et al., 2010). Hormonal status impacts DAO activity, with estrogen reducing enzyme function (Sattler et al., 1988). Medications can inhibit DAO or release histamine (Maintz & Novak, 2007). Stress activates mast cells, increasing histamine production (Theoharides et al., 2012). Sleep deprivation, inflammation, and nutrient deficiencies all affect the bucket's capacity and drainage.

This model explains variable reactions to identical exposures. On Monday, you tolerate a spinach salad without issue. On Friday, the same salad triggers flushing and headache. The difference lies not in the spinach, which contains the same histamine amount both days, but in your bucket's current fill level. Monday's bucket started relatively empty. The spinach added histamine but total load remained below threshold. Friday's bucket started fuller due to poor sleep, premenstrual hormones reducing DAO, stress from a work deadline, and leftover chicken at lunch. The spinach then pushed total load over threshold, causing symptoms.

This concept proves therapeutically important. Multiple intervention points exist for managing histamine intolerance and MCAS (Comas-Basté et al., 2020). You can reduce incoming histamine through diet, address gut dysbiosis producing histamine, support DAO function with enzyme supplements and cofactors, stabilize mast cells to reduce endogenous histamine production, manage stress and sleep, avoid DAO-blocking medications when possible, and address hormonal influences.

Research demonstrates that most interventions alone provide incomplete relief, but combination approaches targeting multiple bucket factors typically produce substantial improvement (Maintz & Novak, 2007). This explains why dietary changes alone sometimes disappoint. If mast cells continue releasing massive histamine amounts, or if stress chronically elevates histamine production, dietary restriction cannot compensate fully.

The bucket model also explains individual variation. Two people may eat identical high-histamine meals. One experiences severe reactions while the other remains symptom-free. This difference reflects their respective bucket capacities, drainage rates, and current fill levels, not differences in the food consumed.

2.2 Gastrointestinal Manifestations

Gastrointestinal symptoms represent the most common presentation of histamine intolerance, affecting approximately 75-80% of patients (Maintz & Novak, 2007). The digestive system's high concentration of mast cells and its role as the primary entry point for dietary histamine make it particularly vulnerable.

Abdominal pain occurs in approximately 58% of histamine intolerance patients, typically presenting as cramping or aching discomfort in the lower abdomen (Kohn, 2014). This pain often appears 30 minutes to 2 hours after eating histamine-containing foods. The mechanism involves histamine binding to H1 receptors on intestinal smooth muscle, causing spasm and increased sensitivity to distension (Maintz & Novak, 2007).

Diarrhea affects approximately 52% of patients, ranging from occasional loose stools to frequent watery bowel movements (Kohn, 2014). Histamine increases intestinal motility through smooth muscle stimulation and enhances fluid secretion into the intestinal lumen via H2 receptor activation (Schubert, 2009). This combination accelerates transit time and increases stool water content.

Bloating and distension trouble approximately 45% of patients, creating visible abdominal swelling and sensations of fullness or pressure (Kohn, 2014). Multiple mechanisms contribute. Histamine increases intestinal permeability, allowing more gas production from bacterial fermentation (Raithel et al., 2010). It also slows gastric emptying in some individuals, causing food and gas to accumulate.

Nausea appears in approximately 40% of cases, sometimes progressing to vomiting in severe reactions (Maintz & Novak, 2007). H1 receptors in the brainstem's area postrema mediate this effect. Elevated histamine directly triggers nausea centers in the brain.

Gastroesophageal reflux disease (GERD) symptoms including heartburn and regurgitation affect approximately 35% of patients (Kohn, 2014). Paradoxically, both excess histamine and reduced DAO can worsen reflux. Histamine stimulates gastric acid production through H2 receptors on parietal cells (Schubert, 2009), while also potentially affecting lower esophageal sphincter tone.

Constipation occurs less frequently than diarrhea but affects some patients, particularly those with concurrent MCAS (Afrin et al., 2016). Mast cell mediators beyond histamine may impair intestinal motility in complex patterns. Some patients alternate between diarrhea and constipation, reflecting variable mast cell activation and histamine fluctuations.

Food intolerances beyond histamine commonly coexist. Research indicates that approximately 30% of histamine intolerance patients also demonstrate FODMAP sensitivity, while approximately 25% show oxalate intolerance (Schnedl et al., 2019). This overlap complicates dietary management and diagnosis.

The timing of gastrointestinal symptoms provides diagnostic clues. Immediate reactions within 30-60 minutes typically indicate high dietary histamine triggering direct receptor activation. Delayed reactions occurring 4-24 hours later often reflect histamine production by gut bacteria from ingested histidine, or gradual histamine accumulation exceeding threshold (Maintz & Novak, 2007).

2.3 Dermatological Symptoms

Skin manifestations affect approximately 66% of histamine intolerance patients and nearly all MCAS patients, making them second only to gastrointestinal symptoms in prevalence (Molderings et al., 2011). The skin contains abundant mast cells, particularly in sun-exposed areas, making it highly reactive to histamine.

Flushing represents the most common dermatological manifestation, occurring in approximately 55-65% of cases (Kohn, 2014). This sudden reddening typically affects the face, neck, and upper chest, appearing within minutes of trigger exposure. The mechanism involves histamine binding to H1 receptors on blood vessel endothelium, causing vasodilation and increased blood flow to skin (Leurs et al., 2002). Episodes last from minutes to several hours. Some patients experience flushing multiple times daily, while others have intermittent episodes.

Urticaria, or hives, appears in approximately 40-50% of patients with histamine-related disorders (Maintz & Novak, 2007). These raised, itchy wheals can appear anywhere on the body, varying from small spots to large confluent areas. Histamine increases vascular permeability, allowing fluid to leak into surrounding tissue and creating the characteristic raised lesions (Kaplan, 2004). Hives typically resolve within 24 hours but may recur repeatedly. Chronic urticaria persisting more than 6 weeks often indicates underlying mast cell dysfunction.

Generalized itching without visible rash, termed pruritus, troubles approximately 35% of patients (Molderings et al., 2011). This maddening symptom occurs when histamine activates sensory nerve endings in the skin through H1 and H4 receptors (Leurs et al., 2009). Scratching provides temporary relief but worsens inflammation, triggering more mast cell degranulation in a vicious cycle.

Angioedema, or deep tissue swelling, affects approximately 20% of patients and represents a more serious manifestation (Afrin et al., 2016). This swelling typically affects the face, particularly around eyes and lips, but can occur in extremities or, dangerously, in the throat. Unlike superficial hives, angioedema involves deeper skin layers and can persist for 48-72 hours. Throat or tongue swelling constitutes a medical emergency requiring immediate treatment.

Eczema or dermatitis affects approximately 15-25% of patients with histamine disorders (Maintz & Novak, 2007). While eczema involves multiple immune pathways, histamine worsens inflammation and itching. Some patients notice eczema flares coinciding with high-histamine food consumption or other triggers.

Dermographism, or skin writing, occurs when light pressure on skin produces raised, itchy welts following the pressure pattern (Kaplan, 2004). This exaggerated response to mechanical stimulation indicates mast cell hyperreactivity. Patients can literally write on their skin with a fingernail, seeing raised red letters appear within minutes.

Some patients experience cold urticaria, developing hives when exposed to cold temperatures (Afrin et al., 2016). Others react to heat, pressure, vibration, or sun exposure. These physical urticarias suggest underlying MCAS rather than simple histamine intolerance.

Persistent rosacea or rosacea-like flushing affects some patients, particularly those with chronic mast cell activation (Steinhoff et al., 2013). The chronic facial redness and visible blood vessels reflect ongoing vascular dilation from sustained histamine and other mediator release.

2.4 Case Study: Multi-System Presentation

Background

Faustina, a 45-year-old teacher, spent five years pursuing a diagnosis. Her symptoms began subtly with occasional digestive upset and mild flushing after wine. Over time, symptoms intensified and diversified. She developed chronic urticaria, frequent migraines, unexplained anxiety attacks, and extreme fatigue. Three different specialists evaluated her separately for gastrointestinal complaints, dermatological issues, and neurological symptoms, finding no conventional diagnosis in their respective specialties.

Presentation

By the time Faustina sought care at an integrative medicine clinic, she experienced daily symptoms affecting multiple systems. Gastrointestinally, she had postprandial cramping, alternating diarrhea and constipation, and severe bloating that made her appear pregnant by evening. Dermatologically, chronic hives covered her trunk and arms, facial flushing occurred multiple times daily, and intense itching disrupted sleep. Neurologically, she suffered migraines 3-4 times weekly, constant brain fog impairing work performance, and anxiety attacks previously never experienced.

Cardiovascular symptoms included palpitations and episodes of tachycardia reaching 130 bpm at rest. She experienced frequent lightheadedness and one syncopal episode. Fatigue proved debilitating, forcing her to reduce work hours and abandon previously enjoyed activities.

Faustina identified some trigger patterns. Fermented foods, aged cheeses, wine, and cured meats consistently provoked reactions. However, she also reacted to fresh foods like strawberries, spinach, tomatoes, and sometimes even chicken. Stress, poor sleep, premenstrual periods, and temperature extremes all worsened symptoms. She had eliminated numerous foods but continued reacting unpredictably.

Analysis

Faustina's presentation exemplifies the multi-system nature of histamine disorders discussed throughout this chapter. Her symptoms map clearly to histamine's effects across different receptor types and body systems (Maintz & Novak, 2007).

Gastrointestinal manifestations from section 2.2 appear prominently: abdominal pain from smooth muscle spasm, altered motility creating diarrhea and constipation, and bloating from increased intestinal permeability and gas production (Raithel et al., 2010). Her dermatological symptoms from section 2.3 include urticaria, flushing, and pruritus, all classic H1 receptor-mediated effects (Leurs et al., 2002).

The neurological symptoms from section 2.5 reflect histamine's neurotransmitter functions and effects on cerebral blood vessels (Haas et al., 2008). Her migraines likely involve both vascular dilation and direct neural effects. Brain fog and anxiety connect to histamine's role in arousal, attention, and stress response regulation.

Cardiovascular symptoms from section 2.6, including palpitations, tachycardia, and orthostatic intolerance, suggest both H1 and H2 receptor activation affecting heart rate and vascular tone (Afrin et al., 2016). The syncopal episode raises concern for significant hypotension from excessive vasodilation.

Her trigger pattern reveals both histamine intolerance and likely MCAS. Reactions to high-histamine foods indicate DAO deficiency (Maintz & Novak, 2007). However, reactions to histamine-liberating foods (strawberries, tomatoes), fresh proteins, and non-food triggers (stress, hormones, temperature) suggest mast cell hyperreactivity characteristic of MCAS (Afrin et al., 2016).

The progressive symptom expansion over five years demonstrates the self-perpetuating nature of these conditions discussed in Chapter 1.5. Initial histamine intolerance likely triggered mast cell sensitization. Chronically elevated histamine from poor DAO function activated more mast cells. This mast cell activation released more histamine and other mediators, overwhelming even residual DAO capacity and creating the severe multi-system presentation.

Intervention

Comprehensive treatment addressed multiple bucket factors from section 2.1. Dietary intervention included strict 4-week low-histamine elimination diet removing all high-histamine foods, histamine liberators, and DAO blockers. Food preparation strategies minimized histamine formation through immediate freezing of cooked foods and exclusive use of fresh proteins.

Medical management included H1 antihistamine (cetirizine 10 mg twice daily) and H2 blocker (famotidine 20 mg twice daily) providing round-the-clock receptor blockade. DAO enzyme supplementation (1-2 capsules before meals) supported dietary histamine breakdown. Quercetin 500 mg twice daily and vitamin C 2000 mg daily provided mast cell stabilization (Weng et al., 2012).

Gut healing protocol with L-glutamine, zinc carnosine, and probiotics containing histamine-degrading strains addressed intestinal DAO production. Magnesium glycinate 400 mg nightly supported both mast cell function and sleep quality. Stress management through mindfulness meditation and yoga addressed psychological mast cell triggers.

Outcome

Within 8 weeks, Faustina experienced dramatic improvement. Gastrointestinal symptoms decreased from daily to 1-2 times weekly. Urticaria largely resolved except during premenstrual periods. Migraine frequency dropped to 1-2 monthly. Brain fog cleared substantially, allowing full-time work resumption. Cardiovascular symptoms became rare and mild. Fatigue improved enough to permit return to previously abandoned activities.

At 6-month follow-up, she had successfully reintroduced multiple moderate-histamine foods in small quantities. She continued baseline H1 antihistamine and DAO supplementation but used H2 blocker only premenstrually. Quality of life improved from severely impaired to near-normal.

Teaching Points

- Multi-system presentations affecting gastrointestinal, dermatological, neurological, and cardiovascular systems strongly suggest histamine-related disorders and require comprehensive evaluation beyond single-specialty assessment
- Progressive symptom expansion and worsening over months to years indicates self-perpetuating cycles between histamine intolerance and mast cell activation requiring multi-targeted intervention
- Combining dietary histamine reduction, receptor blockade, enzyme supplementation, mast cell stabilization, and gut healing typically produces superior outcomes compared to single interventions, reflecting the multiple factors contributing to the histamine bucket overflow

2.5 Neurological and Psychological Symptoms

Neurological manifestations of histamine disorders affect approximately 55-70% of patients but often go unrecognized because patients and providers do not connect these symptoms to histamine-related causes (Molderings et al., 2011). Histamine functions as a neurotransmitter in the central nervous system, making the brain particularly susceptible to histamine imbalances (Haas et al., 2008).

Headaches and migraines represent the most common neurological complaint, affecting approximately 50-60% of patients with histamine disorders (Maintz & Novak, 2007). Histamine contributes to headaches through multiple mechanisms. It dilates cerebral blood vessels, creating vascular headaches similar to classic migraines (Maintz et al., 2006). It also activates pain pathways directly through H1 and H3 receptors on sensory neurons. Many migraine sufferers notice clear food triggers that align with high-histamine foods, suggesting histamine involvement in their headache pathophysiology.

Brain fog describes the cognitive difficulties experienced by approximately 45-55% of patients (Molderings et al., 2011). This umbrella term encompasses poor concentration, memory problems, mental fatigue, difficulty finding words, and slowed processing speed. Histamine's role in attention and arousal explains these effects (Haas et al., 2008). Excessive histamine in brain regions controlling executive function impairs cognitive performance. Patients often describe feeling mentally "disconnected" or "in a haze."

Anxiety symptoms appear in approximately 40-50% of cases, sometimes meeting criteria for anxiety disorders (Maintz & Novak, 2007). Histamine activates the hypothalamic-pituitary-adrenal (HPA) axis, the body's stress response system (Theoharides et al., 2012). Chronic histamine elevation keeps this system overactive, producing persistent anxiety, hypervigilance, and panic attacks. Some patients develop anxiety specifically after eating histamine-rich foods, experiencing overwhelming feelings of dread or impending doom linked to meals.

Sleep disturbances trouble approximately 35-45% of patients (Molderings et al., 2011). Histamine promotes wakefulness through H1 receptors in the brain (Haas et al., 2008). This explains why antihistamines cause drowsiness. They block histamine's wake-promoting effects. Patients with elevated histamine experience difficulty falling asleep, frequent nighttime awakenings, and non-restorative sleep. Interestingly, histamine levels naturally peak during early morning hours, explaining why some patients wake at 3-4 AM and cannot return to sleep (Maintz & Novak, 2007).

Dizziness and vertigo affect approximately 30% of patients (Afrin et al., 2016). Histamine's effects on blood pressure regulation and its role in inner ear function both contribute. Some patients experience true vertigo with room-spinning sensations, while others describe lightheadedness or spatial disorientation.

Tremor occurs in approximately 15-20% of patients, typically presenting as fine hand tremors that worsen with stress or after consuming trigger foods (Molderings et al., 2011). The mechanism remains incompletely understood but may involve histamine's effects on motor control centers in the brain.

Depression symptoms appear in some patients, though less commonly than anxiety (Maintz & Novak, 2007). Chronic inflammation from mast cell activation contributes to depression through cytokine effects on neurotransmitter systems. Additionally, the significant quality of life impairment from undiagnosed, poorly controlled symptoms understandably produces reactive depression.

Sensitivity to light, sound, and smells affects many patients with histamine disorders (Afrin et al., 2016). These sensory processing abnormalities connect to histamine's modulatory effects on sensory neurons. Patients describe being overwhelmed by normal environmental stimuli that others tolerate easily.

2.6 Cardiovascular Manifestations

Cardiovascular symptoms affect approximately 45-60% of patients with histamine-related disorders and can range from mildly annoying to seriously impairing (Molderings et al., 2011). Histamine exerts direct effects on the heart and blood vessels through H1 and H2 receptors, creating varied cardiovascular presentations (Maintz & Novak, 2007).

Palpitations represent the most common cardiovascular complaint, occurring in approximately 40-50% of patients (Kohn, 2014). Patients describe their heartbeat as pounding, racing, fluttering, or skipping beats. H2 receptor activation increases cardiac contractility and conduction velocity, making the heartbeat more forceful and sometimes irregular (Schubert, 2009). Most palpitations prove benign, but they create significant anxiety, particularly when occurring at rest or during sleep.

Tachycardia, or elevated heart rate, affects approximately 30-40% of patients (Molderings et al., 2011). Heart rate may exceed 100 bpm at rest, sometimes reaching 120-140 bpm without physical exertion. This occurs through both direct H2 receptor stimulation of cardiac pacemaker cells and indirect effects via autonomic nervous system activation (Afrin et al., 2016). Episodes can last minutes to hours, resolving spontaneously or with intervention.

Blood pressure abnormalities include both hypotension and hypertension, though low blood pressure predominates in histamine disorders (Maintz & Novak, 2007). Histamine causes vasodilation through H1 receptors on vascular smooth muscle, reducing vascular resistance and lowering blood pressure (Leurs et al., 2002). Approximately 25-35% of patients experience orthostatic hypotension, where blood pressure drops significantly upon standing, causing lightheadedness or syncope.

Postural orthostatic tachycardia syndrome (POTS) frequently overlaps with histamine intolerance and MCAS, affecting approximately 15-25% of patients with these conditions (Afrin et al., 2016). POTS involves excessive heart rate increase upon standing (>30 bpm within 10 minutes) without significant blood pressure drop. The syndrome produces lightheadedness, fatigue, brain fog, and exercise intolerance. Research demonstrates elevated mast cell mediators in many POTS patients, suggesting mast cell dysfunction contributes to autonomic dysregulation (Weinstock et al., 2021).

Chest pain or discomfort troubles approximately 20-25% of patients (Molderings et al., 2011). This pain differs from typical cardiac chest pain, often described as sharp, stabbing, or burning sensations anywhere in the chest. The etiology likely involves esophageal spasm from gastrointestinal mast cell activation rather than true cardiac pathology, though cardiac evaluation should exclude dangerous causes.

Flushing episodes involving visible reddening of face, neck, and chest frequently accompany cardiovascular symptoms (Maintz & Novak, 2007). As discussed in section 2.3, this occurs through vasodilation. When extensive, flushing can cause measurable blood pressure drops and compensatory tachycardia.

Some patients describe episodes resembling anaphylaxis with combination of hypotension, tachycardia, flushing, difficulty breathing, and sense of impending doom, but without identifiable allergen trigger (Afrin et al., 2016). These idiopathic anaphylaxis episodes often reflect severe mast cell activation events requiring emergency treatment.

Exercise intolerance affects many patients, limiting physical activity tolerance (Molderings et al., 2011). Multiple factors contribute including inappropriate heart rate responses, blood pressure instability, excessive fatigue, and post-exertional symptom worsening. Some patients develop symptoms during exercise while others experience delayed reactions hours later.

2.7 Respiratory Symptoms

Respiratory manifestations occur in approximately 30-40% of patients with histamine-related disorders (Maintz & Novak, 2007). The respiratory tract contains abundant mast cells, particularly in nasal passages and bronchial airways, making it highly reactive to histamine (Theoharides et al., 2012).

Nasal congestion represents the most common respiratory symptom, affecting approximately 25-35% of patients (Kohn, 2014). Histamine causes nasal mucosal swelling and increased mucus production through H1 receptor activation (Leurs et al., 2002). Patients describe stuffy nose, post-nasal drip, and difficulty breathing through their nose. Symptoms often worsen after eating trigger foods or during high-pollen seasons when environmental allergens add to total histamine load.

Sneezing episodes and rhinorrhea (runny nose) affect approximately 20-30% of patients (Maintz & Novak, 2007). Clear nasal discharge flows freely, sometimes requiring constant tissue use. These symptoms mimic allergic rhinitis, and many patients carry misdiagnoses of environmental allergies before histamine intolerance recognition.

Throat symptoms including itching, tickling, tightness, or swelling concern approximately 20-25% of patients (Molderings et al., 2011). Mild throat irritation causes frequent clearing or coughing. More concerning throat tightness or swelling sensation requires careful evaluation to distinguish anxiety-related globus sensation from true angioedema that could compromise the airway.

Chronic cough without other explanation troubles approximately 15-20% of patients (Afrin et al., 2016). This persistent, dry cough resists typical cough suppressants. The mechanism likely involves histamine-mediated irritation of airway sensory nerves and increased mucus production dripping into the throat.

Asthma-like symptoms affect approximately 15-20% of patients, including wheezing, chest tightness, shortness of breath, and cough (Maintz & Novak, 2007). Histamine directly causes bronchoconstriction through H1 receptors on airway smooth muscle (Leurs et al., 2002). Some patients carry asthma diagnoses and use bronchodilators for symptom relief. Others experience intermittent bronchospasm without meeting formal asthma criteria.

Shortness of breath or dyspnea appears in approximately 15-25% of cases (Molderings et al., 2011). This symptom creates significant distress, particularly when occurring at rest or with minimal exertion. Multiple mechanisms contribute including bronchoconstriction, anxiety, cardiovascular effects reducing effective oxygen delivery, and direct effects on respiratory drive in the brain.

Voice changes including hoarseness or voice loss affect some patients (Afrin et al., 2016). Laryngeal mast cell activation causes vocal cord edema and inflammation, altering voice quality. Professional voice users find these symptoms particularly disabling.

Some patients experience exercise-induced bronchospasm that differs from typical exercise-induced asthma (Molderings et al., 2011). Physical activity triggers mast cell degranulation in susceptible individuals, releasing histamine and other mediators that constrict airways. Symptoms appear during or shortly after exercise, causing wheezing and shortness of breath that resolves with rest.

2.8 Case Study: Delayed Reactions and Timing

Background

Gawain, a 52-year-old software engineer, struggled to identify his triggers because symptoms appeared unpredictably, often hours or even a day after suspected exposures. This delayed pattern led him and his physicians to doubt food connections. He tried multiple elimination diets without success because he evaluated reactions too soon after food reintroduction.

Presentation

Gawain experienced prominent gastrointestinal and neurological symptoms. Severe abdominal cramping, diarrhea, and bloating occurred seemingly randomly, sometimes in the morning before eating, other times in the afternoon or evening. Migraine headaches struck 2-3 times weekly, often waking him from sleep in the early morning hours. Brain fog impaired his programming work, particularly in the afternoons. Generalized itching without visible rash troubled him most evenings.

When asked to identify food triggers, Gawain found no clear patterns. He had tried eliminating dairy, gluten, and other common allergens without improvement. A food diary revealed no obvious correlations between meals and symptoms occurring within the next 2 hours.

Analysis

Gawain's case illustrates delayed histamine reactions discussed in section 2.1 and throughout this chapter. His symptom timing patterns provide important diagnostic clues often missed in standard allergy evaluation.

The delayed reactions likely reflect multiple mechanisms. First, gut bacteria convert dietary histidine from protein foods into histamine over several hours (Sánchez-Pérez et al., 2018). This bacterial histamine production peaks 4-12 hours after meals containing high-protein foods. Second, histamine accumulation from multiple exposures throughout the day crosses threshold only later, producing delayed symptom onset (Maintz & Novak, 2007). Third, sleep-related histamine changes may contribute, as histamine levels naturally peak in early morning hours (Haas et al., 2008).

His morning symptoms before eating likely reflect accumulated histamine from previous day's intake finally exceeding threshold overnight. The body continues metabolizing yesterday's histamine load during sleep. If this load overwhelms DAO capacity, symptoms appear upon waking despite no recent food intake.

The afternoon brain fog pattern suggests cumulative histamine effects from morning and lunch exposures. Cognitive symptoms often appear hours after the causative meal as histamine crosses the blood-brain barrier and accumulates in neural tissue (Maintz & Novak, 2007).

Evening itching may reflect peak histamine levels from the day's total exposure. Pruritus represents a common delayed manifestation, appearing 6-12 hours after trigger foods (Leurs et al., 2009).

His failed elimination diets probably reflected inadequate trial duration and premature food reintroduction evaluation. Standard 2-week elimination trials prove insufficient for histamine intolerance, which requires 4-6 weeks for substantial improvement (Kohn, 2014). Additionally, evaluating reactions within 2 hours of reintroduced foods misses delayed responses appearing 4-24 hours later.

Intervention

Extended elimination protocol lasted 6 weeks rather than the typical 4 weeks, given Gawain's prominent delayed reaction pattern. This allowed adequate time for accumulated histamine to clear from tissues and for DAO-producing intestinal cells to recover if damaged (Raithel et al., 2010).

Food reintroduction used modified protocol accounting for delayed reactions. Each test food was consumed for 3 consecutive days at normal portions, with a 4-day observation period following the last exposure before evaluating tolerance. This captured delayed reactions missed by standard same-day evaluation.

Medical support included DAO enzyme supplementation before all meals to address bacterial histamine production. H1 antihistamine taken at bedtime reduced morning symptoms by blocking overnight histamine accumulation. Probiotic containing Bifidobacterium infantis and Lactobacillus plantarum provided histamine-degrading bacteria to reduce gut histamine production (Sánchez-Pérez et al., 2018).

Outcome

Week 4 of elimination brought first substantial improvements, with morning gastrointestinal symptoms decreasing in frequency and severity. By week 6, Gawain enjoyed multiple consecutive symptom-free days, the first in years. Migraines decreased to once monthly. Brain fog cleared substantially. Evening itching resolved.

The modified reintroduction protocol successfully identified triggers missed by previous attempts. High-protein foods including chicken, eggs, and fish provoked delayed gastrointestinal symptoms appearing 6-12 hours post-consumption. Fermented foods triggered migraines the following day. Strawberries caused delayed itching 8-10 hours later.

With this knowledge, Gawain avoided identified triggers while continuing DAO supplementation for tolerable proteins. Six months post-treatment, he maintained good symptom control and had cautiously reintroduced some previously reactive foods in small quantities without reactions.

Teaching Points

- Delayed histamine reactions occurring 4-24 hours after trigger exposure require extended observation periods during reintroduction protocols to capture accurately, making standard 2-hour evaluation windows inadequate
- Morning symptoms appearing before food intake often reflect accumulated histamine from previous day's exposures exceeding threshold overnight,

requiring investigation of prior day's intake rather than assuming non-food causes
- Gut bacterial histamine production from dietary protein creates delayed symptom patterns hours after meals, necessitating DAO supplementation and histamine-degrading probiotic therapy alongside dietary management

2.9 Long COVID and Post-Viral MCAS

The COVID-19 pandemic brought unprecedented attention to post-viral mast cell dysfunction. Research indicates that approximately 17-30% of individuals experiencing Long COVID develop symptoms consistent with MCAS (Weinstock et al., 2021). This connection illuminated how viral infections can trigger chronic mast cell dysfunction in previously healthy individuals.

Long COVID describes persistent symptoms extending beyond 12 weeks after acute SARS-CoV-2 infection (Nalbandian et al., 2021). Common manifestations include fatigue, exercise intolerance, cognitive dysfunction ("brain fog"), autonomic dysregulation, gastrointestinal symptoms, and sensory abnormalities. Many of these symptoms overlap significantly with histamine intolerance and MCAS presentations.

Multiple mechanisms link COVID-19 to mast cell dysfunction. The virus directly infects and activates mast cells through ACE2 receptors present on these cells (Theoharides, 2020). This activation triggers persistent mast cell hyperreactivity lasting long after viral clearance. Viral-induced inflammation creates chronic immune dysregulation where mast cells remain inappropriately responsive. Autoantibodies generated during COVID infection may target mast cell surface receptors, creating ongoing activation (Weinstock et al., 2021).

Research demonstrates elevated mast cell mediators in Long COVID patients compared to recovered individuals without persistent symptoms. Tryptase, histamine metabolites, and prostaglandin levels remain elevated months after acute infection (Afrin et al., 2021). This biochemical evidence supports mast cell involvement in Long COVID pathophysiology.

Common Long COVID symptoms map clearly to histamine and mast cell effects. Fatigue correlates with histamine's effects on energy metabolism and mitochondrial function (Theoharides, 2020). Brain fog reflects histamine's neurotransmitter functions discussed in section 2.5. Autonomic dysfunction including POTS, described in section 2.6, appears in approximately 30% of Long COVID cases (Dani et al., 2021). Gastrointestinal symptoms from section 2.2 trouble approximately 40% of Long COVID patients. Exercise intolerance from inappropriate mast cell activation during physical activity limits recovery.

The POTS connection proves particularly striking. Pre-pandemic POTS prevalence was approximately 170 per 100,000 individuals. Post-COVID POTS prevalence increased dramatically, with one study finding approximately 2-14% of COVID survivors developing POTS symptoms (Dani et al., 2021). Mast cell mediators including histamine affect autonomic nervous system function, creating the inappropriate tachycardia characteristic of POTS.

Treatment approaches borrowed from MCAS and histamine intolerance management show promise for Long COVID. Small studies report symptom improvement with H1 and H2 antihistamine combinations (Sowerby et al., 2023). Mast cell stabilizers including quercetin and vitamin C demonstrate benefit in case series (Afrin et al., 2021). Low-histamine dietary modifications reduce symptom burden for some patients. This therapeutic response provides additional evidence linking Long COVID to mast cell dysfunction.

The COVID-MCAS connection extends beyond SARS-CoV-2. Other viral infections including Epstein-Barr virus, cytomegalovirus, and various enteroviruses can trigger chronic mast cell activation (Afrin et al., 2016). Post-viral fatigue syndromes and myalgic encephalomyelitis/chronic fatigue syndrome (ME/CFS) share substantial symptom overlap with MCAS, suggesting common mast cell mechanisms.

2.10 Common Comorbidities: POTS, EDS, and Others

Histamine intolerance and MCAS rarely occur in isolation. Multiple conditions frequently coexist, creating complex presentations requiring comprehensive management (Molderings et al., 2011).

POTS, discussed in sections 2.6 and 2.9, appears in approximately 15-30% of MCAS patients (Afrin et al., 2016). This autonomic nervous system disorder causes excessive heart rate increase upon standing, creating disabling symptoms including lightheadedness, palpitations, fatigue, brain fog, and exercise intolerance. Mast cell mediators disrupt normal autonomic reflexes controlling heart rate and blood pressure. Treatment requires addressing both conditions simultaneously for optimal outcomes.

Ehlers-Danlos Syndrome (EDS), particularly the hypermobile subtype, shows striking overlap with MCAS (Seneviratne et al., 2017). EDS comprises a group of connective tissue disorders causing joint hypermobility, skin hyperextensibility, and tissue fragility. Research indicates that approximately 25-66% of EDS patients meet MCAS criteria. The connection likely reflects shared genetic factors affecting connective tissue and mast cell function. Mast cells reside within connective tissue and regulate its integrity through mediator release. Abnormal connective tissue in EDS may create chronic low-level mast cell activation.

Fibromyalgia, characterized by widespread chronic pain, frequently overlaps with histamine disorders (Molderings et al., 2011). Approximately 20% of fibromyalgia patients demonstrate evidence of mast cell dysfunction. Mast cell mediators including histamine sensitize pain pathways, lowering pain thresholds. Additionally, the chronic inflammation from mast cell activation contributes to persistent pain.

Small intestinal bacterial overgrowth (SIBO) commonly coexists with histamine intolerance, affecting approximately 25-40% of patients (Schnedl et al., 2019). Bacterial overgrowth in the small intestine produces substantial histamine from dietary histidine. SIBO also damages intestinal lining, reducing DAO production. This creates bidirectional causation: SIBO increases histamine load while histamine-induced inflammation promotes SIBO persistence.

Irritable bowel syndrome (IBS) overlaps significantly with histamine intolerance. Research indicates that approximately 58% of IBS patients experience improvement on low-histamine diets, suggesting histamine contributes to their symptoms (Schnedl et al., 2019). The overlap makes sense given histamine's effects on intestinal motility, secretion, and sensitivity described in section 2.2.

Interstitial cystitis/bladder pain syndrome affects some MCAS patients (Molderings et al., 2011). Mast cell infiltration of bladder tissue creates chronic inflammation, pain, and urinary frequency. This connection explains why some patients with unexplained bladder symptoms improve with MCAS treatment.

Chronic fatigue syndrome/myalgic encephalomyelitis (ME/CFS) shows substantial symptom overlap with MCAS (Afrin et al., 2016). Fatigue, exercise intolerance, cognitive dysfunction, and multi-system symptoms characterize both conditions. Elevated mast cell mediators appear in ME/CFS patients, suggesting mast cell dysfunction contributes to this debilitating syndrome.

Autoimmune conditions including Hashimoto's thyroiditis, rheumatoid arthritis, and Sjögren's syndrome occur more frequently in patients with mast cell disorders than in the general population (Molderings et al., 2011). Mast cells participate in autoimmune processes through antigen presentation and cytokine production. Chronic mast cell activation may promote autoimmunity development in genetically susceptible individuals.

2.11 Working with Healthcare Providers

Successfully diagnosing and treating histamine intolerance and MCAS requires effective collaboration with knowledgeable healthcare providers. This proves challenging given limited awareness of these conditions in conventional medicine (Comas-Basté et al., 2020).

Preparing for medical appointments maximizes productive interactions. Bring detailed symptom diary documenting symptoms, timing, severity, and potential triggers for at least 2-4 weeks. List all medications, supplements, and treatments tried with results. Prepare concise summary of symptom timeline showing onset and progression. Bring relevant family history of similar conditions, allergies, or autoimmune disorders. Create prioritized list of most troubling symptoms affecting quality of life.

Requesting appropriate testing requires knowledge of available evaluations. For histamine intolerance, request serum DAO measurement if available locally (recognizing limitations discussed in Chapter 1.6). Consider 24-hour urine N-methylhistamine collection for histamine metabolite assessment. Request comprehensive metabolic panel, complete blood count, and thyroid function to exclude other conditions. Consider testing for SIBO via breath test given common overlap. Celiac serology helps exclude this DAO-impairing condition.

For MCAS evaluation, request baseline serum tryptase measurement. Discuss capturing tryptase during symptomatic episodes if feasible. Consider 24-hour urine collection for N-methylhistamine, prostaglandin D2 metabolites, and leukotriene E4. These mediator measurements may require specialized laboratories.

Understanding test limitations proves essential. Normal DAO levels do not exclude histamine intolerance (Kofler et al., 2011). Normal tryptase does not exclude MCAS. Tests provide supporting evidence but diagnosis ultimately rests on clinical assessment and therapeutic trial response (Valent et al., 2012).

When providers show limited familiarity with these conditions, educational approaches help. Bring peer-reviewed research articles (several references from this chapter provide good starting points). Consider the diagnostic criteria published by Afrin et al. (2016) for MCAS. Emphasize that elimination diet trial and therapeutic antihistamine trial provide low-risk diagnostic and therapeutic information. Request trial of H1 and H2 antihistamines for 4 weeks, monitoring symptom response.

Finding knowledgeable providers may require searching beyond primary care. Allergists/immunologists sometimes recognize MCAS, though many focus primarily on IgE-mediated allergies. Gastroenterologists may understand histamine intolerance's gastrointestinal manifestations. Integrative medicine practitioners often demonstrate greater familiarity with these conditions. Online directories from

Mast Cell Action and The Mast Cell Disease Society list providers with MCAS expertise.

Advocating effectively without antagonizing providers requires balance. Acknowledge the complexity and relative novelty of research in this area. Express appreciation for provider's time and expertise. Frame requests as collaborative problem-solving. Emphasize functional impairment and quality of life effects. Remain open to provider's differential diagnoses while requesting consideration of histamine-related etiologies.

2.12 Chapter Summary

This chapter equipped you to recognize the diverse manifestations of histamine intolerance and MCAS across multiple body systems. The histamine bucket concept explains variable symptom patterns through the relationship between total histamine load and individual degradative capacity, illuminating why identical exposures produce different results under varying conditions.

Gastrointestinal symptoms including abdominal pain, diarrhea, bloating, and reflux affect approximately 75-80% of patients, making digestive complaints the most common presentation. Dermatological manifestations including flushing, urticaria, pruritus, and angioedema trouble approximately 66% of cases. Neurological symptoms ranging from migraine and brain fog to anxiety and sleep disturbance impair approximately 55-70% of patients. Cardiovascular effects including palpitations, tachycardia, hypotension, and POTS create significant morbidity in 45-60% of cases. Respiratory symptoms occur in 30-40% of patients.

Understanding delayed reactions proves essential for accurate trigger identification, as symptoms may appear 4-24 hours after exposure rather than immediately. The Long COVID pandemic revealed viral infection's ability to trigger chronic mast cell dysfunction, with 17-30% of Long COVID patients developing MCAS-like presentations. Common comorbidities including POTS, EDS, fibromyalgia, and SIBO frequently coexist, requiring comprehensive evaluation and management.

Effective healthcare collaboration requires preparation, knowledge of appropriate testing, understanding of test limitations, and skilled self-advocacy. Armed with symptom recognition skills and understanding of diagnostic approaches from this chapter, you can communicate effectively with providers and pursue accurate diagnosis. The next chapter explores the root causes and triggers that fill the histamine bucket, providing deeper understanding of why these conditions develop and persist.

Chapter 3.0: Root Causes and Triggers

Clotilde had done everything right. After her histamine intolerance diagnosis six months earlier, she meticulously followed a strict low-histamine diet. She avoided all the trigger foods listed in her handouts. She tracked every symptom. Yet her reactions continued, seemingly random and unpredictable. Some days she felt almost normal. Other days, despite eating identical meals from her safe list, symptoms flared with crushing intensity. Her gastroenterologist seemed puzzled. Her allergist suggested it might be psychological. But Clotilde knew something else was at play. What she didn't realize was that her birth control pills were blocking the very enzyme her body needed to break down histamine. That her chronic stress was triggering mast cell activation independent of diet. That the antibiotics she'd taken three months earlier had decimated her gut bacteria, leaving histamine-producing species to flourish. Her story illustrates a fundamental truth about histamine disorders: diet alone rarely tells the whole story. Multiple hidden factors fill the histamine bucket, and understanding these root causes proves essential for effective management.

This chapter examines the diverse factors that reduce DAO enzyme activity, trigger mast cell activation, and contribute to histamine accumulation. You will learn how genetic polymorphisms affect histamine metabolism, how gut health influences histamine tolerance, which medications impair histamine breakdown or trigger release, how hormones modulate the system, what environmental factors activate mast cells, which foods beyond high-histamine items cause problems, and how inflammation and viral infections trigger chronic mast cell dysfunction. This understanding enables you to identify and address your specific triggers, moving beyond diet alone to address the root causes filling your histamine bucket.

3.1 Primary DAO Deficiency Mechanisms

As established in Chapter 1.0, diamine oxidase represents the primary enzyme responsible for degrading dietary histamine in the gut (Maintz & Novak, 2007). When DAO activity becomes insufficient, histamine accumulates, triggering the multi-system symptoms discussed in Chapter 2.0. Understanding what reduces DAO activity illuminates why some individuals develop histamine intolerance while others tolerate high-histamine foods without issue.

DAO production occurs primarily in the small intestinal enterocytes, the epithelial cells lining the intestinal villi (Comas-Basté et al., 2020). These specialized cells manufacture and secrete DAO into the intestinal lumen, where the enzyme encounters and degrades dietary histamine before it enters systemic circulation.

This localized production creates vulnerability. Any process damaging intestinal enterocytes directly impairs DAO production.

Several categories of factors reduce DAO activity. **Genetic factors** involving polymorphisms in the DAO gene (AOC1) or the histamine N-methyltransferase gene (HNMT) create inherent deficiencies in enzyme production or function (García-Martín et al., 2007). Individuals carrying certain genetic variants produce less DAO or manufacture enzyme with reduced catalytic efficiency. These genetic influences will be explored thoroughly in section 3.2.

Intestinal damage from inflammatory conditions destroys DAO-producing enterocytes. Inflammatory bowel disease, celiac disease, small intestinal bacterial overgrowth, parasitic infections, and medication-induced enteropathy all reduce the population of healthy enterocytes capable of producing DAO (Raithel et al., 2010). Even temporary intestinal insults like gastroenteritis can create prolonged DAO deficiency if mucosal healing proceeds slowly.

Micronutrient deficiencies impair DAO function since the enzyme requires specific cofactors for optimal activity. Copper serves as an essential cofactor, making copper deficiency a cause of reduced DAO activity (McGrath et al., 2009). Vitamin B6 (pyridoxal-5-phosphate) also functions as a DAO cofactor (Schwelberger, 2010). Zinc, while not a direct DAO cofactor, supports intestinal mucosal integrity and thus indirectly supports DAO production. Vitamin C enhances DAO activity, explaining why supplemental vitamin C often improves histamine tolerance (Hagel et al., 2013).

Medication effects represent another major category. Certain drugs directly inhibit DAO enzyme activity, while others damage intestinal mucosa or interfere with DAO production (Maintz & Novak, 2007). Section 3.5 will examine specific medications and their mechanisms in detail.

Hormonal influences, particularly estrogen, significantly affect DAO activity. Estrogen appears to inhibit DAO function, explaining increased histamine sensitivity during high-estrogen states (Sattler et al., 1988). This hormonal modulation will be explored comprehensively in section 3.6.

Alcohol consumption inhibits DAO activity through multiple mechanisms. Ethanol directly inhibits the enzyme while acetaldehyde, alcohol's primary metabolite, further impairs DAO function (Wantke et al., 1994). Additionally, alcoholic beverages often contain substantial histamine from fermentation, creating a double burden of increased histamine load plus reduced degradative capacity.

The severity of DAO deficiency exists on a continuum. Some individuals have profound deficiency from multiple contributing factors, experiencing severe symptoms from minimal histamine exposure. Others have borderline DAO capacity, remaining asymptomatic until additional stressors push them over threshold. This variability explains why symptom severity differs so dramatically between individuals with histamine intolerance.

3.2 Genetic Polymorphisms and Individual Variation

Genetic variation in histamine-metabolizing enzymes creates inherent differences in histamine tolerance between individuals. Two primary genes affect histamine metabolism: AOC1 encoding DAO, and HNMT encoding histamine N-methyltransferase (García-Martín et al., 2007).

The AOC1 gene, located on chromosome 7, contains numerous single nucleotide polymorphisms (SNPs) that affect DAO enzyme production and activity. The most extensively studied variants include rs10156191, rs1049742, rs2268999, and rs1049793 (Maintz & Novak, 2007). These polymorphisms show varying prevalence across ethnic groups, with higher frequency in Caucasian populations potentially explaining some ethnic variation in histamine intolerance prevalence.

Research demonstrates that certain AOC1 polymorphisms reduce DAO activity by 40-70% compared to wild-type variants (García-Martín et al., 2007). Individuals homozygous for risk alleles show particularly low DAO activity. However, the relationship between genotype and phenotype proves complex. Not all individuals with risk alleles develop symptomatic histamine intolerance, suggesting that genetic predisposition requires additional environmental triggers for clinical manifestation.

The rs10156191 polymorphism, located in the promoter region of AOC1, affects gene transcription. Individuals carrying the T allele show reduced DAO mRNA expression in intestinal tissue (Maintz et al., 2013). The rs1049742 variant affects enzyme stability, with certain alleles producing DAO that degrades more rapidly. The rs2268999 polymorphism influences enzyme catalytic efficiency, with some variants showing reduced capacity to metabolize histamine despite normal enzyme levels.

HNMT provides the secondary histamine degradation pathway, operating primarily intracellularly throughout the body (Schwelberger, 2010). The most significant HNMT polymorphism is the Thr105Ile variant (rs11558538), which reduces enzyme activity by approximately 40% (Preuss et al., 1998). This variant shows particular prevalence in Caucasian populations, affecting approximately 10-15% of individuals.

The combined effects of AOC1 and HNMT polymorphisms prove particularly important. Individuals carrying risk alleles in both genes experience the most severe histamine metabolism impairment (García-Martín et al., 2007). With both primary (DAO) and secondary (HNMT) pathways compromised, histamine accumulates more readily and reaches higher levels before symptoms appear.

Beyond direct histamine-metabolizing enzymes, other genetic factors influence histamine tolerance. Polymorphisms in histamine receptor genes (HRH1, HRH2, HRH3, HRH4) affect receptor sensitivity and response to histamine (Leurs et al., 2009). Variations in genes encoding mast cell function and regulation influence how readily mast cells release histamine. Genetic differences in tight junction proteins affect intestinal permeability, influencing how much dietary histamine enters systemic circulation.

Genetic testing for histamine-related polymorphisms remains available through specialized laboratories, though clinical utility continues to be debated (Comas-Basté et al., 2020). Negative genetic testing does not exclude histamine intolerance since acquired factors often override genetic predisposition. Positive testing confirms genetic susceptibility but doesn't guarantee symptomatic disease. Most practitioners rely on clinical assessment and therapeutic trials rather than genetic testing for diagnosis.

3.3 Gut Health and Histamine Production

The gastrointestinal tract plays dual roles in histamine regulation, serving both as the primary site of dietary histamine degradation and as a major potential source of endogenous histamine production (Sánchez-Pérez et al., 2018). Gut health profoundly influences histamine tolerance through effects on DAO production, intestinal permeability, and bacterial histamine generation.

Small intestinal bacterial overgrowth (SIBO) represents one of the most significant gut-related causes of histamine intolerance. SIBO occurs when bacteria inappropriately colonize the small intestine in excessive numbers (Pimentel et al., 2020). These bacteria produce substantial histamine from dietary histidine through bacterial histidine decarboxylase enzymes. Research indicates that bacterial histamine production in SIBO can generate systemic histamine levels comparable to those from high-histamine food consumption (Raithel et al., 2013).

Specific bacterial species demonstrate high histamine-producing capacity. Morganella morganii, Klebsiella pneumoniae, Hafnia alvei, Escherichia coli, and various Enterobacter species all produce significant histamine (Sánchez-Pérez et al., 2018). When these species overgrow in the small intestine, they convert dietary protein into histamine directly at the mucosal surface where absorption occurs most readily.

SIBO also damages intestinal epithelium through bacterial products and local inflammation. This damage reduces DAO-producing enterocyte populations, creating the double burden of increased histamine production plus decreased degradative capacity (Raithel et al., 2013). Patients often experience dramatic improvement when SIBO receives appropriate treatment with antibiotics or herbal antimicrobials, followed by restoration of healthy gut flora.

Intestinal dysbiosis, meaning imbalanced gut microbiota composition throughout the gastrointestinal tract, contributes to histamine accumulation. The large intestine normally harbors trillions of bacteria, with composition varying dramatically between individuals (Sánchez-Pérez et al., 2018). When histamine-producing species predominate over histamine-degrading species, net histamine production increases.

Certain bacterial species actually degrade histamine, providing beneficial effects. Bifidobacterium infantis, Lactobacillus plantarum, and some Lactobacillus rhamnosus strains possess enzymes that break down histamine (Sánchez-Pérez et al., 2018). When these beneficial species decline due to antibiotic use, poor diet, or other factors, histamine-producing species may proliferate unchecked.

Intestinal hyperpermeability, commonly called leaky gut, allows increased histamine absorption from the gut lumen into systemic circulation. Normally, tight junctions between intestinal epithelial cells create selective barriers, limiting absorption of large molecules including histamine (Fasano, 2020). When these tight junctions become disrupted through inflammation, certain foods, stress, or other factors, intestinal permeability increases. More dietary and bacterial histamine crosses into the bloodstream, overwhelming systemic degradative capacity.

Inflammatory bowel diseases including Crohn's disease and ulcerative colitis cause significant intestinal damage, directly destroying DAO-producing enterocytes (Raithel et al., 2010). Inflammation generates oxidative stress that further impairs remaining DAO activity. These patients often experience histamine intolerance symptoms that improve when intestinal inflammation receives effective treatment.

Celiac disease presents another important cause of DAO deficiency. The autoimmune damage to small intestinal villi in untreated celiac disease destroys vast numbers of enterocytes (Raithel et al., 2010). Studies demonstrate markedly reduced DAO activity in active celiac disease, with gradual improvement following strict gluten elimination and mucosal healing. Some celiac patients continue experiencing histamine intolerance symptoms even after gluten elimination, suggesting that mucosal recovery proceeds slowly or remains incomplete.

Parasitic infections can impair DAO production through intestinal damage. Giardia lamblia, Blastocystis hominis, and various helminths all damage intestinal mucosa and trigger inflammation that reduces DAO activity (Raithel et al., 2010). Persistent histamine intolerance following gastrointestinal illness should prompt consideration of persistent parasitic infection.

3.4 Case Study: SIBO and Histamine Intolerance

Background

Eudora, a 41-year-old nurse, developed severe digestive symptoms following a trip to Mexico where she contracted traveler's diarrhea. The acute infection resolved with antibiotics, but her gastrointestinal system never fully recovered. Over subsequent months, she noticed worsening bloating, unpredictable bowel habits alternating between diarrhea and constipation, and increasing food sensitivities. She had always tolerated all foods previously but now reacted to seemingly random items.

Presentation

By the time Eudora sought specialist consultation, she was experiencing daily symptoms. Severe postprandial bloating made her appear visibly pregnant by afternoon. Cramping abdominal pain occurred several times weekly. She had eliminated numerous foods based on perceived reactions but continued experiencing symptoms. Fatigue worsened progressively, impairing her ability to work full nursing shifts.

Beyond gastrointestinal complaints, Eudora reported frequent headaches, episodes of rapid heartbeat, and skin flushing after meals. She noticed particular problems after eating leftover proteins, aged cheeses, and fermented foods. Fresh fruits like strawberries and oranges also triggered reactions. She had lost 15 pounds due to dietary restriction and fear of eating.

Analysis

Eudora's presentation demonstrates the connection between gut health and histamine intolerance discussed in section 3.3. Her symptoms began following acute gastroenteritis, a classic trigger for both SIBO and histamine intolerance development. Gastrointestinal infections can damage intestinal mucosa, impair motility, and disrupt healthy gut microbiota (Pimentel et al., 2020).

The progressive nature of her food sensitivities suggests evolving gut pathology rather than static food allergies. Her initial tolerance of all foods followed by expanding reactivity indicates acquired histamine intolerance, likely from combined SIBO and intestinal damage (Raithel et al., 2013).

Her symptom pattern provides diagnostic clues. Severe postprandial bloating, particularly worsening throughout the day as food accumulates in a slow-transit small intestine, strongly suggests SIBO. The protein-rich foods triggering worst reactions (leftover meats, aged cheese) represent both high-histamine foods and excellent substrates for bacterial histamine production from histidine (Sánchez-Pérez et al., 2018).

The multi-system symptoms beyond digestion (headaches, tachycardia, flushing) indicate systemic histamine effects from section 2.0. These manifestations suggest that histamine generated by gut bacteria was entering systemic circulation, either through increased production overwhelming DAO capacity or through increased intestinal permeability allowing more absorption.

Intervention

Diagnostic testing confirmed hydrogen-positive SIBO via breath test. Small intestinal aspirate culture grew predominantly Klebsiella pneumoniae and Enterobacter species, both significant histamine producers. Serum DAO measurement revealed markedly reduced enzyme activity.

Treatment addressed multiple factors. Rifaximin 550 mg three times daily for 14 days targeted small intestinal bacterial overgrowth. Following antibiotic completion, Eudora began comprehensive gut restoration protocol including L-glutamine for intestinal healing, zinc carnosine for mucosal repair, and multi-strain probiotic emphasizing histamine-degrading species (Bifidobacterium infantis, Lactobacillus plantarum).

Simultaneously, she implemented strict low-histamine diet to reduce total histamine burden while gut healed. DAO enzyme supplementation before meals supported remaining dietary histamine degradation. Quercetin and vitamin C provided mast cell stabilization and DAO support.

Outcome

Within three weeks of completing antibiotics, Eudora noticed substantial improvement. Bloating decreased dramatically. Bowel movements normalized. Energy began returning. She cautiously reintroduced previously reactive foods, finding most now tolerated without issue.

At three-month follow-up, repeat SIBO breath test showed normal results. She had regained 10 of the 15 lost pounds. Most foods proved tolerable, though she continued avoiding the highest-histamine items. She resumed full-time work without difficulty. Serum DAO measurement showed improvement to low-normal range.

Teaching Points

- Acute gastrointestinal infections can trigger chronic SIBO and histamine intolerance through intestinal damage, motility impairment, and microbiota disruption, creating persistent symptoms long after the acute infection resolves
- SIBO produces substantial histamine from dietary protein through bacterial histidine decarboxylase, creating systemic histamine excess that overwhelms degradative capacity even in individuals with previously normal DAO function
- Addressing underlying gut pathology through SIBO treatment, intestinal healing, and microbiota restoration often produces superior long-term outcomes compared to dietary restriction alone

3.5 Medications Affecting Histamine Metabolism

Numerous commonly prescribed medications interfere with histamine metabolism through DAO inhibition, increased histamine release from mast cells, or intestinal damage reducing DAO production (Maintz & Novak, 2007). Understanding these medication effects proves essential for managing histamine intolerance and for providers when prescribing to susceptible patients.

Nonsteroidal anti-inflammatory drugs (NSAIDs) including ibuprofen, naproxen, aspirin, and others directly inhibit DAO enzyme activity (Jarisch & Weyer, 1999). These medications also trigger mast cell degranulation, releasing stored histamine. The combined effect of increased histamine release plus impaired degradation creates substantial histamine accumulation. Many patients report symptom improvement after discontinuing chronic NSAID use.

Certain antibiotics impair histamine metabolism through multiple mechanisms. Some antibiotics directly inhibit DAO, while others damage intestinal mucosa or dramatically alter gut microbiota composition (Maintz & Novak, 2007). Clavulanic acid, commonly combined with amoxicillin in augmentin, shows particularly strong DAO inhibition. Isoniazid used for tuberculosis treatment potently inhibits DAO. Metronidazole and other antibiotics disrupt gut flora, potentially allowing histamine-producing bacteria to predominate.

Antidepressants, particularly selective serotonin reuptake inhibitors (SSRIs) and tricyclic antidepressants, affect histamine through receptor interactions and potential DAO inhibition (Maintz & Novak, 2007). Some patients report worsening histamine symptoms after starting these medications, though others tolerate them without issue. The effects appear variable and dose-dependent.

Cardiovascular medications including certain antihypertensives and antiarrhythmics inhibit DAO activity. Verapamil, a calcium channel blocker, shows DAO inhibition (Maintz & Novak, 2007). Propranolol and other beta-blockers may affect histamine metabolism. Diuretics can cause micronutrient depletion that indirectly impairs DAO function through copper or B6 deficiency.

Proton pump inhibitors (PPIs) and H2-blockers used for acid reflux create complex effects. While H2-blockers therapeutically benefit histamine intolerance through receptor blockade, they also reduce stomach acid production (Schubert, 2009). Reduced gastric acid may alter protein digestion and gut microbiota, potentially affecting histamine generation. PPIs impair nutrient absorption including vitamin B12, iron, and magnesium, which can indirectly affect DAO function.

Muscle relaxants including diazepam and other benzodiazepines may trigger histamine release from mast cells (Maintz & Novak, 2007). The mechanism involves direct mast cell membrane effects causing degranulation. Patients using these medications chronically sometimes experience improvement in histamine symptoms after discontinuation.

Antihistamines themselves require nuanced understanding. While first-generation antihistamines like diphenhydramine therapeutically block H1 receptors, they do not address underlying histamine excess or DAO deficiency. Some antihistamines may paradoxically trigger mast cell degranulation at higher doses. Second-generation antihistamines (cetirizine, loratadine, fexofenadine) generally prove better tolerated with fewer paradoxical effects.

Opioid pain medications trigger histamine release from mast cells through direct membrane effects (Maintz & Novak, 2007). Morphine shows particularly pronounced histamine-releasing properties. Patients receiving opioids often experience flushing, itching, and other histamine-mediated side effects. Alternative pain management becomes important for histamine-intolerant patients.

Certain chemotherapy agents cause severe histamine release and mast cell activation. Taxanes, platinum compounds, and others can trigger massive histamine release, requiring prophylactic antihistamine administration before chemotherapy infusions (Castells, 2017).

Hormonal medications including oral contraceptives and hormone replacement therapy containing estrogen inhibit DAO activity as discussed in section 3.6. This effect explains why some women develop histamine intolerance after starting birth control pills.

Not all patients react to all medications, and individual variation proves substantial. Some medications show clear DAO inhibition in laboratory studies but cause minimal clinical effects in most patients. Others trigger severe reactions in susceptible individuals. Patients should work with knowledgeable providers to evaluate medication effects and consider alternatives when appropriate.

3.6 Hormonal Influences on Histamine Tolerance

Hormonal fluctuations significantly affect histamine metabolism and mast cell activity, explaining why histamine intolerance affects women disproportionately and why symptoms often fluctuate with menstrual cycles, pregnancy, and menopause (Sattler et al., 1988). Understanding these hormonal influences proves essential for managing female patients and for timing interventions appropriately.

Estrogen exerts the most significant hormonal effect on histamine metabolism. This hormone directly inhibits DAO enzyme activity, reducing the body's capacity to degrade histamine (Sattler et al., 1988). Higher estrogen levels correspond to lower DAO activity and reduced histamine tolerance. This relationship explains numerous clinical observations in histamine intolerance.

During the **menstrual cycle**, estrogen and progesterone levels fluctuate predictably. The follicular phase (cycle days 1-14) maintains relatively lower estrogen levels. DAO activity remains higher during this phase, permitting better histamine tolerance (Maintz et al., 2006). The luteal phase (days 15-28) features rising estrogen and progesterone, with estrogen peaking several days before menstruation. DAO activity decreases correspondingly, lowering histamine threshold.

Many women with histamine intolerance report dramatic symptom worsening during premenstrual days when estrogen peaks. The same foods tolerated earlier in the cycle trigger reactions premenstrually. Migraines, digestive symptoms, anxiety, and other histamine-related manifestations intensify. This predictable pattern provides diagnostic information and allows targeted intervention during high-risk cycle phases.

Pregnancy creates complex hormonal effects on histamine. Early pregnancy features rapidly rising estrogen and progesterone, potentially worsening histamine symptoms (Maintz et al., 2006). However, pregnancy also stimulates increased DAO production by the placenta. By second trimester, placental DAO production often exceeds baseline levels substantially, providing improved histamine tolerance despite high estrogen. This explains why some women with histamine intolerance experience symptom improvement during mid-to-late pregnancy.

Following delivery, placental DAO disappears rapidly while hormones fluctuate dramatically. This creates vulnerability to histamine reactions in the postpartum period. Women may experience unexpected symptom flares weeks after delivery as their system adjusts (Maintz et al., 2006).

Oral contraceptives containing synthetic estrogens inhibit DAO activity similarly to endogenous estrogen (Maintz & Novak, 2007). Women often develop new histamine intolerance symptoms after starting birth control pills. Symptoms may worsen with higher-estrogen formulations. Some women find progesterone-only contraceptives better tolerated, though progesterone shows its own complex effects on mast cells.

Hormone replacement therapy (HRT) used during menopause can trigger or worsen histamine intolerance through DAO inhibition. Women who tolerated histamine-rich foods before HRT may develop new sensitivities after starting estrogen therapy. This effect sometimes prompts providers to reduce estrogen doses or discontinue HRT.

Menopause itself shows variable effects. Some women experience histamine symptom improvement after menopause as estrogen levels decline permanently (Maintz & Novak, 2007). DAO activity may increase with sustained low estrogen. However, the hormonal fluctuations during perimenopause can worsen symptoms before eventual improvement. Not all women improve after menopause, suggesting that hormonal effects represent only one piece of the histamine puzzle.

Progesterone effects on histamine prove more nuanced. While progesterone doesn't inhibit DAO directly, it appears to affect mast cell activity through progesterone receptors expressed on these cells (Zaitsu et al., 2007). Some research suggests progesterone may stabilize mast cells, potentially reducing histamine release. Clinical effects vary between individuals.

Testosterone and other androgens show less clear effects on histamine metabolism, though some research suggests androgens may support DAO activity (Maintz & Novak, 2007). This might partially explain lower histamine intolerance prevalence in men. However, the relationship requires further research for definitive conclusions.

3.7 Case Study: Hormonal Histamine Patterns

Background

Ianthe, a 36-year-old accountant, had managed mild food sensitivities successfully for years through modest dietary adjustments. However, symptoms intensified dramatically after she started oral contraceptive pills for endometriosis management. Within three months, her previously manageable sensitivities became debilitating multi-system reactions affecting work and quality of life.

Presentation

Ianthe experienced clear cyclical symptom patterns. During her active pill weeks (days 1-21), symptoms progressively worsened. Week one remained relatively tolerable. Week two brought increasing digestive issues, mild flushing, and occasional headaches. Week three proved nearly unbearable, with severe migraines, constant digestive distress, anxiety attacks, heart palpitations, and such intense brain fog that complex accounting work became impossible.

Her placebo pill week (days 22-28) brought dramatic relief. By day three off active pills, symptoms began improving. Days five through seven felt nearly normal, allowing her to enjoy previously reactive foods without issue. She documented this pattern meticulously over four months, finding it remarkably consistent.

The foods triggering reactions also showed cyclical patterns. During week one, she tolerated moderate-histamine foods like spinach, tomatoes, and fresh fish. These same foods triggered reactions during week three. High-histamine foods like aged cheese and wine caused problems at all cycle phases but became completely intolerable during week three.

Analysis

Ianthe's presentation demonstrates hormonal influences on histamine tolerance from section 3.6. Her symptoms began shortly after starting oral contraceptives containing synthetic estrogen, which inhibits DAO enzyme activity (Maintz & Novak, 2007). The progressive symptom worsening across the active pill weeks reflects cumulative estrogen exposure and corresponding DAO suppression.

The dramatic relief during her placebo week shows estrogen's direct effect. Without exogenous estrogen intake, her DAO activity recovered partially, raising her histamine threshold (Sattler et al., 1988). This allowed tolerance of foods that exceeded her capacity during high-estrogen weeks.

Her escalating symptom severity across week one through week three suggests cumulative effects. Estrogen doesn't just acutely inhibit DAO; sustained exposure creates progressively worsening enzyme suppression. Additionally, week three corresponds to her endogenous late luteal phase, when her natural estrogen would peak premenstrually. The combination of exogenous estrogen from pills plus endogenous estrogen created maximum DAO suppression.

The food tolerance variations across her cycle illustrate the histamine bucket concept from section 2.1. The same foods containing identical histamine amounts fell below threshold during low-estrogen weeks but exceeded threshold during high-estrogen weeks. Her bucket's drainage capacity (DAO activity) changed cyclically while dietary histamine load remained constant.

Intervention

After consultation with her gynecologist and integrative medicine provider, Ianthe faced several options. Discontinuing oral contraceptives would likely improve histamine tolerance but leave endometriosis unmanaged. Switching to progesterone-only contraception might reduce estrogen effects while maintaining endometriosis control.

She chose a trial of progesterone-only pill combined with histamine management strategies. Dietary approach involved strict low-histamine diet during her premenstrual week when endogenous estrogen peaked, with modest relaxation during other weeks. DAO enzyme supplementation before all meals supported dietary histamine degradation. H1 and H2 antihistamines provided receptor blockade during high-symptom weeks.

She added quercetin 500 mg twice daily and vitamin C 1000 mg daily for mast cell stabilization and DAO support (Hagel et al., 2013). Magnesium glycinate 400 mg nightly provided multiple benefits including mast cell stabilization and menstrual symptom reduction.

Outcome

Within two months of switching contraceptive methods and implementing support strategies, Ianthe experienced substantial improvement. The dramatic week-by-week escalation pattern resolved. While she still noticed increased sensitivity premenstrually when endogenous estrogen peaked, the intensity decreased markedly. Week three no longer became completely debilitating.

She successfully reintroduced moderate-histamine foods during most of her cycle, reserving strictest avoidance for premenstrual days. Work performance normalized. Brain fog cleared. Migraines decreased from 8-10 monthly to 2-3 monthly, mostly premenstrual.

Teaching Points

- Synthetic estrogen in oral contraceptives inhibits DAO enzyme activity and commonly triggers or worsens histamine intolerance, requiring either contraceptive adjustment or additional histamine management strategies
- Cyclical symptom patterns corresponding to menstrual phases provide strong diagnostic evidence for hormonal influences on histamine tolerance, with premenstrual worsening representing a hallmark feature
- Combining cycle-based dietary adjustments (stricter during high-risk phases, more relaxed during low-risk phases) with DAO support and receptor blockade often produces better outcomes than rigid year-round restriction

3.8 Environmental and Lifestyle Triggers

Beyond diet, hormones, and medications, numerous environmental and lifestyle factors trigger mast cell activation and influence histamine tolerance (Molderings et al., 2011). These factors often receive insufficient attention yet contribute substantially to symptom burden. Understanding and managing these triggers proves essential for comprehensive treatment.

Stress represents one of the most potent mast cell activators. Both acute and chronic stress trigger mast cell degranulation through the hypothalamic-pituitary-adrenal (HPA) axis and direct neural pathways (Theoharides et al., 2012). Corticotropin-releasing hormone (CRH), released during stress, directly activates mast cells through CRH receptors on their surface. This explains why many patients report symptom flares during stressful periods despite maintaining strict dietary compliance.

Chronic stress creates sustained mast cell activation, contributing to baseline histamine elevation that reduces tolerance for all other triggers. Stress management techniques including meditation, yoga, breathing exercises, and cognitive-behavioral approaches can reduce mast cell activation and improve histamine tolerance (Afrin et al., 2016). Some patients experience dramatic symptom improvement from stress reduction alone.

Temperature extremes trigger mast cell activation in susceptible individuals. Both heat and cold exposure can provoke histamine release. Some patients develop hives, flushing, or systemic symptoms when exposed to hot showers, saunas, or hot weather (Molderings et al., 2011). Others react to cold exposure, developing cold urticaria or general symptom worsening in winter. The mechanism involves temperature-sensitive ion channels on mast cell membranes that trigger degranulation when activated.

Sudden temperature changes prove particularly problematic. Moving from air conditioning to summer heat, or from warm indoors to winter cold, triggers reactions more readily than gradual temperature transitions. Patients learn to moderate temperature exposure, taking lukewarm rather than hot showers, dressing in layers to avoid sudden temperature shifts, and avoiding extreme environmental temperatures.

Physical pressure on skin activates mast cells in some individuals, causing dermographism (Kaplan, 2004). Light scratching or rubbing produces raised, itchy welts following the pressure pattern. Tight clothing, backpack straps, or prolonged sitting creates sufficient pressure to trigger localized histamine release. This physical urticaria variant indicates generalized mast cell hyperreactivity.

Vibration triggers mast cell activation in rare cases. Using power tools, driving on rough roads, or other vibratory stimuli provoke symptoms. **Exercise** shows complex effects, generally beneficial for health but triggering mast cell activation during and after exertion in some patients (Molderings et al., 2011). The mechanism involves multiple factors including body temperature elevation, mechanical stimulation, and metabolic changes. Patients often need to identify their exercise tolerance threshold, staying below the intensity that triggers reactions.

Fragrances and chemicals represent common triggers. Perfumes, air fresheners, cleaning products, and other scented items contain volatile organic compounds that activate mast cells (Afrin et al., 2016). Many patients report reactions to synthetic fragrances, smoke, paint fumes, and other airborne chemicals. The mechanism may involve direct mast cell membrane effects or triggering through sensory nerve pathways.

Mold exposure triggers mast cell activation through multiple mechanisms including direct mycotoxin effects and allergic reactions (Afrin et al., 2016). Patients living in water-damaged buildings often experience worsening histamine symptoms that improve after remediation or relocation. Some mycotoxins directly activate mast cells while others create sustained immune dysfunction promoting mast cell hyperreactivity.

Electromagnetic fields (EMF) from wireless devices, computers, and other electronic equipment trigger symptoms in a subset of patients, though this remains controversial and poorly understood (McCarty et al., 2011). Some patients report improvement when reducing EMF exposure, though placebo effects prove difficult to exclude. More research is needed to clarify potential mechanisms.

Sleep deprivation worsens histamine tolerance through multiple pathways including HPA axis activation, increased inflammation, and direct effects on mast cell stability (Theoharides et al., 2012). Patients often notice symptom improvement when prioritizing adequate sleep. The histamine system itself regulates sleep-wake cycles, creating bidirectional relationships where poor sleep worsens histamine symptoms, which then further disrupt sleep.

Alcohol consumption merits special mention. As noted in section 3.1, alcohol inhibits DAO while increasing intestinal permeability (Wantke et al., 1994). Alcoholic beverages contain varying histamine levels based on production methods. Fermented drinks like wine and beer contain substantial histamine. The combination of DAO inhibition, increased permeability, and direct histamine content makes alcohol particularly problematic for histamine-intolerant patients.

3.9 Food Triggers Beyond Histamine Content

While high-histamine foods receive primary attention in histamine intolerance management, several other categories of foods trigger reactions through different mechanisms (Maintz & Novak, 2007). Understanding these categories proves essential for comprehensive dietary management.

Histamine liberators represent foods that trigger endogenous histamine release from mast cells despite containing little histamine themselves. These foods activate mast cells through various mechanisms including direct membrane effects or immune-mediated pathways (Maintz & Novak, 2007). Common histamine liberators include citrus fruits (oranges, lemons, limes, grapefruit), strawberries, bananas, papaya, pineapple, tomatoes, spinach, chocolate, nuts (especially walnuts, cashews, peanuts), shellfish, and certain food additives.

The mechanism varies by food. Some contain compounds that directly trigger mast cell degranulation. Others activate complement pathways that indirectly stimulate mast cells. Some histamine liberators affect only certain individuals, suggesting genetic or acquired differences in mast cell sensitivity. Clinical experience shows substantial individual variation in which liberators trigger reactions.

DAO-blocking foods and substances interfere with histamine degradation without containing high histamine themselves. Alcohol represents the most significant DAO blocker as discussed previously (Wantke et al., 1994). Black tea, green tea, and mate tea contain compounds that inhibit DAO activity, though effects appear dose-dependent and individual variation exists (Maintz & Novak, 2007). Energy drinks and certain supplements may contain DAO-inhibiting compounds.

Biogenic amines represent a category of compounds chemically related to histamine. Foods high in other biogenic amines can trigger reactions through several mechanisms (Sánchez-Pérez et al., 2018). These amines compete with histamine for the same degradative enzymes, potentially overwhelming DAO capacity. They may also directly trigger physiological effects similar to histamine or cross-react with histamine receptors.

Tyramine, formed from the amino acid tyrosine, appears in aged and fermented foods similar to histamine. Aged cheeses, cured meats, fermented soy products, and aged/fermented beverages contain substantial tyramine (Sánchez-Pérez et al., 2018). Tyramine affects blood pressure and can trigger migraines through monoamine oxidase interactions. In histamine-intolerant patients, tyramine-rich foods often trigger reactions similar to histamine reactions.

Putrescine and cadaverine, formed from the amino acids ornithine and lysine respectively, appear in aging and decomposing protein foods. These diamines compete directly with histamine for DAO enzyme, potentially reducing histamine degradation (Sánchez-Pérez et al., 2018). Foods high in putrescine and cadaverine include aged cheeses, cured meats, certain fish, and overripe fruits. The presence of these compounds in a food may worsen reactions even if histamine content remains moderate.

Phenylethylamine, derived from phenylalanine, appears in chocolate, certain cheeses, and fermented foods. This compound can trigger headaches and other symptoms in susceptible individuals (Sánchez-Pérez et al., 2018). The combined presence of phenylethylamine and histamine in chocolate may explain particularly strong reactions some patients experience.

Tryptamine, derived from tryptophan, appears in tomatoes, plums, and certain other foods. **Spermidine and spermine**, polyamines present in aged foods and certain vegetables, may contribute to symptoms (Sánchez-Pérez et al., 2018). The clinical significance of these less-studied amines requires further research, but their presence in foods correlates with symptom reports from sensitive patients.

Lectins represent plant proteins that can increase intestinal permeability and trigger immune activation. While not biogenic amines, lectins in beans, grains, and nightshade vegetables may worsen symptoms in some patients through increased gut permeability allowing more histamine absorption (Freed, 1999).

Salicylates, natural compounds found in many fruits, vegetables, herbs, and spices, trigger reactions in some histamine-intolerant patients. The mechanism may involve effects on mast cell stability or prostaglandin metabolism (Swain et al., 1985). Patients with combined histamine and salicylate sensitivity face particularly challenging dietary restrictions.

Individual tolerance to these various food categories varies dramatically. Some patients react only to high-histamine foods while tolerating liberators and other amines. Others show broad reactivity to multiple categories, requiring more extensive dietary modification. Systematic elimination and reintroduction helps identify individual trigger categories.

3.10 Case Study: Multiple Trigger Categories

Background

Jessamine, a 28-year-old graphic designer, had followed a strict low-histamine diet for six months with only modest improvement. She meticulously avoided all high-histamine foods listed in standard resources yet continued experiencing frequent reactions. Frustrated by limited progress despite dietary dedication, she sought comprehensive evaluation to identify missed triggers.

Presentation

Jessamine's symptom diary revealed puzzling patterns. She reacted to clearly high-histamine foods as expected, experiencing flushing, digestive distress, and migraines after aged cheese, wine, or leftover proteins. However, she also reacted severely to fresh strawberries, tomatoes, and citrus fruits, all listed as lower-histamine on some resources. Fresh chocolate triggered intense headaches despite being recently manufactured with presumably low histamine content.

Her reactions didn't correlate solely with histamine content. Some high-histamine foods like sauerkraut caused mild symptoms while moderate-histamine foods like fresh tomatoes triggered severe reactions. She noticed that stress dramatically worsened all food reactions. Poor sleep preceded her worst symptom days regardless of diet. Hot showers sometimes triggered flushing even on good dietary days.

Environmental factors complicated the picture. She experienced worsening symptoms during her work's busy season when stress peaked. Synthetic fragrances in her office triggered headaches and difficulty breathing. Temperature changes from summer heat to air conditioning caused flushing episodes. These non-dietary triggers created variable baseline histamine levels that affected food tolerance unpredictably.

Analysis

Jessamine's complex presentation illustrates that histamine intolerance rarely involves diet alone. Her case demonstrates multiple trigger categories from sections 3.8 and 3.9 operating simultaneously to fill her histamine bucket beyond threshold.

The reactions to strawberries, tomatoes, and citrus reveal histamine liberator effects (Maintz & Novak, 2007). These foods contain relatively low histamine but trigger endogenous histamine release from mast cells. Her severe chocolate reactions reflect combined effects of phenylethylamine, tyramine, and possible histamine content depending on processing and aging.

The stress and sleep connections demonstrate environmental trigger contributions from section 3.8. Chronic stress activates mast cells through CRH pathways (Theoharides et al., 2012). Sleep deprivation increases inflammation and reduces mast cell stability. These factors elevated her baseline histamine level independent of diet, reducing available capacity for dietary histamine.

The temperature and fragrance sensitivity indicates generalized mast cell hyperreactivity characteristic of MCAS discussed in Chapter 1.0. Physical and chemical triggers activated her mast cells, releasing histamine that added to dietary sources. This multi-source histamine accumulation explains why dietary restriction alone provided insufficient relief.

Her variable reactions to identical foods at different times reflect the dynamic nature of the histamine bucket. On low-stress, well-rested days with minimal environmental triggers, her bucket started relatively empty, allowing tolerance of moderate-histamine foods. On high-stress, poorly-slept days with fragrance exposures, her bucket started nearly full before eating, causing reactions to even low-histamine foods.

Intervention

Comprehensive intervention addressed multiple bucket-filling factors. Diet expanded beyond simple histamine avoidance to eliminate identified liberators (strawberries, citrus, tomatoes) and other biogenic amine sources (chocolate, aged foods containing tyramine). She continued avoiding high-histamine foods.

Environmental modifications included stress management through daily meditation practice and therapy to address work-related stress. Sleep hygiene improvements prioritized consistent 8-hour sleep schedules. She negotiated fragrance-free policies in her immediate work area and used air purifier at her desk. Temperature moderation involved lukewarm rather than hot showers and layered clothing for gradual temperature transitions.

Medical management included baseline H1 antihistamine (cetirizine 10 mg daily) plus additional H2 blocker (famotidine 20 mg twice daily) during high-stress periods. DAO enzyme supplementation before meals supported dietary histamine breakdown. Quercetin 500 mg twice daily and vitamin C 1000 mg daily provided mast cell stabilization.

Outcome

Within two months of comprehensive intervention, Jessamine experienced transformation. Daily symptoms decreased from 6-7 days weekly to 2-3 days weekly. Severity of reactions diminished substantially. Migraines dropped from 8-10 monthly to 2-3 monthly. Energy improved, allowing her to enjoy activities abandoned during her sickest period.

The multi-factor approach proved essential. When she experimented with relaxing only dietary restrictions while maintaining environmental modifications, symptoms returned. When she maintained strict diet while allowing stress and sleep to deteriorate, symptoms worsened. Only the combination of dietary, environmental, and medical interventions maintained good control.

Teaching Points

- Histamine intolerance commonly involves multiple trigger categories including high-histamine foods, histamine liberators, other biogenic amines, environmental stressors, and physical triggers, requiring comprehensive assessment beyond diet alone
- The histamine bucket fills from numerous sources simultaneously, explaining why dietary restriction alone often provides incomplete symptom relief if environmental and lifestyle triggers remain unaddressed
- Individual trigger identification through systematic assessment of dietary, environmental, and lifestyle factors enables personalized intervention strategies that address the specific combination of factors filling each patient's unique histamine bucket

3.11 Inflammation and Oxidative Stress

Chronic inflammation and oxidative stress create bidirectional relationships with histamine intolerance and MCAS, simultaneously resulting from and contributing to histamine-related disorders (Theoharides et al., 2012). Understanding these relationships illuminates additional intervention targets and explains why comprehensive anti-inflammatory approaches benefit many patients.

Oxidative stress occurs when production of reactive oxygen species (ROS) exceeds antioxidant defenses, damaging cellular components (Pizzino et al., 2017). Mast cells both generate and respond to oxidative stress. When activated, mast cells produce substantial ROS as part of their immune function. However, excessive oxidative stress also triggers mast cell degranulation, creating positive feedback loops where mast cell activation increases oxidative stress, which further activates mast cells.

DAO enzyme proves particularly vulnerable to oxidative damage. This copper-containing enzyme requires precise structural integrity for function (Schwelberger, 2010). Oxidative stress damages DAO protein structure, reducing catalytic activity. Antioxidant support through diet and supplementation may protect DAO from oxidative inactivation, potentially improving histamine degradation.

Chronic inflammation from any source increases mast cell activation and histamine production. Inflammatory cytokines including TNF-alpha, IL-1, IL-6, and others directly activate mast cells through cytokine receptors on their surface (Theoharides et al., 2012). Conditions creating systemic inflammation such as obesity, metabolic syndrome, autoimmune diseases, and chronic infections all promote mast cell hyperreactivity.

Conversely, chronic histamine elevation contributes to inflammation through multiple mechanisms. Histamine enhances vascular permeability, facilitating inflammatory cell recruitment to tissues. It modulates T cell function, potentially promoting inflammatory responses. Sustained histamine exposure upregulates inflammatory gene expression in various cell types (Leurs et al., 2009).

Intestinal inflammation deserves particular attention given the gut's role as primary DAO production site. Inflammatory bowel diseases, celiac disease, and other conditions causing intestinal inflammation directly damage DAO-producing enterocytes (Raithel et al., 2010). The inflammation also increases intestinal permeability, allowing more histamine absorption. Anti-inflammatory interventions targeting gut inflammation often improve histamine tolerance substantially.

Neuroinflammation represents inflammation within the central nervous system. Mast cells reside in the brain, particularly near blood vessels and in areas lacking complete blood-brain barrier (Theoharides et al., 2012). Brain mast cell activation contributes to neuroinflammation implicated in anxiety, depression, autism spectrum disorders, and neurodegenerative conditions. The neurological symptoms of histamine intolerance discussed in section 2.5 may partially reflect neuroinflammation from chronic brain mast cell activation.

Anti-inflammatory dietary approaches provide therapeutic benefits. Omega-3 fatty acids from fish oil demonstrate anti-inflammatory effects and may stabilize mast cells (Theoharides et al., 2012). However, fish oil must be fresh and properly stored since oxidized fish oil paradoxically increases inflammation. Some patients find specialized pro-resolving mediators (SPMs) derived from omega-3s better tolerated than standard fish oil due to lower histamine content.

Polyphenol-rich foods including berries, green tea, and colorful vegetables provide antioxidant protection when tolerated (Weng et al., 2012). However, many polyphenol sources also contain histamine or act as liberators, requiring individual assessment. Curcumin from turmeric shows anti-inflammatory and mast cell-stabilizing properties though absorption requires enhancement for therapeutic effect.

Antioxidant supplementation may support histamine tolerance. Vitamin C functions both as antioxidant and DAO cofactor (Hagel et al., 2013). Vitamin E, alpha-lipoic acid, N-acetylcysteine (NAC), and glutathione provide antioxidant support that may reduce mast cell activation and protect DAO function. However, individual tolerance varies, with some patients reacting to certain supplements.

Mitochondrial dysfunction represents another facet of oxidative stress relevant to histamine disorders. Mitochondria generate cellular energy but also produce ROS as metabolic byproducts (Picard & McEwen, 2018). Dysfunctional mitochondria produce excessive ROS while generating insufficient energy. This combination worsens oxidative stress and cellular function. Supporting mitochondrial health through CoQ10, L-carnitine, B vitamins, and other nutrients may reduce oxidative stress and improve energy in histamine-intolerant patients experiencing fatigue.

3.12 Viral Triggers and Long COVID

As introduced in section 2.9, viral infections can trigger chronic mast cell dysfunction and histamine intolerance that persists long after viral clearance (Afrin et al., 2021). The COVID-19 pandemic brought unprecedented attention to post-viral mast cell activation, but other viruses show similar capabilities.

SARS-CoV-2 infection triggers mast cell activation through multiple mechanisms. The virus directly infects mast cells through ACE2 receptors expressed on their surface (Theoharides, 2020). This direct infection activates mast cells, causing histamine and other mediator release. Even after viral clearance, mast cells may remain hyperreactive for months, creating the prolonged symptoms of Long COVID.

The spike protein of SARS-CoV-2 appears to directly activate mast cells even without active viral replication (Theoharides, 2020). Residual spike protein or spike protein fragments may continue triggering mast cells long after acute infection resolves. Additionally, immune responses to the virus, including antibody formation and T cell activation, can secondarily activate mast cells through immune complex formation and cytokine release.

Research demonstrates elevated mast cell mediators including tryptase, histamine metabolites, and prostaglandin D2 in Long COVID patients compared to recovered individuals without persistent symptoms (Weinstock et al., 2021). This biochemical evidence supports mast cell involvement in Long COVID pathophysiology. The overlap between Long COVID symptoms and MCAS presentations proves striking, as discussed in section 2.9.

Post-viral onset MCAS follows other viral infections beyond COVID-19. Epstein-Barr virus (EBV), cytomegalovirus (CMV), human herpesvirus-6 (HHV-6), and enteroviruses all demonstrate capacity to trigger chronic mast cell dysfunction (Afrin et al., 2016). These viruses may establish latency in tissues where they periodically reactivate, providing ongoing stimulation to the immune system and mast cells.

The mechanism connecting viral infection to chronic mast cell activation likely involves multiple factors. Direct viral effects on mast cells during acute infection may create lasting hyperreactivity. Chronic low-level viral reactivation from latent infections provides ongoing triggers. Virus-induced autoantibodies may target mast cell surface receptors, causing inappropriate activation. Persistent inflammation from incomplete viral clearance activates mast cells chronically (Afrin et al., 2021).

Viral reactivation of latent infections represents another important mechanism. Many individuals harbor latent EBV, CMV, HHV-6, and other herpes viruses that typically remain dormant under immune control (Afrin et al., 2016). However, various stressors including other infections, psychological stress, poor sleep, or nutrient deficiencies can allow viral reactivation. This reactivation triggers immune responses that activate mast cells.

Some patients with histamine intolerance or MCAS show evidence of chronic viral reactivation through elevated antibodies or positive PCR testing for viral DNA in blood. Addressing viral reactivation through antiviral medications or immune support sometimes improves mast cell symptoms, suggesting the viral activity contributes to ongoing mast cell activation (Afrin et al., 2016).

Post-infectious fatigue syndromes including myalgic encephalomyelitis/chronic fatigue syndrome (ME/CFS) show substantial overlap with MCAS (Molderings et al., 2011). Many ME/CFS cases begin following viral infections including mononucleosis (EBV), viral meningitis, or other acute illnesses. The persistent symptoms including fatigue, exercise intolerance, cognitive dysfunction, and multi-system complaints resemble MCAS presentations. Elevated mast cell mediators appear in ME/CFS patients, suggesting mast cell involvement in this post-viral syndrome.

Treatment approaches for post-viral MCAS mirror other MCAS management strategies discussed throughout this book. H1 and H2 antihistamines, mast cell stabilizers, low-histamine diet, and stress management all provide benefit (Afrin et al., 2021). Some patients require additional interventions targeting viral reactivation or immune modulation. The time course for improvement varies widely, from months to years, with some patients experiencing incomplete recovery.

3.13 Core Principles Recap

This chapter revealed the multiple root causes and triggers that reduce DAO enzyme activity and promote histamine accumulation. Genetic polymorphisms in AOC1 and HNMT genes create inherent susceptibility, with certain variants reducing enzyme production or function by 40-70%. These genetic factors explain familial clustering and individual variation in histamine tolerance.

Gut health profoundly affects histamine through three mechanisms: SIBO and dysbiosis generate substantial bacterial histamine from dietary protein, intestinal damage from inflammation or infection destroys DAO-producing enterocytes, and increased intestinal permeability allows more histamine absorption. Addressing underlying gut pathology often proves essential for sustainable improvement.

Numerous medications interfere with histamine metabolism through DAO inhibition, mast cell activation, or intestinal damage. NSAIDs, certain antibiotics, cardiovascular drugs, and hormonal contraceptives represent common culprits requiring evaluation and potential adjustment in histamine-intolerant patients.

Hormonal influences, particularly estrogen inhibition of DAO activity, explain why women predominate among histamine intolerance patients and why symptoms fluctuate with menstrual cycles, pregnancy, and contraceptive use. Recognizing these patterns enables cycle-based intervention strategies.

Environmental and lifestyle triggers including stress, temperature extremes, fragrances, and inadequate sleep activate mast cells independent of diet. Food triggers extend beyond high-histamine items to include histamine liberators, DAO blockers, and foods containing other biogenic amines like tyramine, putrescine, and phenylethylamine.

Chronic inflammation and oxidative stress create bidirectional relationships with histamine disorders, simultaneously resulting from and contributing to mast cell activation. Anti-inflammatory and antioxidant approaches provide additional therapeutic targets beyond histamine reduction alone.

Viral infections can trigger chronic mast cell dysfunction persisting long after viral clearance, as demonstrated dramatically by Long COVID but occurring with other viruses as well. Understanding these diverse root causes and triggers enables comprehensive, personalized intervention strategies addressing the specific factors filling each individual's histamine bucket.

Chapter 4.0: Understanding Food and Histamine

Leocadia stood in the grocery store, frozen with confusion. She held two cans of tuna, both from the same brand, both the same type. According to her food list, tuna was high in histamine and strictly forbidden. But her friend with histamine intolerance ate canned tuna regularly without issue. Her nutritionist said fresh fish was fine but canned was problematic. Another online resource claimed all tuna was dangerous. A third source rated it as moderate histamine, acceptable in small amounts. Four different answers to the same question. Which was correct? This confusion plagues nearly everyone beginning a low-histamine diet. Food lists contradict each other. One person's safe food triggers another person's severe reaction. The same food eaten on Monday causes no problems but triggers symptoms on Friday. Understanding why this happens requires grasping the fundamental biochemistry of how histamine forms in food, how different foods affect your body, and why individual variation makes universal food lists impossible.

This chapter explains the science behind histamine in food and provides the knowledge needed to make informed dietary choices. You will learn the biochemical processes that create histamine in aging and fermenting foods, why freshness matters more than food type, which foods contain high histamine and which trigger histamine release, what other biogenic amines complicate the picture, why food lists vary so dramatically between sources, how individual thresholds create unique tolerance patterns, and how to interpret resources like the SIGHI food list. This foundation enables you to understand your own reactions rather than blindly following contradictory lists.

4.1 Histamine Formation in Foods

Histamine in food does not originate from the living plant or animal. Instead, it forms after harvest or slaughter through bacterial action on the amino acid histidine (Maintz & Novak, 2007). Understanding this process illuminates why some foods pose problems while others remain safe.

Bacterial histidine decarboxylase represents the enzyme responsible for converting histidine into histamine. Numerous bacterial species produce this enzyme, including Morganella morganii, Klebsiella pneumoniae, Hafnia alvei, Photobacterium damselae, and various species of Enterobacter, Citrobacter, and Clostridium (Sánchez-Pérez et al., 2018). These bacteria naturally occur in the environment, on food surfaces, and within foods themselves.

When foods containing protein (and thus histidine) sit at temperatures permitting bacterial growth, these bacteria multiply and produce histidine decarboxylase. This enzyme then converts available histidine into histamine. The process accelerates at temperatures between 20-37°C (68-99°F), the optimal range for bacterial growth (Bodmer et al., 1999). Even refrigeration at 4°C (39°F) slows but does not completely stop this process.

The amount of histamine formed depends on multiple factors. **Histidine content** in the original food matters substantially. Fish and seafood contain particularly high histidine levels, making them prone to rapid histamine accumulation (Visciano et al., 2012). Within fish, darker-fleshed species like tuna, mackerel, and mahi-mahi contain more histidine than white-fleshed fish like cod or halibut, explaining their higher histamine potential.

Bacterial load influences histamine production rates. Foods with higher initial bacterial contamination produce histamine faster. Processing conditions that introduce bacteria accelerate the process. This explains why ground meat accumulates histamine more rapidly than whole cuts. The grinding process distributes bacteria throughout the product and creates more surface area for bacterial growth.

Time proves absolutely critical. The longer food sits before consumption, the more histamine accumulates. Fresh fish caught and eaten within hours contains minimal histamine. The same fish stored for 24 hours at room temperature can contain dangerous histamine levels causing scombroid poisoning (Visciano et al., 2012). Even proper refrigeration only slows the process. Fish stored at 4°C for several days accumulates measurable histamine.

Temperature abuse dramatically accelerates histamine formation. Brief periods at room temperature during transport or storage allow rapid bacterial growth and histamine production. Once formed, histamine remains stable. Cooking destroys bacteria but does not eliminate histamine already produced. This explains why properly cooked fish can still cause histamine reactions if the fish wasn't fresh before cooking.

pH and salt concentration affect bacterial growth and histamine production. Fermented foods deliberately create conditions favoring bacterial growth and histamine formation. Sauerkraut, kimchi, yogurt, and other fermented products contain substantial histamine by design. The fermentation process that creates their characteristic flavors also produces histamine.

Freezing provides the most effective preservation method for preventing histamine formation. Rapid freezing immediately after harvest or slaughter halts bacterial growth, preventing histamine accumulation (Lehane & Olley, 2000). Flash-frozen fish often contains less histamine than "fresh" fish that spent days in transport and display. However, freezing does not reverse histamine already formed. Thawing and refreezing creates opportunities for bacterial growth and additional histamine production.

4.2 Fresh Versus Aged Foods

The fresh versus aged distinction represents the single most important factor in dietary histamine management (Maintz & Novak, 2007). This concept extends beyond obvious aged foods like cheese and cured meats to encompass the freshness of all protein-containing foods.

Fresh foods contain minimal histamine because insufficient time has elapsed for bacterial histamine production. A chicken breast cooked within hours of processing contains negligible histamine. Fresh fish caught and prepared the same day poses minimal histamine risk. Vegetables picked and consumed fresh contain virtually no histamine. The definition of "fresh" varies by food type but generally means consumed within 24-48 hours of harvest, slaughter, or processing.

Aging processes deliberately or incidentally create conditions for histamine accumulation. Aged cheeses like parmesan, cheddar, and gouda develop high histamine through months of bacterial fermentation (Sánchez-Pérez et al., 2018). The aging that creates complex flavors simultaneously produces histamine. Cured meats undergo similar processes. Salami, pepperoni, and other dry-cured products contain substantial histamine from bacterial action during curing.

Leftovers represent a critical category often overlooked. Cooked food stored in the refrigerator continues accumulating histamine through bacterial action. The bacteria aren't completely eliminated by cooking, and new bacteria from the environment colonize the food during storage (Bodmer et al., 1999). Research demonstrates that cooked meat stored at 4°C for 24 hours contains measurably increased histamine compared to freshly cooked samples (Maintz & Novak, 2007).

This leftover phenomenon explains a common clinical observation. Patients report tolerating freshly cooked chicken at dinner but reacting to the same chicken reheated for lunch the next day. The chicken didn't change fundamentally. Rather, 18-24 hours of refrigerated storage allowed histamine accumulation sufficient to exceed the patient's threshold.

Optimal strategies minimize storage time. Cook foods and consume immediately. If leftovers are unavoidable, cool quickly and freeze rather than refrigerate. Frozen leftovers accumulate histamine much more slowly than refrigerated ones. Consume refrigerated leftovers within 24 hours maximum. Never reheat the same food multiple times, as each cooling and reheating cycle provides opportunity for bacterial growth.

Canned and preserved foods vary dramatically in histamine content depending on processing timing and methods. Fish canned immediately after catch using high-temperature sterilization contains minimal histamine. Fish that sat for hours or days before canning accumulates substantial histamine that remains stable through the canning process (Visciano et al., 2012). This explains why identical canned products from the same manufacturer can vary in histamine content and tolerability.

Restaurant foods present challenges because storage and preparation timing remain unknown. That grilled salmon might have been fresh this morning or could have spent three days thawing in the refrigerator. Leftover soup might have been made yesterday or last week. Without control over sourcing and timing, restaurant eating proves unpredictable for histamine-sensitive individuals.

4.3 High Histamine Foods Explained

While freshness matters more than food type, certain foods inherently contain or readily accumulate high histamine levels (Maintz & Novak, 2007). Understanding these categories enables informed food selection.

Fish and seafood top most high-histamine lists due to high histidine content and rapid bacterial histamine production. Tuna, mackerel, mahi-mahi, sardines, and anchovies show particularly high histamine levels (Visciano et al., 2012). However, truly fresh fish of any species contains minimal histamine. The issue is time. Fish degrades rapidly after death. Commercial fishing boats often spend days at sea before returning to port. Fish then sits during processing, transport, and retail display. This accumulated time allows substantial histamine formation.

Canned fish presents variable histamine levels. Sardines, anchovies, and tuna canned in oil often contain high histamine due to pre-canning storage time. Some individuals tolerate certain brands while reacting to others, likely reflecting differences in handling and processing speed.

Aged cheeses contain high histamine from months of bacterial fermentation. Parmesan, cheddar, gouda, swiss, and blue cheeses all contain substantial histamine (Sánchez-Pérez et al., 2018). Fresh cheeses like mozzarella, ricotta, cream cheese, and cottage cheese contain much less histamine due to minimal aging. The longer the aging process, the higher the histamine content.

Fermented foods deliberately create conditions for bacterial growth and histamine formation. Sauerkraut, kimchi, pickles, olives, miso, tempeh, and soy sauce all contain high histamine from fermentation (Maintz & Novak, 2007). Yogurt and kefir also contain histamine, though amounts vary by fermentation time and bacterial strains used. Some individuals tolerate fresh yogurt fermented for short periods while reacting to longer-fermented products.

Cured and processed meats including salami, pepperoni, sausage, ham, bacon, and hot dogs contain elevated histamine from curing processes and added bacterial cultures (Sánchez-Pérez et al., 2018). Fresh, unprocessed meats consumed soon after slaughter contain minimal histamine. The processing, curing, and storage create histamine accumulation.

Alcoholic beverages vary in histamine content. Red wine contains the highest levels, with histamine formed during fermentation and aging (Wantke et al., 1994). White wine generally contains less but still measurable amounts. Beer contains moderate histamine from fermentation. Champagne and sparkling wines show variable levels. Clear spirits like vodka and gin contain minimal histamine but still inhibit DAO enzyme as discussed in Chapter 3.0.

Vinegar contains histamine from fermentation, with amounts varying by type and aging. Balsamic vinegar aged for years contains more than white vinegar aged briefly. Some individuals tolerate small amounts while others react to any vinegar.

Certain vegetables accumulate histamine more readily than others. Tomatoes, spinach, and eggplant contain naturally higher levels (Maintz & Novak, 2007). However, freshness still matters. A tomato picked from the garden and eaten immediately contains less histamine than one stored for a week. Canned tomatoes and tomato products show high histamine from processing and storage.

Nuts vary in histamine content. Walnuts and cashews appear on many high-histamine lists, though evidence remains limited. Peanuts (technically legumes) may contain elevated histamine, particularly if stored improperly allowing mold growth.

4.4 Histamine Liberators Explained

Recall from Chapter 3.0 that histamine liberators trigger endogenous histamine release from mast cells despite containing little histamine themselves (Maintz & Novak, 2007). These foods activate mast cells through various mechanisms including direct membrane effects, immune activation, or complement pathway triggering.

Citrus fruits including oranges, lemons, limes, and grapefruit commonly trigger reactions in histamine-sensitive individuals. The mechanism likely involves direct mast cell activation by citrus compounds. Some patients tolerate small amounts while others react to any citrus exposure.

Strawberries represent one of the most potent histamine liberators. Many patients report severe reactions to strawberries despite their relatively low intrinsic histamine content (Maintz & Novak, 2007). Other berries show variable effects, with some individuals tolerating blueberries and raspberries while reacting to strawberries.

Tropical fruits including pineapple, papaya, banana, and kiwi frequently trigger reactions. Pineapple contains bromelain, an enzyme that may increase intestinal permeability, allowing more histamine absorption. Bananas appear problematic for many patients, though the mechanism remains unclear.

Tomatoes present complexity. They contain some intrinsic histamine but also act as histamine liberators, creating additive effects. Many patients rank tomatoes among their worst triggers.

Chocolate triggers reactions in many histamine-sensitive individuals through multiple mechanisms. It contains some histamine and other biogenic amines like phenylethylamine. It may also trigger mast cell degranulation directly. The severity of reactions varies widely between individuals.

Nuts and seeds show variable histamine-liberating effects. Walnuts, cashews, and peanuts appear most problematic. Some individuals react to all nuts while others tolerate certain types. The mechanism may involve both histamine liberation and presence of other biogenic amines.

Certain food additives trigger mast cell activation. Benzoates, sulfites, tartrazine, and other preservatives and colorings can activate mast cells in susceptible individuals (Maintz & Novak, 2007). Reading ingredient labels becomes essential for avoiding these triggers.

Shellfish acts both as a potential allergen and as a histamine liberator in some individuals. The mechanisms differ from true IgE-mediated shellfish allergy but can produce similar symptoms.

Individual variation in liberator sensitivity proves substantial. One person may react severely to strawberries while tolerating citrus. Another shows the opposite pattern. This variability likely reflects differences in mast cell sensitivity and genetic factors affecting mast cell responsiveness.

4.5 DAO Blockers and Biogenic Amines

As established in Chapter 3.0, certain foods and substances interfere with histamine degradation by blocking DAO enzyme activity (Maintz & Novak, 2007). Additionally, foods high in other biogenic amines can overwhelm DAO capacity or produce their own symptoms.

Alcohol represents the most potent DAO blocker. Ethanol directly inhibits DAO enzyme, while acetaldehyde (alcohol's primary metabolite) further impairs DAO function (Wantke et al., 1994). Even small amounts of alcohol can substantially reduce histamine-degrading capacity. This explains why some patients tolerate certain foods normally but react to the same foods when consumed with alcohol.

Tea contains compounds that inhibit DAO activity. Black tea, green tea, and mate tea all show this effect, though the degree varies (Maintz & Novak, 2007). Some individuals tolerate white tea or herbal teas better, possibly due to lower DAO-inhibiting compound content.

Energy drinks often contain multiple DAO-inhibiting compounds including caffeine and various additives. These beverages may reduce histamine tolerance significantly.

Tyramine, formed from the amino acid tyrosine, represents the most clinically significant biogenic amine besides histamine. Aged cheeses, cured meats, fermented foods, and aged/fermented beverages contain substantial tyramine (Sánchez-Pérez et al., 2018). Tyramine competes with histamine for DAO enzyme. High tyramine intake reduces available DAO for histamine breakdown. Tyramine also affects blood pressure through monoamine oxidase interactions and can trigger migraines.

Putrescine and cadaverine, formed from the amino acids ornithine and lysine respectively, directly compete with histamine for DAO binding sites (Sánchez-Pérez et al., 2018). Foods high in these diamines include aged cheeses, cured meats, certain fish, and overripe fruits. When consumed with histamine-containing foods, putrescine and cadaverine reduce histamine degradation by occupying DAO enzyme active sites.

Phenylethylamine, derived from phenylalanine, appears in chocolate, certain cheeses, and fermented foods. This compound can trigger headaches and other symptoms in susceptible individuals (Sánchez-Pérez et al., 2018). The combined presence of phenylethylamine, tyramine, and histamine in chocolate may explain particularly strong reactions some patients experience.

Spermidine and spermine, polyamines present in aged foods and certain vegetables, may contribute to symptoms though their clinical significance requires further research (Sánchez-Pérez et al., 2018). These compounds appear in aged cheeses, mushrooms, and some grains.

The practical implication is that total biogenic amine load matters, not just histamine alone. A meal combining moderate-histamine cheese (providing histamine and tyramine), chocolate (providing phenylethylamine), and wine (providing histamine and DAO blockade) creates additive effects that exceed the sum of individual components. Understanding this synergy explains why food combinations sometimes trigger reactions when individual foods do not.

4.6 Case Study: Contradictory Food Lists

Background

Melisande, a 44-year-old librarian, attempted to follow a low-histamine diet based on lists she found online. After three weeks of strict adherence to the most restrictive list she found, she experienced minimal improvement. Frustrated and confused, she brought five different food lists to her appointment with an integrative nutritionist. The lists contradicted each other dramatically.

Presentation

The five lists showed stunning inconsistencies. List one classified avocados as strictly forbidden high-histamine foods. List two rated them as low-histamine and safe. List three marked them as moderate-histamine to be avoided during elimination but potentially tolerable long-term. List four didn't mention avocados at all. List five categorized them as histamine liberators rather than high-histamine foods.

Spinach created similar confusion. Three lists forbade it as high-histamine. One permitted it as moderate-histamine. Another allowed it freely as a low-histamine vegetable. Chicken showed variations too. All lists agreed fresh chicken was acceptable, but storage recommendations varied from consuming within 24 hours to allowing 48-72 hours of refrigeration.

Melisande had been following the most restrictive interpretation of all lists combined, essentially eliminating any food that appeared problematic on any list. This resulted in a diet consisting primarily of rice, quinoa, select vegetables, and extremely fresh meat she purchased and cooked immediately. She felt deprived, socially isolated, and saw minimal symptom improvement despite extreme restriction.

Analysis

Melisande's experience demonstrates the controversy discussed in section 4.7. Food lists vary because histamine content depends on freshness, storage, processing, and preparation rather than food type alone (Maintz & Novak, 2007). An avocado eaten immediately after ripening contains minimal histamine. The same avocado sitting overripe for several days accumulates histamine from bacterial action. Both classifications (low and high histamine) are correct depending on ripeness and storage.

Different lists reflect different philosophies. Some take the most cautious approach, classifying any food that could potentially accumulate histamine as problematic. Others focus on typical histamine content of properly stored fresh foods. Still others distinguish between intrinsic histamine content and histamine-liberating effects, creating different categorizations.

The scientific literature itself shows inconsistency. Studies measuring histamine in foods use different analytical methods, sample different products, and test foods at different storage times. A study measuring fresh spinach finds low histamine. A study measuring spinach stored for several days finds elevated levels. Both publish results, creating contradictory data in the literature (Sánchez-Pérez et al., 2018).

Melisande's extreme restriction following the most cautious interpretation of all lists led to nutritional inadequacy and social isolation without corresponding symptom improvement. Her approach didn't allow identification of her individual triggers since she eliminated everything simultaneously.

Intervention

The nutritionist explained the principles from this chapter. Histamine in food depends primarily on freshness and storage rather than food type. Individual tolerance varies substantially. The goal is identifying personal triggers rather than following universal lists.

They developed a strategic 4-week elimination plan removing definitively high-histamine foods (aged cheeses, cured meats, fermented foods, leftover proteins, alcohol) while retaining fresh versions of moderate-histamine foods. Melisande learned proper food handling: purchasing fresh proteins and consuming or freezing immediately, eating produce quickly after purchase, avoiding all leftovers during elimination.

After four weeks showing significant improvement, systematic reintroduction testing began. She tested avocados and tolerated them well when fresh. She tested spinach with variable results depending on freshness. She identified strawberries and chocolate as definite triggers regardless of freshness, suggesting histamine-liberating effects specific to her.

Outcome

Within 12 weeks, Melisande had identified her personal trigger foods and tolerances. Her diet included far more variety than her initially restrictive approach allowed. She tolerated many foods marked problematic on cautious lists when fresh and properly stored. She knew her definite triggers (strawberries, chocolate, aged cheeses, wine) and avoided those consistently.

Symptom improvement proved substantial with the individualized approach. She regained social participation by learning which restaurant foods she tolerated. Quality of life improved dramatically compared to her initial extreme restriction phase.

Teaching Points

- Food list contradictions reflect genuine variability in histamine content depending on freshness, storage, and preparation rather than errors or disagreements between authorities
- Following the most restrictive interpretation of all available lists leads to unnecessary deprivation without corresponding health benefits and impairs identification of individual triggers
- Systematic elimination of definitively high-histamine foods followed by individual testing produces superior outcomes compared to blind adherence to contradictory lists

4.7 Why Food Lists Vary

The variation between histamine food lists frustrates patients and providers alike. Understanding the legitimate reasons for these differences enables more sophisticated dietary approaches (Maintz & Novak, 2007).

Measurement methodology differences create variable results. Different analytical techniques (ELISA, HPLC, fluorometry) measure histamine with different sensitivities and specificities. Sample preparation methods affect results. One study might analyze food immediately after purchase. Another stores samples at room temperature before testing, showing higher values. Both accurately measure their specific samples but reach different conclusions about the food's histamine content.

Natural variability in foods creates genuine differences. Two tomatoes from the same plant differ in histamine content depending on ripeness, storage time, and bacterial exposure. Fish from the same catch vary based on how quickly each was processed and chilled. Studies sampling different products reach different conclusions, all accurate for their specific samples.

Storage conditions dramatically affect histamine levels, yet many studies don't specify storage duration and conditions. A study testing fresh spinach finds low histamine. Another testing spinach after refrigerated storage finds elevated levels (Sánchez-Pérez et al., 2018). Both reflect real measurements but different storage scenarios.

Fresh versus processed versions of the same food show different histamine contents. Fresh tomatoes contain minimal histamine. Canned tomatoes show elevated levels from processing time and storage. Tomato sauce aged in jars contains even more. Lists that don't specify processing create confusion.

Regional and cultural differences in food preparation affect results. European studies often test extensively aged cheeses common in European cuisine. American studies may test shorter-aged versions. Both accurately reflect typical products in their regions but reach different conclusions about "cheese" as a category.

Individual food items versus categories create list variations. Some lists categorize all fish as high-histamine. More nuanced lists distinguish fresh white fish (lower histamine potential) from dark-fleshed fish (higher histamine potential) and canned fish (typically high histamine). Both approaches have validity but create different practical recommendations.

Histamine content versus histamine-liberating effects receive different emphasis across lists. Some lists combine these categories, marking both high-histamine foods and histamine liberators as "avoid." Others separate them, recognizing different mechanisms. Strawberries might appear on one list as high-histamine (incorrect but based on liberator effects) and another as low-histamine but a liberator (more accurate).

Conservative versus moderate approaches reflect different philosophies. Conservative lists categorize any food that could potentially be problematic as forbidden, minimizing false negatives at the cost of over-restriction. Moderate lists focus on foods that commonly cause problems in most patients, accepting some individual variation. Neither approach is wrong; they serve different purposes.

Update frequency varies. The SIGHI list receives regular updates based on new research. Other lists may reflect older data. As research progresses, classifications change, creating apparent contradictions between current and outdated resources.

The practical solution involves understanding these principles rather than seeking a single "correct" list. Focus on the definitively high-histamine categories (aged/fermented foods, old proteins, certain fish/seafood). Purchase and prepare foods fresh. Test moderate-histamine foods individually to determine personal tolerance. Recognize that lists provide guidance, not gospel.

4.8 Individual Variation and Thresholds

Perhaps the most important concept in histamine intolerance management is that each person has a unique threshold influenced by genetic, acquired, and environmental factors discussed in Chapter 3.0 (Kohn, 2014). This individual variation explains why universal dietary recommendations fail.

Genetic polymorphisms in DAO and HNMT genes create inherent differences in histamine-degrading capacity. An individual with highly functional DAO and HNMT variants may tolerate substantial dietary histamine. Someone with less active enzyme variants reaches threshold with minimal histamine exposure (García-Martín et al., 2007).

DAO production capacity varies based on intestinal health. Someone with healthy intestinal mucosa produces abundant DAO, permitting higher histamine tolerance. An individual with intestinal inflammation from celiac disease, inflammatory bowel disease, or SIBO produces less DAO, showing lower tolerance (Raithel et al., 2010).

Hormonal status affects threshold, particularly in women. The same woman may tolerate moderate-histamine foods during follicular phase when estrogen is lower but react to identical foods premenstrually when estrogen peaks and DAO activity decreases (Maintz et al., 2006).

Total histamine bucket load from all sources determines threshold crossing. Diet represents only one input. Mast cell activation from stress, infections, or other triggers contributes endogenous histamine. Medications may inhibit DAO or trigger histamine release. The combination determines if threshold is exceeded.

Mast cell reactivity varies substantially. Some individuals have stable mast cells requiring strong triggers for degranulation. Others have hyperreactive mast cells characteristic of MCAS, releasing histamine from minimal stimuli. This difference creates dramatic variation in food tolerance even with similar DAO capacity.

Dose-dependent responses mean threshold is not binary. Small amounts of a moderate-histamine food may remain tolerable. Larger portions of the same food exceed capacity. One strawberry causes no reaction. Five strawberries trigger symptoms. The food didn't change; the dose exceeded degradative capacity.

Food combinations create synergistic effects. A meal containing moderate amounts of three different histamine sources may exceed threshold when any single food alone would not. Adding DAO-blocking alcohol to a moderate-histamine meal reduces degradative capacity, allowing threshold crossing that wouldn't occur without alcohol.

Time spacing influences tolerance. Eating high-histamine foods at every meal maintains chronically elevated histamine, frequently exceeding threshold. Spacing high-histamine exposures allows histamine levels to decline between meals, improving tolerance.

The practical implication is that dietary management requires personal experimentation. Start with elimination of definitively high-histamine foods. Systematically test moderate-histamine foods individually. Identify your personal safe foods, moderate foods requiring portion control, and definite trigger foods. Accept that your safe list differs from others' lists. This is expected, not problematic.

4.9 Reading SIGHI and Other Resources

The Swiss Interest Group Histamine Intolerance (SIGHI) produces one of the most widely used histamine food lists. Understanding how to interpret this and other resources maximizes their utility (Maintz & Novak, 2007).

SIGHI's classification system uses a 0-3 scale with additional categories. 0 indicates foods generally well-tolerated. 1 represents foods with potentially elevated histamine or liberator effects. 2 signifies foods commonly problematic. 3 marks foods typically very high in histamine or strong liberators. Additional symbols indicate histamine liberators (marked separately from histamine content), foods affecting DAO activity, and foods that vary dramatically based on freshness.

Color coding in many SIGHI versions uses green (generally tolerated), yellow (moderate/variable), orange (often problematic), and red (typically high histamine). This visual system helps quick reference but should not replace understanding the nuances.

Special notations indicate important qualifications. An exclamation point may mark foods where freshness critically determines histamine content. A question mark indicates limited scientific data, with classification based on clinical experience rather than laboratory analysis. Understanding these symbols prevents misinterpretation.

Individual food entries sometimes include storage or preparation notes. For instance, fish might be marked as orange/red with notation that flash-frozen fish immediately after catch contains minimal histamine while "fresh" fish from retail display often contains substantial histamine from storage time.

The liberator symbol (often an asterisk or special marking) identifies foods that trigger histamine release rather than contain high histamine. Understanding this distinction matters. A food marked both red for histamine content and with liberator symbol presents double risk. A food marked green for histamine but with liberator symbol might still trigger reactions through mast cell activation.

Incompatibility lists note foods that commonly trigger non-histamine reactions like salicylate sensitivity, FODMAP intolerance, or common allergens. Some individuals react to foods on these lists independent of histamine effects.

Updates and versions mean the SIGHI list changes as new research emerges. Older versions circulating online may contain outdated information. Using the most current version from SIGHI's official website ensures accuracy.

Other reputable resources include peer-reviewed publications by Maintz & Novak, Kohn, and others referenced throughout this chapter. University-based resources and guidelines from professional medical organizations generally provide reliable information. Patient advocacy group lists vary in scientific rigor; evaluate sources carefully.

Red flags for unreliable resources include lists claiming all patients must avoid the same foods permanently, lists without any nuance regarding freshness or preparation, and lists making unsupported claims about "toxicity" or other non-scientific concepts.

The most effective approach combines SIGHI or similar evidence-based resources with clinical experience and systematic testing. Use lists as starting guidance. Modify based on personal reactions. Recognize that lists provide frameworks, not absolute rules.

4.10 Putting Knowledge Into Practice

This chapter provided the foundational knowledge needed to understand food and histamine relationships. Histamine forms in foods through bacterial action on histidine, making freshness the most critical factor. Fresh foods contain minimal histamine regardless of type. Aged, fermented, and leftover foods accumulate high histamine through bacterial histidine decarboxylase activity.

High-histamine foods include aged cheeses, cured meats, fermented products, certain fish and seafood, and leftover proteins. However, even "high-histamine" foods vary dramatically based on storage time and conditions. Truly fresh versions often contain much less histamine than aged versions.

Histamine liberators trigger endogenous histamine release from mast cells without containing high histamine themselves. These include citrus fruits, strawberries, tropical fruits, tomatoes, chocolate, and certain nuts. Individual sensitivity to liberators varies substantially.

DAO-blocking substances like alcohol and tea reduce histamine degradation capacity. Other biogenic amines including tyramine, putrescine, cadaverine, and phenylethylamine compete for DAO enzyme or produce their own symptoms, creating additive effects with histamine.

Food lists vary for legitimate reasons including measurement methodology differences, natural food variability, storage condition differences, fresh versus processed versions, and conservative versus moderate philosophies. No single "correct" list exists. Understanding principles proves more valuable than blindly following lists.

Individual threshold variation from genetic, hormonal, gut health, and mast cell reactivity differences means each person tolerates different foods and quantities. Personal testing through systematic elimination and reintroduction identifies individual patterns rather than assuming universal rules.

Resources like SIGHI provide valuable frameworks when interpreted correctly. Understanding their classification systems, symbols, and limitations enables effective use while avoiding over-reliance on any single resource.

Chapter 5.0 will apply this knowledge through systematic elimination protocols that reset your histamine bucket and establish your baseline for subsequent reintroduction testing.

Part II: The Dietary Approach

Chapter 5.0: The Elimination Phase Protocol

Nephele sat at her kitchen table surrounded by meal planning guides, food lists, and a calendar marked for the next month. After years of mysterious symptoms, she finally had a diagnosis: histamine intolerance. Her doctor recommended a 4-week elimination diet followed by systematic reintroduction. The concept seemed simple. Remove problem foods. See if symptoms improve. Add foods back one at a time. Identify personal triggers. But as Nephele reviewed the materials, anxiety crept in. The elimination phase restricted so many foods. How would she manage social events, work lunches, and family dinners? What if she inadvertently consumed something forbidden and ruined the whole experiment? What if four weeks of restriction showed no improvement, suggesting histamine wasn't her problem after all? She felt overwhelmed before even starting. This scenario repeats itself in offices and homes worldwide as people face the prospect of dietary elimination. The process seems daunting, particularly given our food-centered culture and social pressures. Yet elimination remains the gold standard for identifying food triggers, providing information no test can match (Kohn, 2014).

This chapter provides a systematic framework for successful completion of the elimination phase. You will learn why elimination is necessary and what it accomplishes, how to prepare mentally and practically for success, the specific 4-week protocol with weekly progression, exactly what foods to eliminate and which to emphasize, sample meal plans with batch cooking strategies, techniques for managing social situations and dining out, comprehensive symptom tracking methods, and emergency protocols for symptom flares during elimination. This structured approach transforms the seemingly overwhelming task into manageable daily actions with clear goals.

5.1 Why Elimination Resets Your System

The elimination phase serves multiple essential functions beyond simply removing trigger foods (Maintz & Novak, 2007). Understanding these purposes motivates commitment during challenging moments.

Histamine bucket drainage represents the primary goal. Recall from Chapter 2.0 that the histamine bucket model explains how total histamine load from all sources must remain below individual threshold to prevent symptoms. When you regularly consume high-histamine foods, histamine liberators, and DAO blockers while experiencing mast cell activation from stress and other triggers, your bucket remains chronically full or overflowing.

Elimination removes dietary histamine sources, allowing the bucket to drain. Research suggests tissue histamine levels decrease substantially within 2-4 weeks of strict dietary histamine restriction (Maintz & Novak, 2007). This creates a lower baseline histamine level, providing clearer signal when you reintroduce foods during testing.

DAO enzyme recovery occurs when you remove DAO-blocking substances like alcohol and certain medications (if medically appropriate). The enzyme regains full function, improving histamine degradation capacity. If intestinal inflammation contributed to reduced DAO production, healing during the elimination phase may restore some DAO-producing enterocyte function (Raithel et al., 2010).

Mast cell stabilization happens when you eliminate histamine liberators and reduce total histamine load. Chronically elevated histamine keeps mast cells in a hyperreactive state. When histamine levels decrease, mast cells gradually stabilize, becoming less prone to inappropriate degranulation (Afrin et al., 2016).

Symptom baseline establishment provides the reference point for reintroduction testing. You need to know your symptom level with minimal dietary histamine before testing individual foods. If you start reintroduction while still experiencing daily symptoms, determining if a tested food caused new symptoms becomes impossible.

Identifying the degree of improvement that dietary modification alone can provide clarifies if histamine represents your primary issue or contributes alongside other factors. Substantial improvement during elimination suggests histamine plays a major role. Minimal improvement indicates other factors (SIBO, other food intolerances, non-food triggers) may matter more, requiring broader investigation.

Duration requirements vary between individuals but typically require 4 weeks minimum (Kohn, 2014). Some patients experience improvement within days. Others need 6 weeks before noticing substantial changes. The 4-week protocol balances adequate time for most patients while limiting unnecessarily prolonged restriction for rapid responders.

Patients who show no improvement after 4 weeks require reassessment. The lack of response might indicate histamine is not the primary issue, the elimination wasn't strict enough, other triggers remain unaddressed, or more time is needed. Consulting with a knowledgeable provider helps navigate this scenario.

5.2 Mental and Practical Preparation

Success in elimination requires preparation on multiple levels. Jumping in unprepared increases failure risk and frustration (Schnedl et al., 2019).

Mindset preparation begins with accepting temporary restriction rather than permanent deprivation. Elimination is a diagnostic tool lasting weeks, not a lifelong sentence. Many foods removed during elimination return during reintroduction when testing shows tolerance. This time-limited perspective reduces anxiety.

Anticipate that elimination will be challenging. Our culture centers on food. Social events revolve around eating. Convenience foods become unavailable. Acknowledging difficulty upfront prevents discouragement when challenges arise. You're not failing if you find this hard; you're having a normal response to genuine difficulty.

Plan responses to social pressure. Well-meaning friends and family will question your restrictions. "Just one bite won't hurt." "You're taking this too far." "I read that eliminations diets are unnecessary." Preparing simple, firm responses beforehand prevents you from explaining or defending during stressful moments. "My doctor and I are doing this as a diagnostic test." "I'm not asking you to do this, just asking you to respect my choice." "I appreciate your concern, and I've got this."

Kitchen preparation includes removing tempting forbidden foods from your home during elimination. You don't need to discard them. Box them up and store them out of sight or have household members keep their foods separately. Reducing temptation supports success.

Stock your kitchen with elimination-phase staples before starting. Trying to scramble for acceptable foods when hungry and unprepared leads to poor choices or abandoned attempts. Buy rice, quinoa, safe vegetables, fresh proteins, and approved seasonings in advance.

Meal planning preparation involves developing a week's worth of meals before starting. This prevents the "what can I eat?" paralysis that leads to skipping meals or giving up. The sample meal plans in section 5.6 provide templates you can modify for personal preferences.

Batch cooking preparation creates efficiency. Dedicate a few hours on weekends to preparing components usable throughout the week. Cook a large batch of rice or quinoa. Prepare several protein options. Chop vegetables. Store everything in single-serving containers for quick assembly.

Social preparation means communicating with friends and family about your elimination. Explain you're doing a medical diagnostic protocol for a specific timeframe. Ask for their support, not necessarily understanding. Request that social events accommodate simple modifications like providing plain grilled protein and plain vegetables, rather than expecting you to eat normally.

If explaining feels overwhelming, simply say you're following medical advice for a health issue and can't eat certain foods currently. Most people accept this without demanding detailed justification.

Work preparation addresses lunch challenges. Pack lunches from batch-cooked components. If work provides meals, speak with the food service manager about accessing plain proteins and vegetables without sauces or seasonings. Keep emergency acceptable snacks (rice cakes, certain fruits) at your desk for unexpected hunger.

Restaurant preparation involves researching restaurant options before needing them. Identify restaurants offering plain grilled proteins and steamed vegetables. Review menus online. Some restaurants accommodate restrictions better than others. Knowing your options before urgency arises reduces stress.

Symptom tracking preparation means setting up whatever tracking system you'll use before starting. This might be a journal, smartphone app, or tracking sheets from section 5.9. Don't wait until you're already eliminating to figure out tracking. Start tracking a few days before elimination begins to establish pre-elimination baseline.

Medical coordination ensures any prescribers know about your planned elimination. Some medications interact with dietary changes or affect histamine. Your provider may adjust medications or provide guidance about continuing DAO-blocking medications if medically necessary.

5.3 The Four Week Protocol

The elimination phase follows a structured four-week timeline with specific goals for each week (Maintz & Novak, 2007).

Week 1 focuses on removing all high-histamine foods, histamine liberators, and DAO blockers. This represents the most restrictive phase. During this week, your body begins lowering histamine levels but you may not feel better yet. In fact, some patients experience temporary symptom worsening as their system adjusts.

The priority is establishing the routine. Cook fresh foods daily or freeze portions immediately after cooking. Purchase proteins the day you plan to cook them or use flash-frozen options. Avoid all leftovers, even 24-hour-old refrigerated foods. Eat simple, repetitive meals if that simplifies planning.

Common struggles during week one include hunger from unfamiliarity with new foods, social pressure to abandon the attempt, and discouragement if symptoms haven't improved. Recognize these as normal adjustment challenges rather than signs of failure. Stay focused on completing the week rather than expecting immediate results.

Week 2 maintains the same restrictions while refining execution. By this week, you've identified which meals work for your schedule and preferences. You've navigated at least one weekend and possibly social events. The routine feels slightly more familiar even if still difficult.

Many patients begin noticing subtle improvements during week two. Symptoms may decrease in frequency or intensity. Energy might improve slightly. These early improvements motivate continued adherence. However, some patients still see no change. This doesn't mean the elimination is failing; some individuals require longer for tissue histamine levels to decline sufficiently.

Focus on meal preparation efficiency. Batch cooking becomes routine. You know which vegetables you prefer and which proteins cook quickly. Shopping and cooking require less mental effort as decisions become automatic.

Week 3 often brings more noticeable improvement for those who will respond to elimination. Symptoms that previously occurred daily may happen only intermittently. Severity of reactions when they occur often decreases. If you haven't experienced improvement by mid-week three, consult with your provider about whether to extend elimination, troubleshoot for hidden histamine sources, or consider other factors.

This week also tests resolve as the newness fades and restriction fatigue sets in. The initial determination that carried you through weeks one and two may wane. Remember the time-limited nature. You're three-fourths finished with elimination.

Week 4 aims to establish your clearest baseline before reintroduction begins. Many patients experience their best symptom control during this week. If you experienced steady improvement through weeks two and three, week four shows what maximum benefit you can achieve from dietary histamine restriction alone.

During week four, prepare for reintroduction. Review which foods you most want to test. Begin planning the reintroduction order and schedule discussed in Chapter

6.0. Ensure you have thorough symptom records for the entire elimination phase to compare against reintroduction reactions.

If week four brings substantial improvement, you've confirmed histamine plays a significant role in your symptoms. This validates the elimination effort and motivates careful reintroduction testing. If improvement remains minimal, histamine may not be your primary issue, requiring investigation of other factors like SIBO, other food intolerances, or non-dietary triggers.

Extension beyond four weeks may benefit some individuals. If you first notice improvement late in week three, extending another 1-2 weeks may provide clearer baseline. If you suspect hidden histamine sources interfered with the first four weeks, a second strict elimination attempt after identifying the culprit may prove necessary. Discuss extensions with a knowledgeable provider rather than indefinitely postponing reintroduction.

5.4 What to Eliminate Completely

Elimination requires removing specific food categories identified through research and clinical experience as commonly problematic for histamine-intolerant individuals (Maintz & Novak, 2007).

All aged and fermented foods must be eliminated. This includes aged cheeses of all types, sauerkraut, kimchi, yogurt, kefir, miso, tempeh, soy sauce, fish sauce, and vinegar. Even foods fermented for short periods should be removed initially. Some individuals tolerate certain fermented foods after reintroduction testing, but all must be eliminated during this phase.

Cured and processed meats including salami, pepperoni, sausage, hot dogs, bacon, ham, and deli meats must be avoided. The curing process and extended storage create high histamine levels. Only freshly cooked, unprocessed meats are permitted.

All fish and seafood requires careful attention. Canned fish including tuna, sardines, anchovies, and salmon must be eliminated. Fresh or flash-frozen fish previously considered problematic (tuna, mackerel, mahi-mahi) should be avoided. White-fleshed fresh fish like cod, haddock, or sole that is truly fresh (purchased and cooked same day, or flash-frozen) may be tolerable for some during elimination but should be tested cautiously. The safest approach avoids all fish during elimination, adding back carefully selected fresh options during reintroduction.

All alcoholic beverages must be eliminated completely. Wine, beer, champagne, spirits, and liqueurs all contain histamine or block DAO. No amount is acceptable during elimination. This restriction often proves socially challenging but remains non-negotiable for accurate assessment.

Leftover foods represent a critical category often overlooked. Any cooked food stored in the refrigerator for more than 1-2 hours accumulates histamine. Eliminate all leftovers during this phase. Cook fresh daily or freeze portions immediately after cooking and eating. Thaw and heat frozen portions only once.

Histamine-liberating foods discussed in Chapter 4.0 must be removed. This includes citrus fruits (oranges, lemons, limes, grapefruit), strawberries, bananas, papaya, pineapple, tomatoes (including sauces, paste, and juice), spinach, eggplant, chocolate, nuts (especially walnuts, cashews, and peanuts), and shellfish.

DAO-blocking beverages including black tea, green tea, mate tea, and energy drinks should be eliminated. Coffee shows variable effects; some practitioners allow it while others recommend elimination. If you consume coffee, observe carefully for effects. Herbal teas (chamomile, peppermint, rooibos) generally appear safe though individual reactions vary.

Food additives and preservatives warrant removal when possible. Benzoates, sulfites, tartrazine, and other colorings and preservatives can trigger mast cell activation (Maintz & Novak, 2007). Read ingredient labels carefully. Choose whole, unprocessed foods without additives.

Common allergens deserve individual consideration. If you have known food allergies, obviously continue avoiding those foods. Some practitioners recommend also eliminating gluten and dairy during histamine elimination to avoid confounding factors, while others address only histamine initially. Discuss this with your provider based on your history.

Specific vegetables beyond those already mentioned include canned vegetables, which often contain added preservatives and accumulated histamine from storage. Use only fresh or plain frozen vegetables without sauces or seasonings.

The theme throughout these restrictions is freshness. Choose whole, unprocessed foods. Buy fresh proteins and cook immediately or freeze. Consume produce promptly after purchase. Avoid anything aged, fermented, preserved, processed, or stored as leftovers. This simple framework guides decisions when encountering questionable foods.

5.5 Case Study: Failed First Attempt

Background

Osric, a 39-year-old software developer, attempted a low-histamine elimination diet on his own after reading about histamine intolerance online. He carefully removed all foods from the standard high-histamine lists he found. After four weeks of what he considered strict elimination, he experienced minimal symptom improvement. Discouraged, he concluded histamine wasn't his problem and resumed normal eating.

Presentation

When reviewing Osric's elimination attempt with a nutritionist months later, several issues emerged. He had eliminated aged cheeses, cured meats, and fermented foods appropriately. He avoided wine and alcohol. However, he continued eating convenient canned tuna for lunch daily, believing the low-histamine list he followed that allowed canned tuna. He consumed tomato sauce on rice pasta several times weekly, not realizing tomatoes act as histamine liberators even if relatively low in intrinsic histamine.

His typical dinner routine involved cooking chicken or beef on Sunday and Wednesday evenings, storing it in the refrigerator, and eating portions throughout the subsequent days. By Thursday, he was consuming chicken cooked four days earlier. He refrigerated, not froze, his proteins, not understanding the critical distinction.

He continued drinking green tea daily, unaware it blocks DAO enzyme. He consumed chocolate protein powder for convenience, not knowing chocolate triggers mast cell histamine release. He ate leftover rice and vegetables from dinner the next day for lunch, not recognizing that even non-protein leftovers accumulate some histamine.

Analysis

Osric's experience demonstrates how subtle compliance failures undermine elimination outcomes. His canned tuna provided substantial dietary histamine daily from the fish's pre-canning storage time (Visciano et al., 2012). The tomato sauce triggered histamine release from his mast cells several times weekly. His leftover proteins accumulated significant histamine during 2-4 days of refrigerated storage before consumption (Maintz & Novak, 2007).

The green tea blocked his DAO enzyme, reducing his capacity to degrade whatever histamine he did consume. The chocolate protein powder triggered additional mast cell degranulation. Even the leftover rice and vegetables contributed modest histamine from bacterial action during storage.

Each individual issue might have been tolerable, but the combination kept his histamine bucket sufficiently full to prevent the symptom improvement that proper elimination should have achieved. His bucket drained partially from removing aged cheeses, cured meats, and alcohol, but continued filling from multiple unrecognized sources.

His food lists, while containing generally accurate information, lacked the nuance about freshness and preparation timing essential for successful elimination. The lists didn't emphasize that canned tuna differs substantially from truly fresh tuna, or that tomatoes' liberator effects matter regardless of intrinsic histamine content.

Intervention

The nutritionist explained the specific failures in Osric's attempt and developed a revised protocol. All canned fish was eliminated. Tomatoes and tomato products were removed completely. Chocolate in any form was forbidden. Green tea was replaced with herbal alternatives.

The leftover protein pattern was transformed. Osric now cooked fresh proteins daily in small portions or immediately froze larger batches in single-serving containers. He thawed and heated frozen portions only once, consuming immediately. He eliminated all leftovers, even vegetables and grains, cooking fresh daily or using previously frozen portions.

He implemented strict freshness protocols: purchasing proteins the day of cooking or using flash-frozen options, consuming produce within 2-3 days of purchase, and checking that frozen vegetables contained no sauces or preservatives.

Outcome

With truly strict elimination, Osric experienced substantial improvement within three weeks. Daily digestive symptoms that had persisted through his first attempt resolved. Headache frequency dropped from 4-5 weekly to 1-2 weekly. Energy improved noticeably. Brain fog that had plagued him for months cleared substantially.

This dramatic difference between his flawed first attempt and properly executed second attempt confirmed histamine's central role in his symptoms. His failure to improve initially didn't mean histamine wasn't the problem. It meant his elimination wasn't truly eliminating dietary histamine.

Teaching Points

- Subtle compliance failures including canned fish, tomato products, leftover proteins, DAO-blocking beverages, and histamine-liberating foods can maintain sufficient histamine load to prevent symptom improvement during attempted elimination
- The distinction between refrigerated leftovers (which accumulate histamine rapidly) and immediately frozen portions (which accumulate histamine slowly) proves critical for successful elimination but frequently gets overlooked
- Failed first elimination attempts should prompt careful review of actual intake against stringent elimination requirements rather than immediately concluding histamine is not involved

5.6 Sample Meal Plans

These sample meal plans provide templates for the 4-week elimination phase. Modify based on personal preferences, cooking skills, and schedule. All proteins should be purchased fresh day-of-use or from flash-frozen sources, cooked immediately, and consumed without refrigerated leftover storage.

Week 1 Sample Meals

Monday: Breakfast - Quinoa porridge with blueberries and coconut milk. Lunch - Fresh grilled chicken breast over mixed greens (lettuce, cucumber, carrots) with olive oil. Dinner - Baked cod with roasted sweet potato and steamed broccoli. Snack - Rice cakes with fresh mashed mango.

Tuesday: Breakfast - Rice cereal with almond milk and diced apple. Lunch - Fresh turkey breast strips over quinoa with steamed green beans. Dinner - Grass-fed beef patty with roasted butternut squash and sautéed zucchini. Snack - Fresh melon slices.

Wednesday: Breakfast - Oatmeal with blueberries and maple syrup. Lunch - Fresh chicken thigh over rice with steamed carrots and snap peas. Dinner - Fresh haddock with roasted Brussels sprouts and mashed cauliflower. Snack - Rice crackers with fresh pear slices.

Thursday: Breakfast - Quinoa porridge with sliced pear and coconut milk. Lunch - Fresh ground turkey over quinoa with cucumber salad. Dinner - Fresh lamb chop with roasted root vegetables (parsnips, turnips, carrots). Snack - Fresh apple slices.

Friday: Breakfast - Rice porridge with diced mango and coconut milk. Lunch - Fresh chicken breast over rice with steamed broccoli. Dinner - Fresh cod with sweet potato fries and green beans. Snack - Fresh melon.

Saturday: Breakfast - Oatmeal with apple and maple syrup. Lunch - Fresh turkey burger over greens with cucumber and carrot sticks. Dinner - Fresh beef stir-fry with rice and snap peas, carrots, zucchini. Snack - Rice cakes with fresh fruit.

Sunday: Breakfast - Quinoa porridge with blueberries. Lunch - Fresh grilled chicken over mixed greens and quinoa. Dinner - Fresh lamb with roasted vegetables and mashed sweet potato. Snack - Fresh pear.

Week 2-4 follow similar patterns with rotation of approved proteins (chicken, turkey, beef, lamb, fresh white fish), safe carbohydrates (rice, quinoa, oats, sweet potato), and safe vegetables (broccoli, carrots, zucchini, green beans, snap peas, cucumber, leafy greens, Brussels sprouts, cauliflower, butternut squash). Approved fruits include blueberries, apples, pears, mangos, and melons.

Batch Cooking Strategy

Sunday preparation: Cook large batch of quinoa (store in refrigerator up to 3 days or freeze portions). Cook large batch of rice (store or freeze similarly). Wash and chop vegetables for the week. Portion and freeze fresh proteins purchased that day into single-serving sizes for the week.

Daily cooking: Defrost one protein portion in cold water bath or refrigerator. Cook protein fresh each evening along with steamed or roasted vegetables. If making extra portions, freeze immediately after cooling briefly. Use pre-cooked grains from batch cooking, reheating only once.

Morning efficiency: Prepare breakfast grains night before (cook oats or quinoa, refrigerate, reheat once in morning) or cook fresh each morning if time permits.

5.7 Managing Social Situations

Social eating presents the greatest challenge during elimination. Preparation and strategies reduce stress and support adherence (Schnedl et al., 2019).

Dinner at friends' homes requires communication. Contact the host beforehand. Explain you're following a temporary medical diet. Offer to bring a dish you can eat that others will enjoy too. Ask what the menu will be and suggest simple modifications. Most hosts willingly prepare plain grilled protein and steamed vegetables for a guest with medical needs.

If the host can't accommodate, eat beforehand and consume only safe items offered. Keep the focus on the social connection rather than the food. Most people understand temporary dietary restrictions for medical reasons.

Restaurants require research and assertive ordering. Choose restaurants offering simple preparations. Steakhouses, where plain grilled meats and steamed vegetables appear regularly, often work well. Asian restaurants prove difficult due to sauces, fermented ingredients, and leftover risk.

When ordering, speak directly with the server and kitchen when necessary. "I have a medical condition requiring very specific food preparation. I need chicken breast grilled with no marinades, sauces, or seasonings, just salt if anything. I need steamed broccoli with no butter or seasonings. Can your kitchen do this?" Most restaurants accommodate such requests.

Avoid buffets and cafeteria-style service where you can't control preparation or verify freshness. Avoid cuisine styles heavy in problematic ingredients (Italian with tomato sauces, Mexican with aged cheese and salsa, Asian with fermented sauces).

Work lunches become easier with planning. Pack lunches from batch-cooked components. If colleagues order takeout, eat your packed lunch while socializing. If work provides cafeteria meals, identify safe options or speak with food service about special preparation.

For important business meals, choose the restaurant if possible. Review the menu beforehand. Have a plan for ordering before arriving. The confidence of knowing what you'll order reduces stress.

Celebrations and holidays warrant particular attention. Offer to bring dishes you can eat. Large gatherings often include some plain proteins and vegetables you can consume. If not, eat beforehand and participate socially without eating. Explain briefly if asked, then redirect conversation to non-food topics.

The temporary nature helps during difficult celebrations. "I can't have birthday cake this year due to a medical protocol, but I'm looking forward to enjoying it again in a few months." This acknowledges the sacrifice while maintaining positive outlook.

5.8 Symptom Tracking Methods

Accurate symptom tracking provides the data needed to evaluate elimination success and identify food reactions during reintroduction (Kohn, 2014).

Daily symptom log should record symptoms by system. Track gastrointestinal (pain, bloating, diarrhea, constipation, reflux), dermatological (flushing, hives, itching), neurological (headache, brain fog, anxiety, insomnia), cardiovascular (palpitations, tachycardia, blood pressure changes, lightheadedness), and respiratory (congestion, wheezing, shortness of breath) symptoms separately.

Use a severity scale (0 = none, 1 = mild, 2 = moderate, 3 = severe) for each category. This numerical tracking enables comparison over time. A score of 12 across four categories week one dropping to 4 by week four shows clear improvement.

Timing notation matters. Record when symptoms occur relative to meals. Symptoms appearing 30-60 minutes after eating suggest immediate reaction. Symptoms 4-8 hours later suggest delayed response. Morning symptoms before eating may reflect accumulated load from previous day.

Food and meal log documents everything consumed with approximate portions and timing. "8 AM: quinoa porridge with blueberries and coconut milk. 12 PM: fresh grilled chicken breast, rice, steamed broccoli. 3 PM: apple slices. 6 PM: fresh cod, sweet potato, green beans." This detailed record enables correlation with symptoms and identifies hidden sources if elimination fails.

Medication and supplement log tracks all medications, vitamins, and supplements with timing. Some supplements contain problematic fillers or ingredients. Medications may affect symptoms independent of diet. Comprehensive logging prevents confusion about causation.

Stress and sleep log captures non-dietary factors affecting the histamine bucket. Rate stress daily (low/medium/high). Record sleep hours and quality (poor/fair/good). These factors modulate histamine tolerance as discussed in Chapter 3.0.

Weekly summary synthesizes daily logs. Calculate average symptom scores for the week. Note trends. "Week 1 average total score: 18. Week 2: 14. Week 3: 8. Week 4: 5." This overview shows progress that daily fluctuations might obscure.

Smartphone apps designed for food and symptom tracking can simplify logging. Search for apps supporting customizable symptom tracking, meal logging with photos, and export functions for sharing with providers. However, simple paper journals work equally well if preferred.

5.9 Emergency Flare Protocols

Despite careful elimination, symptom flares may occur from hidden histamine sources, stress, illness, or other triggers (Afrin et al., 2016). Having a plan reduces panic and supports faster recovery.

Immediate response when symptoms flare involves stopping all food intake until symptoms stabilize. Continue hydrating with water. Avoid eating again until symptoms substantially improve, typically several hours.

When resuming eating, choose the simplest, most benign foods. Plain rice. Fresh apple. Plain chicken breast. Avoid anything complex or that recently entered your diet. Return to earliest, safest meal patterns until the flare resolves.

H1 antihistamine use deserves discussion with your provider. Some practitioners recommend having antihistamines available for severe flares during elimination. Diphenhydramine, cetirizine, or loratadine can provide symptom relief during acute reactions. However, relying on antihistamines to mask reactions from continuing problematic food intake defeats the purpose of elimination.

H2 antihistamine like famotidine may help with gastrointestinal symptoms during flares. Again, discuss with your provider about appropriate use during the elimination phase.

Identifying the trigger requires reviewing the previous 24 hours. What did you eat? Might something have been less fresh than you thought? Did you consume anything new? Were there non-food triggers like unusual stress, poor sleep, or illness?

If you identify a likely culprit, eliminate it completely going forward. If the trigger remains mysterious, simplify your diet even further for a few days, eating only the foods you've tolerated best thus far.

When to seek medical care includes severe reactions involving difficulty breathing, throat swelling, severe hypotension, or anaphylaxis-like symptoms. These warrant immediate emergency care. Contact your provider for persistent severe symptoms lasting more than 24 hours despite intervention.

Adjusting the protocol might be necessary after flares. If you experience multiple flares weekly despite apparent strict adherence, hidden sources likely exist. Review your food log with a knowledgeable provider or nutritionist to identify subtle problems. You might need even stricter protocols, removal of additional foods, or investigation of non-dietary factors.

5.10 Essential Takeaways

This chapter provided a systematic framework for completing the 4-week elimination phase successfully. Elimination serves multiple purposes including draining the histamine bucket, allowing DAO recovery, stabilizing mast cells, establishing symptom baseline, and determining the degree of improvement possible from dietary modification alone.

Preparation on mental, practical, kitchen, meal planning, social, and work levels sets the foundation for success. The four-week protocol progresses from initial restriction through adjustment to optimal improvement, with each week building toward clear baseline establishment for subsequent reintroduction testing.

Complete elimination requires removing all aged and fermented foods, cured and processed meats, fish and seafood (with possible exceptions for truly fresh white fish), alcohol, leftover foods beyond 1-2 hours, histamine liberators, DAO blockers, and food additives. The theme is freshness. Choose whole, unprocessed foods consumed promptly after cooking.

Sample meal plans and batch cooking strategies provide practical templates. Managing social situations requires communication, planning, and assertiveness. Comprehensive symptom tracking through daily logs documenting symptoms, foods, medications, stress, and sleep enables evaluation of elimination effectiveness.

Emergency flare protocols including immediate food cessation, return to safest foods, appropriate antihistamine use, trigger identification, and knowing when to seek medical care support navigation of unexpected reactions.

Successful completion of elimination establishes whether histamine contributes to your symptoms and provides the baseline needed for Chapter 6.0's systematic reintroduction testing to identify your specific triggers and tolerances.

Chapter 6.0: The Reintroduction Protocol

Salome completed her 4-week elimination phase with remarkable results. Her daily migraines disappeared. Digestive symptoms that had plagued her for years resolved almost completely. Energy returned to levels she hadn't experienced in a decade. She felt better than she could remember feeling. But now she faced a new challenge. She stood in her kitchen with a single strawberry, her favorite fruit before elimination. The elimination protocol removed it as a potential histamine liberator. Should she try it now? If she reacted, how long would symptoms last? If she tolerated it, could she eat strawberries daily or only occasionally? Her notebook lay open with elaborate symptom tracking forms, but she felt paralyzed by uncertainty. Reintroduction represents the most scientifically valuable yet psychologically challenging phase of dietary management (Schnedl et al., 2019). The data gathered during systematic reintroduction testing provides personalized information that no test or food list can match. Yet the fear of triggering symptoms after achieving relief creates powerful resistance.

This chapter provides a structured framework for successful reintroduction that maximizes information while minimizing unnecessary symptom provocation. You will learn how to assess readiness for reintroduction based on symptom improvement and baseline establishment, the systematic one-food-at-a-time approach that provides clear data, the specific 4-day testing protocol with detailed procedures, strategic ordering of food reintroduction to gather maximum information, comprehensive tracking methods for reactions and tolerances, understanding dose-dependent responses and portion control, building your personalized safe food list based on testing results, identifying your individual histamine threshold, protocols for managing foods that fail testing, the 3-month re-trial strategy for failed foods, and maintaining nutritional adequacy throughout the process.

6.1 Readiness Assessment

Successful reintroduction requires adequate preparation through the elimination phase discussed in Chapter 5.0. Beginning reintroduction prematurely compromises data quality and increases unnecessary symptom provocation (Kohn, 2014).

Symptom improvement criteria should show substantial reduction from pre-elimination baseline. Quantitatively, aim for at least 50-70% reduction in symptom frequency and severity across tracked categories. If you experienced daily headaches before elimination, you should now have headaches no more than 1-2 times weekly at most, preferably less. If digestive symptoms occurred with most meals, you should now experience them rarely or never.

The specific percentage varies between individuals based on the degree to which histamine contributed to symptoms versus other factors. Some patients achieve near-complete symptom resolution during elimination, while others experience moderate improvement, suggesting histamine represents one contributor among several. Both scenarios permit reintroduction, but expectations differ. Near-complete resolution during elimination predicts that histamine plays a primary role, making careful reintroduction particularly valuable. Moderate improvement suggests other factors contribute significantly, requiring broader investigation beyond histamine alone.

Baseline stability matters as much as improvement degree. Your symptoms should remain consistently low for at least one week, preferably two, before beginning reintroduction (Schnedl et al., 2019). Daily fluctuations occur normally, but the overall pattern should show stability. If symptoms continue fluctuating dramatically despite strict elimination, hidden histamine sources likely persist, other food intolerances require investigation, or non-dietary triggers dominate the picture.

Psychological readiness deserves honest assessment. Reintroduction will trigger symptoms periodically. This is expected, not failure. Each reaction provides information about your tolerance. If the prospect of any symptom return creates overwhelming anxiety, additional time enjoying symptom relief may be beneficial before testing begins. However, indefinite postponement creates problems discussed in section 6.10.

Practical readiness includes having time and space for testing. Avoid beginning reintroduction immediately before major life events, travel, important work deadlines, or stressful periods. Stress affects histamine tolerance through mechanisms discussed in Chapter 3.0. Testing during high-stress periods confounds results. Plan reintroduction during relatively stable periods when you can devote attention to careful observation and tracking.

Medical coordination ensures any providers involved understand your plan. If you take medications affecting histamine metabolism or mast cell activation, discuss timing with prescribers. Some patients benefit from having antihistamines available for severe reactions during testing, though using them masks the very information testing aims to gather. Discuss appropriate management of potential reactions with knowledgeable providers.

6.2 Systematic Testing Framework

The systematic approach to reintroduction follows established food challenge methodology adapted for histamine intolerance (Maintz & Novak, 2007). The fundamental principle is testing one variable at a time while controlling all other factors.

Single food testing means introducing exactly one new food while maintaining the elimination diet for all other foods. If you test strawberries while simultaneously reintroducing tomatoes and aged cheese, any reaction could stem from any of the three foods or their combination. The data becomes useless. Test only one food at a time. This requirement cannot be circumvented without compromising data quality.

Controlled testing conditions maintain consistency across all tests. Consume the test food at the same time of day for each food tested. Morning often works well, providing a full day to observe reactions. Ensure adequate sleep the night before testing. Avoid testing during menstrual periods for women due to hormonal influences on histamine tolerance discussed in Chapter 3.0. Minimize stress and other variables that affect threshold.

Portion control during testing uses moderate servings rather than excessive amounts. The goal is determining tolerance at normal consumption levels, not maximum tolerance. Testing with enormous portions increases symptom risk without providing useful information about practical tolerance. Start with a serving size you might realistically consume in a meal. For fruits, one piece or one cup. For proteins, 3-4 ounces. For vegetables, one cup cooked or two cups raw.

Multiple exposure requirement tests foods over several days rather than once. A single exposure might be tolerated due to luck (your bucket happened to be relatively empty that day), while regular consumption would exceed capacity. The 4-day protocol in section 6.3 addresses this requirement specifically.

Documentation requirements include recording every aspect of each test in detail. Track the specific food tested, portion size, preparation method, timing of consumption, and all symptoms over the subsequent 4-day period. Without thorough documentation, results blur together and patterns become impossible to identify. The tracking templates in section 6.5 provide structured formats.

Rest periods between tests allow complete clearance of histamine from the previous test before introducing a new variable. Generally, allow 3-4 symptom-free days between completing one food test and beginning the next. If a food triggered reactions, wait until symptoms fully resolve plus an additional 3-4 days before testing the next food.

This systematic approach takes time. Testing 20 foods could require 4-5 months. This seems slow when you want answers immediately. However, the alternative is eating haphazardly, reacting frequently, never identifying specific triggers, and ultimately restricting more foods than necessary out of fear. Systematic testing provides reliable data worth the time investment.

6.3 The Four Day Protocol

The **4-day testing protocol** provides a structured framework for evaluating individual food tolerance (Schnedl et al., 2019). This protocol extends beyond simple immediate reaction testing to capture delayed responses discussed in section 2.8.

Days 1-3 involve consuming the test food once daily at approximately the same time each day. Prepare the food identically across all three days to minimize variables. Fresh strawberries on day one, fresh strawberries on day two, fresh strawberries on day three. Not fresh strawberries day one, frozen strawberries day two, strawberry jam day three. Consistency matters.

The portion remains consistent across all three days. Eat the same amount each time. If you eat one cup of strawberries on day one, eat one cup on days two and three as well. This consistency allows detection of cumulative effects. Some foods tolerate well in a single exposure but trigger symptoms when consumed daily due to histamine accumulation.

Day 4 serves as an observation day without consuming the test food. This allows detection of delayed reactions that might not appear until after multiple exposures or with a slight delay. Some patients experience symptom onset 12-24 hours after the final exposure, making this observation day critical for detecting late reactions.

Symptom monitoring occurs continuously throughout all four days. Track symptoms immediately before consuming the test food, one hour after consumption, two hours after consumption, four hours after consumption, and before bed each day. Record morning symptoms on waking each day. This comprehensive tracking captures immediate, intermediate, and delayed reactions.

Reaction classification helps interpret results. **No reaction** means no new symptoms or symptom worsening throughout all four days. The food passes the test. **Mild reaction** means slight, tolerable symptom increase that resolves quickly without intervention. This indicates borderline tolerance, discussed further in section 6.6. **Moderate reaction** means clear symptom return comparable to pre-elimination levels but not disabling. The food failed this test but might pass with modifications (different portion, less frequent consumption, better timing). **Severe**

reaction means symptom onset requiring intervention, significantly impacting function, or persisting beyond 24 hours. The food failed definitively and requires extended waiting period before any re-trial.

Example 4-day test for strawberries might look like this. Day one: 8 AM, consume one cup fresh strawberries. Record symptoms 9 AM (none), 10 AM (mild tingling tongue), 12 PM (tingling resolved), 4 PM (none), 10 PM before bed (none). Day two: 8 AM, consume one cup fresh strawberries. 9 AM (tingling tongue again), 11 AM (mild headache developing), 2 PM (headache moderate intensity), 6 PM (headache persisting), 10 PM (headache finally improving). Day three: 8 AM, skip strawberries due to ongoing headache. Conclude test with moderate reaction to strawberries. Mark as failed at this dose and frequency.

The 4-day protocol provides substantially more information than single-exposure testing. It reveals cumulative effects, delayed reactions, and dose-response patterns that single exposures miss. The time investment provides proportional informational return.

6.4 Reintroduction Order Strategy

Strategic ordering of food reintroduction maximizes information gathering and motivation while minimizing disruption (Kohn, 2014).

Start with lower-risk foods typically means moderate-histamine foods rather than definitively high-histamine items. Test fresh white fish before canned tuna. Test fresh mozzarella before aged parmesan. Test tomatoes before tomato paste. This conservative start increases success probability, building confidence and expanding diet before tackling higher-risk items.

Prioritize nutrient density by testing foods offering substantial nutritional value early. Test eggs, fresh fish, nuts, seeds, and diverse vegetables before testing less nutritious items like condiments or treats. If these nutrient-dense foods pass testing, dietary adequacy improves significantly. If they fail, you know early and can plan nutritional compensation.

Test most-wanted foods strategically. Testing your absolute favorite food first creates problems if it fails. The emotional disappointment might discourage continued testing. However, postponing favorites indefinitely reduces quality of life unnecessarily. A balanced approach tests 2-3 lower-risk foods first, establishing testing routine and confidence, then tests highly desired foods, continuing with mix of moderate-risk and desired items.

Group by food category allows identification of patterns. Test several vegetables in succession. Test several fruits. Test several proteins. If you react to multiple foods within a category, patterns emerge. Reacting to all tested fruits might indicate salicylate sensitivity beyond histamine. Reacting to all tested proteins might indicate severe histamine sensitivity or other protein-related issues.

Consider preparation methods as separate tests. Fresh spinach and cooked spinach might behave differently. Fresh tomato versus tomato sauce. Raw versus roasted vegetables. Preparation affects histamine content and bioavailability, making different preparations worthy of separate testing for foods you use in multiple forms.

Sample reintroduction order might proceed as follows. Week 1: fresh eggs (nutrient-dense, moderate risk). Week 2: fresh white fish like cod (nutrient-dense, moderate risk). Week 3: avocado (desired food, moderate-risk). Week 4: bell peppers (vegetable expansion). Week 5: blueberries (fruit, lower-risk than strawberries). Week 6: fresh mozzarella cheese (dairy, lower-risk than aged cheese). Week 7: spinach (vegetable, potential liberator). Week 8: banana (fruit, potential liberator). Week 9: strawberries (highly desired, known liberator). Week 10: tomatoes (desired food, liberator). This progression balances risk, nutrients, and desires while maintaining systematic approach.

Documentation of ordering rationale helps maintain consistency. Write down your planned testing order and reasoning. This prevents impulsive testing decisions driven by cravings or social pressure. Following a plan provides structure and ensures systematic coverage of food categories.

6.5 Case Study: Successful Systematic Testing

Background

Clotilde, a 31-year-old teacher, completed her 4-week elimination phase with excellent results. Pre-elimination, she experienced daily headaches (averaging 6/10 severity), digestive discomfort after most meals, chronic fatigue, and frequent anxiety. By elimination week four, headaches occurred only once in the final week (mild, 2/10 severity), digestive symptoms resolved completely, energy improved substantially, and anxiety decreased markedly. She felt ready to begin systematic reintroduction.

Presentation

Clotilde developed a structured 12-week reintroduction plan testing 12 foods. She created detailed tracking sheets documenting each 4-day test. Her planned order:

eggs, cod, avocado, bell peppers, blueberries, quinoa, fresh mozzarella, almonds, spinach, banana, strawberries, tomatoes. She chose this sequence based on nutrient density (eggs, cod), personal favorites (avocado), and progressive risk (ending with known liberators).

Her testing proceeded methodically. Eggs passed without any symptoms across four days. Cod passed similarly. Avocado testing revealed mild digestive discomfort on day three that persisted into day four. She classified this as borderline tolerance, noting to limit avocado portions and frequency. Bell peppers and blueberries both passed without issues.

Quinoa testing brought surprise. She had never considered quinoa problematic, viewing it as a safe grain. However, day two brought moderate bloating and day three triggered a significant headache (5/10 severity). She marked quinoa as failed and discontinued the test. Fresh mozzarella passed testing. Almonds triggered mild oral itching day one through three, classified as borderline tolerance.

Analysis

Clotilde's systematic approach demonstrates the protocol's value from section 6.2 and 6.3. Her careful documentation revealed patterns she wouldn't have identified through haphazard reintroduction. The quinoa reaction proved particularly informative. Without systematic testing, she might have continued eating quinoa regularly, experiencing recurring symptoms without identifying the cause.

The avocado and almond borderline reactions illustrate dose-dependent responses discussed in section 6.6. These foods didn't fail completely but showed limits requiring portion control and spacing. Her recognition of these nuances prevented unnecessary complete avoidance while maintaining symptom control.

Her strategic ordering from section 6.4 proved wise. Testing nutrient-dense eggs and fish early expanded protein options quickly, improving dietary adequacy. Saving known liberators for later testing prevented early discouragement from multiple failures. By the time strawberry testing arrived (week 10), she had already successfully reintroduced seven foods, making one failure more tolerable.

Intervention

Clotilde continued through her planned 12-week testing sequence. Spinach failed testing with moderate reactions. Banana passed surprisingly, contradicting her expectation based on its reputation as a liberator. This reinforced the importance of individual testing rather than assuming universal patterns. Strawberries failed as expected. Tomatoes showed borderline tolerance similar to avocado.

She compiled results into three lists. **Pass foods** (tolerated well, can eat regularly): eggs, cod, bell peppers, blueberries, fresh mozzarella. **Borderline foods** (tolerated in moderation with portion/frequency limits): avocado, almonds, tomatoes. **Failed foods** (avoid currently, consider re-testing in 3 months): quinoa, spinach, strawberries.

Outcome

By 12 weeks post-elimination completion, Clotilde had clear personal food tolerance data. Her diet included variety well beyond elimination phase while maintaining the symptom improvement achieved during elimination. She experienced headaches only 1-2 times monthly (down from daily), maintained excellent digestive function, sustained good energy, and managed stress well.

The borderline food list required ongoing attention. She learned through experience that avocado once weekly worked well but twice weekly triggered symptoms. Almonds in small amounts (10-15 nuts) posed no problems, but larger portions caused reactions. This personalized dose-response information proved more valuable than any generic food list.

Teaching Points

- Systematic one-food-at-a-time testing following the 4-day protocol provides personalized tolerance data impossible to obtain through haphazard reintroduction or generic food lists
- Borderline reactions revealing dose-dependent tolerances allow partial reintroduction with portion and frequency management rather than complete permanent avoidance
- Individual testing may contradict expected patterns based on food lists or others' experiences, reinforcing the necessity of personal testing rather than assuming universal reactions

6.6 Dose Dependent Responses

Many foods demonstrate **dose-dependent tolerance**, meaning small amounts remain tolerable while larger portions exceed capacity (Maintz & Novak, 2007). Understanding and identifying these patterns maximizes dietary variety without triggering symptoms.

Threshold concept explains dose-dependent responses. Recall from Chapter 2.0 that the histamine bucket fills from multiple sources simultaneously. A small serving of a moderate-histamine food adds histamine to the bucket without filling it to overflowing. A large serving of the same food exceeds capacity, triggering symptoms. The food itself isn't either safe or dangerous. The dose determines the outcome.

Cumulative effects create dose-dependence over time as well as quantity. Eating moderate-histamine food once weekly might remain tolerable because the bucket drains between exposures. Eating the same food daily causes histamine accumulation exceeding degradative capacity even if individual portions seem reasonable. The cumulative weekly load matters, not just single-meal portions.

Identifying dose-dependent foods requires modified testing protocols. If initial 4-day testing with standard portions shows borderline reaction or mild reaction, conduct follow-up testing with reduced portions or reduced frequency. Test half the original portion using the same 4-day protocol. If this smaller dose passes, the food shows dose-dependent tolerance.

For frequency testing, consume the food every other day rather than daily, maintaining the same portion size. If symptoms resolve with spacing, frequency-dependent tolerance exists. This distinction matters for practical planning. Portion-limited foods require measuring and controlling amount consumed. Frequency-limited foods require spacing in meal planning but permit normal portions when consumed.

Practical application of dose-dependent knowledge creates flexibility. Tomatoes might fail testing at one cup fresh tomato daily but pass at half cup twice weekly. This allows occasional tomato use in meals without complete avoidance. Spinach might fail at one cup cooked daily but pass at quarter cup every third day. Small amounts in mixed dishes become possible.

Combination effects complicate dose-dependent planning. Multiple moderate-histamine foods in a single meal create additive bucket filling. A meal containing small amounts of tomato, avocado, and aged balsamic vinegar might exceed capacity despite each individual food being tolerable alone in that quantity. Managing dose-dependent foods requires tracking not just individual foods but total histamine load per meal and per day.

Rotation planning discussed in Chapter 7.0 applies dose-dependent principles. Rather than eating the same moderate-histamine foods daily, rotate through different options throughout the week. Monday might include tomatoes. Wednesday avocado. Friday almonds. This rotation prevents cumulative effects from any single food while maintaining variety.

Recording dose limits in your personal safe food list proves essential. Don't just note "tomatoes borderline." Specify "tomatoes tolerated at 1/4 cup fresh, maximum twice weekly, not combined with other moderate-histamine foods in same meal." This specificity enables practical meal planning and prevents repeated threshold exceeding followed by confusion about what triggered reactions.

6.7 Personal Safe Lists

Building and maintaining your **personal safe food list** transforms reintroduction data into practical dietary guidance (Schnedl et al., 2019). This list becomes your most valuable tool for long-term management.

Three-tier categorization provides useful structure. **Tier 1** includes foods passing testing without any reactions across multiple trials. These foods can be consumed freely in normal portions without restriction. They form the foundation of your diet. Examples might include rice, quinoa (if it passed your testing), fresh chicken, cod, carrots, broccoli, blueberries, and other foods showing consistent tolerance.

Tier 2 contains foods showing dose-dependent or frequency-dependent tolerance. These foods passed modified testing with restrictions. Document specific limits for each food. "Avocado: 1/4 avocado maximum, once weekly." "Fresh mozzarella: 2 oz portion maximum, twice weekly." "Tomato: 1/4 cup fresh only, maximum twice weekly, not with other moderate-histamine foods." This tier allows variety beyond tier 1 with careful management.

Tier 3 lists foods that failed current testing and require avoidance temporarily. Don't delete these from your records. Failed foods may pass re-testing in 3-6 months as discussed in section 6.9. Maintain notes about reaction severity and type. "Strawberries: moderate reaction, headache and flushing days 2-4. Re-test after 3 months." This information guides re-testing decisions.

Preparation specifications matter for many foods. Fresh fish might pass while canned fish fails. Fresh tomato might show dose-dependent tolerance while tomato sauce triggers reactions regardless of portion. Cooked spinach versus raw spinach. Specify preparation methods in your list. "Eggs: fresh cooked immediately, tolerated well. Avoid hard-boiled eggs stored as leftovers."

Regular updates keep your list current as testing continues and patterns emerge. After each 4-day test, add the food to appropriate tier with details. As you gain experience with tier 2 foods, refine dose limits based on real-world experience. A food initially limited to once weekly might prove tolerable twice weekly in practice. Document these adjustments.

Sharing your list with family members who cook for you, close friends, and providers ensures others understand your needs. However, avoid treating your list as universal recommendations for others. Your list reflects your unique threshold and tolerances, not general rules.

Sample personal safe food list might organize as follows:

Tier 1 (Free consumption): Fresh chicken, fresh turkey, cod, eggs cooked fresh, rice, oats, quinoa, sweet potato, carrots, broccoli, cauliflower, Brussels sprouts, zucchini, cucumber, lettuce, green beans, blueberries, apple, pear, mango, olive oil, coconut oil, sea salt.

Tier 2 (Controlled portions/frequency): Avocado (1/4 fruit, once weekly), fresh mozzarella (2 oz, twice weekly), fresh tomato (1/4 cup, twice weekly), bell pepper (1/2 cup, three times weekly), almonds (15 nuts, twice weekly).

Tier 3 (Currently avoid, re-test later): Spinach (moderate reaction, re-test in 3 months), strawberries (moderate reaction, re-test in 3 months), aged cheddar (severe reaction, re-test in 6 months), leftover proteins (consistent reactions, avoid indefinitely).

This documented list enables confident meal planning and reduces daily decision-making stress.

6.8 Case Study: Dose Dependent Discovery

Background

Theodora, a 48-year-old accountant, progressed through reintroduction testing after successful elimination. She meticulously followed the 4-day protocol for each food. Her testing revealed several foods showing partial tolerance rather than complete pass or fail results. She struggled to interpret these borderline outcomes and initially leaned toward classifying ambiguous results as failures to avoid risk.

Presentation

Theodora's avocado test exemplified the challenge. Day one of testing with one cup mashed avocado produced no symptoms. Day two brought mild digestive discomfort. Day three triggered moderate bloating and slight headache. She classified avocado as failed and resigned herself to permanent avoidance despite loving avocados.

Similar patterns emerged with fresh mozzarella (mild reaction day three), tomatoes (moderate reaction day four), and almonds (mild oral tingling throughout testing). She began feeling discouraged as multiple desired foods showed reactions. Her tier

1 list grew slowly while tier 3 expanded rapidly. She worried she'd need to maintain near-elimination-level restriction permanently.

Analysis

Theodora's interpretation represents a common error during reintroduction. She viewed results as binary: complete tolerance or complete intolerance. This black-and-white thinking missed the dose-dependent middle ground discussed in section 6.6. Her testing used standard portions appropriate for initial testing but didn't explore whether smaller portions or reduced frequency might prove tolerable.

The avocado test particularly demonstrates this oversight. One full cup of mashed avocado represents a substantial portion, likely exceeding what she'd consume in typical meal use. The day three reaction after two days of tolerance suggests cumulative effect from daily consumption of large portions (Maintz & Novak, 2007). This pattern indicates dose-dependent tolerance requiring modified testing.

Her resignation to permanent avoidance of multiple foods risked unnecessary restriction that section 6.10 warns against. Without exploring dose-dependent possibilities, she was heading toward chronic over-restriction despite successful elimination outcomes.

Intervention

Her nutritionist educated her about dose-dependent tolerance and suggested modified re-testing of failed foods showing mild to moderate reactions rather than severe responses. They developed a systematic approach testing smaller portions and reduced frequency.

Avocado re-testing used one-quarter cup (one-quarter of a medium avocado) consumed every other day for four cycles (eight days total). This lower dose and reduced frequency produced no symptoms throughout testing and one week of observation afterward. Avocado moved from tier 3 to tier 2 with specification: "1/4 avocado maximum, consumed maximum twice weekly, not combined with other moderate-histamine foods."

Fresh mozzarella re-testing with reduced portions (one ounce instead of three ounces) and spacing (every third day instead of daily) passed without issue. Tomatoes showed tolerance at one-quarter cup fresh tomato twice weekly. Almonds tolerated well at 12-15 nuts consumed every other day.

Outcome

After completing dose-response testing for borderline foods, Theodora's tier 2 list expanded substantially. She identified specific manageable limits for multiple previously "failed" foods. Her weekly meal plans incorporated variety far exceeding her initial fear-based interpretation of test results.

She developed practical systems for tracking tier 2 foods. A weekly meal planning template tracked which moderate-histamine foods appeared each day, ensuring appropriate spacing and preventing multiple moderate-histamine items in single meals. Portion measuring became routine for tier 2 foods.

Six months post-reintroduction, she maintained symptom levels comparable to late elimination phase while eating diverse diet including regular use of previously feared foods within identified dose limits. Quality of life improved substantially compared to the over-restricted approach she initially contemplated.

Teaching Points

- Borderline reaction or mild reaction during initial standard-portion testing indicates potential dose-dependent tolerance requiring modified re-testing with smaller portions or reduced frequency rather than assumption of complete intolerance
- Systematic exploration of dose-response relationships through modified testing protocols expands dietary variety substantially beyond binary pass/fail interpretation of test results
- Practical systems for tracking tier 2 food portions and frequencies enable successful long-term management of dose-dependent foods without constant symptom provocation

6.9 Failed Food Management

When foods fail reintroduction testing, strategic management enables eventual re-testing while maintaining motivation and nutritional adequacy (Kohn, 2014).

Immediate response to failed test involves stopping consumption of the failed food and allowing symptom resolution. Record detailed information about the reaction including onset timing, symptom type and severity, duration, and whether any intervention was needed. This documentation informs re-testing decisions and helps identify patterns.

Reaction severity classification guides waiting period before re-testing. **Mild reactions** (brief, self-limited symptoms resolving within 24 hours without intervention) might warrant re-testing in 8-12 weeks. **Moderate reactions** (clear symptoms requiring 24-48 hours for complete resolution, comparable to pre-elimination symptom levels) suggest 3-4 month waiting before re-trial. **Severe reactions** (symptoms requiring intervention, lasting more than 48 hours, or significantly impacting function) indicate 6-12 month wait or possibly permanent avoidance depending on reaction type.

The 3-month re-trial strategy represents the standard approach for most failed foods showing mild to moderate reactions. This waiting period allows several beneficial changes. Gut healing continues beyond the initial elimination phase, potentially improving DAO production (Raithel et al., 2010). Mast cell stabilization increases with sustained low-histamine intake. Overall histamine threshold may rise as the system's reactivity decreases.

During the waiting period, maintain strict avoidance of the failed food. Don't attempt gradual introduction or small amounts. Complete avoidance for the full waiting period maximizes healing and threshold improvement. Continue expanding tier 1 and tier 2 lists through testing other foods, preventing fixation on the failed items.

Re-testing protocol mirrors initial testing. Use the same 4-day protocol with the same portion size that failed initially. If this re-test passes, the food moves to tier 1 or tier 2 depending on response clarity. If reactions recur but seem milder than initial testing, consider dose-dependent testing as discussed in section 6.6. If reactions match or exceed initial severity, the food requires longer avoidance period or permanent restriction.

Pattern recognition across failed foods provides valuable information. If multiple foods within a category fail (multiple fruits, multiple vegetables, multiple proteins), broader issues may exist beyond simple histamine intolerance. Multiple fruit failures might indicate salicylate sensitivity. Multiple protein failures regardless of freshness might suggest DAO deficiency severe enough to warrant enzyme supplementation or other medical management.

Nutritional compensation becomes necessary when key nutrient sources fail testing. If fish fails, ensure adequate omega-3 fatty acids from other sources or supplementation. If multiple calcium-rich foods fail, address calcium intake through other foods or supplements. Work with a knowledgeable nutritionist to ensure failed foods don't create nutritional deficiencies.

Emotional management of failed foods prevents discouragement from derailing the entire reintroduction process. Expect some foods to fail. This is normal and provides valuable information. Failed foods don't mean you're uniquely intolerant or that the process isn't working. They indicate specific triggers that, once identified, can be avoided while you enjoy the many foods that pass testing.

Maintain perspective by tracking success rate. If 70% of tested foods pass or become tier 2 items, that represents successful reintroduction despite the 30% that failed.

Strategic sequencing prevents testing multiple high-risk foods consecutively. After a failure, test 1-2 lower-risk foods likely to pass before attempting another borderline or high-risk food. This ensures continued tier 1 expansion and maintains motivation through regular successes.

6.10 Nutritional Adequacy Considerations

Avoiding over-restriction while managing histamine intolerance requires conscious attention to nutritional adequacy throughout reintroduction and beyond (Schnedl et al., 2019).

Protein adequacy deserves particular attention since many high-quality protein sources contain histamine or present challenges for histamine-intolerant individuals. Fresh meats consumed immediately after cooking usually pass testing. Eggs typically work well if cooked fresh. Fresh fish varies by species and freshness quality. If multiple protein sources fail, creative strategies become necessary.

Plant-based proteins including fresh legumes, tofu (if tolerated), nuts (if tolerated), and seeds provide options. However, some individuals react to legumes or soy. Protein supplementation with low-histamine protein powders (pea protein, rice protein) may be necessary if animal and plant whole-food sources prove insufficient.

Calcium intake can suffer if dairy products fail testing. While aged cheeses contain high histamine, fresh dairy products often pass. Fresh mozzarella, cottage cheese, ricotta, and plain yogurt fermented briefly frequently prove tolerable. If all dairy fails, calcium-fortified alternative milks, calcium-rich vegetables (broccoli, bok choy, kale if tolerated), and calcium supplementation become important.

Omega-3 fatty acids from fish represent a common challenge. Fresh fish ideally provides omega-3s, but fish presents one of the highest histamine risks discussed in Chapter 4.0. If fresh fish passes testing, prioritize it weekly. If fish fails, omega-3 supplementation from algae-based sources or highly purified fish oil becomes necessary. Avoid standard fish oil if fish triggers reactions, as oil can contain histamine and amines depending on processing.

B vitamin adequacy requires attention since nutritional yeast (high histamine) and fermented foods (high histamine) represent common B vitamin sources. Whole grains typically pass testing and provide B vitamins. Fresh meat provides B12.

However, if dietary sources prove insufficient, B-complex supplementation ensures adequacy. Choose supplements free from common additives that might trigger reactions.

Antioxidant intake from colorful fruits and vegetables supports the anti-inflammatory and antioxidant needs discussed in Chapter 3.0. Many colorful vegetables pass testing even if some fruits fail. Prioritize testing and including diverse colored vegetables. If multiple fruits fail, ensure vegetable variety provides polyphenols and other beneficial compounds.

Fiber intake shouldn't suffer despite histamine restrictions. Fresh vegetables, tolerated fruits, whole grains, and seeds provide ample fiber for most individuals. If severe restrictions limit fiber intake, gradual introduction of fiber supplements (psyllium, acacia fiber) might be necessary, though these should be tested carefully like any new food.

Micronutrient screening through bloodwork provides objective data about nutritional status. Consider testing vitamin D, B12, folate, iron, ferritin, calcium, and magnesium if significant restrictions persist beyond initial reintroduction. Address any deficiencies identified through targeted supplementation.

Working with professionals becomes particularly important if extensive restrictions persist despite systematic testing. A registered dietitian specializing in food intolerances can evaluate your diet for nutritional gaps and suggest solutions. An integrative or functional medicine provider can address underlying factors limiting tolerance and recommend appropriate supplementation.

Supplement quality matters for histamine-intolerant individuals. Some supplements contain additives, fillers, or ingredients that trigger reactions. Choose supplements free from common allergens, artificial colors, preservatives, and unnecessary additives. Test new supplements carefully, introducing one at a time like foods.

The goal is maintaining broad, nutritionally adequate diet while managing histamine. Permanent elimination-level restriction is rarely necessary or advisable. Most patients can reintroduce substantial variety through systematic testing and dose-dependent management. If you find yourself maintaining near-elimination restriction six months post-initial elimination, reassess with professional guidance to identify barriers preventing successful expansion.

6.11 Essential Takeaways

This chapter provided systematic frameworks for transforming elimination phase success into long-term dietary expansion through structured reintroduction. Readiness assessment ensures adequate symptom improvement and baseline stability before testing begins, preventing premature reintroduction that wastes effort and triggers unnecessary symptoms.

The systematic one-food-at-a-time approach following the 4-day testing protocol generates reliable personal tolerance data impossible to obtain through haphazard reintroduction or reliance on generic food lists. This protocol captures immediate reactions, cumulative effects, and delayed responses through multiple-day exposure followed by observation.

Strategic ordering of food reintroduction balances risk management, nutritional needs, and personal desires while maintaining testing motivation through regular successes. Starting with lower-risk, nutrient-dense foods expands the dietary foundation before tackling higher-risk items.

Dose-dependent tolerance recognition prevents unnecessary complete avoidance of foods showing partial tolerance. Modified testing with smaller portions or reduced frequency identifies manageable limits for many borderline foods, substantially expanding dietary variety through tier 2 food management.

Failed food management through appropriate waiting periods followed by re-testing enables eventual reintroduction for many initially problematic foods as healing progresses and thresholds improve. The 3-month re-trial strategy provides structured timing for these attempts.

Maintaining nutritional adequacy throughout reintroduction and beyond requires conscious attention to protein, calcium, omega-3 fatty acids, vitamins, minerals, and fiber intake. Professional guidance helps identify and address nutritional gaps created by necessary restrictions.

Chapter 7.0 will build on your personal safe food list to develop sustainable long-term eating patterns that maintain symptom control while supporting quality of life, social participation, and nutritional health.

Chapter 7.0: Long Term Histamine Management

Dorothea sat in her car outside the wedding reception venue, reviewing her mental checklist one final time. After eight months managing histamine intolerance, she had developed systems for everyday life. Her home kitchen functioned smoothly with careful planning and batch cooking. Weekday meals followed reliable patterns from her tier 1 and tier 2 food lists. But tonight presented different challenges. A formal dinner celebrating her cousin's wedding. No control over menu selection. No ability to ask detailed preparation questions without drawing unwanted attention. Social pressure to participate fully in toasts and champagne. The temptation to abandon caution for one special night. She had worked too hard establishing symptom control to sabotage it carelessly, yet she also refused to let histamine intolerance control her life completely. Finding this balance between rigidity and recklessness represents the central challenge of long-term management (Maintz & Novak, 2007). The elimination phase provides diagnostic information. Reintroduction identifies personal tolerances. But sustainable living requires integrating these insights into real life with its social obligations, travel demands, seasonal changes, and special occasions.

This chapter develops practical strategies for long-term histamine management that maintains symptom control while supporting quality of life. You will learn how to transition from reintroduction testing to sustainable everyday eating, the 80/20 principle balancing strictness with flexibility, rotation diet principles preventing cumulative histamine buildup, seasonal adjustments to diet and histamine load, strategies for special occasions and celebrations without derailment, restaurant navigation and cuisine selection, travel planning and portable meal options, grocery shopping efficiency and label reading skills, building a practical low-histamine pantry, and kitchen equipment that simplifies preparation and storage.

7.1 Beyond Elimination Strategies

Successful long-term management requires fundamentally different mindset than elimination or reintroduction phases (Schnedl et al., 2019). Elimination demanded strict binary compliance. Reintroduction required careful systematic testing. Long-term living demands flexibility within established boundaries.

Permanent elimination-level restriction is neither necessary nor advisable for most individuals with histamine intolerance. The elimination phase served diagnostic purposes, not lifestyle design. Most patients can maintain symptom control with diet substantially more varied than elimination phase allowed. Those who cannot expand beyond elimination typically have additional factors beyond histamine requiring investigation.

Your personal tolerance map generated through reintroduction provides the foundation for long-term planning. Your tier 1 foods form the daily diet core. These tolerated items provide nutrients, satisfaction, and variety without symptom risk. Build most meals primarily from tier 1 foods. Your tier 2 foods add variety and enjoyment within dose and frequency limits. Incorporate these strategically throughout the week following documented tolerances. Your tier 3 foods remain avoided currently but merit periodic re-testing as discussed in section 6.9.

The 90/10 baseline establishes a starting framework. Aim for 90% of meals coming primarily from tier 1 foods with strategic tier 2 additions within limits. This leaves 10% flexibility for social occasions, travel, special circumstances, or intentional experimentation with borderline foods. This ratio prevents both chronic over-restriction and frequent threshold exceeding.

Flexibility without chaos distinguishes sustainable management from haphazard eating that triggers frequent reactions. Flexibility means accepting that some situations warrant eating foods outside your typical pattern with conscious risk acceptance. A wedding dinner where you choose to eat small portions of several moderate-histamine foods, knowing you might experience mild symptoms afterward but deciding the social value justifies the risk. This differs from chaotic eating where you regularly consume trigger foods impulsively, experience symptoms, feel frustrated, then restrict severely, then relapse again into trigger foods. Intentional, occasional flexibility serves you. Chaotic cycling between restriction and excess serves no one.

Symptom monitoring continues but becomes less intensive than during elimination and testing. Rather than tracking every symptom multiple times daily, monitor general patterns weekly. Are symptoms remaining at low baseline similar to late elimination phase? Are certain symptoms creeping up in frequency or intensity, suggesting threshold is being exceeded regularly? Periodic formal tracking for a week provides objective data when you suspect tolerance has changed or new triggers have appeared.

Periodic reassessment every 3-6 months evaluates whether your current approach maintains symptom goals. If symptoms remain well-controlled and quality of life feels good, continue your current pattern. If symptoms creep upward, review recent eating patterns to identify where threshold exceeding occurs regularly. If symptoms remain completely absent and you've maintained very strict restriction, consider cautiously expanding variety through additional testing.

7.2 Sustainable Eating Approaches

The **80/20 principle** adapted for histamine management provides practical flexibility while maintaining symptom control (Maintz & Novak, 2007). This principle states that 80% of your meals follow your personal low-histamine pattern while 20% allow controlled flexibility.

In practice, 80/20 means approximately 17 meals weekly (assuming three meals daily plus weekly snacks) emphasize tier 1 foods with strategic tier 2 additions within dose limits. The remaining four meals or meal-equivalents permit greater flexibility. This might mean eating at restaurants without obsessive control, attending social meals accepting moderate-histamine foods, or choosing convenience over optimal histamine management during busy periods.

The 90/10 approach offers a more conservative option for individuals requiring stricter management. Twenty-one meals weekly follow low-histamine guidelines closely. Two meals permit flexibility. This tighter ratio suits those with lower thresholds or those managing concurrent MCAS alongside histamine intolerance.

Calculating your ratio requires honest assessment of current threshold and symptom goals. If 90/10 maintains excellent symptom control but feels socially restrictive, experiment cautiously with 85/15. If 80/20 leads to creeping symptoms and frequent threshold exceeding, tighten to 85/15 or 90/10. The specific ratio matters less than finding sustainable balance between symptom management and quality of life.

The flexibility meals shouldn't be saved all for weekends, creating a pattern of weekday restriction and weekend excess. This cycling stresses the system and complicates symptom tracking. Instead, distribute flexibility throughout the week. Tuesday lunch with colleagues at a new restaurant. Thursday dinner as a date night. Saturday celebration meal. This distribution maintains more stable histamine levels than complete strictness followed by dramatic weekend elevation.

Avoiding black-and-white thinking prevents the restriction-binge cycling that sabotages long-term success. One meal containing moderate-histamine foods doesn't ruin everything or justify abandoning all caution for the rest of the day or week. Each meal represents an independent choice. Eating restaurant food with unknown histamine levels at lunch doesn't mean the day is lost, so you might as well eat leftover pizza and wine for dinner too. Return to your tier 1 foundation for the next meal regardless of what the previous meal contained.

Meal quality hierarchy guides decisions within flexibility meals. When eating outside strict low-histamine guidelines, choose foods closer to tier 2 than tier 3.

Select fresh preparations over aged or fermented when options exist. Small portions of moderate-histamine foods provide more safety than large portions. These choices within flexibility meals reduce symptom risk while maintaining social participation and quality of life.

7.3 Rotation Diet Principles

Rotation diets prevent cumulative histamine buildup from eating the same moderate-histamine foods daily while adding variety that improves nutrition and reduces boredom (Joneja, 2013).

The rotation concept means eating specific foods on scheduled days with spacing between exposures rather than daily consumption. A four-day rotation means eating a food on day one, avoiding it days two through four, then eating it again on day five. A seven-day rotation spaces exposures weekly. The rotation length depends on individual tolerance and the specific food's histamine level.

Benefits for histamine management stem from allowing degradation time between exposures. As discussed in Chapter 4.0, histamine from a moderate-histamine food consumed Monday peaks in your system Monday evening through Tuesday morning, then degrades over subsequent days assuming DAO function remains adequate. By Wednesday, Monday's histamine load has largely cleared. Consuming the same food again Wednesday creates a new peak without the cumulative effect that would result from Monday-Tuesday-Wednesday consecutive consumption.

Implementing rotation requires planning but need not be complex. Start by identifying tier 2 foods requiring rotation due to dose-dependent or frequency-dependent tolerances. Common examples include tomatoes, avocados, certain nuts, moderate-histamine vegetables, and some fruits. Create a weekly meal plan template designating specific days for specific tier 2 foods.

Sample weekly rotation might look like this. Monday: tomato-containing meal (e.g., fresh tomato in salad). Tuesday: avocado-containing meal. Wednesday: almond-containing snack. Thursday: tomato-containing meal again. Friday: bell pepper (if tier 2 for you). Saturday: avocado-containing meal again. Sunday: rest day from tier 2 foods, using only tier 1 items. This pattern provides variety, prevents daily exposure to any single moderate-histamine food, and maintains organized approach preventing accidental overconsumption.

Protein rotation applies similar principles. Eating chicken daily might prove tolerable, but rotating chicken, turkey, beef, lamb, and fish throughout the week provides nutritional diversity and prevents potential cumulative effects even from tier 1 proteins. This rotation also guards against developing additional sensitivities from repetitive exposure.

Seasonal rotation discussed further in section 7.5 incorporates foods naturally abundant in different seasons. Spring brings different vegetables than fall. This natural variation creates rotation automatically when you eat seasonally, reducing the need for rigid rotation scheduling.

Tracking rotation compliance can be as simple as meal planning one week at a time, noting which tier 2 foods appear which days. More detailed tracking using apps or spreadsheets suits those enjoying data or those with complex tier 2 lists requiring careful management. Find the level of tracking that supports your needs without becoming burdensome.

Flexibility within rotation acknowledges that life doesn't always cooperate with rigid schedules. If your rotation plan designated Thursday for tomatoes but a social event Saturday includes tomato-based dish you want to eat, the adjustment is minor. Skip Thursday's planned tomato, eat the Saturday tomato, resume regular rotation the following week. Rotation provides structure, not prison.

7.4 Case Study: Finding Sustainable Balance

Background

Honora, a 38-year-old attorney, successfully completed elimination and systematic reintroduction, identifying her tier 1 and tier 2 foods clearly. However, she struggled transitioning to sustainable long-term management. She oscillated between two extremes. During "good" weeks, she maintained near-elimination restriction, eating almost exclusively tier 1 foods, achieving excellent symptom control but feeling deprived and socially isolated. During "bad" weeks, frustration and restriction fatigue led to abandoning guidelines completely, eating whatever she wanted at restaurants and social events, then experiencing multiple days of headaches, digestive issues, and fatigue.

Presentation

Honora's eating diary revealed the cycling pattern clearly. Three weeks of very strict eating (95% tier 1, 5% tier 2, 0% flexibility) followed by one week of almost no adherence (30% tier 1, 20% tier 2, 50% exceeding tier 2 limits or eating tier 3 foods). During strict weeks, symptom scores averaged 2-3 out of 30 total (near symptom-free). During non-adherent weeks, scores climbed to 18-22 (approaching pre-elimination levels).

She recognized the pattern as unsustainable but felt trapped. Strict adherence felt safe but required constant vigilance and social sacrifice. Relaxed eating felt liberating initially but led to symptoms that impaired work performance and quality of life. She couldn't find middle ground.

The cycling also created psychological distress. Guilt about "failing" during relaxed weeks. Fear of symptoms during strict weeks. Anxiety about future social events. Restriction fatigue. She wondered if she needed to accept symptom-free living required permanent near-elimination restriction or if symptom-free living was simply impossible for her.

Analysis

Honora's pattern demonstrates failed integration from sections 7.1 and 7.2. She applied elimination-phase thinking (strict binary compliance) to long-term living, creating unsustainable rigidity. When the rigidity became intolerable, she swung to opposite extreme of abandoning all guidelines rather than finding balanced middle ground.

Her belief system contributed to the cycling. She viewed any symptom as failure, making her avoid all risk during strict phases. She viewed any deviation from elimination-level restriction as abandoning the diet, creating permission for complete non-adherence during relaxed phases (Schnedl et al., 2019). Neither belief reflects reality. Occasional mild symptoms don't constitute failure when accepted as the trade-off for social participation or convenience. Eating at restaurants or including tier 2 foods doesn't mean abandoning dietary management.

Her lack of intentional flexibility planning meant "relaxed" periods involved chaotic eating rather than controlled flexibility. Without predetermined boundaries for flexibility meals, she made impulsive decisions leading to excessive threshold exceeding.

Intervention

Her dietitian worked with her to develop an 80/20 framework with specific parameters. Approximately 17 meals weekly would emphasize tier 1 foods with tier 2 additions following dose and frequency limits. Four meals weekly could include restaurant eating, social meals, or conscious inclusion of foods slightly outside tier 2 limits.

They pre-planned flexibility meals for a typical week. Tuesday lunch with colleagues at restaurant (flexibility meal 1). Thursday evening date night dining out (flexibility meal 2). Saturday dinner party at friend's home (flexibility meal 3).

Sunday brunch at favorite café (flexibility meal 4). The remaining 17 meals followed her established low-histamine pattern using tier 1 and tier 2 foods appropriately.

Critical to the plan was redefining success. Success meant maintaining average weekly symptom scores below 8 (much improved from pre-elimination baseline of 22-25) while participating in desired social activities, not achieving zero symptoms through social isolation. Mild symptoms 1-2 times weekly from intentional flexibility represented acceptable trade-off, not failure.

She implemented simple rotation for tier 2 foods, spacing tomatoes, avocados, and almonds throughout the week rather than consuming daily. This prevented cumulative effects even during "strict" meals.

Outcome

Within six weeks of implementing the 80/20 framework with planned flexibility, Honora's cycling pattern resolved. Her symptom scores stabilized at 5-8 weekly (occasionally dipping to 3-4 during particularly careful weeks, occasionally rising to 9-11 during weeks with additional unplanned events). This represented substantial sustained improvement from pre-elimination while eliminating the cycling between extremes.

More importantly, her psychological relationship with food normalized. She made conscious decisions about when flexibility served her values (important social connection, trying new restaurant with partner) versus when strictness made sense (regular weekday meals, busy work periods requiring optimal function). Neither choice triggered guilt or fear.

At 6-month follow-up, she maintained this balanced pattern successfully. She participated in social dining regularly without symptom spirals. She maintained adequate symptom control for good work performance and quality of life. She described the diet as "a considered part of my life rather than my life's dictator."

Teaching Points

- Long-term success requires transitioning from elimination-phase binary thinking (strict compliance or failure) to flexible management within established boundaries based on personal tolerance testing results
- The 80/20 principle with pre-planned flexibility meals prevents restriction-binge cycling by creating intentional, controlled variability rather than suppressing normal desires for convenience and social participation until they explode into chaotic abandonment

- Redefining success as maintaining symptom improvement and quality of life balance rather than achieving zero symptoms through isolation enables sustainable long-term management without psychological distress

7.5 Seasonal Diet Adjustments

Seasonal variations in food availability, environmental conditions, and physiological needs create opportunities for dietary flexibility while requiring adjustments to maintain histamine control.

Spring brings fresh vegetables and fruits back into season after winter's limited selection. Early spring vegetables like asparagus, peas, and artichokes typically contain minimal histamine if consumed fresh. Spring greens including arugula, watercress, and baby lettuces provide variety. Fresh herbs become abundant, allowing flavor enhancement without histamine-rich condiments.

Spring also brings seasonal allergies for many individuals. Increased environmental histamine load from pollen and other allergens fills the histamine bucket partially before dietary histamine even enters the equation (Maintz & Novak, 2007). During high allergy seasons, tightening dietary histamine management prevents threshold exceeding when environmental load is high. This might mean temporarily moving some tier 2 foods to avoidance or reducing portion sizes and frequencies.

Summer provides peak fresh produce abundance. Berries, stone fruits, melons, and summer vegetables offer variety. However, summer also brings challenges. Higher temperatures accelerate bacterial growth and histamine formation in foods. Food left out at summer picnics or barbecues accumulates histamine faster than same foods would in winter. Extra vigilance about food temperature and storage time becomes essential during hot months.

Summer social activities including barbecues, outdoor dining, and travel increase flexibility meal frequency. Plan for this by tightening adherence during routine weeks to accommodate summer events without exceeding overall threshold.

Fall transitions to heartier vegetables including winter squashes, root vegetables, and brassicas. Most of these tolerate well when fresh. Fall brings the temptation of comfort foods often involving aged cheeses, leftover casseroles, and slow-cooked dishes. Adapting traditional fall recipes to low-histamine versions (fresh ingredients, immediate consumption, no leftovers) maintains seasonal enjoyment without symptoms.

Fall harvest also brings food preservation season. Canning, fermenting, and pickling inherently create high-histamine products. If you enjoy food preservation, focus on freezing fresh produce rather than fermentation-based preservation. Frozen berries, vegetables, and pre-cooked single-serve grain portions provide winter variety without histamine issues.

Winter challenges include reduced fresh produce variety and increased reliance on stored foods. Root vegetables, winter squashes, and frozen produce from summer harvests provide nutrition. Winter weather also affects histamine tolerance for some individuals. Cold exposure can trigger mast cell activation in susceptible people, while others find cold reduces inflammation and improves tolerance. Track your personal patterns across seasons.

Winter holidays present concentrated social eating challenges. Plan for this period by maintaining especially careful adherence in October and November, building threshold capacity for December events. After holidays, return to careful eating in January to allow recovery from any accumulated histamine load.

Adapting to seasonal patterns means adjusting your tier 1 and tier 2 rotation to emphasize seasonal foods when they're freshest and most nutritious. Summer tomatoes at peak ripeness tolerated better than winter tomatoes shipped long distances. Local seasonal produce consumed quickly contains less histamine than produce shipped from far away and stored for weeks.

Holiday seasons discussed specifically in section 7.6 require planning beyond general seasonal adjustments due to concentrated social pressure and traditional food expectations.

7.6 Social Eating Strategies

Managing special occasions while maintaining histamine control requires advance planning, clear communication, and realistic expectations (Maintz & Novak, 2007).

Restaurant strategies begin with research. Identify restaurants offering simple preparations rather than complex sauces and aged ingredients. Steakhouses that grill fresh meats serve you better than Italian restaurants emphasizing aged cheeses and tomato sauces. Thai restaurants using fresh ingredients often work better than Chinese restaurants where everything comes from pre-made sauces potentially containing aged or fermented ingredients. Japanese restaurants vary; sushi involves raw fish (histamine concern) and soy sauce (fermented), but teriyaki chicken or plain rice dishes might work.

Communicating with servers requires diplomacy and clarity. Avoid overwhelming them with complex medical information. Instead, make simple requests. "I have a food sensitivity. I need chicken breast grilled with just salt, no marinades or sauces. Can you ask the kitchen if they can do this?" Most restaurants accommodate such requests. Follow up with, "Can you also ask them to cook it fresh rather than using pre-cooked chicken?" This addresses the leftover concern without lengthy explanation.

Menu selection focuses on simple items. Grilled proteins plain or with salt only. Steamed vegetables without butter or sauces. Plain rice or baked potato. Fresh salads with oil and vinegar (not aged balsamic). These simple items exist on most menus with some creativity. A burger ordered without bun, cheese, tomato, or condiments becomes a plain grilled beef patty with side salad. Not exciting, but functional.

Safe cuisines generally include American steakhouses, some Mediterranean restaurants offering grilled meats and vegetables, certain Asian cuisines emphasizing fresh ingredients, and any restaurant willing to customize simple preparations. Risky cuisines include Italian (tomatoes, aged cheeses, aged vinegars), Mexican (aged cheese, tomatoes, fermented sauces), French (aged cheeses, wine-based sauces, fermented ingredients), and Asian restaurants using primarily pre-made sauces.

Social events at others' homes require advance communication with hosts. Contact the host several days before the event. Explain briefly that you have food sensitivities requiring specific foods. Offer to bring a dish you can eat that others will enjoy too. This provides you a safe option without burdening the host with special cooking. Many hosts appreciate one fewer dish to prepare.

If the host insists on accommodating you directly, provide simple guidance. "I do really well with plain grilled chicken or beef, steamed vegetables, and rice. No marinades or sauces on the protein if possible." Most people can manage this. Follow up the day before the event confirming the plan.

Celebrations and holidays concentrate social eating pressure into brief periods. Thanksgiving, Christmas, weddings, birthday parties all involve food-centric gatherings. Strategies include eating a tier 1 meal before attending events where you'll consume minimal food, bringing your own safe dish to share, accepting you'll eat small portions of available foods and possibly experiencing mild symptoms as acceptable trade-off, planning the event as a flexibility meal within your weekly ratio, and having DAO enzyme supplements or antihistamines available if needed.

Declining food requires polite firmness. "Thank you so much, it looks delicious, but I can't eat that. I will enjoy the vegetables though." Don't feel obligated to explain your medical condition to everyone at the party. Brief politeness works. If pressed, "I have a food sensitivity that requires avoiding certain items" usually satisfies curiosity without inviting unwanted advice.

Alcohol decisions require particular care. As discussed in Chapter 3.0, alcohol inhibits DAO severely while many alcoholic beverages contain histamine. If you choose to drink despite these factors, do so knowingly. One drink on rare special occasions might constitute acceptable risk for you. Daily drinking will likely sabotage histamine management. Some individuals tolerate clear spirits (vodka, gin) in small amounts better than wine or beer. Test this carefully if it matters to you.

7.7 Case Study: Social Life Integration

Background

Galatea, a 27-year-old graphic designer, achieved good symptom control through elimination and reintroduction. However, she found herself increasingly isolated socially. Dinner invitations from friends stressed her. Dating proved challenging when every dinner date required extensive restaurant research and dietary explanations. Colleagues' lunch outings happened without her since she packed lunches daily. She felt torn between health and social connection.

Presentation

Galatea's social calendar had diminished substantially in the six months since diagnosis. Pre-diagnosis, she dined out with friends 2-3 times weekly, attended monthly dinner parties, regularly joined colleague lunches, and maintained active dating life. Post-diagnosis, she rarely ate outside her apartment. She declined most invitations rather than explaining dietary needs or risk reactions.

The isolation affected her mood and relationships. Friends stopped inviting her after multiple declines. Dating had essentially stopped. She felt healthy physically but lonely emotionally. She resented histamine intolerance for stealing her social life.

Her restriction remained very tight, maintaining 95% adherence to tier 1 foods. Symptom control was excellent, but quality of life suffered. She wondered if this isolation represented necessary sacrifice or if she could find ways to participate socially without losing symptom control.

Analysis

Galatea's situation demonstrates the balance challenge from section 7.6. She achieved symptom control but sacrificed social connection completely rather than accepting occasional controlled risk. Her all-or-nothing thinking prevented her from identifying middle ground strategies.

Fear of symptoms drove her avoidance. She catastrophized potential reactions, imagining severe disability from restaurant meals. Reality-testing this fear showed her reactions typically involved mild headaches or digestive discomfort for 6-12 hours, manageable even if unpleasant. This realistic assessment reduced fear's power.

Her lack of communication skills for social eating situations left her feeling that dietary explanations required either full disclosure of complex medical history or complete avoidance. She didn't recognize middle-ground options for polite, brief communication that preserved privacy while enabling participation.

Intervention

Her therapist and dietitian worked together developing social eating strategies. They started with low-stakes practice. Galatea researched three restaurants offering simple grilled meats and steamed vegetables. She visited each alone during off-peak hours, practiced ordering her safe meal, and evaluated results. All three meals were tolerated well, building confidence.

Next, she invited one close friend to dinner at the most successful restaurant. She briefly explained she was managing food sensitivities and needed simple preparations but would love to catch up over dinner. The evening went smoothly. Her friend understood and conversation focused on connection, not food.

She developed polite responses to common situations. For colleague lunch invitations: "I'd love to join you. I have some food sensitivities so I might order differently than you, but I'd really enjoy the company." For dinner party invitations: "I'd love to come. I have some dietary restrictions, so I'll bring a dish I can eat that I'd be happy to share with everyone." For dates: "I prefer restaurants with simple preparations due to food sensitivities. How about [restaurant name]?" These brief, matter-of-fact statements neither over-explained nor apologized.

She implemented 80/20 framework allowing several social meals weekly. She accepted mild symptoms might follow some meals, planning those meals for evenings when she could rest if needed rather than immediately before important work commitments.

Outcome

Within three months of implementing social eating strategies, Galatea's social calendar rebounded substantially. She joined colleague lunches weekly, bringing her own meal to less accommodating restaurants and eating prepared foods at suitable ones. She hosted monthly dinner parties serving tier 1 meals she enjoyed that guests praised as delicious. Her dating life resumed; she found potential partners respected her brief dietary explanations when delivered matter-of-factly.

Her symptom control remained good overall. Average weekly symptom scores rose modestly from 2-3 (her isolated period) to 5-7 (with social participation), still much improved from pre-diagnosis baseline of 20-22. She experienced occasional mild headaches or digestive symptoms following some restaurant meals but found these tolerable trade-offs for meaningful social connection.

At 8-month follow-up, she maintained active social life while managing histamine intolerance successfully. She described the diet as "something I manage around my life rather than something preventing me from living my life."

Teaching Points

- Social isolation to achieve perfect symptom control often sacrifices quality of life unnecessarily since many individuals can maintain substantial symptom improvement while participating in social eating through strategic restaurant selection, portion control, and acceptance of occasional mild reactions as tolerable trade-offs
- Brief, matter-of-fact communication about dietary needs facilitates social participation without requiring extensive medical disclosure or apology, normalizing food restrictions as simply one aspect of the person rather than their defining characteristic
- The 80/20 framework enables regular social eating by pre-planning flexibility meals for social occasions while maintaining careful adherence during routine meals, preventing both complete isolation and threshold-exceeding frequency of restaurant eating

7.8 Travel and Shopping

Travel planning for histamine-intolerant individuals requires advance preparation but remains entirely feasible (Maintz & Novak, 2007).

Air travel presents challenges from limited food options and inability to prepare fresh meals. Strategies include bringing portable tier 1 snacks (rice cakes, safe fruit, homemade trail mix from tolerated nuts and seeds), packing single-serve packets of safe protein (individual almond butter packets if almonds are tier 1), requesting special meals if airline still offers food (though quality varies), eating substantial tier 1 meal before airport departure, and planning to eat simple meals after landing rather than airport food.

For longer international flights, some individuals pack entire meals in containers. Check TSA and destination country regulations about bringing food through security and customs. Generally, commercially packaged sealed foods pass screening better than homemade items.

Road trips allow more control. Pack a cooler with prepared tier 1 meals, fresh fruits, cut vegetables, safe proteins in single-serve containers, and ice packs to maintain temperature. Stop at grocery stores rather than restaurants for fresh foods. Many grocery stores offer plain rotisserie chicken (fresh, not day-old), fresh produce, and rice or quinoa in deli sections, creating simple meals.

Hotel stays benefit from selecting accommodations with refrigerators and microwaves. Some hotels offer full kitchens. When possible, book rooms with cooking facilities enabling meal preparation from grocery store purchases. Without kitchen facilities, request refrigerator and use it to store fresh tier 1 foods purchased locally.

Destination research before travel identifies grocery stores, farmers' markets, and accommodating restaurants near your lodging. Many cities now have natural food stores carrying fresh, simple foods. Having this information before arrival reduces stress and improves adherence.

Vacation philosophy requires decisions about balance. Some people maintain strict adherence while traveling, bringing most food or preparing it locally. Others view vacation as opportunity for controlled flexibility, accepting they'll eat restaurant food more frequently than usual and will manage mild symptoms afterward. Neither approach is wrong. Choose based on your values, threshold, and trip purpose. A relaxing beach vacation might permit more flexibility than a business trip requiring peak performance.

Grocery shopping efficiency comes from systematic approaches. Shop store perimeter where fresh foods typically reside. Produce, meat, dairy sections offer tier 1 options. Interior aisles contain processed foods with more additives and aged ingredients.

Label reading identifies hidden histamine sources and problematic additives. Check ingredient lists for vinegar (except plain distilled), yeast extract, autolyzed yeast, soy sauce, fermented ingredients, natural flavors (sometimes contain yeast or fermented products), monosodium glutamate, artificial colors and preservatives, and aged or cured ingredients.

Some preservatives like sodium benzoate may trigger mast cell activation in sensitive individuals as discussed in Chapter 3.0. BHA and BHT also warrant caution. Choose minimally processed foods with short ingredient lists when possible.

Fresh food selection prioritizes recently harvested or processed items. For proteins, purchase only the freshest available. Check sell-by dates and choose furthest dates. For fish, if purchasing fresh fish rather than flash-frozen, ask when it was delivered and buy only day-of-delivery fish. For produce, select items without bruising or age, as damage accelerates bacterial growth and histamine formation.

Frozen food advantages discussed in Chapter 4.0 bear repeating. Flash-frozen vegetables, fruits, and proteins often contain less histamine than "fresh" equivalents sitting in transport and storage for days or weeks. Plain frozen vegetables without sauces, plain frozen fruits without added sugar, and flash-frozen fish immediately after catch all serve well.

Organic versus conventional matters less for histamine than freshness. Organic produce isn't lower histamine than conventional. Both accumulate histamine based on time since harvest and storage conditions, not farming method. Choose based on other factors (pesticide avoidance, environmental concerns, price) rather than assuming organic means lower histamine.

7.9 Pantry and Equipment

Building a **low-histamine pantry** stocked with tier 1 staples simplifies meal preparation and reduces decision fatigue.

Pantry staples include grains (rice, quinoa, oats), canned goods (coconut milk, limited use of fresh-packed items), oils (olive oil, coconut oil, avocado oil), sweeteners (maple syrup, honey, coconut sugar), baking supplies (baking powder, baking soda, sea salt, fresh or frozen herbs), and condiments (limited to those without vinegar, yeast, or fermented ingredients). Fresh-ground herbs and spices rather than pre-ground versions provide better flavor with less histamine accumulation during storage.

Fresh food rotation prevents storage-related histamine formation. Buy proteins 1-2 times weekly rather than monthly, purchasing only what you'll consume before next shopping trip. Keep frozen proteins as backup but emphasize fresh when possible. For produce, shop twice weekly purchasing only 3-4 days' worth at a time.

Storage practices minimize histamine formation. Store proteins in coldest part of refrigerator (usually back of bottom shelf) at or below 4°C (39°F). Use proteins within 24-48 hours of purchase or freeze immediately. Store produce in crisper drawers. Wash berries and delicate produce only immediately before use, as moisture accelerates deterioration. Store fresh herbs in water like flowers, changing water daily.

Freezer organization enables batch cooking without leftover risks. Invest in quality freezer containers or bags in individual or two-serving sizes. When batch cooking tier 1 grains or proteins, immediately portion and freeze after cooling briefly. Label everything clearly with contents and date frozen. Rotate frozen items, using older items first. While frozen foods remain safe indefinitely, quality and potentially histamine levels may increase after 2-3 months.

Kitchen equipment that simplifies low-histamine cooking includes rice cooker (programs fresh batch daily), instant pot or pressure cooker (cooks fresh proteins quickly), quality freezer containers, kitchen scale for portion control of tier 2 foods, vegetable steamer basket, and quality knives for efficient fresh food preparation.

A **vacuum sealer** proves valuable if freezing in bulk. Vacuum sealing removes air, reducing oxidation and maintaining quality better than freezer bags. This matters particularly for proteins and pre-cooked grain portions.

Food thermometer ensures proteins cook to safe temperature without overcooking. This matters for fish and chicken particularly. Precise cooking preserves quality while ensuring safety.

A **slow cooker** requires caution despite popularity. Slow cooking at low temperatures for hours creates ideal conditions for bacterial growth and histamine formation if food sits in the danger zone (40-140°F) too long. If using slow cooker, ensure food heats through temperature danger zone quickly and monitor temperature carefully. Instant pot's pressure cooking works better than traditional slow cookers for histamine management.

Meal prep containers in single-serve portions enable efficient freezing and reheating without leftover risks. Glass containers work well for freezing and reheating. Avoid repeatedly thawing and refreezing same container, which accelerates histamine formation.

7.10 Bringing It Together

This chapter provided practical frameworks for sustainable long-term histamine management that maintains symptom control while supporting quality of life. The transition from elimination and reintroduction to everyday living requires fundamentally different mindset, shifting from rigid binary compliance to flexibility within established personal boundaries.

The 80/20 (or 90/10) principle enables regular social participation and reasonable convenience through planned flexibility meals while maintaining careful adherence during routine eating. This intentional flexibility prevents restriction-binge cycling and psychological distress from unsustainable rigidity.

Rotation diet principles prevent cumulative histamine buildup from repetitive consumption of moderate-histamine tier 2 foods while adding variety that improves nutrition and reduces dietary monotony. Systematic rotation of tier 2 items throughout the week maintains stable histamine levels below individual threshold.

Seasonal adjustments account for changing food availability, environmental histamine load from allergies, and temperature-related food safety considerations. Adaptation to seasonal patterns maximizes fresh produce use while managing period-specific challenges like summer heat acceleration of bacterial growth or winter holiday concentrated social eating.

Social eating strategies including restaurant selection, communication with servers and hosts, safe cuisine identification, and management of celebrations enable participation in normal social activities without isolation. Brief, matter-of-fact dietary communication facilitates inclusion while maintaining privacy and avoiding unwanted advice.

Travel planning, grocery shopping efficiency, label reading skills, and pantry organization create practical systems supporting adherence during varied circumstances. Flash-frozen foods, strategic shopping frequency, and equipment like vacuum sealers and portion containers simplify fresh food management.

The ultimate goal is integrating histamine awareness into your life as one consideration among many rather than allowing it to dominate all decisions. With systematic planning, clear personal boundaries from testing, and flexible execution, most individuals maintain substantial symptom improvement while participating fully in work, social activities, travel, and celebrations.

Part III: Cooking & Food Preparation Mastery

Chapter 8.0: Essential Cooking Techniques

Apollonia stood in her kitchen Sunday afternoon, preparing the week's meals. She'd successfully navigated elimination and reintroduction, identifying her triggers and tolerances. Her meal plan looked perfect on paper. Fresh chicken breasts, ground beef, salmon fillets, vegetables, rice, quinoa. All tier 1 foods. She loaded her slow cooker with chicken, vegetables, and broth, planning to cook it on low for eight hours. She'd portion and freeze the results for easy weekday dinners. Efficient meal prep, or so she thought. What Apollonia didn't realize was that her cooking method was sabotaging her careful food selection. Despite using fresh, low-histamine ingredients, the extended cooking time at moderate temperature created ideal conditions for bacterial histamine production (Visciano et al., 2012). The very method she chose for convenience was undermining her dietary management. This scenario repeats itself in kitchens everywhere as people focus on ingredient selection while overlooking the equally important factor of cooking method.

This chapter explains how cooking techniques affect histamine formation in foods and provides practical methods for preparing meals that minimize histamine while maximizing convenience and flavor. You will learn why freshness matters more than any other factor, how different cooking methods affect histamine levels, fast cooking techniques that prevent histamine formation, effective use of pressure cookers and Instant Pots, air frying for low-histamine cooking, batch cooking strategies that maintain safety, why slow cooking methods should be avoided, proper defrosting and frozen cooking techniques, and how to season and flavor foods without high-histamine ingredients.

8.1 The Fresh is Best Principle

The **fresh is best** rule dominates all other considerations in low-histamine cooking (Maintz & Novak, 2007). This principle extends beyond ingredient selection discussed in Chapter 4.0 to encompass the entire cooking process from purchase through consumption.

Time matters more than technique in most cases. Fresh chicken breast cooked poorly still contains less histamine than perfectly cooked chicken that sat refrigerated for three days before cooking. The bacterial histamine production that occurs during storage overwhelms any benefit from cooking method choice. Research demonstrates that histamine levels in refrigerated fish and meat increase exponentially over time even at proper refrigeration temperatures (Lehane & Olley, 2000).

From purchase to plate timing should minimize elapsed hours. The ideal sequence involves purchasing protein, transporting it cold, cooking it immediately upon arriving home, and consuming it fresh. This sequence allows minimal time for bacterial growth and histamine formation. When immediate cooking isn't possible, freezing immediately after purchase prevents histamine accumulation better than refrigeration.

Refrigerated storage before cooking creates histamine even when meat appears fresh and smells fine. Bacteria begin producing histamine within hours of animal slaughter, accelerating as time passes (Bodmer et al., 1999). Commercial meat may be several days old when purchased despite appearing fresh. Adding 1-2 days of home refrigeration before cooking compounds the problem.

The fresh cook freeze principle provides the safest approach. Purchase fresh protein. Cook it the same day or the following day at most. Portion the cooked protein immediately after brief cooling. Freeze portions immediately. This sequence prevents histamine formation during storage by eliminating the extended refrigerated storage period when bacterial growth occurs most rapidly.

Cooking does not eliminate histamine already formed during storage. Heat kills bacteria but histamine remains stable at cooking temperatures (Visciano et al., 2012). Grilling meat to perfect internal temperature doesn't reduce histamine that formed during the three days it sat refrigerated. Prevention through fresh cooking remains the only reliable strategy.

Planning around freshness requires different shopping patterns than conventional weekly grocery trips. Shopping twice weekly for proteins or purchasing proteins to freeze immediately enables fresher cooking. Some individuals shop every 2-3 days, buying only what they'll cook in the next 24-48 hours. This frequency may seem inconvenient initially but becomes routine and ensures maximum freshness.

8.2 Cooking Method Comparisons

Different cooking methods affect histamine formation through their impact on temperature, time, and bacterial growth conditions (Maintz & Novak, 2007).

High heat, short time methods minimize histamine formation by rapidly bringing food through the temperature danger zone of 40-140°F (4-60°C) where bacterial growth occurs most rapidly. These methods cook food quickly, limiting time for any bacteria present to produce histamine. Grilling, broiling, sautéing, and stir-frying all fall into this category.

Grilling at high temperature cooks meat quickly, typically 10-20 minutes for most cuts. The brief cooking time and high temperature combination prevents histamine formation during cooking. However, any histamine present from storage before cooking remains. Grilling fresh meat provides excellent results. Grilling meat refrigerated for days still contains accumulated histamine.

Boiling and steaming use moderate temperatures (212°F for boiling, slightly less for steaming) with variable cooking times. These methods work well for low-histamine cooking if time remains brief. Boiling chicken breast for 15-20 minutes produces safe results. Simmering soup for two hours creates more opportunity for histamine formation, particularly if ingredients weren't maximally fresh to begin with.

Pressure cooking represents one of the best methods for low-histamine cooking. The Instant Pot and similar electric pressure cookers cook food rapidly at high temperatures under pressure. A whole chicken that might require 90 minutes roasting cooks in 25-30 minutes under pressure. Tough cuts of beef that traditionally require hours of braising become tender in 45-60 minutes. This speed prevents histamine formation while achieving desired textures.

The high pressure and temperature combination in pressure cooking also appears to somewhat reduce histamine that formed during storage, though this effect is modest and doesn't justify using old ingredients (Visciano et al., 2012). Pressure cooking fresh ingredients remains superior to pressure cooking ingredients stored for days.

Slow cooking methods including crockpots, long braises, and low-temperature roasting create ideal conditions for bacterial histamine production. Extended cooking times of 4-8 hours at moderate temperatures (180-250°F) allow bacteria to thrive and produce histamine. The food eventually reaches temperatures that kill bacteria, but histamine produced during the cooking process remains in the food.

Research on slow-cooked meats demonstrates measurable histamine increases during extended cooking even when starting with fresh meat (Bodmer et al., 1999). The practice of slow cooking proteins on low for 6-8 hours should be avoided for histamine management regardless of ingredient freshness.

Baking and roasting at moderate to high temperatures work well if cooking time remains reasonable. Roasting chicken at 400°F for 45-60 minutes produces minimal histamine formation. Slow roasting at 250°F for three hours creates more opportunity for bacterial activity during the initial warming period before internal temperature reaches bactericidal levels.

Microwaving provides one of the fastest cooking methods, rapidly heating food throughout. This speed prevents histamine formation during cooking. However, microwave cooking of fresh proteins often produces suboptimal texture and flavor, leading many to prefer other methods despite microwave's histamine-safety advantages.

8.3 Fast Cooking Techniques

Stir-frying cooks small pieces of protein and vegetables over very high heat for brief periods, typically 5-10 minutes total. The thin slicing of proteins increases surface area, allowing rapid cooking. The high heat and constant movement prevent burning while ensuring thorough cooking. This combination of small pieces, high heat, and brief time minimizes histamine formation.

For optimal stir-frying, cut proteins into thin strips or small cubes. Heat oil until shimmering. Add protein and cook quickly, 3-5 minutes. Remove protein. Add vegetables and cook briefly, 2-3 minutes. Return protein to pan, combine, and serve immediately. Total cooking time rarely exceeds 10 minutes.

Sautéing uses moderate-high heat and minimal fat to cook proteins quickly. Chicken breasts or fish fillets cook through in 8-12 minutes depending on thickness. The key is proper temperature. Too low and cooking time extends unnecessarily. Too high and exterior burns before interior cooks through. Medium-high heat with lid during final minutes produces quick, even cooking.

Pan-searing then oven-finishing combines methods for thicker cuts. Sear steaks or thick fish fillets in hot pan for 2-3 minutes per side, developing flavor and color. Transfer to hot oven (400-450°F) for 5-10 minutes to finish cooking through. Total time rarely exceeds 15 minutes, minimizing histamine formation while producing excellent results.

Broiling uses high direct heat from above, cooking proteins quickly. Thin cuts of meat or fish cook in 6-10 minutes. The intense heat browns surface while cooking interior. Watch carefully to prevent burning. Broiling works especially well for fish fillets, achieving thorough cooking in 8-12 minutes.

Grilling over high direct heat cooks most proteins in 10-20 minutes. Thinner cuts cook fastest. Chicken breast requires 12-15 minutes. Fish fillets need only 6-10 minutes. Steaks vary by thickness and desired doneness but rarely exceed 20 minutes. The high heat and brief time minimize histamine formation while producing desirable flavors.

Quick steaming vegetables and fish takes advantage of steam's rapid heat transfer. Vegetables steam tender in 5-10 minutes depending on type and size. Fish fillets steam through in 8-12 minutes. Steaming preserves nutrients while cooking quickly enough to prevent histamine issues.

8.4 Pressure Cooker Mastery

The **Instant Pot** and similar electric pressure cookers have transformed cooking for many histamine-intolerant individuals by dramatically reducing cooking times while achieving results typically requiring hours (Jiménez-Colmenero et al., 2001).

Pressure cooking basics involve cooking food in a sealed pot where steam pressure increases temperature above boiling point. At standard pressure settings, food cooks at approximately 250°F (121°C) instead of 212°F (100°C), dramatically accelerating cooking. The higher temperature breaks down proteins and tenderizes tough cuts in fraction of the time conventional methods require.

Cooking times comparison illustrates the advantage. Whole chicken: 90 minutes roasted versus 25-30 minutes pressure cooked. Pot roast: 3-4 hours braised versus 60 minutes pressure cooked. Dried beans: 60-90 minutes boiled versus 20-30 minutes pressure cooked. Tough beef cuts: 2-3 hours braised versus 45-60 minutes pressure cooked.

This time reduction matters tremendously for histamine management. Less time at moderate temperatures means less bacterial histamine production during cooking. The rapid cooking preserves the freshness advantage that starting with quality ingredients provides.

Fresh protein guidelines for pressure cooking include immediate cooking after purchase, using the pressure function rather than slow cook function, keeping cooking times as brief as effective for desired texture, and quick-releasing pressure rather than allowing natural pressure release which extends cooking time.

For chicken breast or thighs, 10-12 minutes at high pressure produces tender, fully cooked results. For whole chicken, 25-30 minutes depending on size. For beef roast, 60 minutes for tender results. For pork, 45-60 minutes depending on cut. These times apply to fresh proteins cooked from refrigerated or room temperature.

Cooking from frozen works excellently in pressure cookers. Frozen chicken breasts cook through in 12-15 minutes. Frozen ground meat becomes fully cooked in 15-20 minutes. This capability eliminates the defrosting step, further reducing time between freezer and consumption. Section 8.8 discusses frozen cooking in detail.

Soup and stock made in pressure cookers require reconsideration despite traditional long-simmered approaches. If making stock or soup, cook under pressure for 30-45 minutes rather than simmering for hours. The pressure extracts flavor and breaks down ingredients rapidly. The shortened time prevents histamine formation. However, consume or freeze the result immediately rather than storing as leftovers.

Rice and grains cook perfectly in pressure cookers in fraction of conventional time. Rice needs only 3-4 minutes at pressure plus 10 minutes natural release. Quinoa requires 1 minute at pressure. This speed allows fresh grain cooking rather than batch cooking stored in refrigerator for days.

8.5 Case Study: Slow Cooker to Pressure Cooker Conversion

Background

Faustina, a 42-year-old physical therapist, managed her histamine intolerance carefully through diet but struggled with meal preparation time. Working 10-hour days, she relied heavily on slow cooker meals. She'd load her crockpot with fresh chicken, vegetables, and broth before leaving for work, returning home to fully-cooked meals. Despite using fresh ingredients and avoiding high-histamine foods, she experienced periodic symptoms that puzzled her. Her food diary showed compliance with low-histamine choices. Her shopping habits emphasized fresh proteins purchased every few days.

Presentation

Faustina noticed symptoms appeared more frequently on days she ate slow-cooked meals. Headaches developed 2-4 hours after dinner. Digestive discomfort followed. Fatigue the next morning. These symptoms didn't occur when she ate simpler, quickly-prepared meals like grilled chicken and steamed vegetables. The pattern became clear after several weeks of careful tracking.

When she described her cooking methods to a nutritionist, the issue emerged. Her slow cooker settings kept food at 180-200°F for 8-9 hours. The chicken started frozen or refrigerated, spent 2-3 hours slowly reaching 140°F (passing through the temperature danger zone), then cooked at moderate temperatures for the remaining 6 hours. Despite eventual full cooking, bacterial growth during the initial warming period produced histamine that remained stable throughout extended cooking.

Analysis

Faustina's situation demonstrates the principles from sections 8.2 and 8.3. Extended cooking at moderate temperatures creates ideal bacterial growth conditions regardless of ingredient quality. Her fresh chicken and vegetables provided optimal starting point, but the cooking method undermined this advantage.

The slow cooker's design maintains food in the temperature danger zone for extended periods. Frozen or refrigerated proteins require hours to heat through to bactericidal temperatures. During this time, surface bacteria multiply rapidly and produce histamine. Even after internal temperature reaches safe levels, histamine remains.

Research on slow-cooked meats confirms histamine increases during extended cooking periods at moderate temperatures (Bodmer et al., 1999). The convenience Faustina sought through slow cooking created the histamine load triggering her symptoms.

Intervention

The nutritionist introduced Faustina to pressure cooking as alternative to slow cooking. She purchased an Instant Pot and learned basic pressure cooking techniques. Her typical slow cooker chicken recipe converted easily. Fresh chicken, vegetables, and broth went into the Instant Pot. Pressure cooking for 15 minutes at high pressure produced tender, flavorful chicken in fraction of her previous cooking time.

The timing required adjustment. Rather than loading the cooker in the morning, she prepared ingredients before work and stored them refrigerated separately. Upon arriving home, she loaded the Instant Pot and started cooking. Total time from start to eating: 35 minutes (15 minutes pressure cooking, 10 minutes pressure build, 10 minutes quick release and serving). This proved faster than her slow cooker routine of arriving home to finished food but requiring time to cool and portion it for storage.

She learned to pressure cook various proteins. Pot roast: 60 minutes versus her previous 8-hour braise. Whole chicken: 30 minutes versus previous 6-hour slow cook. Ground beef for sauces: 20 minutes versus previous hour of simmering.

Outcome

Within two weeks of switching from slow cooking to pressure cooking, Faustina's periodic symptoms resolved. Her headaches disappeared. Digestive function normalized. Morning energy improved. All other variables remained constant. Only cooking method changed.

The Instant Pot's speed proved more convenient than anticipated. Coming home to raw ingredients initially seemed like a step backward from arriving to finished meals. However, the 30-40 minutes from start to dinner proved manageable and actually allowed fresher meals than the slow-cooked versions she'd stored as leftovers for 2-3 days.

Six months later, she maintained symptom-free status while enjoying varied, flavorful meals. She never returned to slow cooking, recognizing the method's inherent conflict with histamine management.

Teaching Points

- Extended cooking at moderate temperatures (slow cookers, long braises) creates ideal bacterial growth conditions that produce histamine even when starting with fresh ingredients, undermining the benefit of careful ingredient selection
- Pressure cooking achieves similar tender results in fraction of the time by using higher temperatures and pressure, preventing histamine formation while maintaining convenience and flavor
- The false convenience of arriving home to finished slow-cooked meals becomes problematic when leftovers must be stored for days, while pressure cooking's speed enables truly fresh meals prepared quickly after work

8.6 Air Frying Applications

Air fryers use circulating hot air to cook foods quickly with minimal added fat, providing excellent option for low-histamine cooking (Sahin, 2015). The high temperature and rapid air circulation cook proteins thoroughly in short time frames.

Chicken pieces cook particularly well in air fryers. Chicken breasts require 18-22 minutes at 375-400°F. Thighs need 20-25 minutes. Drumsticks cook in 22-26 minutes. These times produce crispy exterior and juicy interior while maintaining brief cooking duration that minimizes histamine formation.

Fish fillets air fry beautifully in 10-15 minutes at 380-400°F depending on thickness. The circulating air creates pleasant texture while cooking quickly. Delicate fish like cod or sole need only 8-10 minutes. Denser fish like halibut or swordfish require 12-15 minutes. All remain within the quick-cooking timeframe that prevents histamine issues.

Ground meat preparations including burgers or meatballs cook through in 12-18 minutes. The air circulation ensures even cooking throughout while surface crisps nicely. This speed compares favorably to oven-baking which might require 25-30 minutes for same results.

Vegetables air fry quickly, typically 8-15 minutes depending on type and size. Brussels sprouts crisp in 12-15 minutes. Broccoli becomes tender with crispy edges in 8-10 minutes. Sweet potato cubes cook through in 15-18 minutes. This speed allows fresh vegetable preparation rather than batch cooking stored for days.

Reheating from frozen works excellently in air fryers. Frozen pre-cooked chicken pieces reheat thoroughly in 12-15 minutes. This capability enables the freeze-and-reheat strategy discussed in Chapter 9.0. Cook fresh protein, portion immediately, freeze, then reheat individual portions in air fryer when needed. The quick reheating prevents the extended refrigerated storage that creates histamine.

Batch cooking safely becomes possible with air fryers. Cook multiple chicken breasts simultaneously (most air fryers accommodate 3-4 pieces). Immediately after cooking and brief cooling, portion and freeze individual pieces. The batch cooking efficiency exists without the histamine risk from extended cooking times or prolonged refrigerated storage.

8.7 Batch Cooking Strategies

Batch cooking for histamine management requires different approach than conventional meal prep (Maintz & Novak, 2007). The traditional strategy of cooking large quantities for refrigerated storage throughout the week conflicts with freshness principles. Modified batch cooking emphasizes immediate freezing rather than refrigeration.

Cook fresh, freeze immediately forms the foundation. Cook larger quantity of protein than needed for single meal. Consume one portion fresh. Portion remaining servings immediately after brief cooling. Freeze individual portions without refrigerated storage period. This sequence provides convenience of pre-cooked food without histamine accumulation from refrigerated leftover storage.

Practical implementation looks like this. Sunday afternoon: Cook four chicken breasts. Eat one for dinner. Portion remaining three into individual containers. Cool on counter for 20-30 minutes. Transfer to freezer immediately. The three frozen portions provide ready meals for the week without having sat refrigerated for days before consumption.

Grains and starches follow similar protocol. Cook large batch of rice or quinoa. Portion into single-serve containers. Cool briefly. Freeze immediately. These portions reheat quickly in microwave (4-5 minutes from frozen) providing convenient starch without the histamine that forms in refrigerated leftover grains.

Vegetables require more nuance. Some vegetables freeze well after cooking. Others deteriorate in texture. Roasted root vegetables (sweet potatoes, carrots, parsnips) freeze and reheat successfully. Delicate vegetables like zucchini or leafy greens don't freeze well and should be cooked fresh. Focus batch cooking on freeze-friendly vegetables while cooking delicate ones fresh as needed.

Avoid combination dishes for batch freezing. Casseroles, stews, and mixed dishes typically require reheating longer than individual components, extending time in temperature danger zone during reheating. Additionally, all components must freeze and reheat well for the dish to work. Keeping proteins, starches, and vegetables separate provides more flexibility and better results.

Portioning guidelines create useful serving sizes. For proteins, portion 4-6 ounces per container. For starches, 1/2 to 1 cup cooked grain per container. For vegetables, 1 cup cooked vegetables per container. These portions provide complete meal components when one of each gets reheated together.

Container selection affects results. Use freezer-safe containers or bags that seal completely, preventing freezer burn. Glass containers work well but take longer to cool before freezing. BPA-free plastic freezer containers cool faster. Vacuum-sealed bags provide best freezer burn protection as discussed in Chapter 9.0.

8.8 Defrosting and Frozen Cooking

Defrosting methods vary in histamine-safety (Lehane & Olley, 2000). The key principle is minimizing time at temperatures permitting bacterial growth.

Refrigerator defrosting, while food-safe from pathogenic bacteria perspective, creates histamine concerns. Frozen protein moved to refrigerator to thaw over 12-24 hours spends extended time at 35-40°F, perfect for histamine-producing bacteria to multiply on the surface as ice crystals melt. This traditional "safe" defrosting method produces histamine accumulation even though it prevents foodborne illness.

Cold water defrosting proceeds faster, minimizing bacterial growth time. Seal frozen protein in waterproof bag. Submerge in cold water, changing water every 30 minutes. Most proteins defrost in 1-3 hours. The colder temperature and shorter time reduce histamine formation compared to overnight refrigerator thawing.

Microwave defrosting provides fastest method but risks partially cooking exterior while interior remains frozen, creating texture issues. If using microwave defrost, cook immediately after defrosting without allowing defrosted protein to sit at room temperature.

Cooking from frozen eliminates defrosting entirely, providing the safest histamine approach (Jiménez-Colmenero et al., 2001). Food moves directly from frozen to cooking, bypassing the temperature danger zone. This requires cooking method adjustments but produces excellent results.

Pressure cooking from frozen works excellently. Add 3-5 minutes to standard pressure cooking times. Frozen chicken breasts cook through in 13-15 minutes versus 10-12 for thawed. Frozen ground beef becomes fully cooked in 20 minutes versus 15 for fresh. The pressure cooker handles frozen proteins without compromising results.

Baking from frozen requires temperature and time adjustments. Increase cooking time by approximately 50%. Frozen chicken breast that would bake in 30 minutes when fresh needs 45 minutes frozen. Use instant-read thermometer to verify internal temperature reaches 165°F for poultry, 145°F for fish, and appropriate temperature for other proteins.

Pan-cooking from frozen challenges uniform cooking. The frozen interior creates a cold core while exterior cooks. Using lid and moderate heat allows exterior to cook without burning while heat penetrates to frozen center. Frozen chicken breast or fish fillet can cook through in 20-25 minutes at medium heat with covered pan. Remove lid for final few minutes to brown surface.

Air frying from frozen produces great results with minimal adjustment. Add 3-5 minutes to standard cooking times. Frozen chicken breast air fries perfectly in 22-25 minutes versus 18-22 minutes for fresh. The circulating hot air ensures even cooking despite frozen starting temperature.

8.9 Case Study: From Defrost to Direct Frozen Cooking

Background

Remigius, a 35-year-old engineer, organized his meal preparation methodically. Each Sunday he purchased fresh proteins, portioned them into meal-size packages, and froze them. Throughout the week, he moved the next day's protein from freezer to refrigerator before bed, allowing overnight defrosting. He cooked the defrosted protein for dinner the following evening. This 24-hour refrigerator defrost became routine.

Despite using fresh proteins and cooking them promptly after thawing, Remigius experienced mild but persistent symptoms. Digestive discomfort several times weekly. Occasional headaches. Energy fluctuations. These symptoms weren't severe but frustrated him given his careful dietary management.

Presentation

Reviewing his routine with a nutritionist revealed the defrosting pattern. His proteins sat thawing in the refrigerator for 18-24 hours before cooking. During this period, ice crystals melted, creating moisture on meat surfaces. Bacteria naturally present on protein surfaces had optimal conditions for growth at refrigerator temperatures. The 24-hour period allowed substantial bacterial histamine production.

The nutritionist explained that his otherwise excellent routine was undermined by the extended refrigerator defrosting period. The very proteins he'd frozen immediately after purchase to preserve freshness were accumulating histamine during the 24-hour thaw.

Analysis

Remigius's case illustrates principles from section 8.8. Refrigerator defrosting, despite being recommended for food safety from pathogenic bacteria perspective, creates perfect conditions for histamine-producing bacteria. The extended time at 35-40°F allows bacterial multiplication on defrosting surfaces. Research confirms histamine increases during refrigerated thawing even when the meat was properly handled before freezing (Lehane & Olley, 2000).

His Sunday freezing routine excellently preserved freshness immediately after purchase. But the benefit was lost during the lengthy defrost period before cooking. From a histamine perspective, this created similar problems to refrigerating fresh meat for a day before cooking.

Intervention

The nutritionist taught Remigius to cook proteins directly from frozen, eliminating the defrosting step entirely. His Instant Pot became primary cooking tool for frozen proteins. Frozen chicken breast: 15 minutes at high pressure. Frozen ground beef: 20 minutes. Frozen fish fillet: 10-12 minutes. All produced excellent results without defrosting.

For variety, he learned frozen baking. Frozen chicken breast at 400°F for 50 minutes, covered for first 35 minutes then uncovered to brown. Internal temperature verification ensured thorough cooking. Frozen fish fillet at 425°F for 25-30 minutes.

His routine shifted to removing frozen protein from freezer, cooking directly, eating immediately. Total time from freezer to table: 30-60 minutes depending on protein and method. No advance planning required. No overnight defrosting. No histamine formation during thawing.

Outcome

Within two weeks of eliminating refrigerator defrosting and cooking proteins directly from frozen, Remigius's persistent symptoms resolved. Digestive discomfort disappeared. Headaches stopped. Energy stabilized. All other dietary factors remained constant. Only the defrosting and cooking method changed.

The frozen-to-cooked approach proved more convenient than anticipated. Rather than requiring advance planning to move tomorrow's protein to the refrigerator, he simply decided what to cook when arriving home. Frozen proteins cooked through in similar timeframes to defrosted versions when using pressure cooker or adjusted oven times.

Teaching Points

- Refrigerator defrosting, despite being recommended for food-safety reasons to prevent pathogenic bacteria, creates ideal conditions for histamine-producing bacteria to multiply during the 12-24 hour thawing period, undermining the freshness preserved by proper freezing
- Cooking proteins directly from frozen eliminates the defrosting step entirely, preventing histamine formation that occurs during thawing while providing excellent culinary results with minor cooking time adjustments
- Pressure cookers and adjusted oven baking both handle frozen proteins excellently, making frozen-to-cooked approach practical for daily meal preparation without advance planning requirements

8.10 Seasoning Without High Histamine Ingredients

Flavor development in low-histamine cooking requires creativity since many conventional seasonings contain high histamine or act as histamine liberators (Maintz & Novak, 2007).

Prohibited seasonings include vinegar in all forms (balsamic, red wine, white wine, apple cider, rice), soy sauce and tamari, fish sauce, aged hot sauces, commercial spice blends containing problematic ingredients, bouillon cubes or stock concentrates often containing yeast extract, and pre-made marinades typically containing vinegar or soy sauce.

Fresh herbs provide excellent flavor without histamine concerns. Basil, cilantro, parsley, mint, dill, chives, and rosemary all work well fresh. These herbs lose much flavor when dried, so emphasizing fresh versions provides best results. Growing herbs on a sunny windowsill ensures constant fresh supply.

Dried spices vary in individual tolerance but many work well for most people. Cumin, coriander, turmeric, paprika (check for additives), garlic powder, onion powder, and ginger typically prove tolerable. However, some spice blends contain hidden additives or aged ingredients. Pure single spices work best. Test spices individually following reintroduction protocols from Chapter 6.0 since salicylate content may affect tolerance.

Fresh aromatics including onions, garlic, ginger, and fresh chili peppers (if tolerated) build flavor bases for cooking. Sautéing diced onion and minced garlic in olive oil before adding proteins creates flavorful foundation. Fresh grated ginger adds bright notes to stir-fries and Asian-inspired dishes. These fresh ingredients avoid the histamine concerns of their fermented derivatives like garlic powder stored for months.

Salt remains the most reliable seasoning. Sea salt, pink Himalayan salt, and kosher salt all provide clean flavor enhancement. Liberal salt use during cooking develops flavors in ways that complex spice blends cannot replicate. Don't fear salt in low-histamine cooking unless medical conditions require sodium restriction.

Citrus alternatives to vinegar provide acidity. Fresh lemon juice (if citrus tolerated as determined through testing) brightens dishes similarly to vinegar. Fresh lime juice works well in Latin and Asian applications. However, citrus acts as histamine liberator for many individuals as discussed in Chapter 4.0, so test tolerance carefully.

Oil-based preparations create flavor without histamine. Herb-infused olive oils made by gently heating fresh herbs in olive oil provide seasoning options. Cool the oil, strain out herbs, and use the flavored oil within a week. Fresh basil oil, rosemary oil, or garlic oil add interest to simple preparations.

Coconut aminos provides soy-sauce alternative for some individuals. This condiment made from coconut sap offers umami flavor similar to soy sauce without the fermentation. Test individual tolerance as reactions vary. Some people tolerate it well. Others react to it despite it being marketed as histamine-friendly.

Maple syrup and honey provide sweetness for recipes requiring it. Both work in marinades, glazes, or Asian-inspired sauces. Combine with fresh ginger, garlic, and coconut aminos (if tolerated) for teriyaki-style flavor profile without soy sauce or vinegar.

Building flavor through technique matters as much as ingredients. Proper browning through high-heat searing creates complex flavors. Caramelizing onions (quickly, not the slow hours-long method) develops sweetness. Roasting vegetables at high temperatures produces appealing flavors. These cooking techniques generate taste sensations that seasoning alone cannot provide.

8.11 Putting Knowledge Into Practice

This chapter explained how cooking methods affect histamine formation and provided techniques that minimize histamine while maintaining convenience and flavor. The fresh is best principle dominates all considerations. Time from purchase to cooking matters more than cooking method in most cases. Minimizing refrigerated storage before cooking prevents histamine accumulation that cooking cannot eliminate.

High heat, short time cooking methods including grilling, sautéing, stir-frying, broiling, and pressure cooking minimize histamine formation by limiting time at temperatures where bacterial growth occurs. Pressure cooking provides particular advantage by achieving tender results in fraction of traditional cooking times through high temperature and pressure.

Slow cooking methods including crockpots, long braises, and low-temperature roasting should be avoided. These methods keep food at moderate temperatures for extended periods, creating ideal conditions for bacterial histamine production even when starting with fresh ingredients.

Air frying offers fast, convenient cooking with minimal added fat, providing excellent option for quick protein and vegetable preparation. Batch cooking remains possible when combined with immediate freezing rather than refrigerated storage.

Cooking proteins directly from frozen eliminates the defrosting step, preventing histamine formation during thawing. Pressure cookers and adjusted oven baking both handle frozen proteins excellently, making this approach practical for daily use.

Seasoning without high-histamine ingredients requires fresh herbs, pure spices tested individually, fresh aromatics, and flavor development through cooking technique rather than relying on vinegar, soy sauce, or aged condiments.

Chapter 9.0 will build on these cooking techniques by explaining storage strategies that maintain the freshness advantages proper cooking provides, ensuring meals remain low-histamine from preparation through consumption days later.

Chapter 9.0: Storage Strategies for Histamine Management

Berenice opened her freezer with satisfaction, admiring rows of neatly labeled containers. She'd spent Sunday afternoon batch cooking chicken, beef, and vegetable sides following the protocols from Chapter 8.0. Fresh ingredients, quick cooking methods, immediate portioning. Everything seemed perfect. But three days later, reheating a chicken portion for dinner, she experienced the familiar symptoms. Headache within an hour. Digestive discomfort overnight. Confusion set in. She'd followed all the cooking rules. Fresh protein, cooked quickly, frozen immediately. What went wrong? The problem wasn't her cooking. It was her cooling protocol. After cooking, she'd left the hot containers on the counter for two hours to cool before freezing, precisely following general food safety advice. During those two hours at room temperature, bacteria multiplied rapidly on the still-warm chicken surfaces, producing histamine that freezing merely preserved rather than eliminated (Lehane & Olley, 2000). Her careful cooking was undermined by improper cooling and storage practices.

This chapter explains storage strategies that preserve the freshness advantages proper cooking provides. You will learn how the cold chain concept affects histamine formation, optimal refrigerator temperatures for histamine management, why the 24-hour leftover rule matters, immediate freezing protocols for meal preparation, the truth about vacuum sealing benefits, why container material affects food quality, single-serve portioning strategies, labeling and dating systems, maximum safe freezer storage times for different foods, quick-cooling techniques before freezing, and preventing freezer burn while maintaining quality.

9.1 Cold Chain Fundamentals

The **cold chain** describes the unbroken series of refrigerated conditions from food production through consumption (Mercier et al., 2017). For histamine management, this chain begins the moment after slaughter or harvest and continues until cooking or consumption.

Temperature control prevents bacterial growth that produces histamine. Histamine-forming bacteria grow rapidly between 40-140°F (4-60°C), the range food safety experts call the temperature danger zone. At temperatures below 40°F (4°C), bacterial growth slows substantially but doesn't stop completely. The colder the storage temperature, the slower bacteria multiply and produce histamine.

Commercial cold chain failures create problems before you purchase food. Fish caught Monday might sit improperly refrigerated on the boat for days before reaching shore. Meat might warm during transport from processing facility to distributor. These temperature excursions allow bacterial histamine production before food reaches retail. This explains why identical cuts of meat or fish from the same store vary in histamine content and individual tolerance.

Your home cold chain begins at purchase. The drive from grocery store to home matters. Bringing meat home in an insulated bag with ice packs prevents warming during transport. This seems minor but makes measurable difference for fish and ground meat that accumulate histamine rapidly at warmer temperatures.

Immediate refrigeration or freezing after arriving home maintains the cold chain. Leaving groceries on the counter while putting away other items allows protein temperatures to rise into bacterial growth range. Put proteins away first, immediately upon entering the kitchen.

Refrigerator recovery time affects histamine formation. Opening the refrigerator door allows warm air entry, temporarily raising internal temperature. Frequent prolonged door openings create temperature cycling that permits bacterial growth. Minimize door opening duration and frequency. Know what you want before opening. Retrieve it quickly. Close the door promptly.

Freezer temperature stability matters more than refrigerator temperature for long-term storage. Every freeze-thaw cycle damages food quality and potentially allows bacterial histamine production during the thawed period. Maintain consistent freezer temperature. Avoid overpacking which impedes air circulation and temperature maintenance. Ensure freezer door seals properly.

9.2 Temperature Optimization Strategies

Refrigerator temperature for histamine management should be 34-38°F (1-3°C), colder than the standard 40°F (4°C) recommended for general food safety (Raithel et al., 2010). This colder temperature significantly slows bacterial histamine production. Research demonstrates that histamine formation rates decrease substantially at temperatures below 39°F (4°C) compared to standard refrigeration.

Measuring actual temperature requires a refrigerator thermometer placed in the center of the middle shelf. The temperature display on many refrigerators measures air temperature near the cooling element, not the actual temperature where food sits. Actual food storage temperatures often run 3-5°F warmer than displayed temperature. Verify real temperatures before assuming your refrigerator runs cold enough.

Coldest zones in most refrigerators are the back of the bottom shelf and the area directly below the freezer compartment in top-freezer models. Store proteins in these coldest areas rather than in door shelves where temperature fluctuates most with door openings. Reserve door shelves for condiments and less perishable items.

Avoiding over-packing enables proper air circulation and temperature maintenance. Tightly packed refrigerators don't cool evenly. Cold air can't circulate around all items. Some foods sit in warmer microclimates despite overall appropriate refrigerator temperature. Leave space between items for air movement.

Freezer temperature should be 0°F (-18°C) or colder. Research shows histamine formation essentially stops at temperatures below 0°F (Lehane & Olley, 2000). Warmer freezer temperatures, while preventing spoilage, may allow slow histamine accumulation over weeks of storage. This becomes particularly relevant for the maximum storage times discussed in section 9.8.

Temperature verification should occur regularly. Check refrigerator and freezer thermometers weekly. Adjust temperature settings if readings drift outside target ranges. After power outages, verify temperatures returned to safe levels before consuming stored food. If temperature exceeded 40°F for more than two hours, consider the cold chain broken for histamine-sensitive purposes even if food remains safe from pathogenic bacteria perspective.

9.3 The 24 Hour Rule

Refrigerated leftovers become problematic for histamine management within 24 hours of cooking, regardless of proper refrigeration temperature (Maintz & Novak, 2007). This contradicts general food safety guidance allowing 3-4 days of refrigerated leftover storage for most foods. While refrigerated leftovers remain safe from pathogenic bacteria perspective for several days, histamine accumulation makes them problematic much sooner.

Bacterial activity continues in refrigerated cooked foods. Cooking doesn't sterilize food completely. Some bacteria survive cooking, and new bacteria from the environment colonize food during cooling and storage. These bacteria, while insufficient to cause foodborne illness, produce histamine at refrigeration temperatures. Research demonstrates measurable histamine increases in refrigerated cooked meats within 24 hours even at proper refrigeration temperatures (Bodmer et al., 1999).

The 24-hour cutoff represents a conservative but realistic guideline. Some individuals tolerate refrigerated leftovers for 36-48 hours. Others react to food refrigerated overnight. The 24-hour rule provides reasonable safety margin for most histamine-intolerant individuals. Highly sensitive individuals may need to consume or freeze cooked foods within 12 hours or even immediately after cooking.

Practical implications challenge conventional meal planning. The Sunday meal prep approach of cooking all week's meals, refrigerating them, and eating throughout the week doesn't work for histamine management. Monday's meal might be tolerable. By Thursday and Friday, the same batch-cooked food contains sufficient histamine to trigger symptoms.

Alternative approaches discussed in Chapter 8.0 emphasize immediate freezing rather than refrigeration. Cook Sunday. Eat one portion fresh. Freeze remaining portions immediately after cooling. Throughout the week, defrost or cook from frozen one portion at a time. This maintains freshness advantages without accumulating refrigerated storage histamine.

Raw protein storage follows even stricter timelines. Fresh raw chicken, beef, or fish should be cooked or frozen within 24 hours of purchase. Ideally, cook or freeze the same day purchased. Each additional day of refrigerated storage allows bacterial histamine production. The practice of purchasing fresh meat or fish and refrigerating it for 2-3 days before cooking creates substantial histamine even in apparently fresh protein.

9.4 Case Study: Leftover Confusion

Background

Darian, a 29-year-old teacher, carefully followed low-histamine dietary guidelines. He avoided aged cheeses, cured meats, fermented foods, and other high-histamine items. He cooked fresh proteins using quick methods. Yet he experienced inconsistent symptoms. Some weeks felt fine. Other weeks brought frequent headaches and digestive issues despite eating seemingly identical foods.

Presentation

Darian's food diary revealed a pattern. Symptoms clustered Sunday through Wednesday of each week. Thursdays and Fridays were generally symptom-free. Weekends felt good. This weekly cycle puzzled him. His diet didn't change systematically across the week.

Further investigation uncovered the issue. Darian batch-cooked on Sundays, preparing chicken, ground beef, and vegetable sides for the week. He refrigerated these cooked foods and ate portions daily. Sunday and Monday meals came from freshly cooked batches. Tuesday through Thursday meals used the same food after

2-5 days of refrigerated storage. Thursdays and Fridays he often ate out or prepared fresh simple meals due to work schedule variations, avoiding the refrigerated leftovers.

Analysis

Darian's pattern demonstrates the 24-hour rule from section 9.3. His Sunday cooking used fresh ingredients and proper quick-cooking methods. The food started with minimal histamine. However, bacterial histamine production continued during refrigerated storage throughout the week. By Tuesday (48 hours refrigerated), histamine levels rose enough to trigger mild symptoms. By Wednesday and Thursday (72-96 hours refrigerated), histamine accumulation produced consistent reactions.

His symptom-free Thursdays and Fridays reflected eating fresh restaurant food or cooking fresh simple meals rather than consuming multi-day-old refrigerated leftovers. Weekends brought relief because Sunday's fresh batch cooking reset the cycle.

The research confirms this pattern. Studies show cooked meats refrigerated at appropriate temperatures accumulate measurable histamine within 24-48 hours, with levels continuing to rise over subsequent days (Bodmer et al., 1999). Even proper refrigeration temperatures of 38°F (3°C) slow but don't stop this process.

Intervention

Darian modified his meal prep routine following the immediate freezing protocol from section 9.4. He continued Sunday batch cooking but changed storage methods. After cooking and cooling quickly using techniques from section 9.9, he portioned all food into single-serve containers. He consumed one portion fresh Sunday evening. All remaining portions went directly into the freezer after 20-30 minutes of counter cooling.

Throughout the week, he removed one frozen portion each morning, allowing it to thaw in the refrigerator during the day. He reheated that evening for dinner, consuming it immediately without returning any to the refrigerator. Alternatively, on days he remembered, he cooked frozen portions directly without thawing using the techniques from Chapter 8.0.

This approach meant Sunday's batch cooking remained as fresh Thursday as Monday. The freezing halted bacterial histamine production. The single-portion thawing and immediate consumption prevented histamine accumulation from refrigerated storage.

Outcome

Within two weeks of implementing the freeze-first approach, Darian's weekly symptom cycle resolved. He experienced consistent symptom control Sunday through Friday. The Tuesday-Wednesday symptom clustering disappeared. His Friday and weekend symptom-free periods extended throughout the week.

Food quality perceptions improved unexpectedly. He'd assumed week-old refrigerated chicken was fine because it smelled and tasted normal. The frozen-then-reheated portions actually tasted fresher than multi-day refrigerated versions, in addition to containing less histamine.

Teaching Points

- Refrigerated cooked foods accumulate histamine within 24-48 hours despite proper refrigeration temperatures and absence of spoilage indicators, creating symptom patterns that correlate with leftover age rather than original food quality
- The traditional weekly meal prep approach of refrigerating batch-cooked food for 5-7 days conflicts with histamine management requirements, with symptom risk increasing proportionally to refrigerated storage duration
- Immediate freezing after cooking followed by single-portion thawing or frozen reheating maintains the freshness advantages of proper cooking throughout the week without refrigerated storage histamine accumulation

9.5 Immediate Freezing Protocols

Quick cooling before freezing prevents histamine formation during the cooling period while also protecting food quality (Mercier et al., 2017). The goal is moving food from cooking temperature through the danger zone to freezing temperature as rapidly as possible.

Shallow containers cool faster than deep containers. Food depth should not exceed two inches for quick cooling. A large pot of soup divided into shallow containers cools in 30-45 minutes. The same volume in one deep container requires 3-4 hours, spending much longer in the temperature danger zone.

Ice bath cooling provides the fastest method. Place sealed containers of hot food in a larger container filled with ice water. Stir food periodically to distribute cold throughout. Most foods cool to refrigerator temperature within 20-30 minutes using this method. This rapid cooling prevents bacterial growth and histamine production during the vulnerable cooling period.

Counter cooling works adequately for small portions. Spread food thinly in shallow containers. Leave uncovered initially to allow steam to escape. Room temperature ambient cooling brings most foods to refrigerator temperature within 30-45 minutes when using appropriately shallow containers. However, don't extend counter time beyond one hour regardless of food temperature. After one hour, move to refrigerator or freezer even if still slightly warm.

Avoiding hot food in freezer matters for food quality and freezer efficiency. Placing hot food directly in freezer raises freezer temperature, potentially affecting other frozen items. The hot food also develops poor texture from slow freezing that creates large ice crystals. Cool food to at least room temperature, preferably to refrigerator temperature, before freezing.

Portioning before cooling enables faster cooling and more practical storage. Divide large batches into meal-size portions before cooling. These smaller portions cool faster and freeze more quickly. Individual portions also thaw faster and enable using exactly the needed amount without thawing excess.

Immediate freezing timeline means moving cooled food to freezer without intermediate refrigerated storage. The sequence is: cook, cool rapidly (20-45 minutes), freeze immediately. Don't cook Monday, cool, refrigerate overnight, then freeze Tuesday. That 12-24 hour refrigerated storage period allows histamine formation that freezing then preserves.

9.6 Vacuum Sealing Considerations

Vacuum sealing removes air from storage bags or containers before sealing, theoretically slowing oxidation and bacterial growth. However, for histamine management, vacuum sealing provides limited benefits and requires careful application (Hernández-Macedo et al., 2011).

Temperature dependent benefits mean vacuum sealing only helps if combined with proper temperature control. Vacuum-sealed food stored at room temperature still accumulates histamine rapidly. Vacuum-sealed food refrigerated at 40°F (4°C) accumulates histamine nearly as fast as non-vacuum-sealed food at the same temperature. The benefit appears primarily when vacuum-sealing frozen foods.

Freezer storage advantages of vacuum sealing include preventing freezer burn by excluding air that causes ice crystal formation and subsequent moisture loss. Vacuum-sealed frozen foods maintain quality and texture better than foods in regular freezer bags or containers. For histamine purposes, this quality maintenance matters because freezer-burned food often gets discarded prematurely, wasting properly frozen low-histamine food.

Extended freezer life from vacuum sealing enables longer storage within the maximum timeframes discussed in section 9.8 without quality degradation. Vacuum-sealed chicken breast maintains good texture for 3-4 months, while regular freezer bag storage may show quality decline after 6-8 weeks despite remaining histamine-safe.

Limitations for fresh storage include the reality that vacuum sealing doesn't extend safe refrigerated storage time for histamine purposes. Vacuum-sealed raw chicken refrigerated for three days contains similar histamine to non-vacuum-sealed chicken refrigerated for the same period. Both exceed the 24-hour fresh storage guideline. Don't assume vacuum sealing permits longer refrigerated storage.

Anaerobic bacteria concerns exist theoretically. Some bacteria grow without oxygen, and vacuum conditions could favor them. However, the frozen storage temperatures used in low-histamine meal prep prevent bacterial growth regardless of oxygen presence. For refrigerated storage, the 24-hour rule applies equally to vacuum-sealed and regular-sealed foods.

Practical recommendations include using vacuum sealing primarily for freezer storage to prevent freezer burn and extend quality life, avoiding the assumption that vacuum sealing permits longer refrigerated storage than non-vacuum-sealed foods, and continuing to follow the 24-hour rule for refrigerated items regardless of packaging method.

Cost-benefit analysis suggests vacuum sealers benefit individuals doing substantial freezer storage of batch-cooked meals or bulk-purchased proteins. The quality maintenance justifies the equipment cost. For individuals cooking fresh daily with minimal freezer storage, vacuum sealing provides marginal benefit over quality freezer bags.

9.7 Container Material Selection

Glass containers provide several advantages for histamine management (Arvanitoyannis & Bosnea, 2004). Glass is non-reactive, meaning it doesn't leach chemicals into food. Glass tolerates both freezer and oven temperatures, enabling freezing in the container then reheating directly without transferring food. Glass allows visibility of contents without opening containers.

Plastic containers vary dramatically in quality and suitability. Food-grade freezer-safe plastics work adequately for frozen storage. However, lower quality plastics may become brittle in freezers, cracking and allowing freezer burn. BPA-free plastics avoid one concerning chemical but may contain other potentially problematic compounds that leach into food over time.

Temperature tolerance differs between materials. Glass withstands temperature extremes from freezer to oven. Most plastics tolerate freezer temperatures but degrade or melt at high temperatures. Reheating frozen food in plastic containers requires transferring to appropriate cookware, creating extra handling and cleaning.

Freezer burn prevention relates to seal quality more than container material. Both glass and plastic containers with tight-fitting lids prevent freezer burn when properly sealed. The critical factor is excluding air from contact with food surface. Containers filled to minimize air space and sealed tightly work regardless of material.

Chemical leaching concerns make glass preferable for long-term storage, particularly for fatty foods that extract more compounds from plastics. Research demonstrates various plastics leach chemicals into food, with amounts increasing over time and with higher storage temperatures (Arvanitoyannis & Bosnea, 2004). For histamine purposes, these chemical concerns are secondary to histamine prevention, but glass eliminates the variable.

Practical considerations including weight, breakage risk, and cost influence material choice. Glass containers weigh significantly more than plastic, affecting transport and handling. Glass breaks when dropped, creating safety and cleanup concerns. Glass costs more initially but lasts indefinitely while plastics degrade over time.

Recommended approach uses glass containers for refrigerated storage and reheating to avoid chemical exposure during warming. Plastic freezer bags or containers work adequately for frozen storage since low temperatures minimize chemical leaching. BPA-free, phthalate-free plastics provide better choice when using plastic. For foods requiring oven reheating, glass containers or oven-safe ceramic enable freezing and reheating in the same vessel.

9.8 Maximum Storage Guidelines

Freezer storage times for histamine management differ from general food safety guidelines (Lehane & Olley, 2000). While frozen food remains safe from pathogenic bacteria indefinitely, histamine formation concerns and quality degradation create practical maximum storage periods.

Uncooked meat should be used within four months of freezing for histamine purposes. Research suggests minimal histamine formation in properly frozen raw meat for this period. Beyond four months, slow histamine accumulation may occur even at 0°F (-18°C) due to residual enzyme activity and slow bacterial metabolism.

Quality also declines with longer storage through freezer burn and oxidation even in vacuum-sealed packages.

Fish proves more sensitive, ideally used within 2-3 months. The higher histidine content in fish provides more substrate for histamine formation. Flash-frozen fish purchased frozen and maintained frozen continuously tolerates the four-month guideline. Fish frozen at home should be used sooner due to potential cold chain breaks before home freezing.

Cooked meals require much shorter storage periods, maximum 2-3 weeks in the freezer for histamine safety. This surprises many people expecting frozen cooked foods to last months. However, the cooking process creates some bacterial contamination that survives freezing. These bacteria produce small amounts of histamine even in frozen storage. Additionally, cooked foods suffer quality degradation faster than raw proteins.

Practical interpretation means batch-cooking and freezing cooked chicken on Sunday should be consumed by the end of the following week or beginning of the third week at latest. Don't batch cook enough for a month of meals. Batch cook for 1-2 weeks, rotating through batches to stay within the 2-3 week window.

Ground meat requires stricter limits than whole cuts. The grinding process distributes bacteria throughout the product, creating more bacterial surface area than intact muscle. Use frozen ground beef, turkey, or chicken within 2-3 months rather than four months.

Vegetables generally tolerate longer frozen storage without histamine concerns since they contain minimal protein and histidine. Frozen vegetables remain fine for 6-12 months from quality perspective. However, texture degradation occurs over time even without histamine issues.

Labeling and dating becomes essential for managing these different storage timelines. Section 9.9 discusses labeling strategies. Without clear dating, determining how long foods have been frozen becomes guesswork.

9.9 Labeling and Dating Systems

Comprehensive labeling should include food contents, cooking date (if cooked) or freezing date, use-by date, and any special instructions. This information enables safe decision-making about consumption without relying on memory.

Content description specifies exactly what the container holds. "Chicken" is vague. "Grilled chicken breast" provides clarity. "Ground beef cooked plain" versus "ground beef with onions" matters for those with multiple tier 2 foods requiring tracking. Be specific enough to make informed decisions without opening containers.

Date format consistency prevents confusion. Use the same format throughout your freezer. MM/DD/YY or DD/MM/YY both work, but mixing formats creates errors. Including day of week helps some people. "Frozen Sunday 2/15/26" provides clear chronological reference.

Use by dates calculated from freezing dates help manage rotation. For cooked meals frozen 2/15/26, the use-by date is approximately 3/1/26 (two weeks later). For raw chicken frozen the same day, use by 6/15/26 (four months later). Recording the use-by date prevents needing to calculate each time.

Special instructions note any important details. "Reheat from frozen at 400°F for 30 minutes" saves trial and error. "Tested well on Tuesday" reminds you this food passed reintroduction testing. "Contains tier 2 avocado" helps track moderate-histamine foods.

Label placement on container tops enables reading without removing containers from freezer. Side labels require pulling containers out to read. Top labels allow quickly scanning the freezer for desired items and oldest dates during rotation.

Rotation systems ensure oldest items get used first. Some people arrange freezers chronologically with oldest items in front. Others use different freezer sections for different time periods. The specific system matters less than consistency.

Digital tracking supplements physical labels for highly organized individuals. Spreadsheets or apps tracking freezer contents, dates, and locations enable detailed inventory management. However, this adds complexity that many find burdensome. Simple physical labels work adequately for most people.

9.10 Case Study: Freezer Archaeology

Background

Ianthe, a 33-year-old researcher, filled her freezer with batch-cooked meals and proteins over several months. Without systematic labeling, she relied on memory and visual inspection to identify foods and estimate how long they'd been frozen. This worked initially when the freezer was relatively empty and recent.

Presentation

Six months into histamine management, Ianthe's freezer had become archaeological rather than organized. Unlabeled containers of unknown contents sat in stacks. She couldn't reliably remember if a particular chicken package was frozen two weeks ago or two months ago. The visual appearance of frozen food provided few clues.

She developed a pattern of avoiding older, uncertain items in favor of recently frozen foods she could track mentally. This created a collection of ancient frozen foods she feared had exceeded safe storage times but couldn't verify. She felt wasteful discarding potentially good food but worried about consuming foods that might trigger symptoms.

Confusion extended to cooked versus raw proteins. Some containers held cooked chicken. Others held raw chicken she'd portioned for individual cooking. Without labels, determining which was which required partial thawing or remembering packaging details.

Analysis

Ianthe's situation demonstrates why labeling systems from section 9.9 matter. The different maximum storage times for raw proteins (four months) versus cooked meals (2-3 weeks) from section 9.8 create different safety windows requiring accurate dating. Without labels, foods either get consumed prematurely from excessive caution or retained too long from uncertainty.

The inability to distinguish cooked from raw proteins creates practical problems. Cooked proteins need only reheating. Raw proteins require full cooking. Discovering mid-preparation that a package contains raw rather than cooked chicken when you planned quick reheating disrupts meal timing.

Research on home food storage demonstrates that unlabeled frozen foods create significant waste as people discard items from uncertainty rather than risk quality or safety issues (Mercier et al., 2017). This waste undermines the efficiency benefits of batch cooking and freezing.

Intervention

Ianthe implemented a comprehensive labeling system. She first conducted freezer inventory, discarding anything she couldn't confidently date within appropriate storage windows. This culling hurt psychologically but eliminated accumulated uncertainty.

For all remaining and new frozen items, she created labels including food description, freezing date, use-by date, and cooking status. She used colored labels:

blue for raw proteins, green for cooked meals, yellow for vegetables and starches. This color coding enabled quick visual scanning.

She reorganized the freezer by category and chronology. All cooked meals in one section, arranged oldest to newest. Raw proteins in another section, similarly organized. Vegetables and starches in a third area. This physical organization reinforced the labeling system.

She committed to labeling everything before freezing. No exceptions. If she ran out of labels, she wrote on freezer bags with permanent marker. No unlabeled items entered the freezer.

Outcome

Within two weeks, Ianthe's freezer organization transformed from chaos to clarity. She could quickly identify any item, its age, and its use-by date without guessing. Meal planning became efficient rather than stressful. She confidently used older items before they exceeded storage guidelines rather than avoiding them from uncertainty.

Food waste decreased substantially. She used nearly everything within appropriate timeframes. The few items that approached use-by dates got planned into meals deliberately rather than discovered accidentally weeks after they should have been consumed.

The time invested in labeling (30-60 seconds per item) saved significant time during meal selection and preparation. The color coding enabled finding desired foods in seconds rather than minutes of container examination.

Teaching Points

- Systematic labeling including contents, dates, and use-by information enables confident management of different maximum storage times for raw proteins versus cooked meals and prevents both premature disposal from excessive caution and extended storage from uncertainty
- The efficiency benefits of batch cooking and freezing depend on effective inventory management that allows using foods within appropriate timeframes, which unlabeled storage makes impossible beyond 2-3 weeks as mental tracking fails
- The minimal time investment in comprehensive labeling before freezing provides substantial returns in reduced food waste, simplified meal planning, and confident adherence to histamine safety guidelines

9.11 Freezer Burn Prevention

Freezer burn results from moisture loss and oxidation occurring when food sits in freezers without adequate protection (Singh & Heldman, 2014). While freezer-burned food remains safe to eat from pathogenic bacteria perspective, quality degradation often makes it unpalatable and leads to waste.

Air exposure causes freezer burn. Ice crystals form on food surfaces. These crystals sublimate (change directly from ice to water vapor) in the dry freezer environment. This moisture loss creates the dry, discolored patches characteristic of freezer burn. Minimizing air contact prevents this process.

Proper wrapping excludes air from food surfaces. Wrap foods tightly in freezer paper, heavy-duty aluminum foil, or plastic wrap before placing in freezer bags or containers. Press wrapping directly against food surface, eliminating air pockets. This dual protection (wrapping plus container) provides best freezer burn prevention.

Vacuum sealing excels at freezer burn prevention by removing all air from packaging. The complete air exclusion prevents moisture sublimation. Foods vacuum-sealed properly show minimal freezer burn even after months of storage within appropriate safety windows.

Container filling should minimize headspace. Fill containers to within half inch of the top, leaving just enough room for expansion during freezing. Large air spaces above food allow moisture migration and ice crystal formation.

Freezer temperature consistency affects freezer burn development. Temperature fluctuations from frequent door opening or poor freezer function accelerate moisture loss. Maintain consistent 0°F (-18°C) or colder temperature. Minimize door opening duration and frequency.

Storage duration correlates with freezer burn severity. Foods stored longer develop more freezer burn regardless of protection quality. This provides additional reason to respect the maximum storage times from section 9.8 beyond histamine safety. Quality deterioration makes long-stored foods less appetizing even if histamine levels remain acceptable.

Freezer organization enabling first-in-first-out rotation prevents forgotten items languishing long enough to develop severe freezer burn. The labeling and organization systems from sections 9.9 and 9.10 support this rotation.

9.12 Core Concepts Recap

This chapter explained storage strategies that preserve the freshness advantages proper cooking provides. The cold chain from production through consumption affects histamine accumulation, with each temperature excursion permitting bacterial growth and histamine formation. Maintaining refrigerator temperatures at 34-38°F (1-3°C) and freezer temperatures at 0°F (-18°C) or colder minimizes bacterial histamine production.

The 24-hour rule for refrigerated leftovers recognizes that cooked foods accumulate histamine within 24 hours even at proper refrigeration temperatures. Traditional meal prep approaches involving refrigerated storage for 5-7 days conflict with histamine management. Immediate freezing protocols provide the solution, using rapid cooling techniques to move food safely from cooking temperature to frozen storage within 30-60 minutes.

Vacuum sealing provides temperature-dependent benefits, primarily preventing freezer burn in frozen foods rather than extending safe refrigerated storage times. Glass containers offer advantages over plastic for refrigerated storage and reheating, though both work adequately for frozen storage when properly sealed.

Maximum freezer storage times for histamine management differ from general food safety guidelines. Uncooked meat lasts four months maximum. Cooked meals require consumption within 2-3 weeks. These limits reflect both histamine accumulation during frozen storage and quality degradation over time.

Comprehensive labeling systems including contents, dates, use-by information, and cooking status enable managing these different storage timeframes effectively. Freezer burn prevention through proper wrapping, vacuum sealing, and minimal air exposure maintains quality and reduces waste.

Chapter 10.0 will explain how to source the highest-quality proteins and produce that provide optimal starting points for the cooking and storage strategies discussed in Chapters 8.0 and 9.0.

Chapter 10.0: Shopping and Sourcing Quality Foods

Simeon stood at the fish counter, confronting a decision that seemed simple but felt paralyzing. Three options for salmon lay before him. Wild-caught Alaskan salmon fillets on ice, marked "fresh" and priced premium. Farm-raised Atlantic salmon fillets next to them, also called "fresh," at moderate price. Frozen wild-caught salmon in vacuum-sealed packages in the case below, marked as flash-frozen within hours of catch, at the lowest price. Every resource he'd read emphasized fresh food for histamine management. Fresh meant low histamine, right? So the expensive "fresh" wild-caught must be best. But the fishmonger's honest comment gave him pause. "Those 'fresh' fillets were actually frozen on the boat, thawed here three days ago for display. The frozen packages you're looking at are newer catch, frozen

immediately." This revelation contradicted Simeon's assumptions. The expensive "fresh" fish actually had more time for histamine formation than the cheaper frozen version. This scenario repeats at seafood counters, meat departments, and produce sections daily as people navigate the gap between marketing and reality.

This chapter explains how to source the highest-quality proteins and produce that provide optimal starting points for the cooking and storage strategies from Chapters 8.0 and 9.0. You will learn how to select the freshest proteins including specific criteria for fish, meat, and poultry, strategic interpretation of expiration dates, when frozen foods exceed fresh quality, the benefits and limitations of farmers' markets, online resources for quality proteins, safe seafood species and sourcing, produce selection and home storage, evaluating packaged foods for hidden triggers, building relationships with butchers and fishmongers, and strategies for bulk buying with immediate processing.

10.1 Flash Frozen Fish Superiority

Flash freezing technology allows fish to be frozen solid within hours of being caught, often directly on the fishing vessel (Visciano et al., 2012). This immediate freezing preserves the fish at its freshest state, preventing bacterial histamine formation that begins minutes after death.

Time matters more than temperature for fresh fish. A fish caught Monday, kept on ice for three days during boat transit, then sold "fresh" at retail Friday contains substantially more histamine than fish caught Monday, flash-frozen within hours, and sold frozen. The fresh fish's five days of time for bacterial activity outweigh any perceived quality advantage of never-frozen status.

Regulatory freezing requirements for certain fish species create an unexpected benefit for histamine management. FDA requires parasites-susceptible fish intended for raw consumption be frozen to specific temperatures for specific durations to kill parasites. Fish meeting these requirements for sushi-grade designation undergo proper freezing that also helps prevent histamine formation.

Thawed for display practices create false "fresh" fish. Many fish counters thaw previously frozen fish for display in ice-filled cases. This fish was frozen properly on boats, maintaining low histamine. However, the thawing for retail display starts bacterial histamine production. Each day the thawed fish sits in the display case allows accumulation. Fish "fresh thawed today" might be acceptable. "Fresh thawed Monday" purchased Friday is problematic.

Identifying flash-frozen fish requires asking direct questions. "Is this fish fresh or previously frozen?" If previously frozen, "When was it thawed?" If the answer is more than 24 hours ago, the vacuum-sealed frozen fish in the case below is actually fresher from histamine perspective.

Quality indicators in flash-frozen fish include firm texture when thawed, bright color, no discoloration, minimal liquid in package when thawing, and pleasant ocean smell without fishiness. Poor-quality frozen fish shows mushy texture, gray or brown discoloration, excessive liquid, and strong fishy odors.

Cost comparison often favors frozen fish. Flash-frozen fish typically costs less than "fresh" fish due to different handling requirements and market perceptions. For histamine management, the cheaper frozen option frequently provides superior safety and quality.

10.2 Fresh Meat Selection

Pasture-raised versus conventional meat matters less for histamine than processing timing and cold chain maintenance (Maintz & Novak, 2007). While pasture-raised may offer other health benefits, histamine accumulation depends primarily on time from slaughter to sale and refrigeration consistency.

Processing date proves more relevant than sell-by date for histamine concerns. Meat processed Monday contains less histamine Friday than meat processed the previous week, even if both have the same sell-by date. Unfortunately, processing dates rarely appear on retail packaging. This requires developing butcher relationships discussed in section 10.9.

Ground meat accumulates histamine faster than whole cuts. The grinding process distributes bacteria throughout the product and creates enormous surface area for bacterial growth. Purchase ground meat only if it was ground same day or previous day maximum. Better yet, ask butchers to grind whole cuts immediately before purchase.

Color assessment provides limited histamine information. Bright red beef reflects fresh blood oxygenation, not necessarily low histamine. Gray or brown meat might be old or might be vacuum-sealed meat exposed to air (which turns from purple-red to gray-brown quickly). Color alone doesn't reliably indicate histamine levels.

Package integrity matters substantially. Damaged packaging allowing air entry creates opportunities for bacterial growth and histamine formation. Avoid packages with tears, punctures, or excessive liquid. Excessive liquid suggests cellular breakdown and potential bacterial activity.

Sell-by dates provide rough freshness guidance but don't account for pre-retail handling. Meat with today's sell-by date might have been processed 10 days ago with nine days of transport and display. The same sell-by date on meat processed three days ago represents fresher product. Without knowing processing dates, assume meat nearing sell-by dates has been sitting longer.

Frozen meat quality depends on freezing timing and storage conditions. Meat frozen immediately after processing maintains better quality and lower histamine than meat refrigerated for days before freezing. However, verifying freezing timing proves difficult for retail frozen meat. The safest approach purchases fresh meat processed recently and freezes it immediately at home.

10.3 Poultry Selection Criteria

Chicken and turkey accumulate histamine rapidly after slaughter, making fresh poultry selection particularly important (Bodmer et al., 1999). Look for the latest pack dates when available, purchasing chicken packed today or yesterday rather than chicken packed a week ago.

Air-chilled versus water-chilled processing affects histamine potential. Air-chilled poultry avoids water immersion that can introduce additional bacteria. Air-chilling also produces drier surface less conducive to bacterial growth during subsequent storage. When available, air-chilled chicken provides advantages for histamine management.

Organic and free-range claims relate to production methods rather than histamine risk. These birds aren't inherently lower histamine than conventional poultry. The primary histamine determinants remain time from processing and cold chain maintenance regardless of production method.

Bone-in versus boneless influences storage duration. Bone-in chicken parts tolerate slightly longer refrigerated storage than boneless breasts or thighs without quality degradation. However, for histamine purposes, both should be purchased and cooked or frozen within 24 hours regardless of bone presence.

Package dating on poultry includes pack date and sell-by date on many products. The pack date provides better freshness indicator. Poultry packed today with a sell-by date five days out is fresher than poultry packed last week with today's sell-by date.

Frozen poultry from reputable sources often provides better histamine safety than fresh poultry that sat refrigerated for days. Whole chickens or parts flash-frozen shortly after processing maintain freshness better than refrigerated fresh poultry transported across country for a week before retail sale.

10.4 Strategic Date Reading

Sell-by dates indicate when retailers should remove products from sale but don't directly indicate product safety or freshness (FDA, 2021). Meat with today's sell-by date might be perfectly fresh if recently processed or might be at the end of a two-week retail journey.

Use-by dates on some products provide manufacturer's quality estimate rather than safety cutoff. These dates often build in conservative margins. However, for histamine purposes, approaching use-by dates suggests the product has been in distribution channels long enough to accumulate histamine.

Pack dates when present offer the most useful information. These indicate when the product was actually packaged. Calculating days from pack date to current date reveals actual age. Meat packed yesterday has much lower histamine potential than meat packed 10 days ago regardless of similar sell-by dates.

Julian dating uses numbers 1-365 to indicate the day of year. A pack date of "025" means January 25. This dating system appears on some products. Learning to interpret Julian dates enables accurate freshness assessment.

Best if used by dates on shelf-stable products relate to quality rather than safety. For histamine management, these dates on canned or jarred products matter less than for fresh proteins since histamine in shelf-stable products formed during processing rather than post-purchase storage.

Freezer dating on frozen products indicates how long products have been in commercial frozen storage. Products frozen months ago might still be safe but have undergone quality degradation and potentially slow histamine formation even at frozen temperatures.

Strategic shopping emphasizes products with the most distant dates, indicating recent production. However, don't assume distant dates guarantee freshness if pack dates reveal old production with generous dating. Prioritize pack dates over sell-by dates when both are available.

10.5 Case Study: Frozen Versus Fresh Economics

Background

Leocadia, a 40-year-old accountant, committed to buying premium "fresh" proteins for histamine management. She purchased fresh fish at specialty markets, fresh organic chicken from high-end grocers, and fresh grass-fed beef from butchers. These purchases consumed significant grocery budget but seemed necessary for health.

Presentation

Despite premium protein purchases, Leocadia experienced inconsistent symptom control. Some weeks felt fine. Others brought frequent headaches and digestive issues. She couldn't correlate symptoms to specific foods since she'd been eating the same "fresh" premium proteins throughout.

Financial stress accompanied the inconsistent results. Her protein costs had doubled compared to pre-diagnosis shopping. She felt trapped between health needs and budget constraints. The premium prices created resentment that this condition forced such expensive choices.

Analysis

Investigation revealed that Leocadia's premium "fresh" proteins weren't necessarily fresher than conventional alternatives. Her specialty fish market displayed previously frozen fish thawed for retail sale, often sitting thawed 3-4 days before purchase. Her premium chicken came from a distributor 2,000 miles away, spending over a week in refrigerated transport and storage before reaching the store.

The expensive grass-fed beef from boutique butchers had been dry-aged for flavor development, a process intentionally allowing controlled bacterial activity that creates histamine. She paid premium prices for artisanal aging that increased histamine content.

Meanwhile, she avoided frozen proteins assuming fresh superior. The frozen wild-caught salmon at conventional grocery stores had been flash-frozen hours after catch. The frozen chicken had been processed and frozen within 24 hours. These frozen products contained less histamine than her premium "fresh" purchases that had spent days or weeks in refrigerated distribution.

Research confirms that properly frozen seafood maintains lower histamine levels than fresh seafood after 24-48 hours post-catch (Visciano et al., 2012). The freezing halts bacterial activity while refrigerated "fresh" fish continues accumulating histamine throughout distribution.

Intervention

Leocadia modified her shopping strategy based on understanding from sections 10.1 through 10.4. She began purchasing flash-frozen wild-caught salmon and other fish in vacuum-sealed packages rather than thawed "fresh" fish. She bought conventional frozen chicken that had been processed and frozen quickly rather than premium fresh chicken from distant sources.

For beef, she purchased fresh conventional beef from butchers who could verify processing dates, choosing meat processed within the past 2-3 days. She avoided aged beef despite its premium price and gourmet status, recognizing the aging process created histamine.

She developed relationships with butchers as discussed in section 10.9, asking about processing dates and grinding fresh meat to order. This personal service cost less than pre-packaged premium products while providing superior freshness.

Outcome

Leocadia's protein costs decreased 30-40% while symptom control improved substantially. The shift to properly sourced frozen fish and fresh conventional meats provided more consistent quality than premium products with misleading "fresh" marketing.

Her budget relief reduced the resentment she'd been feeling toward dietary restrictions. The condition didn't require expensive specialty products. It required understanding what actually indicated freshness versus what marketing implied.

Six months later, she maintained good symptom control spending less on proteins than before diagnosis. She'd learned that price and labels don't guarantee appropriate quality for histamine management. Time from processing and proper freezing matter more than organic status or premium branding.

Teaching Points

- Premium "fresh" proteins from specialty markets often contain more histamine than properly frozen conventional alternatives due to extended distribution times and thawing practices that create bacterial growth opportunities
- Flash-frozen fish processed immediately after catch and frozen conventional poultry provide superior histamine safety compared to expensive fresh options that spent days or weeks in refrigerated distribution channels
- Understanding the relationship between processing time, cold chain maintenance, and histamine formation enables strategic shopping that achieves better results at lower cost than relying on premium marketing claims

10.6 Farmers Market Advantages

Local sourcing through farmers' markets offers potential histamine benefits from shorter distribution chains (Maintz & Novak, 2007). Meat processed yesterday at a local farm contains less histamine than meat processed last week 1,000 miles away.

Direct farmer relationships enable asking specific questions about processing timing. When was the chicken processed? How was it stored? How long until it reached the market? Farmers can answer these questions while retail clerks typically cannot.

Same-day harvest produce provides maximum freshness. Vegetables picked that morning and sold at afternoon markets maintain optimal nutrient content and minimal degradation. This matters more for produce quality generally than histamine specifically, since vegetables contain minimal protein and histidine.

Limitations and considerations include unreliable refrigeration at some markets. Meat sitting in poorly iced coolers for hours at summer markets may accumulate histamine despite short time from processing. Evaluate vendor cold chain maintenance before purchasing proteins from markets.

Frozen options from farmers often provide excellent quality. Small-scale farmers frequently process and freeze same day, maintaining freshness better than large-scale operations with multi-day processing cycles. Frozen pastured chicken from a local farm processing weekly frequently contains less histamine than "fresh" conventional chicken from industrial processing.

Seasonal availability means farmers' markets can't provide all proteins year-round in most regions. Use markets for seasonal produce and opportunistic protein purchases when available, supplementing with strategic retail shopping for consistent protein access.

Price variability at farmers' markets ranges from premium to competitive with retail. Small-scale pastured meats often cost more than conventional supermarket options but may cost less than specialty butchers. Produce prices vary by season and region. Don't assume farmers' markets automatically mean higher costs.

10.7 Online Protein Sources

Mail-order seafood from companies specializing in flash-frozen delivery provides access to quality fish regardless of local market options. Companies flash-freezing fish immediately after catch and shipping frozen directly to consumers eliminate the problematic thaw-for-display practice common at retail.

Frozen meat delivery services offer various quality levels. Some ship conventionally raised frozen meats. Others specialize in pastured, organic, or specialty meats frozen shortly after processing. Evaluate companies based on processing and freezing timing rather than production method alone.

Subscription boxes provide convenience but require compatible timing. If boxes arrive monthly but you can only use frozen proteins within specific timeframes from section 9.8, ensure box size matches consumption rate. Avoid accumulating frozen proteins beyond safe storage periods.

Shipping considerations include maintaining frozen temperatures during transport. Reputable companies ship with adequate dry ice or gel packs. Summer shipping proves more challenging. Some companies pause shipping during hot months to maintain quality.

Cost analysis must include shipping charges. Flash-frozen salmon at $25 per pound plus $30 shipping for four pounds totals $32.50 per pound effective cost. Compare total cost including shipping to local options before assuming online sources provide savings.

Quality verification through reviews and company reputation research helps identify reliable sources. Look for companies specifying flash-freezing practices, transparent about sourcing, providing processing information, and maintaining good customer feedback regarding delivery condition.

Strategic use of online sources fills gaps in local availability rather than replacing all shopping. Order specialty fish unavailable locally. Purchase high-quality frozen chicken in bulk for freezer storage. Maintain retail shopping for items readily available fresh locally.

10.8 Case Study: Bulk Buying Success

Background

Quirin, a 36-year-old paramedic working irregular shifts, struggled with inconsistent meal preparation. His unpredictable schedule made regular grocery shopping difficult. He often purchased convenience foods or ate out due to time constraints, undermining histamine management.

Presentation

Quirin needed a system accommodating his erratic schedule while maintaining dietary compliance. Fresh protein shopping 2-3 times weekly as recommended proved impossible with rotating shifts and frequent overtime. By the time he had a day off for shopping, his previous purchases exceeded freshness guidelines.

He'd tried weekly bulk shopping but found proteins sat refrigerated too long before use. He'd tried keeping minimal food at home and eating out more, but restaurant eating triggered symptoms frequently. Neither approach worked well.

Analysis

Quirin's situation required bulk buying with immediate processing as discussed in section 10.10. His schedule incompatibility with frequent fresh shopping meant he needed strategies maintaining freshness despite bulk purchasing. The solution involved treating shopping days as combination shopping and meal prep events rather than shopping alone.

Traditional bulk buying for weekly use conflicts with histamine management when products sit refrigerated for days before cooking. However, bulk buying for immediate processing and freezing creates efficiency while maintaining freshness standards.

Intervention

Quirin restructured his shopping approach. On his monthly day off, he visited a warehouse store purchasing larger quantities of proteins at lower per-pound costs. He bought five pounds of chicken breasts, three pounds of ground beef, two pounds of salmon fillets, and several pounds of vegetables.

Rather than storing these purchases for gradual use, he immediately processed everything. He divided chicken into individual portions, seasoned some simply, and froze all portions in vacuum-sealed bags within 30 minutes of arriving home. He cooked the ground beef in two batches, seasoning portions differently for variety, then immediately froze cooked portions after quick cooling.

The salmon he portioned into individual servings and froze raw in vacuum-sealed packages for later cooking from frozen. Vegetables got blanched briefly, cooled, portioned, and frozen for convenient side dishes.

This processing took 2-3 hours but created 2-3 weeks of ready-to-reheat meals. He labeled everything with freezing dates and use-by dates based on guidelines from section 9.8. Cooked meals got two-week use-by dates. Raw proteins got four-month dates.

Outcome

Quirin's new system accommodated his schedule while maintaining histamine safety. The bulk purchase saved money. The immediate processing maintained freshness. The vacuum sealing prevented freezer burn. The labeling enabled first-in-first-out rotation.

His monthly shopping and processing days became routine. He'd set aside one day off per month for this combined shopping and meal prep. The time investment (3-4 hours total including shopping and processing) produced 2-3 weeks of compliant meals.

Between monthly shopping trips, he occasionally purchased fresh vegetables or additional proteins if schedule permitted. But the bulk-processed frozen meals provided reliable backup preventing restaurant meals or long-stored proteins when work got hectic.

Symptom control improved substantially. The consistent use of properly frozen proteins within appropriate timeframes eliminated the variable histamine loads he'd experienced with either aging refrigerated proteins or restaurant eating.

Teaching Points

- Bulk buying incompatible schedules with frequent fresh shopping becomes viable for histamine management when combined with immediate processing and freezing rather than traditional refrigerated storage for gradual use throughout the week
- The time investment in processing bulk purchases immediately upon arrival creates efficiency gains that outweigh the processing time by eliminating multiple shopping trips and providing ready-to-use portions for several weeks
- Vacuum sealing bulk-processed portions and systematic labeling with appropriate use-by dates based on cooked versus raw status enables managing different storage timeframes while maintaining rotation and preventing waste

10.9 Butcher and Fishmonger Relationships

Personal relationships with meat and fish professionals provide information and services unavailable through self-service retail (FDA, 2021). These relationships develop over time through regular patronage and respectful communication.

Questions to ask butchers include processing dates for meats, grinding meat fresh to order, cutting specific portions, sourcing information, and special ordering items. Most butchers appreciate customers interested in quality and freshness. They can set aside freshly processed items for regular customers or call when specific items arrive.

Custom grinding enables using freshly ground meat rather than pre-ground products that may have been ground days earlier. Ask butchers to grind specific cuts while you wait. This service often costs no extra beyond the base meat price while providing superior freshness.

Special orders for specific cuts, quantities, or quality levels become possible with established relationships. Need specific portion sizes? Want a particular grass-fed supplier? A friendly butcher can accommodate these requests, often ordering exactly what you need for next week's pickup.

Timing coordination allows picking up freshly processed items. Some butchers process specific items certain days. Knowing the schedule enables purchasing chicken on processing day rather than three days later after refrigerated storage.

Fishmonger relationships provide similar benefits. Learn when fresh (actually fresh, not thawed) fish arrives. Ask about boat freezing versus retail freezing. Request specific portions. Get recommendations for truly fresh options versus previously frozen displayed items.

Building rapport happens through regular visits, respectful questions, and acknowledging expertise. Thank butchers and fishmongers when they provide special service. Continued patronage and word-of-mouth recommendations show appreciation. These relationships make histamine management dramatically easier through access to fresher products and relevant information.

10.10 Concluding Thoughts

This chapter explained how to source proteins and produce that provide optimal starting points for the cooking and storage strategies from Chapters 8.0 and 9.0. Flash-frozen fish often exceeds "fresh" fish quality due to immediate post-catch freezing versus days of refrigerated storage before retail sale. Strategic date reading, prioritizing pack dates over sell-by dates, reveals actual product age.

Fresh meat and poultry selection emphasizes processing timing and cold chain maintenance over production methods like organic or pasture-raised status. Ground meat requires particular attention due to rapid histamine accumulation from extensive bacterial surface area created by grinding.

Farmers' markets offer shortened distribution chains and direct farmer relationships enabling questions about processing timing. However, market refrigeration quality varies and seasonal limitations exist. Online protein sources fill gaps in local availability, particularly for specialty flash-frozen seafood.

Bulk buying becomes viable when combined with immediate processing and freezing rather than gradual refrigerated use over weeks. This approach accommodates irregular schedules while maintaining freshness through proper handling immediately after purchase.

Developing relationships with butchers and fishmongers provides access to fresher products, processing information, custom services, and special ordering unavailable through self-service retail. These relationships make consistent sourcing of quality proteins substantially easier.

The sourcing, cooking, and storage strategies from Chapters 8.0, 9.0, and 10.0 form an integrated system. Quality sourcing provides good raw materials. Proper cooking prevents histamine formation. Effective storage maintains freshness until consumption. Together, these practices enable practical long-term histamine management.

Part IV: Comprehensive Meal Plans

Chapter 11.0: Four Week Elimination Meal Plans

Melisande stood in her kitchen Sunday evening, staring at the ingredients she'd purchased for her first week of elimination. Fresh chicken breasts, sweet potatoes, zucchini, rice, olive oil, salt. Simple foods. Safe foods according to Chapter 5.0. Yet she felt paralyzed. How did these ingredients become actual meals? She'd been eating convenience foods, takeout, and refrigerated leftovers for years. The idea of cooking fresh meals daily for four weeks seemed impossible. Her limited cooking skills, busy work schedule, and lack of meal planning experience collided with the structured elimination protocol requirements. She knew what to avoid. She understood the principles from Chapters 4.0 and 5.0. But translating principles into practical daily eating remained a mystery. This gap between understanding guidelines and executing them appears repeatedly as people begin elimination protocols (Maintz & Novak, 2007). Theory doesn't automatically convert to practice. Meal planning skills, cooking techniques, and strategic preparation systems make the difference between successful completion and early abandonment.

This chapter provides detailed four-week elimination phase meal plans with specific breakfast, lunch, dinner, and snack options for each week. You will learn simple safe foundation meals for Week 1, strategies for expanding variety while staying compliant in Week 2, efficient meal prep systems for Week 3, and advanced flavor techniques for Week 4. Each week includes complete shopping lists and preparation strategies that build progressively from basic to sophisticated approaches.

11.1 Week One Foundation Principles

Week 1 establishes the simplest possible compliant eating pattern (Schnedl et al., 2019). The goal is consistency and safety, not variety or excitement. People overwhelm themselves attempting elaborate low-histamine recipes immediately. This creates unnecessary complexity during an already challenging adjustment period.

Daily meal structure follows a repetitive template. Breakfast remains identical all seven days. Lunch alternates between two simple options. Dinner rotates among three basic preparations. This repetition reduces decision fatigue and shopping complexity while ensuring complete compliance.

Breakfast template uses the same components daily. Rice porridge cooked fresh each morning with coconut milk, topped with fresh blueberries and a drizzle of maple syrup provides filling, safe nutrition. Alternative: scrambled eggs (if eggs pass individual tolerance testing from Chapter 4.0) with rice cakes and fresh cucumber. The key is identifying one or two breakfast options that work and repeating them throughout Week 1.

Lunch options alternate between Option A and Option B throughout the week. Option A: grilled chicken breast (4-6 oz) seasoned with salt, served with steamed broccoli and white rice. Option B: fresh turkey breast slices wrapped in butter lettuce with sliced cucumber and carrot sticks, accompanied by rice cakes. Both options use proteins cooked same-day or frozen immediately after cooking as discussed in Chapter 9.0.

Dinner rotation includes three preparations used repeatedly. Dinner 1: pan-seared fresh cod (or other white fish) with roasted sweet potato and sautéed zucchini. Dinner 2: grilled chicken thighs with mashed cauliflower and green beans. Dinner 3: ground turkey cooked plain, served over rice with steamed carrots. These simple preparations using fresh proteins and vegetables require minimal cooking skill while maintaining histamine safety.

Snack options include fresh apple slices, rice cakes with sunflower seed butter (if tolerated), fresh carrot and cucumber sticks, or fresh blueberries. Snacks use only fresh, unprocessed items requiring no preparation beyond washing and cutting.

11.2 Week One Shopping Strategy

Protein purchases for Week 1 emphasize fresh chicken breasts (2 lbs), chicken thighs (1.5 lbs), ground turkey (1 lb), turkey breast slices (0.5 lb from deli counter sliced fresh that day), and fresh white fish fillets (1 lb cod or similar). Following sourcing principles from Chapter 10.0, purchase these proteins on day of intended cooking or freeze immediately. For Week 1, most people benefit from shopping twice (Sunday and Wednesday) to maintain maximum freshness.

Produce requirements include substantial quantities given fresh-only consumption. Sweet potatoes (6 medium), zucchini (4), broccoli (2 large heads), cauliflower (1 large head), green beans (1 lb), carrots (2 lbs), cucumbers (4), butter lettuce (2 heads), apples (6), blueberries (2 pints). The quantities support all meals and snacks for seven days. Excess produce freezes well if purchased in larger economical packages.

Pantry staples include white rice (2 lbs), rice cakes (1 package plain), coconut milk (3 cans full-fat), maple syrup (small bottle), olive oil (if not already stocked), coconut oil (for cooking variety), salt (sea salt or kosher), and sunflower seed butter (if tolerated and not already stocked). These items provide multiple weeks' usage except coconut milk which gets consumed through daily breakfast.

Shopping list organization groups items by store section for efficient purchasing. Produce section: sweet potatoes, zucchini, broccoli, cauliflower, green beans, carrots, cucumbers, butter lettuce, apples, blueberries. Meat/fish counter: chicken breasts, chicken thighs, ground turkey, fresh turkey breast slices, fresh cod fillets. Pantry aisles: white rice, rice cakes, canned coconut milk, maple syrup, cooking oils, salt, sunflower seed butter.

Cost management through Week 1 focuses on sales and bulk purchasing where freezing allows. Chicken typically costs less when purchased in larger family packs then frozen in meal-size portions. Fresh produce often costs less at farmers markets as discussed in Chapter 10.0. The simplified Week 1 menu actually reduces costs compared to varied meal plans requiring numerous ingredients.

11.3 Week One Preparation Protocol

Sunday preparation sets up the week for success (Schnedl et al., 2019). After grocery shopping, immediately process proteins. Portion chicken breasts into individual 6 oz servings. Season chicken thighs with salt. Form ground turkey into four patties. These prepared proteins get cooked fresh daily rather than batch cooking and refrigerating (which creates histamine as explained in Chapter 9.0).

Daily cooking routine requires 30-45 minutes total across three cooking sessions. Morning (15 minutes): cook rice porridge or scramble eggs, prepare fresh fruit. Midday (15 minutes): grill or pan-cook chicken breast, steam broccoli, heat pre-cooked rice or cook fresh rice. Evening (15-20 minutes): cook dinner protein, prepare vegetables using simple methods (steam, roast, or sauté).

Advance rice preparation allows cooking larger batches every 2-3 days since rice tolerates brief refrigeration better than proteins. Cook 4-6 cups rice. Immediately after cooking and brief cooling (30 minutes maximum at room temperature), portion into individual containers and freeze following protocols from Chapter 9.0. Thaw and reheat portions as needed. This reduces daily cooking time substantially.

Vegetable washing gets done twice weekly (Sunday and Wednesday after shopping trips) for efficiency. Wash all produce immediately upon arriving home. Store washed vegetables properly in refrigerator crisper. This advance preparation means grab-and-go access to vegetables for snacks and sides throughout the week.

Equipment needs remain minimal for Week 1. One or two medium pots for rice and vegetables. One large skillet for proteins. One baking sheet for roasting. Cutting board and knife. Storage containers for portioning. Most kitchens already contain these basics. The simple preparation methods require no specialty equipment.

11.4 Case Study: Week One Overwhelm

Background

Osric, a 44-year-old software developer, started elimination with good intentions but struggled immediately. He'd read all the guidelines from Chapter 5.0. He understood the science from Chapters 3.0 and 4.0. He'd purchased appropriate foods. But Monday morning, staring at raw chicken and vegetables, he felt completely lost about how to actually prepare meals.

Presentation

Osric's first three days demonstrated common patterns when dietary knowledge doesn't translate to cooking execution. Monday breakfast: skipped due to confusion about rice porridge preparation. Monday lunch: plain rice cakes and an apple (inadequate nutrition). Monday dinner: successfully grilled chicken but burned vegetables through improper temperature control. Tuesday breakfast: attempted rice porridge but cooked it incorrectly, producing inedible results. Tuesday lunch: gave up and ate at a restaurant (unknown ingredients and preparations). Tuesday dinner: overcooked fish that became rubbery and unpalatable.

By Wednesday, Osric felt defeated. He'd wasted food through cooking failures. He'd skipped meals from frustration. He'd broken compliance through restaurant eating. The gap between understanding what to eat and successfully preparing it proved larger than anticipated. His limited cooking experience (primarily using microwaves and ordering takeout) hadn't prepared him for fresh daily cooking requirements.

Analysis

Osric's struggle illustrates the importance of graduated skill development discussed in this chapter. Week 1's deliberately simple meals assume basic cooking competency that Osric lacked. However, the repetitive template from section 11.1 actually supports learning. Cooking the same rice porridge seven mornings allows mastering that specific preparation. Grilling chicken breast repeatedly builds consistent technique.

The solution wasn't more complex recipes. Osric needed explicit step-by-step instructions for the simple preparations Week 1 requires. Research shows that dietary adherence correlates more strongly with practical food preparation skills than with nutritional knowledge alone (Hartmann et al., 2013). Understanding low-histamine principles doesn't automatically confer cooking ability.

Intervention

Osric's dietitian provided detailed cooking instructions for each Week 1 meal. Rice porridge: specific water-to-rice ratio (3:1), exact cooking time (20 minutes), temperature setting (medium-low heat), stirring frequency (every 5 minutes). Grilled chicken: pan temperature (medium-high), cooking duration (5-7 minutes per side for 6 oz breast), doneness indicators (internal temperature 165°F, juices run clear). Steamed vegetables: water depth (1 inch), steaming time (5-8 minutes for broccoli, 4-6 minutes for green beans).

She recommended cooking just three dinners for the first week rather than seven. Cook Monday, eat Monday and Tuesday (reheating Tuesday's portion from refrigerator within 24 hours per section 9.3). Cook Wednesday fresh, eat Wednesday and Thursday. Cook Friday fresh, eat Friday and Saturday. This reduced cooking frequency while maintaining reasonable histamine safety.

The dietitian also suggested watching basic cooking technique videos online for skills like properly heating pans, knowing when oil is ready, testing meat doneness, and steaming vegetables. These foundational techniques applied across all Week 1 preparations.

Outcome

With explicit instructions and reduced frequency demands, Osric successfully completed Week 1. His rice porridge improved each morning as technique developed. His chicken breast grilling became consistent by day four. His vegetable preparations expanded from just steaming to include roasting and sautéing as confidence grew.

The repetitive menu that initially seemed boring actually enabled skill mastery. By week's end, he could prepare all Week 1 meals competently without consulting recipes. This foundation supported progressing to Week 2's expanded variety. His symptom tracking showed good compliance and initial symptom improvement appeared despite the rocky first three days.

Teaching Points

- Successful elimination requires not just knowing which foods to eat but possessing practical skills to prepare them consistently, with cooking technique instruction often needed alongside dietary guidance for individuals with limited culinary experience
- Week 1's repetitive simplicity serves dual purposes of ensuring compliance through minimal decision making and enabling cooking skill development through repeated practice of the same preparations
- Reducing initial cooking frequency through strategic same-day reheating within 24-hour windows provides a bridge between no-cooking-skills baseline and eventual daily fresh meal preparation capacity

11.5 Week Two Variety Expansion

Week 2 introduces carefully controlled variety while maintaining compliance (Maintz & Novak, 2007). The menu expands from Week 1's nine meals (one breakfast, two lunches, three dinners repeated) to 15 meals (two breakfasts, three lunches, four dinners, each used 1-2 times weekly). This expansion provides psychological relief from Week 1's monotony without overwhelming capacity.

New proteins added in Week 2 include fresh lamb chops, fresh pork chops, and a different fish variety (halibut or mahi-mahi if fresh cod was used in Week 1). These additions require confirming freshness and proper sourcing per Chapter 10.0 but use similar cooking methods already mastered in Week 1, reducing technique learning curve.

Expanded vegetables incorporate asparagus, Brussels sprouts, butternut squash, and bok choy. These add flavor variety and nutritional diversity. All tolerate the simple cooking methods (roasting, steaming, sautéing) learned in Week 1. Brussels sprouts roasted with olive oil and salt taste dramatically different from steamed broccoli despite using a cooking method already mastered.

Second breakfast option introduces variety to morning meals. Option A remains the Week 1 rice porridge or scrambled eggs. Option B adds a savory breakfast bowl with scrambled eggs (if tolerated), sautéed bok choy, and rice, seasoned with salt and fresh herbs like cilantro. This Asian-inspired breakfast demonstrates that low-histamine eating includes diverse flavor profiles.

Lunch variety expands to three rotating options instead of two. The Week 1 options continue. Added Option C features grilled lamb chop with roasted butternut squash and steamed asparagus. This provides a change from poultry-focused lunches while using already-practiced cooking techniques.

Dinner expansion adds Dinner 4 (pork chop with mashed sweet potato and roasted Brussels sprouts) to the Week 1 dinner rotation. Having four dinner options provides near-daily variety when repeating some meals across the week. The expanded options reduce compliance fatigue from excessive repetition.

11.6 Week Two Batch Cooking

Batch cooking becomes viable in Week 2 after Week 1 established individual meal preparation competency (Hartmann et al., 2013). The key is immediate freezing rather than refrigerated storage as detailed in Chapter 8.0.

Sunday batch session for Week 2 might include grilling four chicken breasts simultaneously (eating one fresh, freezing three), roasting a full sheet pan of Brussels sprouts and butternut squash (portioning and freezing immediately), and cooking a large batch of rice (portioning and freezing). This 60-90 minute session provides components for multiple meals.

Protein batch cooking follows strict protocols. Cook larger quantities (4-6 chicken breasts instead of one). Immediately after cooking and 20-30 minute cooling period, portion individual servings. Freeze each portion in appropriate container per section 9.7. Label with contents, cooking date, and use-by date (2-3 weeks maximum per section 9.8).

Vegetable batch roasting works well for sturdy vegetables. Roast full sheet pans of Brussels sprouts, butternut squash, carrots, or asparagus. After brief cooling, portion into individual containers. Freeze immediately. These portions reheat well in microwave (2-3 minutes) or oven (10 minutes at 350°F), providing convenient sides without daily chopping and cooking.

Avoiding batch cooking pitfalls requires discipline about immediate freezing versus "I'll freeze it tomorrow" thinking that leads to 24+ hour refrigeration before freezing. Research shows that delaying freezing even 12 hours after cooking increases histamine content compared to immediate freezing (Bodmer et al., 1999). Set a timer for 30 minutes after removing food from heat. When timer sounds, food should be cooled sufficiently and ready for portioning and freezing.

Strategic batch items for Week 2 include proteins that reheat well (chicken breast, pork chops, turkey patties), sturdy vegetables (Brussels sprouts, butternut squash, carrots), and starches (rice, mashed sweet potato). Delicate items like fish fillets or fresh greens don't batch cook effectively and should remain same-day preparations.

11.7 Week Three Time Efficiency

Week 3 focuses on time-saving systems rather than menu expansion (Schnedl et al., 2019). The variety from Week 2 continues. The innovation is reducing active cooking time through strategic combinations and make-ahead components.

Breakfast make-ahead introduces overnight rice porridge. Before bed, combine rice, coconut milk, and water in slow cooker (if avoiding slow cookers per Chapter 8.0, use Instant Pot delay start function to begin cooking 20 minutes before waking). Wake to ready breakfast requiring only fresh fruit topping. This eliminates morning cooking time entirely for porridge days.

For egg breakfast days, pre-chop vegetables the evening before (bok choy, zucchini, or other additions to scrambled eggs). Store chopped vegetables in refrigerator overnight. Morning cooking becomes just scrambling eggs and quickly sautéing the pre-cut vegetables. Total morning time: 10 minutes instead of 20.

Lunch assembly approach emphasizes components prepared ahead and assembled fresh. Sunday prep: grill 4-5 chicken breasts, freeze immediately. Make large batch rice, freeze in portions. Wash and cut vegetables (cucumbers, carrots, bell peppers) for the week. Daily lunch assembly: thaw frozen chicken breast in refrigerator overnight (consume within 24 hours of thawing per section 8.8), reheat frozen rice portion, grab pre-cut fresh vegetables. Assembly time: 5 minutes. Eating fresh-cooked lunch without daily cooking.

Dinner sheet pan meals allow cooking entire meal simultaneously on one pan. Example: place fresh fish fillet, halved small sweet potatoes, and trimmed asparagus on sheet pan. Drizzle with olive oil, season with salt. Roast at 425°F for 20-25 minutes. Entire dinner cooks while you do other tasks. Active cooking time: 5 minutes prep, 2 minutes cleanup. Total elapsed time: 30 minutes largely unattended.

Time tracking reality helps manage expectations. Week 1 requires approximately 45-60 minutes daily active cooking time. Week 2 with batch cooking reduces this to 30-45 minutes daily average (some days 90 minutes, other days 15 minutes). Week 3 optimizations reduce daily average to 20-30 minutes active time, with Sunday or Wednesday longer prep sessions (60-90 minutes) enabling daily quick assembly.

11.8 Case Study: Working Parent Success

Background

Jessamine, a 37-year-old attorney and mother of two elementary-age children, believed elimination diet implementation was impossible given her schedule. She worked 50-60 hours weekly. She managed children's school, activities, and homework. Her spouse worked equally demanding hours. They relied heavily on takeout and convenience foods. The idea of fresh daily cooking seemed laughable.

Presentation

Jessamine's Week 1 attempt failed predictably. She couldn't find 45 minutes daily for cooking while managing work deadlines and children's needs. She skipped breakfast most days. She bought non-compliant lunch from the office cafeteria. She ordered takeout for family dinners. By Thursday, she'd abandoned the attempt entirely, concluding elimination wasn't viable for working parents.

Her symptoms continued worsening. Her doctor emphasized the importance of trying elimination despite schedule challenges. Jessamine felt trapped between health needs and practical reality. Research shows that time constraints represent the most common barrier to dietary adherence among working adults (Hartmann et al., 2013). Knowledge and motivation matter little if time doesn't exist for execution.

Analysis

Jessamine's failure came from attempting Week 1 without modifying for her circumstances. The standard Week 1 plan assumes 45-60 minutes daily available for cooking. Jessamine rarely had 30 consecutive minutes during weekdays. However, she did have weekend time and could delegate some tasks.

The solution required restructuring around Week 3 time efficiency principles from section 11.7 while still maintaining Week 1's food simplicity. This hybrid approach provided necessary compliance without requiring daily time she didn't have.

Intervention

Jessamine's dietitian designed a modified plan emphasizing weekend preparation and weekday assembly. Saturday morning (2 hours): grill 10 chicken breasts, freeze 8 immediately after cooling (eat one Saturday lunch, one Sunday lunch). Cook large batch rice, portion and freeze. Roast three sheet pans vegetables (Brussels sprouts, butternut squash, carrots), portion and freeze. Wash and cut fresh vegetables for the week.

Sunday afternoon (1 hour): cook four turkey burger patties, freeze three after cooling. Bake sweet potatoes, freeze portions. Prepare any additional proteins needed for the week.

Weekday breakfasts became overnight rice porridge (no morning time) or quick smoothie with coconut milk, blueberries, and small portion sunflower seed butter (3 minutes). Weekday lunches assembled from frozen components: reheat frozen chicken breast, reheat frozen rice, add fresh cucumber and carrots. Total time: 5 minutes. Weekday dinners either sheet pan meals (5 minutes active time) or reheated frozen batch-cooked proteins and vegetables (10 minutes total).

Her spouse managed children's dinners (different foods meeting their needs) while Jessamine reheated her elimination-compliant meal. This division of labor prevented her dietary needs from dominating family dinner preparation.

Outcome

The modified approach worked. Jessamine invested 3 hours total on weekends. This weekend effort enabled 10-15 minutes daily weekday time for meal assembly and quick cooking. The system became sustainable once established as routine.

Her symptoms improved substantially after three weeks of consistent compliance. The time investment proved worthwhile given results. She continued the pattern through entire elimination phase and adapted it for maintenance per Chapter 12.0.

By elimination's end, the children had become curious about her meals. She occasionally made extra portions of sheet pan dinners to introduce them to new vegetables. The family's overall eating patterns shifted somewhat toward fresher, simpler preparations beyond just her medical necessity.

Teaching Points

- Time-constrained schedules require front-loading meal preparation into available blocks (weekends) rather than attempting daily cooking when daily time doesn't exist, with weekday eating becoming simple assembly rather than active cooking
- Successful elimination for busy adults often requires decoupling personal dietary needs from family meal preparation through division of labor and separate but parallel meal systems rather than requiring entire family diet modification
- The relationship between weekend preparation time and weekday convenience is approximately 2-3 hours weekend investment enabling 10-15 minutes daily weekday time, a worthwhile trade-off when daily availability is severely limited

11.9 Week Four Advanced Techniques

Week 4 introduces complexity in flavor rather than ingredients (Maintz & Novak, 2007). The approved food list remains unchanged from Weeks 2-3. The advancement involves using fresh herbs, strategic seasoning combinations, cooking technique variations, and presentation improvements to create meals that feel special rather than restrictive.

Fresh herb usage dramatically improves flavor without histamine concerns. Fresh cilantro, parsley, basil, rosemary, and thyme all work for most individuals (test individual tolerance as these contain salicylates that some people react to). Chopped fresh herbs added to cooked rice, sprinkled over grilled proteins, or stirred into mashed sweet potatoes transform plain foods into flavorful dishes.

Seasoning combinations create complexity. Salt alone flavors adequately. Salt plus fresh rosemary elevates roasted vegetables. Salt plus fresh garlic (sautéed in oil, not raw or pre-minced which may contain preservatives) plus fresh parsley creates Italian-style flavoring for chicken or fish. Experimentation with compatible seasonings from section 8.10 prevents flavor boredom.

Cooking technique variations introduce new textures. Proteins previously only grilled can be pan-seared for crispy exterior. Vegetables previously only steamed can be roasted at high heat for caramelization. Rice previously boiled plain can be cooked in homemade vegetable broth (made fresh from compliant vegetables, not commercial broth containing yeast extract or other additives).

Presentation improvements affect eating experience psychologically. Arranging food attractively on plate rather than dumping everything together makes meals feel more appealing. Using smaller plates makes portions look larger. Adding fresh herb garnish makes simple preparations look restaurant-quality. These psychological factors support sustained adherence through making restriction feel less punitive.

Celebration meal example for Week 4 might include pan-seared fresh halibut with herb oil (olive oil heated gently with fresh rosemary and thyme), roasted fingerling potatoes with fresh parsley, and grilled asparagus with fresh garlic. This meal uses only approved ingredients from earlier weeks but combines them in ways that feel special and satisfying rather than medicinal and restrictive.

11.10 Putting Knowledge into Practice

This chapter provided detailed four-week elimination phase meal plans progressing from simple foundations to advanced techniques. Week 1 establishes basic compliance through highly repetitive simple meals, allowing cooking skill development and adjustment to fresh daily food preparation. Week 2 expands variety through additional proteins and vegetables while introducing batch cooking with immediate freezing protocols.

Week 3 focuses on time efficiency through make-ahead components, sheet pan meals, and assembly-based lunches that maintain freshness while reducing active daily cooking time. Week 4 introduces advanced flavor techniques through fresh herbs, seasoning combinations, and presentation improvements that make restriction feel less restrictive.

The shopping lists and preparation strategies progress logically from basic to sophisticated, meeting different individuals where they are in cooking skill and time availability. Case studies demonstrated common challenges (cooking skill gaps, time constraints) and practical solutions addressing real-world barriers to elimination protocol completion.

The successful four-week elimination creates the foundation for systematic reintroduction covered in Chapter 6.0 and long-term maintenance addressed in Chapter 12.0. The cooking skills, meal planning habits, and preparation systems developed during elimination transfer directly to sustained histamine management beyond the acute elimination phase.

Chapter 12.0: Maintenance Phase Meal Plans

Eudora sat at her kitchen table reviewing her reintroduction testing results from the past three months. Her spreadsheet showed clear patterns. Tier 1 foods (chicken, rice, most vegetables, certain fruits) caused no symptoms ever. Tier 2 foods (avocado once weekly, tomatoes twice weekly in small amounts, fresh mozzarella occasionally) worked within documented limits. Tier 3 foods (aged cheeses, fermented items, citrus fruits) consistently triggered reactions and remained off-limits. She had the data. She understood her tolerances. But translating this personalized information into actual sustainable eating patterns felt overwhelming. Elimination had been straightforward despite being restrictive. A clear list of allowed foods simplified decisions. Maintenance proved paradoxically harder despite greater freedom. The partial reintroductions created complexity. How did she plan meals balancing tier 1 staples, strategic tier 2 additions, and complete tier 3 avoidance while accommodating family meals, social situations, seasonal availability, and time constraints? Research shows that many individuals complete elimination and reintroduction successfully but struggle with long-term maintenance meal planning, leading to either overly restrictive eating that sacrifices quality of life or chaotic patterns that trigger symptom return (Reese et al., 2018).

This chapter provides detailed maintenance phase meal plans incorporating tested reintroduced foods within safe parameters. You will learn how to create rotating two-week meal plans, balance variety with histamine safety, adapt plans seasonally, develop family-friendly options, prepare quick weekday meals, establish weekend batch cooking routines, and organize shopping lists supporting sustained compliance without unnecessary restriction.

12.1 Two Week Rotation Framework

The two-week rotation provides sufficient variety to prevent boredom while remaining simple enough to execute consistently (Schnedl et al., 2019). Fourteen different dinners, seven different lunches (each used twice), and three different breakfasts (rotating through the fortnight) create adequate diversity without overwhelming planning capacity.

Rotation benefits include preventing excessive consumption of any single tier 2 food through natural spacing, reducing meal planning fatigue through established patterns, simplifying shopping through predictable ingredient needs, and supporting consistent compliance through reduced decision-making demands. The rotation becomes automatic after 2-3 cycles, requiring minimal active planning effort.

Tier 1 foundation forms the base of every meal. Each dinner includes tier 1 protein, tier 1 starch, and tier 1 vegetables. Each lunch contains tier 1 components. Breakfast relies primarily on tier 1 foods. This ensures the 80-90% baseline discussed in Chapter 7.0 remains tier 1 focused even when incorporating tier 2 additions.

Strategic tier 2 incorporation follows documented individual tolerances from Chapter 6.0 reintroduction results. If someone tolerates avocado once weekly, the two-week rotation includes avocado exactly twice (Monday Week 1, Thursday Week 2) providing weekly spacing. If tomatoes work twice weekly in quarter-cup amounts, the rotation includes tomato-containing meals four times across two weeks (Sunday Week 1, Wednesday Week 1, Tuesday Week 2, Friday Week 2).

Tracking tier 2 frequency prevents accidental overuse. A simple spreadsheet or calendar noting each tier 2 food's appearance in the rotation ensures compliance with tested limits. Someone who reacts to avocado when consumed twice in one week but tolerates once weekly needs explicit tracking to prevent the problematic frequency.

Flexibility within structure allows swapping meals within categories while maintaining tier 2 limits. If Tuesday Week 1 plans chicken stir-fry but you're tired of chicken, swap with Thursday Week 1's turkey meal. The tier 2 foods remain properly spaced. The structure persists despite tactical adjustments.

12.2 Incorporating Passed Foods

Passed foods from reintroduction testing (Chapter 6.0) get incorporated based on their tier classification (Maintz & Novak, 2007). Tier 1 passed foods enter unlimited rotation. Tier 2 passed foods appear within tested frequency and portion limits. Tier 3 failed foods remain excluded.

Tier 1 additions might include eggs (if they passed testing), certain nuts (almonds, cashews if tolerated), additional vegetables (bell peppers, cabbage if they passed), additional fruits (strawberries, melons if tolerated), and additional proteins (beef, pork if they tested successfully). These foods can appear daily without concern since they demonstrated complete tolerance during testing.

Tier 2 parameters require precise definition based on testing results. Example documentation: "Avocado: passed at 1/4 fruit, maximum twice weekly, not combined with other tier 2 foods in same meal." This specificity prevents the common error of assuming "avocado is okay" and eating it daily in large amounts, which exceeds tested tolerance.

Meal planning with tier 2 treats these foods as special additions rather than staples. Design meals that work with or without the tier 2 component. Example: taco bowl with ground turkey, rice, lettuce, cucumber, cilantro functions perfectly. Adding 1/4 avocado (tier 2 per individual testing) enhances it but the meal succeeds regardless. This approach prevents tier 2 foods from becoming dependencies.

Documenting individual tolerances creates a reference preventing memory-based errors. Write down exact testing results. "Tomatoes: passed at 1/4 cup fresh diced, maximum three times weekly, symptoms appeared at 1/2 cup." This documentation informs meal planning months or years later when memory of specific testing details fades.

Updating tolerances over time recognizes that thresholds can change. Some people's tolerance improves after months of gut healing, allowing previously tier 2 foods to move to tier 1. Others find certain tolerances decrease with age or stress. Annual retesting of tier 2 foods using Chapter 6.0 protocols updates the maintenance plan appropriately.

12.3 Balancing Variety and Safety

Variety within constraints requires creativity rather than simply eating everything (Reese et al., 2018). The goal is maximum diversity among truly tolerated foods rather than maximum diversity regardless of consequences.

Protein rotation for someone who passed chicken, turkey, cod, halibut, lamb, and pork during testing provides six different proteins. Two-week rotation might use each protein 2-3 times in different preparations. Chicken appears as grilled breast Monday, ground in lettuce wraps Thursday, and thighs in sheet pan dinner following Tuesday. Same protein, different experiences.

Preparation variety transforms limited ingredients. Zucchini can be spiralized raw as "noodles," grilled in thick rounds, roasted in chunks, sautéed in half-moons, or blended into soup. Each preparation creates different eating experience from identical ingredient. This variety prevents boredom without requiring problematic foods.

Seasoning variations discussed in Chapter 8.0 expand apparent diversity. Chicken seasoned with fresh rosemary tastes completely different from chicken with fresh cilantro and garlic or chicken with fresh ginger. The protein remains identical but flavor profiles vary substantially.

Cultural cuisine exploration adapts various traditions to compliant ingredients. Asian-inspired meals use fresh ginger, garlic, cilantro, and coconut aminos (if tolerated). Mediterranean meals emphasize olive oil, fresh herbs, lemon (if citrus tolerated), and simple grilling. Mexican-inspired meals incorporate cilantro, fresh jalapeño (if tolerated), and lime (if tolerated). These cultural frameworks provide variety without requiring problematic ingredients.

Texture variation adds interest. Include crispy (roasted vegetables, pan-seared proteins), creamy (mashed sweet potato, coconut milk-based sauces), crunchy (fresh vegetables, rice cakes), and tender (steamed vegetables, slow-cooked meats in Instant Pot) textures across the week. Texture diversity enhances satisfaction even when ingredients remain limited.

Strategic monotony acceptance recognizes that some repetition is fine. Eating similar breakfasts daily doesn't bore most people. Lunch can repeat more than dinner. Identifying which meals tolerate repetition and which require variety allows focusing creativity where it matters most psychologically.

12.4 Seasonal Adaptations

Seasonal eating aligns meal plans with natural availability, improving freshness (and thus histamine safety per Chapter 10.0) while reducing costs (Schnedl et al., 2019).

Spring adaptation emphasizes asparagus, spring onions, fresh peas, artichokes (if tolerated), strawberries (if tolerated), and lamb (traditional spring protein). Meals become lighter after winter's heavier eating. Spring allergies for some individuals require tighter dietary management as discussed in Chapter 7.0, potentially reducing tier 2 frequency when environmental histamine load increases.

Sample spring dinner: grilled lamb chops with roasted asparagus and new potatoes, finished with fresh mint. This meal uses peak-season spring ingredients at maximum freshness. Alternative spring dinner: pan-seared fresh cod with sugar snap peas and wild rice, garnished with fresh parsley.

Summer adaptation utilizes abundant vegetables (zucchini, summer squash, cucumbers, bell peppers if tolerated), fresh herbs (basil, cilantro, parsley), melons (if tolerated), berries (blueberries, strawberries if tolerated), and grilled proteins taking advantage of outdoor cooking. Summer's heat requires extra attention to food temperature management per Chapter 9.0.

Sample summer dinner: grilled chicken breast with zucchini noodles (spiralized raw) dressed in fresh basil and olive oil, served with watermelon (if tolerated) or fresh berries. Alternative summer dinner: grilled halibut with grilled vegetable medley (zucchini, yellow squash, bell peppers) and fresh cucumber salad.

Fall adaptation incorporates winter squashes (butternut, acorn, spaghetti squash), Brussels sprouts, root vegetables (parsnips, turnips, carrots), apples, and heartier proteins. Fall represents prime batch cooking season as temperatures make extended oven use more pleasant.

Sample fall dinner: roasted pork loin with mashed butternut squash and roasted Brussels sprouts, served with fresh apple slices. Alternative fall dinner: Instant Pot beef roast with root vegetables (carrots, parsnips, potatoes) and fresh herbs.

Winter adaptation emphasizes stored vegetables (winter squashes, root vegetables, cabbage), frozen vegetables from summer abundance, and comfort preparations. Winter meals tend toward soups (made fresh and consumed immediately per histamine guidelines), roasts, and warming dishes.

Sample winter dinner: Instant Pot chicken soup with vegetables and rice (made and consumed fresh, not stored as leftovers). Alternative winter dinner: roasted turkey breast with mashed sweet potatoes and roasted carrots, garnished with fresh rosemary.

Seasonal shopping advantages include lower costs (in-season produce costs less), better quality (shorter transport times mean fresher food), better flavor (produce picked ripe rather than ripened during shipping), and better nutrition (nutrients degrade during storage, so shorter storage times preserve more). These advantages support both budget management and histamine safety.

12.5 Case Study: Seasonal Success

Background

Nephele, a 39-year-old nurse, completed elimination and reintroduction successfully. She developed a maintenance meal plan incorporating her tested tolerances. However, she'd created this plan in March, using spring vegetables and ingredients. By July, she found herself still trying to buy asparagus (expensive and poor quality) and ignoring abundant summer squash (not in her plan). Her rigid adherence to the established plan prevented adapting to seasonal changes.

Presentation

Nephele's summer grocery bills increased substantially as she purchased out-of-season vegetables at premium prices. The quality suffered. Asparagus in July came from distant countries, spent weeks in refrigerated transport, and cost three times spring prices. Following Chapter 10.0 principles, this extended transport time created higher histamine risk than locally-grown seasonal alternatives.

Simultaneously, she ignored plentiful local summer squash, cucumbers, and fresh herbs at farmers' markets. These peak-season items would have cost less and provided better quality than her out-of-season purchases. Her meal plan's rigidity created unnecessary expense and potentially reduced quality.

Analysis

Nephele's situation demonstrates a common maintenance phase pattern. The effort invested in creating an initial maintenance plan creates psychological attachment to that specific plan. The idea of modifying it feels like starting over. However, seasonal adaptation doesn't require complete replanning. It requires strategic ingredient substitution within established meal frameworks.

Her spring meal plan's structure remained sound. The specific vegetables needed swapping. Research shows that seasonal eating supports better nutrient intake and lower costs while improving environmental sustainability through reduced transportation (Reese et al., 2018). For histamine management, the fresher local seasonal produce provides safety advantages over shipped out-of-season alternatives.

Intervention

Nephele's dietitian explained the concept of framework constancy with ingredient flexibility. Her meal structures could remain while vegetables rotated seasonally. Spring meal: "grilled chicken with roasted asparagus and new potatoes" becomes summer meal: "grilled chicken with roasted zucchini and new potatoes." The framework (grilled protein, roasted vegetable, starch) persists. Only the specific vegetable changes.

They created a seasonal substitution guide. Spring vegetables (asparagus, peas, spring onions) map to summer alternatives (zucchini, green beans, regular onions). Fall vegetables (butternut squash, Brussels sprouts) map to winter alternatives (acorn squash, cabbage). This guide allowed updating meal plans quarterly without complete reconstruction.

Nephele began shopping at farmers' markets Saturday mornings, purchasing whatever looked best that week rather than shopping from a rigid list. She'd identify 3-4 peak-season vegetables, then plan the week's meals around those items using her established frameworks (grilled protein plus roasted vegetables, sheet pan meals, stir-fries, etc.).

Outcome

Nephele's summer grocery costs decreased 30% compared to her rigid spring-plan continuation. Quality improved dramatically. Local summer squash harvested that morning tasted better and contained less histamine than asparagus shipped internationally for two weeks. Her meal satisfaction increased despite using the "same" basic meal structures with different seasonal vegetables.

She maintained this seasonal adaptation pattern through fall and winter. Each season she identified that season's best local produce and adapted her established meal frameworks accordingly. The variety across seasons prevented boredom while the framework constancy prevented decision fatigue.

Teaching Points

- Successful long-term maintenance requires seasonal adaptation rather than rigid year-round meal plans, with ingredient flexibility within consistent meal frameworks preventing both expense and quality issues from out-of-season purchasing
- Seasonal local produce provides histamine safety advantages through shorter transport times and fresher products compared to internationally shipped out-of-season alternatives, supporting the fresh-is-best principle from Chapter 8.0
- Framework thinking (grilled protein plus roasted vegetable plus starch) enables ingredient substitution without complete meal plan reconstruction, reducing the cognitive burden of seasonal transitions

12.6 Family Friendly Strategies

Family meals for histamine-intolerant individuals with non-restricted family members require strategic approaches preventing dietary needs from dominating household (Schnedl et al., 2019).

Component meal strategy prepares meal elements separately, allowing customization at serving. Example: taco night provides seasoned ground turkey (compliant), rice (compliant), lettuce (compliant), cucumber (compliant), fresh cilantro (compliant), plus separate bowls of cheese (non-compliant), sour cream (non-compliant), and salsa (non-compliant). Each family member builds their plate from available components.

Parallel cooking makes two versions of the same meal simultaneously. Example: making pasta for family using jarred sauce (contains histamine from tomatoes and preservatives) while making fresh ground turkey with fresh tomatoes (if tolerated in tested amounts) for yourself. Both meals feature ground meat and tomato-based sauce, creating similar eating experience with different histamine profiles.

Compliant base with optional additions creates meals that work for everyone in basic form, with non-compliant additions available for family members without restrictions. Example: sheet pan dinner with roasted chicken, potatoes, and vegetables works for everyone. Family members can add purchased salad dressing (often contains vinegar) while you use olive oil and fresh lemon.

Child acceptance strategies for families where children eat the compliant meals include involving children in meal preparation (children eat foods they helped create), starting with naturally kid-friendly compliant items (grilled chicken strips, roasted sweet potato fries, fresh berries), and avoiding forcing issues (if children won't eat compliant meals, maintain parallel cooking rather than battling).

Spouse involvement dramatically improves sustainability. Spouses who understand the medical necessity, participate in meal planning, and occasionally cook compliant meals reduce the burden on the restricted individual. This prevents resentment from feeling solely responsible for complex meal management.

Social meal solutions within family include accepting that holiday meals or special occasions may involve more tier 2 foods (planned flexibility per Chapter 7.0) or preparing personal compliant versions of traditional dishes (sweet potato casserole without marshmallows and brown sugar, green bean casserole without cream of mushroom soup).

12.7 Quick Weekday Solutions

Weekday meals require 30 minutes or less total time from starting cooking to sitting down eating (Hartmann et al., 2013). This necessitates strategic planning and preparation.

Sheet pan dinners discussed in Chapter 11.0 provide the fastest cooking method. Place protein and vegetables on pan, season, roast 20-25 minutes at 425°F. Active time: 5 minutes. Examples: chicken breast with Brussels sprouts and sweet potato chunks; cod with asparagus and new potatoes; pork chops with butternut squash and green beans.

Instant Pot weeknight meals cook quickly under pressure. Frozen chicken breast becomes tender in 15 minutes. Ground beef cooks from frozen in 20 minutes. Add vegetables and rice for complete meals. Example: frozen ground turkey, frozen vegetables, rice, and broth cook together in Instant Pot for 20 minutes, producing complete meal with 3 minutes active prep time.

Pre-prepped assembly meals use components prepared during weekend batch cooking. Reheat frozen grilled chicken (10 minutes in oven from frozen), microwave frozen rice (3 minutes), steam fresh vegetables (5 minutes). Total time: 15 minutes with minimal active effort. All components reach table simultaneously.

Breakfast for dinner utilizes quick breakfast preparations for dinner when time is extremely limited. Scrambled eggs with sautéed vegetables and rice cakes provides adequate dinner nutrition in 10 minutes total time. Not exciting but functional for high-stress weeknights.

Strategic leftovers within the 24-hour window from section 9.3 provide quick meals. Cook double portion Monday evening. Eat one portion fresh. Refrigerate second portion immediately. Consume Tuesday within 24 hours of cooking. This twice-weekly strategy (Monday/Tuesday and Thursday/Friday) reduces cooking frequency while maintaining histamine safety.

Emergency backup meals for truly chaotic days include compliant frozen dinners (if commercially available options meeting individual tolerances exist), rotisserie chicken from grocery store (consumed same day of purchase, only if purchase timing known), or extremely simple assemblies (rice cakes with sunflower seed butter, fresh apple, carrot sticks).

12.8 Weekend Batch Cooking

Weekend preparation enables weekday convenience (Hartmann et al., 2013). The time investment (2-4 hours) creates streamlined weeknight meals for the following week.

Saturday morning routine might include grocery shopping (1 hour) followed by immediate processing. Returning from grocery store triggers the preparation sequence: proteins go into refrigerator briefly while produce gets washed. Then immediate protein portioning and first cooking session begins.

Protein processing includes portioning chicken breasts into individual servings, forming ground meat into patties or seasoning for later cooking, and deciding which proteins cook immediately versus later in the week. Proteins intended for early week use (Monday/Tuesday) might cook Saturday. Proteins for later week (Thursday/Friday) might remain raw, portioned, and frozen for cooking fresh mid-week.

Vegetable preparation includes washing everything immediately, pre-cutting hardy vegetables (carrots, bell peppers if tolerated, cucumbers) for the week's snacks and salads, and roasting 2-3 sheet pans of vegetables for freezing. Delicate vegetables (leafy greens, zucchini) get washed but not cut until day of use.

Starch preparation batch cooks rice, quinoa (if tolerated), or other grains in large quantities. Portion into individual servings while still hot. Cool on counter 20-30 minutes. Freeze immediately per Chapter 9.0 protocols. These portions provide quick sides all week.

Sauce and condiment preparation makes week's worth of compliant dressings and flavor enhancers. Fresh herb oil (olive oil gently heated with fresh herbs, strained), fresh salsa (if tomatoes tolerated), fresh cucumber dressing (blended cucumber, olive oil, fresh dill), or other compliant sauces get prepared and refrigerated for week use.

Sunday session supplements Saturday preparation. Sunday afternoon (1-2 hours) might focus on assembling freezer meals for following week or preparing any items not completed Saturday. Some people prefer splitting preparation across both weekend days rather than one long Saturday session.

Batch cooking schedule variation recognizes different preferences. Some people prefer the focused 4-hour Saturday marathon getting all preparation done at once. Others prefer 2 hours Saturday, 2 hours Sunday for less intensity. Both approaches work equally well. Choose based on personal preference and schedule.

12.9 Case Study: Batch Cooking Transformation

Background

Salome, a 41-year-old project manager, maintained decent compliance through elimination and early maintenance phases but found the daily cooking burden increasingly exhausting. Working full days then cooking 45 minutes nightly left no time for exercise, hobbies, or relationships. She'd lost 15 pounds during elimination (not deliberately, just from reduced eating due to time constraints). Her quality of life had decreased despite symptom improvement.

Presentation

By month six of maintenance, Salome considered abandoning dietary management despite good results. The daily cooking demand felt unsustainable. She'd tried quick meals but they became monotonous. She'd tried assembly meals but lacked prepared components. Her weeknight routine involved arriving home exhausted at 7pm, cooking until 8pm, eating quickly, cleaning up, and collapsing by 9pm. No social life. No activities. Just work and cooking.

Research shows that long-term dietary adherence depends heavily on integration with desired lifestyle rather than dietary compliance becoming the dominant life activity (Hartmann et al., 2013). When diet management consumes all discretionary time, abandonment becomes likely regardless of symptom control success.

Analysis

Salome's failure was strategic rather than motivational. She understood the diet. She tolerated the food restrictions. She valued her symptom relief. But she couldn't sustain the time investment indefinitely. The issue wasn't will but method.

Weekend batch cooking from section 12.8 could transform her weeknight experience. Instead of 45 minutes cooking nightly (315 minutes weekly), she could invest 3-4 hours one weekend day and reduce weeknight cooking to 10-15 minutes (50-75 minutes weekly). Total weekly time might even decrease while weeknight burden dropped dramatically.

Intervention

Salome's dietitian walked her through a Saturday batch cooking session. They created a detailed schedule: 9am grocery shopping. 10am return home, wash produce, portion proteins. 10:30am start first protein cooking (grilling chicken breasts). While chicken cooks, roast vegetables. While vegetables roast, cook rice. 11:30am portion and freeze cooked items as they finish. 12:30pm prepare second protein batch. 1pm finish freezing everything, clean up.

The 4-hour session produced: 10 grilled chicken breasts (frozen individually), 8 turkey burger patties (frozen individually), 3 sheet pans roasted vegetables (portioned and frozen), 12 cups cooked rice (portioned and frozen), pre-cut raw vegetables for the week's snacks and salads.

This preparation enabled weeknight meals assembled in 10-15 minutes. Monday: reheat frozen chicken, frozen rice, frozen roasted vegetables, add fresh cucumber. Tuesday: cook frozen turkey patty fresh, reheat frozen rice, steam fresh broccoli. Wednesday: sheet pan meal (only night requiring actual cooking, 5 minutes active time). Thursday and Friday similar to Monday and Tuesday.

Outcome

Salome's weeknight routine transformed. Arriving home at 7pm, she had dinner on table by 7:15pm. Eating and cleanup finished by 8pm. She now had 1-2 hours nightly for other activities. She rejoined a book club. She started walking 3-4 evenings weekly. She reconnected with friends she'd been "too busy" to see.

Her Saturday mornings now included 4 hours of meal prep, but this felt worthwhile given weeknight freedom. She eventually refined her process to 3 hours through efficiency improvements. Some Saturdays she'd invite friends to help, turning meal prep into social activity.

Six months later she maintained excellent dietary compliance without the lifestyle sacrifice. The time investment shifted from distributed daily burden to consolidated weekly session, creating psychological and practical sustainability.

Teaching Points

- Long-term dietary adherence depends on time management strategies that prevent diet from consuming all discretionary time, with consolidated batch cooking creating weeknight freedom that distributed daily cooking cannot provide
- The shift from 45 minutes nightly cooking to 3-4 hours weekend preparation plus 10-15 minutes weeknight assembly actually reduces total weekly time investment while dramatically improving quality of life through weeknight availability
- Successful maintenance requires finding the specific time management approach matching individual preferences and constraints, with some people preferring daily cooking while others need batch approaches

12.10 Complete Shopping Organization

Shopping list structure for maintenance phase organizes by frequency and category (Schnedl et al., 2019). Weekly staples, biweekly items, and monthly pantry restocking each get separate list sections.

Weekly protein shopping for two-week rotation includes approximately: 4-6 chicken breasts, 2-3 pounds other poultry (turkey, game hen if tolerated), 2-3 pounds fish (variety based on seasonal availability and sales), 1-2 pounds red meat if tolerated (beef, lamb, pork), and 1 pound ground meat (turkey, chicken, or beef). Quantities assume batch cooking and freezing per Chapter 9.0.

Weekly produce shopping varies seasonally but generally includes: 3-4 pounds mixed vegetables for roasting (Brussels sprouts, butternut squash, zucchini, asparagus depending on season), 2-3 pounds vegetables for steaming (broccoli, green beans, carrots), 2 pounds vegetables for raw consumption (cucumbers, carrots, bell peppers if tolerated), fresh herbs (cilantro, parsley, basil depending on planned meals), and 2-3 pounds fruit if tolerated (apples, berries, melons seasonally).

Biweekly staples include items consumed regularly but not requiring weekly purchase: rice (5 pounds every 2-3 weeks), coconut milk (6 cans), olive oil if running low, cooking oil (coconut, avocado if running low), and any tolerated nuts or seeds (almonds, sunflower seeds).

Monthly pantry restocking replenishes shelf-stable items: salt, basic spices that passed testing (garlic powder, onion powder if tolerated), maple syrup or honey, and any other condiments meeting individual tolerances (coconut aminos if tolerated).

Seasonal bulk buying takes advantage of peak season abundance. Summer: buy extra zucchini, berries, and cucumbers when cheap and plentiful (freeze excess). Fall: purchase winter squashes in bulk (store in cool dry place for months). This reduces costs and ensures supply during less abundant seasons.

List organization by store section speeds shopping. Produce section first (largest category, best when fresh). Meat/fish counter second (while still early for best selection). Pantry aisles last (shelf-stable, timing less critical). Frozen section final stop (stays coldest until checkout).

12.11 Essential Points to Remember

This chapter provided maintenance phase meal planning strategies supporting long-term histamine management. The two-week rotation framework creates adequate variety while maintaining plannable simplicity, with tier 1 foods forming the foundation and tier 2 foods appearing within tested frequency limits.

Seasonal adaptations align meal plans with natural availability, improving freshness, reducing costs, and supporting histamine safety through shorter transport times for local seasonal produce. Framework constancy with ingredient flexibility allows seasonal transitions without complete meal plan reconstruction.

Family-friendly strategies including component meals, parallel cooking, and compliant bases with optional additions enable dietary management without dominating household eating patterns. Quick weekday solutions emphasizing sheet pan meals, Instant Pot preparations, and assembly from batch-cooked components maintain compliance without excessive daily time investment.

Weekend batch cooking provides the strategic approach enabling weeknight convenience, with 3-4 hours weekend preparation reducing weeknight active time to 10-15 minutes while maintaining histamine safety through immediate freezing protocols.

Shopping organization by frequency and category streamlines purchasing while controlling costs through seasonal bulk buying and strategic planning. The maintenance phase represents the sustainable long-term approach, balancing histamine management with quality of life, social participation, and practical constraints.

Part V: Recipes By Category

Chapter 13.0: Breakfast and Brunch Recipes

Dorothea stood in her kitchen at 6:30 AM, already running late for work. Pre-diagnosis, she'd grabbed a yogurt parfait and coffee, eating while getting ready. Those options no longer worked. Yogurt contained aged dairy. Her usual granola included dried fruits and nuts that now triggered symptoms. Even her coffee ritual had ended when she discovered caffeine's histamine-liberating effects. She'd managed elimination phase breakfasts (rice porridge, scrambled eggs, fresh fruit) but they felt monotonous after three months. She craved variety without spending hours on morning meal prep. The breakfast challenge affects nearly everyone managing histamine intolerance (Schnedl et al., 2019). Morning meals require speed and convenience. Most conventional breakfast foods (yogurt, cheese, processed meats, leftover pizza, commercial baked goods) contain high histamine or problematic additives. Creating satisfying, varied, quick breakfast options using only fresh low-histamine ingredients requires planning and tested recipes.

This chapter provides 13 breakfast and brunch recipes designed for histamine management. You will learn smoothie and smoothie bowl recipes using DAO-supporting ingredients, hot cereal and grain bowl preparations, egg-based dishes including frittatas and scrambles, pancake and waffle recipes with freezer-friendly variations, breakfast cookies and muffins for grab-and-go convenience, and quick assembly options for rushed mornings.

13.1 Smoothie Foundation Principles

Smoothies provide quick nutrition but require careful ingredient selection for histamine safety (Maintz & Novak, 2007). Most commercial smoothie recipes include bananas (histamine liberators for many), berries (high salicylates), citrus (histamine liberators), and yogurt or aged protein powders (high histamine).

DAO-supporting ingredients form the foundation of histamine-safe smoothies. Research suggests certain nutrients support diamine oxidase function, the enzyme that degrades histamine (Wantke et al., 1998). These include vitamin C from fresh sources (if citrus is tolerated, otherwise from fresh bell peppers or other vegetables), vitamin B6 from fresh proteins and certain vegetables, copper from fresh meats and some vegetables, and adequate protein from fresh sources.

Base liquid options include fresh coconut milk (not canned which may contain preservatives), fresh coconut water (if tolerated individually), rice milk made fresh from cooked rice, or filtered water. Avoid dairy milk, aged nut milks with preservatives, and citrus juices unless individually tested and tolerated per Chapter 6.0.

Fresh fruit selections emphasize low-histamine options tested during reintroduction. Blueberries work for most people. Fresh mango (if tolerated) provides tropical flavor and natural sweetness. Fresh apple (peeled to reduce pesticide exposure) adds mild sweetness. Avoid bananas (histamine liberators), strawberries (high histamine for many), and all citrus unless specifically tested and tolerated.

Vegetable additions boost nutrition without flavor dominance. Fresh spinach (if tolerated, test carefully as it's high oxalate) blends invisibly in fruit smoothies. Fresh cucumber adds hydration and mild flavor. Fresh zucchini (cooked briefly and cooled) provides creamy texture. Fresh cauliflower rice (steamed and cooled) adds thickness without flavor.

Protein sources for smoothies require freshness emphasis. Fresh cooked chicken breast (cooled and diced) blends surprisingly well in non-sweet smoothies. Plain rice protein powder (check ingredients carefully for additives and preservatives) works if tolerated. Fresh cooked and cooled white fish provides omega-3s in savory smoothies. Avoid all aged protein powders, whey proteins, and commercial blends containing multiple ingredients.

13.2 Smoothie Bowl Recipes

Coconut Blueberry Smoothie Bowl (Serves 1)

Ingredients: 1 cup fresh or frozen blueberries, 1 cup fresh coconut milk, 1/2 cup cauliflower rice (steamed and cooled), 1 tablespoon maple syrup, 1/4 teaspoon vanilla extract (alcohol-free if available).

Instructions: Combine all ingredients in blender. Blend until smooth and thick. Pour into bowl. Top with additional fresh blueberries, unsweetened coconut flakes (check for preservatives), and rice cereal (plain, no additives).

Nutritional notes: Provides antioxidants from blueberries, healthy fats from coconut, and hidden vegetables from cauliflower. The cauliflower rice creates smoothie bowl thickness without bananas.

Mango Coconut Cream Bowl (Serves 1)

Ingredients: 1 cup fresh mango chunks (frozen after cutting fresh), 1 cup coconut milk, 1/2 fresh zucchini (cooked and cooled), 1 tablespoon honey.

Instructions: Blend all ingredients until very smooth. Texture should be thick like soft-serve. Top with diced fresh mango, coconut flakes, and compliant granola if available.

Green Protein Smoothie Bowl (Serves 1)

Ingredients: 1 cup fresh cucumber (peeled), 1/2 cup fresh apple (peeled), 1/4 cup cooked chicken breast (cooled), 1 cup coconut water, 1 cup fresh spinach (if tolerated), 1 tablespoon sunflower seed butter (if tolerated).

Instructions: Blend cucumber, apple, and coconut water first until smooth. Add remaining ingredients. Blend until completely smooth. Serve immediately for freshness per Chapter 8.0 cooking principles.

13.3 Hot Cereal Preparations

Rice porridge forms the foundation of low-histamine hot breakfast (Schnedl et al., 2019). The basic preparation discussed in Chapter 11.0 adapts infinitely through topping variations and cooking liquid changes.

Classic Coconut Rice Porridge (Serves 2)

Ingredients: 1 cup white rice, 3 cups coconut milk (or 2 cups coconut milk plus 1 cup water for thinner consistency), 1/4 teaspoon salt, 2 tablespoons maple syrup, fresh blueberries for topping.

Instructions: Combine rice, coconut milk, and salt in medium pot. Bring to boil over medium-high heat. Reduce to low simmer. Cover. Cook 20 minutes, stirring every 5 minutes to prevent sticking. Add maple syrup. Serve hot topped with fresh blueberries.

Storage: Make fresh daily. Do not store cooked rice porridge refrigerated due to histamine formation from bacterial activity on cooked grains.

Savory Rice Bowl (Serves 1)

Ingredients: 1 cup cooked rice (fresh, not refrigerated leftovers), 1/2 cup cooked chicken (fresh or frozen-reheated per Chapter 9.0), 1 cup fresh bok choy (sautéed), 1 teaspoon coconut oil, salt to taste, fresh cilantro (if tolerated).

Instructions: Heat coconut oil in pan. Sauté bok choy until tender (3-4 minutes). Heat rice and chicken separately (microwave or stovetop). Combine in bowl. Top with fresh cilantro. Season with salt.

Quinoa Breakfast Bowl (Serves 2)

Ingredients: 1 cup quinoa (if tested and tolerated), 2 cups water, 1/2 teaspoon salt, 1 cup fresh blueberries, 2 tablespoons sunflower seed butter (if tolerated), 2 tablespoons maple syrup.

Instructions: Rinse quinoa thoroughly. Combine with water and salt. Bring to boil. Reduce heat and simmer covered 15 minutes until water absorbs. Remove from heat. Let stand 5 minutes covered. Fluff with fork. Divide between bowls. Top with blueberries, sunflower seed butter, and maple syrup drizzle.

13.4 Egg Based Dishes

Eggs provide complete protein and cook quickly, making them ideal for breakfast if individually tolerated (Maintz & Novak, 2007). Test eggs carefully during reintroduction per Chapter 6.0 as some histamine-intolerant individuals react to them.

Basic Vegetable Frittata (Serves 4)

Ingredients: 8 eggs (if tolerated), 1/4 cup coconut milk, 1/2 teaspoon salt, 2 cups mixed vegetables (zucchini, bell peppers if tolerated, spinach if tolerated, all diced), 2 tablespoons coconut oil, fresh herbs (basil, parsley, or chives if tolerated).

Instructions: Preheat oven to 375°F. Heat coconut oil in oven-safe skillet over medium heat. Sauté vegetables until tender (5-7 minutes). Whisk eggs, coconut milk, salt, and fresh herbs. Pour over vegetables. Cook on stovetop 2 minutes until edges begin setting. Transfer to oven. Bake 12-15 minutes until center sets. Let cool 5 minutes. Cut into wedges.

Storage: Consume fresh or freeze individual portions immediately after cooling per Chapter 9.0. Use frozen portions within 2 weeks.

Simple Scrambled Eggs (Serves 1)

Ingredients: 2-3 eggs, 1 tablespoon coconut milk, salt, 1 teaspoon coconut oil, fresh vegetables (optional: diced zucchini, bell peppers if tolerated, fresh herbs).

Instructions: Whisk eggs, coconut milk, and salt. Heat coconut oil in pan over medium heat. Add vegetables if using. Cook until tender (2-3 minutes). Pour in eggs. Cook slowly, stirring gently, until just set (2-3 minutes). Serve immediately.

Baked Egg Cups (Makes 6)

Ingredients: 6 eggs, 1/4 cup coconut milk, 1/2 cup diced vegetables (zucchini, bell pepper), 1/4 teaspoon salt, fresh herbs, coconut oil for greasing muffin tin.

Instructions: Preheat oven to 350°F. Grease 6 muffin cups with coconut oil. Divide vegetables among cups. Whisk eggs, coconut milk, salt, and herbs. Pour over vegetables, filling each cup 3/4 full. Bake 18-20 minutes until centers set. Cool briefly. Remove from tin.

Storage: Freeze immediately after cooling. Reheat individual cups from frozen in microwave (1 minute) or toaster oven (10 minutes at 350°F).

13.5 Case Study: Breakfast Variety Success

Background

Theophilus, a 45-year-old teacher, struggled with breakfast monotony during maintenance phase. He'd successfully completed elimination and reintroduction. His tier 1 foods included eggs, rice, certain vegetables, blueberries, and fresh chicken. Tier 2 included small amounts of mango and sunflower seed butter. However, his breakfast routine had calcified into scrambled eggs and rice cakes daily for six months.

Presentation

Theophilus reported good symptom control but increasing breakfast dissatisfaction. He'd begun skipping breakfast some mornings from boredom, then feeling hungry and tired mid-morning. This led to poor food choices at lunch (eating whatever looked appealing at the cafeteria, sometimes non-compliant items). His afternoon symptoms occasionally returned despite overall good management.

Analysis revealed that breakfast boredom was undermining his otherwise successful maintenance. He'd never developed varied breakfast options beyond elimination phase basics. He didn't realize his tolerated foods could create different breakfast experiences through varied preparations and combinations.

Analysis

Theophilus's situation demonstrates a common maintenance phase pattern. People develop minimal rotation during elimination's restrictive phase, then never expand despite successful reintroduction adding options. The psychological pattern of "this works, don't change it" creates unnecessary restriction even when more variety becomes safe.

Research shows that dietary variety supports long-term adherence better than monotonous eating, even when the monotonous pattern is technically compliant (Raynor & Epstein, 2001). Humans crave sensory variety. Providing it within compliant parameters prevents the rebellion that excessive monotony triggers.

Intervention

A dietitian worked with Theophilus to develop 10 different breakfast options using only his tested tier 1 and tier 2 foods. Week 1: scrambled eggs with sautéed zucchini (Monday), rice porridge with blueberries (Tuesday), egg frittata with mixed vegetables (Wednesday), smoothie bowl with mango and coconut (Thursday), savory rice bowl with chicken (Friday), leftover frittata reheated (Saturday), coconut rice porridge with sunflower seed butter (Sunday).

This simple 7-day rotation used only foods he'd eaten for months, just combined differently or prepared through varied techniques. The frittata provided make-ahead convenience. The smoothie bowl felt treat-like despite being compliant. The savory rice bowl transformed breakfast into a mini-meal rather than traditional breakfast foods.

He batch-prepared frittatas Sunday (making two, freezing one for later in week). He pre-portioned smoothie bowl ingredients into freezer bags (Sunday prep, quick blending weekday mornings). This minimal weekend prep enabled weekday variety without daily extensive cooking.

Outcome

Within two weeks, Theophilus reported renewed breakfast enjoyment. He stopped skipping meals. His mid-morning hunger disappeared. His lunch choices improved because he arrived satisfied rather than ravenous. The variety prevented the boredom-driven non-compliance that had been creeping in.

Six months later, he'd expanded his rotation to 14 different breakfasts, rotating through a two-week cycle. His symptom control remained excellent while his quality of life improved through simple variety within established tolerances.

Teaching Points

- Breakfast monotony during maintenance phase often reflects failure to translate tested food tolerances into varied meal options rather than actual dietary restriction necessity, with people continuing elimination-phase minimal rotation despite reintroduction expanding choices

- Developing 7-10 different breakfast preparations using tier 1 and tier 2 tested foods prevents boredom-driven non-compliance while maintaining histamine safety through variety within established tolerances
- Minimal weekend batch preparation of freezer-friendly breakfast items like frittatas or pre-portioned smoothie ingredients enables weekday variety without daily extensive cooking time investment

13.6 Pancakes and Waffles

Pancakes and waffles require flour alternatives since wheat hasn't been discussed as tested. Rice flour, oat flour (if oats tested successfully), and cassava flour provide options.

Basic Rice Flour Pancakes (Serves 2, makes 8 small pancakes)

Ingredients: 1 cup rice flour, 1 tablespoon maple syrup, 1 teaspoon baking powder (aluminum-free), 1/4 teaspoon salt, 1 cup coconut milk, 2 eggs (if tolerated), 2 tablespoons melted coconut oil plus more for cooking.

Instructions: Mix dry ingredients (rice flour, baking powder, salt). Whisk wet ingredients (coconut milk, eggs, maple syrup, melted coconut oil). Combine wet and dry. Mix until just combined (lumps okay). Heat griddle or large skillet over medium heat. Lightly grease with coconut oil. Pour 1/4 cup batter per pancake. Cook until bubbles form and edges look dry (2-3 minutes). Flip. Cook until golden (1-2 minutes). Serve hot with maple syrup and fresh blueberries.

Freezing instructions: Cool completely. Stack with parchment paper between pancakes. Place in freezer bag. Freeze up to 2 weeks per Chapter 9.0 guidelines. Reheat from frozen in toaster or toaster oven.

Blueberry Pancakes (Serves 2)

Ingredients: Basic rice flour pancake batter (above), 1 cup fresh blueberries.

Instructions: Prepare batter as directed. Fold in 3/4 cup blueberries gently. Cook as directed. Top finished pancakes with remaining fresh blueberries and maple syrup.

Simple Waffles (Serves 3, makes 6 waffles)

Ingredients: 1.5 cups rice flour, 2 teaspoons baking powder, 1/4 teaspoon salt, 2 tablespoons maple syrup, 1.5 cups coconut milk, 2 eggs, 3 tablespoons melted coconut oil.

Instructions: Preheat waffle iron. Mix dry ingredients. Whisk wet ingredients. Combine. Pour appropriate amount onto waffle iron (varies by iron size). Cook according to waffle iron instructions until golden (typically 3-5 minutes). Serve immediately or cool completely and freeze per pancake instructions.

13.7 Grab and Go Options

Breakfast cookies and **muffins** provide portable options when properly formulated and stored (Schnedl et al., 2019).

Coconut Blueberry Breakfast Cookies (Makes 12)

Ingredients: 2 cups oat flour (if oats tolerated) or rice flour, 1/2 cup coconut oil (softened), 1/3 cup maple syrup, 1 egg, 1 teaspoon vanilla extract, 1/2 teaspoon baking soda, 1/4 teaspoon salt, 1 cup fresh blueberries, 1/2 cup unsweetened coconut flakes.

Instructions: Preheat oven to 350°F. Line baking sheet with parchment. Mix coconut oil and maple syrup until combined. Add egg and vanilla. Mix well. Combine flour, baking soda, and salt. Add to wet ingredients. Mix until just combined. Fold in blueberries and coconut. Drop by 1/4 cup portions onto prepared sheet. Flatten slightly. Bake 12-15 minutes until edges golden. Cool completely.

Storage: Freeze individually immediately after cooling. Use within 2 weeks per Chapter 9.0.

Basic Muffins (Makes 12)

Ingredients: 2 cups rice flour, 1/2 cup maple syrup, 1/2 cup coconut oil (melted), 2 eggs, 1 cup coconut milk, 2 teaspoons baking powder, 1/2 teaspoon salt, 1 teaspoon vanilla.

Instructions: Preheat oven to 375°F. Line muffin tin with papers or grease well. Mix wet ingredients (coconut oil, maple syrup, eggs, coconut milk, vanilla). Mix dry ingredients (rice flour, baking powder, salt). Combine wet and dry. Mix until just combined. Divide among muffin cups. Bake 18-22 minutes until toothpick comes out clean. Cool completely before freezing.

Variations: Add 1 cup fresh blueberries, or 1 cup grated zucchini (squeeze out excess moisture first), or 1/2 cup sunflower seed butter (if tolerated).

13.8 Quick Assembly Options

Quick breakfast assemblies require no cooking, just strategic pantry and freezer stocking.

Rice Cake Plate: 2-3 rice cakes topped with sunflower seed butter (if tolerated), fresh apple slices, fresh blueberries, drizzle of maple syrup.

Fresh Fruit Bowl: 1 cup fresh blueberries, 1 fresh apple (diced), 1/2 cup mango (if tolerated), top with coconut flakes and sunflower seed butter.

Coconut Yogurt Alternative: Blend fresh coconut milk with fresh mango until smooth and thick. Top with fresh blueberries and compliant granola (if available).

Breakfast Wrap (if tolerated wraps available): Fill compliant wrap with scrambled eggs (pre-cooked and reheated), fresh vegetables, fresh herbs. Roll and eat.

Smoothie: Simplest option using recipes from section 13.1. Blend and consume immediately.

13.9 Chapter Summary

This chapter provided 25 breakfast and brunch recipes emphasizing histamine safety through fresh ingredients and immediate consumption or proper freezing protocols. Smoothies and smoothie bowls use DAO-supporting ingredients like fresh coconut milk, blueberries, and hidden vegetables for nutrition density. Hot cereals including rice porridge and quinoa bowls adapt through varied toppings and sweet versus savory preparations.

Egg-based dishes from simple scrambles to batch-prepared frittatas provide protein-rich options for those who tolerate eggs. Freezer-friendly pancakes and waffles using rice flour enable make-ahead convenience. Breakfast cookies and muffins offer grab-and-go solutions when properly frozen immediately after cooling and used within appropriate timeframes.

Quick assembly options like rice cake plates and fruit bowls require zero cooking while providing adequate nutrition for busy mornings. The case study demonstrated how breakfast variety supports long-term compliance by preventing monotony-driven non-adherence. Chapter 14.0 will provide soup and salad recipes that maintain similar safety principles while expanding mealtime options.

Chapter 14.0: Soups and Salads

Cyril stood before the soup aisle at his grocery store, a practice he'd abandoned three months into histamine management. Every can contained tomatoes, aged cheese, yeast extract, or vinegar. The "healthy" options boasted bone broth (aged during long simmering), fermented vegetables, and nutritional yeast. Even the simple chicken soup contained "natural flavors" (code for MSG and yeast extracts) and had been packaged weeks earlier. He'd once relied on canned soup for quick lunches and easy dinners. Now the entire category seemed off-limits. His dietitian had suggested making fresh soups, but the recipes he found online all required long simmering (creating histamine per Chapter 8.0) or problematic ingredients. Salads seemed safer until he considered that most dressings contained vinegar, aged cheeses, or commercial mayonnaise with preservatives. The soup and salad category that had once represented healthy convenience eating now felt completely inaccessible. This frustration is common among people managing histamine intolerance (Maintz & Novak, 2007). Conventional soup and salad preparation relies heavily on aged ingredients, long cooking times, and commercial products designed for extended shelf life rather than freshness.

This chapter provides 21 soup and salad recipes designed for histamine safety. You will learn pressure cooker soup techniques that minimize cooking time, fresh vegetable soup preparations, protein-packed salad formulas, grain-based salad options, homemade low-histamine dressings, and vegetable-based cream soup alternatives to dairy-based versions.

14.1 Pressure Cooker Soup Principles

Pressure cooking transforms soup preparation for histamine management by drastically reducing cooking time (Schnedl et al., 2019). Traditional soup recipes simmer 2-4 hours, creating ideal conditions for bacterial histamine production discussed in Chapter 8.0. Pressure cooking achieves similar flavor development and vegetable tenderness in 15-30 minutes.

Instant Pot soup method follows specific protocols. Sauté vegetables briefly in Instant Pot using sauté function (5-7 minutes). This step develops flavor without long cooking. Add liquid and remaining ingredients. Seal lid. Cook on high pressure for appropriate time (10-20 minutes for most vegetable soups, 15-25 minutes for soups with proteins). Quick release pressure. Serve immediately or cool rapidly and freeze portions per Chapter 9.0.

Fresh broth alternatives replace traditional bone broth (which requires extended simmering that creates histamine). Fresh vegetable broth made in pressure cooker provides flavor without histamine risk. Combine 4 cups water, 2 carrots (chopped), 2 celery stalks (chopped), 1 onion (quartered), fresh herbs, salt. Pressure cook 10 minutes. Strain. Use immediately.

Immediate consumption protocol remains critical. Soup cooked fresh and eaten immediately contains minimal histamine. Soup refrigerated as leftovers accumulates histamine within 24 hours per Chapter 9.0. The solution is portioning soup into individual servings and freezing immediately after rapid cooling.

Rapid cooling technique for soup uses ice bath method. Place pot in larger container filled with ice water. Stir soup frequently to distribute cold throughout. Soup should reach refrigerator temperature within 30 minutes. Then portion immediately and freeze. Don't leave soup sitting at room temperature for hours cooling slowly.

14.2 Fresh Vegetable Soup Recipes

Quick Vegetable Soup (Serves 6)

Ingredients: 2 tablespoons coconut oil, 1 onion (diced), 2 carrots (diced), 2 celery stalks (diced), 2 zucchini (diced), 2 cups cauliflower florets, 6 cups fresh vegetable broth or water, 1 teaspoon salt, 1/2 teaspoon garlic powder (if tolerated), fresh parsley, fresh basil.

Instructions: Set Instant Pot to sauté. Heat coconut oil. Add onion, carrots, celery. Sauté 5 minutes until softened. Add remaining vegetables, broth, salt, garlic powder. Seal lid. Cook high pressure 10 minutes. Quick release. Stir in fresh herbs. Serve immediately or cool rapidly and freeze portions.

Butternut Squash Soup (Serves 4)

Ingredients: 1 large butternut squash (peeled and cubed), 1 onion (diced), 3 cups fresh vegetable broth, 1 cup coconut milk, 1 teaspoon salt, 1/4 teaspoon fresh ginger (grated), fresh sage.

Instructions: Sauté onion in coconut oil using Instant Pot sauté function (5 minutes). Add squash, broth, salt, ginger. Seal lid. Pressure cook 12 minutes. Quick release. Blend soup until smooth using immersion blender. Stir in coconut milk. Garnish with fresh sage.

Chicken Vegetable Soup (Serves 6)

Ingredients: 1 pound fresh chicken breast (diced), 2 tablespoons coconut oil, 1 onion (diced), 3 carrots (sliced), 3 celery stalks (sliced), 2 zucchini (diced), 6 cups fresh broth or water, 1 cup rice, 2 teaspoons salt, fresh parsley, fresh dill.

Instructions: Sauté onion, carrots, celery in coconut oil (Instant Pot sauté function, 5 minutes). Add chicken, remaining vegetables, broth, rice, salt. Seal lid. Pressure cook 15 minutes. Quick release. Stir in fresh herbs. Serve immediately.

Storage note: This soup must be consumed fresh or frozen immediately. The combination of cooked rice and chicken creates rapid bacterial growth if refrigerated.

Zucchini Basil Soup (Serves 4)

Ingredients: 4 medium zucchini (chopped), 1 onion (diced), 3 cups fresh vegetable broth, 1 cup coconut milk, 1 teaspoon salt, 2 cups fresh basil leaves, 2 tablespoons olive oil.

Instructions: Sauté onion in olive oil (5 minutes). Add zucchini, broth, salt. Pressure cook 8 minutes. Quick release. Add basil leaves. Blend until smooth. Stir in coconut milk. Serve hot or cold.

14.3 Protein Packed Salad Formulas

Protein salads provide complete meals when properly constructed (Maintz & Novak, 2007). The formula combines fresh greens, cooked protein, fresh vegetables, and homemade dressing.

Grilled Chicken Salad (Serves 2)

Ingredients: 4 cups mixed greens (butter lettuce, romaine), 8 ounces grilled chicken breast (fresh or frozen-reheated), 1 cup cucumber (diced), 1 cup bell pepper (diced, if tolerated), 1/2 cup carrots (shredded), 1/4 cup fresh herbs (basil, cilantro, or parsley), homemade dressing (see section 14.5).

Instructions: Arrange greens on plates. Top with sliced chicken, vegetables, and herbs. Drizzle with dressing. Serve immediately.

Turkey and Apple Salad (Serves 2)

Ingredients: 4 cups mixed greens, 8 ounces cooked turkey breast (fresh), 1 fresh apple (diced), 1/2 cup cucumber (diced), 1/4 cup sunflower seeds (if tolerated), fresh parsley, olive oil and fresh lemon dressing (if lemon tolerated).

Instructions: Combine greens, turkey, apple, cucumber. Top with sunflower seeds and parsley. Dress just before serving.

Salmon and Vegetable Salad (Serves 2)

Ingredients: 4 cups mixed greens, 8 ounces fresh salmon (cooked same day and cooled), 1 cup cherry tomatoes (if tolerated, otherwise substitute bell pepper), 1 cup cucumber, 1 avocado (if tolerated in tested portions), fresh dill, homemade creamy dressing.

Instructions: Flake cooled salmon over greens. Add vegetables. Garnish with fresh dill. Dress immediately before eating.

14.4 Grain Based Salad Options

Grain salads use freshly cooked grains rather than refrigerated leftovers to minimize histamine (Schnedl et al., 2019). Cook grains fresh for each salad or use frozen pre-cooked portions reheated immediately before assembly.

Rice and Vegetable Salad (Serves 4)

Ingredients: 3 cups cooked rice (fresh or frozen-reheated), 1 cup cucumber (diced), 1 cup bell pepper (diced, if tolerated), 1 cup carrots (shredded), 1/2 cup fresh parsley (chopped), 1/4 cup olive oil, 2 tablespoons fresh lemon juice (if tolerated) or apple cider substitute, 1 teaspoon salt.

Instructions: Cook rice fresh or reheat frozen portion. Cool to room temperature (don't refrigerate overnight). Combine with vegetables. Mix olive oil, lemon juice, salt for dressing. Toss together. Serve within 2 hours of preparation.

Quinoa Salad with Herbs (Serves 4)

Ingredients: 3 cups cooked quinoa (fresh), 1 cup cucumber (diced), 1 cup cherry tomatoes (halved, if tolerated), 1/2 cup fresh mint (chopped), 1/2 cup fresh parsley (chopped), 1/4 cup olive oil, juice of 1 lemon (if tolerated), 1 teaspoon salt.

Instructions: Cook quinoa fresh. Cool to room temperature. Combine with vegetables and herbs. Whisk oil, lemon juice, salt. Toss together. Serve within 2 hours.

Mediterranean Rice Bowl (Serves 2)

Ingredients: 2 cups cooked rice (fresh), 1 cup cucumber (diced), 1/2 cup fresh herbs (parsley, mint, basil), 1/4 cup olive oil, 1 tablespoon fresh lemon juice (if tolerated), 1 teaspoon salt, optional: 4 ounces grilled chicken.

Instructions: Combine all ingredients. Toss gently. Serve immediately. If adding protein, grill chicken fresh and add warm over room-temperature rice salad.

14.5 Homemade Low Histamine Dressings

Commercial dressings almost universally contain vinegar, aged cheese, yeast extract, or preservatives incompatible with histamine management (Maintz & Novak, 2007). Homemade versions using fresh ingredients and alternative acids provide flavor without triggers.

Basic Olive Oil Dressing (Makes 1/2 cup)

Ingredients: 1/3 cup olive oil, 2 tablespoons fresh lemon juice (if tolerated) or 1 tablespoon apple cider (fresh, not vinegar), 1/2 teaspoon salt, 1/4 teaspoon garlic powder (if tolerated), fresh herbs (optional).

Instructions: Whisk all ingredients. Store refrigerated up to 3 days (brief storage acceptable for dressings as bacterial growth is inhibited by acidity and oil).

Creamy Cucumber Dressing (Makes 1 cup)

Ingredients: 1 cup cucumber (peeled and roughly chopped), 1/4 cup olive oil, 2 tablespoons fresh lemon juice (if tolerated), 1/4 teaspoon salt, 1 tablespoon fresh dill, 2 tablespoons coconut milk.

Instructions: Blend all ingredients until smooth. Use immediately or refrigerate up to 2 days.

Fresh Herb Vinaigrette (Makes 1/2 cup)

Ingredients: 1/3 cup olive oil, 2 tablespoons fresh lemon juice, 2 tablespoons fresh herbs (basil, parsley, or cilantro), 1/2 teaspoon salt, 1/4 teaspoon maple syrup (optional for slight sweetness).

Instructions: Blend or whisk all ingredients. Best used fresh.

Sunflower Seed Dressing (Makes 3/4 cup, if sunflower seeds tolerated)

Ingredients: 1/4 cup sunflower seed butter, 1/4 cup olive oil, 2 tablespoons fresh lemon juice, 2 tablespoons water (to thin), 1/2 teaspoon salt, 1 clove fresh garlic (if tolerated).

Instructions: Blend until smooth. Add water as needed for desired consistency. Refrigerate up to 3 days.

14.6 Case Study: Soup Solution Success

Background

Gawain, a 38-year-old accountant, felt restricted by his inability to enjoy soups during cold weather. He'd completed elimination and reintroduction successfully. His tier 1 foods included chicken, various vegetables, rice, and fresh herbs. However, he avoided soup entirely, believing it required ingredients or preparation methods incompatible with histamine management.

Presentation

During a November dietitian appointment, Gawain expressed frustration about missing comfort foods as weather cooled. He described soup as representative of foods that "just don't work" for histamine management. When asked what specifically prevented him from making soup, he listed: need for bone broth (requires long simmering), use of canned tomatoes (aged and preserved), extended cooking times (2-3 hours standard for soup), and leftovers (soup recipes make large batches requiring days of refrigerated storage).

His assumptions, while understandable, reflected incomplete understanding of how pressure cooking and freezing strategies from Chapters 8.0 and 9.0 applied to soup preparation. He'd never attempted soup using compliant methods because he assumed the entire category was off-limits.

Analysis

Gawain's avoidance pattern demonstrates how people create unnecessary restrictions through incomplete application of principles. He correctly identified that traditional soup preparation conflicts with histamine management. But he didn't realize that modified techniques eliminate these conflicts while preserving soup's essential character.

Research shows that perceived dietary restriction often exceeds actual restriction when people fail to adapt cooking techniques to their requirements (Reese et al., 2018). Gawain's restriction was perceptual rather than actual. Soup works perfectly for histamine management when prepared using fresh vegetable broth, pressure cooking for short durations, and immediate portioning for freezing.

Intervention

The dietitian taught Gawain pressure cooker soup preparation. They made fresh vegetable broth in his Instant Pot (10 minutes start to finish). Using that broth, they prepared chicken vegetable soup with rice (total time from starting to cook: 30 minutes including sauté time and pressure cooking). The soup tasted rich and flavorful despite brief cooking.

They discussed immediate freezing protocols. Rather than making one pot to eat all week (creating the refrigerated leftover problem), Gawain learned to portion soup into individual containers immediately after rapid cooling and freeze all portions except that evening's dinner.

He developed a rotation of four soups made monthly: chicken vegetable with rice, butternut squash with coconut milk, zucchini basil, and simple vegetable. Each recipe made 6 servings. He'd make one soup, freeze 5 portions, eat 1 fresh. Throughout the month, he'd accumulate 20-24 frozen soup portions (variety across four recipes). These provided quick lunches and easy dinners by reheating single frozen portions.

Outcome

Gawain's perceived restriction decreased substantially. Having soup back in his rotation improved his satisfaction with the diet. The frozen individual portions provided convenience rivaling the canned soups he'd previously relied on, but with fresh ingredients and proper histamine management.

He reported that soup success motivated investigating other foods he'd assumed were off-limits. If soup worked with proper technique, what else might work? This shift from "what can't I eat" to "how can I make this work" transformed his relationship with dietary management.

Teaching Points

- Perceived dietary restriction often exceeds actual restriction when people assume entire food categories are incompatible without investigating how modified techniques can preserve the food's essential character while eliminating problematic elements

- Pressure cooking enables soup preparation that achieves traditional flavor development in 15-30 minutes rather than 2-4 hours, preventing the bacterial histamine production that extended simmering creates
- Batch cooking soups for immediate freezing in individual portions provides convenience comparable to commercial canned soups while maintaining complete control over ingredients and freshness

14.7 Vegetable Cream Soups

Cream soups traditionally use dairy cream, aged cheese, or commercial cream substitutes containing preservatives. Vegetable-based versions using coconut milk create similar texture without problematic ingredients.

Cauliflower Cream Soup (Serves 4)

Ingredients: 1 large head cauliflower (chopped), 1 onion (diced), 3 cups fresh vegetable broth, 1 cup coconut milk, 2 tablespoons coconut oil, 1 teaspoon salt, fresh chives for garnish.

Instructions: Sauté onion in coconut oil (Instant Pot sauté function, 5 minutes). Add cauliflower, broth, salt. Pressure cook 10 minutes. Quick release. Blend until completely smooth. Stir in coconut milk. Garnish with fresh chives.

Broccoli Soup (Serves 4)

Ingredients: 4 cups broccoli florets, 1 onion (diced), 3 cups fresh broth, 1 cup coconut milk, 2 tablespoons olive oil, 1 teaspoon salt, 1/2 teaspoon garlic powder (if tolerated).

Instructions: Sauté onion in olive oil (5 minutes). Add broccoli, broth, salt, garlic powder. Pressure cook 8 minutes. Quick release. Blend until smooth. Add coconut milk. Serve hot.

Carrot Ginger Soup (Serves 4)

Ingredients: 6 large carrots (chopped), 1 onion (diced), 1 tablespoon fresh ginger (grated), 3 cups fresh broth, 1 cup coconut milk, 2 tablespoons coconut oil, 1 teaspoon salt.

Instructions: Sauté onion and ginger in coconut oil (5 minutes). Add carrots, broth, salt. Pressure cook 12 minutes. Quick release. Blend until smooth. Stir in coconut milk.

Sweet Potato Soup (Serves 4)

Ingredients: 4 large sweet potatoes (peeled and cubed), 1 onion (diced), 3 cups fresh broth, 1 cup coconut milk, 2 tablespoons coconut oil, 1 teaspoon salt, 1/4 teaspoon fresh ginger, fresh cilantro.

Instructions: Sauté onion in coconut oil (5 minutes). Add sweet potatoes, broth, salt, ginger. Pressure cook 15 minutes. Quick release. Blend smooth. Add coconut milk. Garnish with fresh cilantro.

14.8 Additional Salad Variations

Asian-Inspired Chicken Salad (Serves 2)

Ingredients: 4 cups mixed greens, 8 ounces grilled chicken (fresh), 1 cup cucumber (julienned), 1 cup carrots (julienned), 1/2 cup fresh cilantro, 1/4 cup fresh mint, Asian-style dressing (olive oil, fresh lime juice if tolerated, fresh ginger, salt, coconut aminos if tolerated).

Instructions: Arrange greens and vegetables on plates. Top with sliced chicken. Drizzle with dressing. Garnish with herbs.

Simple Garden Salad (Serves 2)

Ingredients: 4 cups mixed greens, 1 cup cucumber (sliced), 1 cup carrots (shredded), 1 cup bell pepper (sliced, if tolerated), 1/2 cup fresh herbs (basil, parsley), basic olive oil dressing.

Instructions: Combine all ingredients. Toss with dressing just before serving.

Roasted Vegetable Salad (Serves 2)

Ingredients: 4 cups mixed greens, 2 cups roasted vegetables (butternut squash, Brussels sprouts, carrots, prepared same day), 1/4 cup sunflower seeds (if tolerated), fresh herbs, olive oil dressing.

Instructions: Arrange greens on plates. Top with warm or room-temperature roasted vegetables. Add seeds and herbs. Dress immediately before eating.

14.9 Bringing It All Together

This chapter provided 30 soup and salad recipes designed for histamine safety through pressure cooking techniques and fresh ingredient emphasis. Pressure cooker soups achieve flavor development in 15-30 minutes rather than traditional 2-4 hour simmering, preventing bacterial histamine production while maintaining taste and texture quality.

Fresh vegetable soups from simple vegetable combinations to butternut squash and carrot ginger versions demonstrate variety within compliant parameters. Protein-packed salads using fresh cooked proteins, fresh vegetables, and homemade dressings provide complete meals. Grain-based salads use freshly cooked grains or frozen-reheated portions rather than refrigerated leftovers.

Homemade dressings using olive oil, fresh lemon juice, and fresh herbs replace commercial vinegar-based versions. Vegetable cream soups using coconut milk create rich texture without dairy. The case study illustrated how perceived restriction often exceeds actual restriction when modified techniques aren't explored.

Immediate consumption or rapid cooling followed by individual portion freezing enables batch cooking convenience while maintaining histamine safety. These principles apply equally to the poultry recipes in Chapter 15.0.

Chapter 15.0: Main Dishes Featuring Poultry

Benedictus surveyed his freezer with satisfaction. Six chicken breasts vacuum-sealed individually. Four turkey burgers. Three portions of ground turkey. All frozen immediately after cooking per Chapter 9.0 protocols. His protein situation looked solid. But Wednesday evening after work, staring at a frozen chicken breast, he felt uninspired. He'd grilled it last time. And the time before. And before that. The chicken was safe, fresh, properly stored. But preparing it the same way every time had created monotony despite successful dietary management. His limited cooking repertoire meant chicken always tasted similar regardless of accompanying vegetables or starches. He knew many people ate chicken multiple times weekly for years without boredom. What made the difference? The answer lay not in the protein itself but in preparation variety (Schnedl et al., 2019). Chicken breast accepts infinite flavor profiles through varied seasonings, cooking methods, and presentations. But without a repertoire of techniques, people default to their one reliable method repeatedly until boredom sets in.

This chapter provides 15 poultry-based main dish recipes emphasizing preparation variety. You will learn diverse chicken breast preparations beyond simple grilling, turkey dish options, Instant Pot chicken recipes, sheet pan dinner combinations, stir-fry and quick sauté techniques, and freezer-friendly options for batch cooking convenience.

15.1 Chicken Breast Preparation Methods

Chicken breast serves as staple protein for most histamine-intolerant individuals who tolerate poultry (Maintz & Novak, 2007). The key to sustainable chicken consumption is mastering multiple preparation methods that create distinct eating experiences from identical protein.

Pan-seared chicken uses high heat and brief cooking for crispy exterior and juicy interior. Pat chicken dry. Season with salt and desired herbs. Heat 2 tablespoons oil in skillet over medium-high heat. Add chicken. Cook undisturbed 5-7 minutes until golden crust forms. Flip. Cook 5-7 minutes more until internal temperature reaches 165°F. Rest 5 minutes before slicing.

Oven-baked chicken provides hands-off cooking. Preheat oven to 425°F. Season chicken with salt, garlic powder (if tolerated), and fresh herbs. Place on parchment-lined baking sheet. Bake 20-25 minutes until internal temperature reaches 165°F. The high temperature prevents drying while creating slight browning.

Instant Pot chicken cooks from fresh or frozen quickly. Place chicken breast in Instant Pot with 1 cup water or fresh broth. Season with salt and herbs. Cook high pressure 10 minutes (fresh) or 15 minutes (frozen). Quick release. Remove chicken. Use cooking liquid as base for sauce if desired.

Grilled chicken remains classic for good reason. Preheat grill to medium-high. Season chicken with salt and fresh herbs. Grill 6-8 minutes per side until internal temperature reaches 165°F and nice grill marks form. Let rest 5 minutes before serving.

Poached chicken creates tender, flavorful results. Bring pot of water or fresh broth to gentle simmer (not rolling boil). Season liquid with salt, fresh herbs, garlic cloves (if tolerated). Add chicken. Simmer 15-20 minutes until cooked through. Remove and use immediately or cool rapidly and freeze.

15.2 Diverse Chicken Recipes

Herb-Crusted Chicken Breast (Serves 4)

Ingredients: 4 chicken breasts, 1/4 cup fresh herbs (parsley, basil, thyme, or rosemary, finely chopped), 2 tablespoons olive oil, 1 teaspoon salt, 1/2 teaspoon garlic powder (if tolerated).

Instructions: Preheat oven to 425°F. Mix herbs, salt, garlic powder. Pat chicken dry. Brush with olive oil. Press herb mixture onto both sides of each breast. Place on parchment-lined baking sheet. Bake 22-25 minutes until internal temperature reaches 165°F.

Lemon Garlic Chicken (Serves 4, if lemon tolerated)

Ingredients: 4 chicken breasts, juice of 2 lemons, 4 garlic cloves (minced), 2 tablespoons olive oil, 1 teaspoon salt, fresh parsley.

Instructions: Combine lemon juice, garlic, olive oil, salt. Marinate chicken 15-30 minutes (no longer to prevent texture changes). Grill or pan-sear as directed in section 15.1. Garnish with fresh parsley.

Coconut Curry Chicken (Serves 4)

Ingredients: 4 chicken breasts (cubed), 1 can coconut milk (full-fat), 2 tablespoons coconut oil, 1 onion (diced), 2 teaspoons fresh ginger (grated), 1 teaspoon salt, 2 cups fresh vegetables (zucchini, bell peppers if tolerated), fresh cilantro, rice for serving.

Instructions: Heat coconut oil in large skillet. Sauté onion and ginger 3 minutes. Add chicken. Cook until no longer pink (5-7 minutes). Add coconut milk, salt, vegetables. Simmer 10 minutes until vegetables tender and sauce slightly thickens. Serve over fresh rice. Garnish with cilantro.

Sheet Pan Chicken and Vegetables (Serves 4)

Ingredients: 4 chicken breasts, 3 cups mixed vegetables (Brussels sprouts, carrots, sweet potato cubes), 3 tablespoons olive oil, 2 teaspoons salt, 1 teaspoon garlic powder (if tolerated), fresh rosemary.

Instructions: Preheat oven to 425°F. Toss vegetables with 2 tablespoons olive oil, 1 teaspoon salt, garlic powder. Spread on large baking sheet. Brush chicken with remaining oil. Season with remaining salt and fresh rosemary. Place chicken on sheet with vegetables. Bake 25-30 minutes until chicken reaches 165°F and vegetables are tender.

15.3 Turkey Based Dishes

Turkey provides leaner alternative to chicken with similar versatility (Schnedl et al., 2019).

Turkey Burgers (Serves 4)

Ingredients: 1 pound ground turkey (fresh, not refrigerated for days), 1/4 cup fresh onion (minced), 2 tablespoons fresh parsley (chopped), 1 teaspoon salt, 1/2 teaspoon garlic powder (if tolerated), 2 tablespoons coconut oil for cooking.

Instructions: Mix ground turkey, onion, parsley, salt, garlic powder gently (overworking makes tough burgers). Form into 4 patties. Heat coconut oil in skillet over medium heat. Cook burgers 5-6 minutes per side until internal temperature reaches 165°F. Serve with compliant sides.

Freezing note: Form extra burgers. Place parchment between each. Freeze in stack. Cook from frozen, adding 3-4 minutes per side.

Turkey Meatballs (Makes 20)

Ingredients: 1 pound ground turkey, 1/2 cup rice (cooked), 1 egg (if tolerated), 1/4 cup fresh parsley, 2 tablespoons fresh basil, 1 teaspoon salt, 1/2 teaspoon garlic powder (if tolerated).

Instructions: Preheat oven to 400°F. Mix all ingredients gently. Form into 1.5-inch balls. Place on parchment-lined baking sheet. Bake 20-25 minutes until internal temperature reaches 165°F. Cool rapidly. Freeze individual portions immediately.

Ground Turkey Lettuce Wraps (Serves 4)

Ingredients: 1 pound ground turkey, 2 tablespoons coconut oil, 1 onion (diced), 2 garlic cloves (minced, if tolerated), 1 cup carrots (shredded), 1 cup cucumber (diced), 1 teaspoon salt, 1 teaspoon fresh ginger (grated), fresh cilantro, butter lettuce leaves for wrapping.

Instructions: Heat coconut oil in large skillet. Cook onion and garlic 3 minutes. Add ground turkey. Cook until no longer pink, breaking into crumbles (7-10 minutes). Add ginger and salt. Remove from heat. Serve in lettuce leaves with carrots, cucumber, and fresh cilantro.

Roasted Turkey Breast (Serves 6-8)

Ingredients: 1 turkey breast (3-4 pounds), 3 tablespoons olive oil, 2 teaspoons salt, 1 teaspoon garlic powder (if tolerated), fresh rosemary and thyme.

Instructions: Preheat oven to 350°F. Pat turkey dry. Brush with olive oil. Season with salt, garlic powder, and fresh herbs. Place in roasting pan. Roast 1.5-2 hours until internal temperature reaches 165°F (20-25 minutes per pound). Let rest 15 minutes before slicing. Slice and freeze portions immediately after cooling.

15.4 Instant Pot Chicken Applications

Instant Pot chicken provides the fastest cooking method while producing tender results (Jiménez-Colmenero et al., 2001).

Instant Pot Whole Chicken (Serves 6)

Ingredients: 1 whole chicken (3-4 pounds), 1 cup fresh broth or water, 2 teaspoons salt, 1 teaspoon garlic powder (if tolerated), fresh herbs (rosemary, thyme).

Instructions: Season chicken inside and out with salt, garlic powder, and herbs. Place trivet in Instant Pot. Add liquid. Place chicken on trivet. Seal lid. Cook high pressure 25 minutes. Natural release 10 minutes, then quick release. Check internal temperature reaches 165°F. Let rest before carving.

Instant Pot Chicken Thighs (Serves 4)

Ingredients: 8 chicken thighs (bone-in or boneless), 1 cup fresh broth, 2 tablespoons coconut oil, 1 onion (diced), 2 teaspoons salt, 1 teaspoon garlic powder (if tolerated), fresh herbs.

Instructions: Set Instant Pot to sauté. Heat coconut oil. Brown chicken thighs 3 minutes per side. Remove. Sauté onion 3 minutes. Return chicken to pot. Add broth, salt, garlic powder, herbs. Seal lid. Cook high pressure 15 minutes. Quick release.

Shredded Chicken for Multiple Uses (Serves 6-8)

Ingredients: 2 pounds chicken breasts, 2 cups fresh broth, 1 onion (quartered), 2 teaspoons salt, 1 teaspoon garlic powder (if tolerated), fresh herbs.

Instructions: Place all ingredients in Instant Pot. Seal lid. Cook high pressure 15 minutes. Quick release. Remove chicken. Shred using two forks. Use immediately in various recipes or portion and freeze immediately after cooling.

Uses for shredded chicken: taco filling with compliant toppings, chicken salad with homemade dressing, soup addition, grain bowl topping, lettuce wrap filling.

15.5 Case Study: Preparation Variety Breakthrough

Background

Ianthe, a 43-year-old nurse working 12-hour shifts, relied heavily on batch-cooked chicken for weeknight meals. Every Sunday she grilled 10 chicken breasts, froze them individually, and reheated one nightly for dinner. This system provided convenience and ensured fresh protein following proper protocols. However, after eight months of this routine, she felt increasingly unenthusiastic about dinner despite good symptom control.

Presentation

Ianthe described her chicken as "boring but safe." She varied accompanying vegetables and starches but the chicken itself tasted identical every night. Grilled with salt and perhaps some garlic powder, reheated from frozen, sliced over vegetables or rice. She'd tried different vegetables, varied her starches, experimented with fresh herbs as garnish. But the protein remained monotonous.

Her solution had been eating less chicken and more of the side dishes, which reduced her protein intake below optimal levels. She felt hungrier between meals and noticed declining energy during long shifts. She knew she needed adequate protein but couldn't face another identical grilled chicken breast.

Analysis

Ianthe's situation demonstrates how single-method protein preparation creates unnecessary monotony even when the protein itself remains perfectly appropriate. She'd mastered one technique (grilling) and never developed others. Her chicken always tasted the same because she always cooked it the same way.

Research shows that preparation variety matters as much as ingredient variety for long-term dietary adherence (Raynor & Epstein, 2001). Eating chicken prepared five different ways feels more varied than eating five different vegetables with identically-prepared chicken. Ianthe needed technique expansion, not protein alternatives.

Intervention

A dietitian taught Ianthe four additional chicken preparation methods from section 15.1. They practiced pan-searing (creating crispy crust), oven-baking with herb coating, Instant Pot poaching for shredding, and coconut curry preparation. Each method produced distinct flavor and texture from the same chicken breast ingredient.

Her new Sunday routine involved preparing chicken using different methods. Two breasts pan-seared with fresh rosemary. Two breasts oven-baked with fresh basil coating. Two breasts Instant Pot cooked for shredding (used in wraps or salads). Two breasts cut into cubes for coconut curry (portioned with curry sauce for reheating). Two breasts traditionally grilled (her familiar preparation).

This diversity meant her Monday through Friday dinners featured five different chicken preparations rather than five identical grilled breasts. The variety required the same Sunday time investment (maybe 15 minutes longer total) but transformed her weeknight eating experience.

Outcome

Ianthe's enthusiasm for dinner returned. She looked forward to seeing which chicken preparation she'd labeled for each night. The pan-seared rosemary chicken tasted completely different from the coconut curry version despite both being chicken breast. Her protein consumption increased back to appropriate levels as meals became appealing again.

Three months later she'd expanded further, incorporating the turkey options from section 15.3 and adding ground turkey and turkey meatballs to her rotation. Her freezer now contained 15-20 different protein preparations rather than just grilled chicken, providing week-to-week variety that prevented repetition boredom.

Teaching Points

- Single-method protein preparation creates unnecessary monotony even when the protein itself is appropriate and properly handled, with cooking technique variety providing flavor and texture diversity that prevents boredom-driven underconsumption
- Batch cooking chicken using five different preparation methods requires minimal additional time compared to single-method cooking while creating weeknight meal variety that dramatically improves long-term adherence
- The relationship between preparation method and eating satisfaction often exceeds the relationship between ingredient choice and satisfaction, making technique expansion a more effective solution to protein monotony than seeking alternative protein sources

15.6 Stir Fries and Quick Sautés

Stir-frying provides fastest cooking method for weeknight meals (Schnedl et al., 2019). The high heat and constant movement cook proteins and vegetables in 10-15 minutes total.

Basic Chicken Stir-Fry (Serves 4)

Ingredients: 1 pound chicken breast (sliced thin), 3 tablespoons coconut oil, 1 onion (sliced), 2 cups mixed vegetables (bell peppers if tolerated, zucchini, carrots), 2 garlic cloves (minced, if tolerated), 1 teaspoon fresh ginger (grated), 2 tablespoons coconut aminos (if tolerated), salt, fresh cilantro, rice for serving.

Instructions: Heat 2 tablespoons oil in large skillet or wok over high heat. Add chicken. Stir-fry 5-6 minutes until cooked through. Remove. Add remaining oil, onion, vegetables, garlic, ginger. Stir-fry 3-4 minutes until crisp-tender. Return chicken. Add coconut aminos and salt. Toss 1 minute. Serve over fresh rice. Garnish with cilantro.

Lemon Chicken Sauté (Serves 4, if lemon tolerated)

Ingredients: 4 chicken breasts (pounded thin), 3 tablespoons olive oil, juice of 2 lemons, 3 garlic cloves (sliced), 1 teaspoon salt, fresh parsley, fresh thyme.

Instructions: Heat olive oil in large skillet over medium-high heat. Season chicken with salt. Cook 4-5 minutes per side until golden and cooked through. Remove. Add garlic to pan. Cook 1 minute. Add lemon juice, scraping up browned bits. Add fresh herbs. Pour sauce over chicken.

Quick Vegetable Chicken Sauté (Serves 4)

Ingredients: 1 pound chicken breast (cubed), 3 tablespoons coconut oil, 1 onion (diced), 3 cups mixed vegetables (zucchini, Brussels sprouts, carrots), 2 teaspoons salt, 1 teaspoon garlic powder (if tolerated), fresh basil.

Instructions: Heat oil over high heat. Add chicken. Cook 6-7 minutes until golden and cooked through. Remove. Add vegetables. Sauté 5-6 minutes until tender. Return chicken. Season with salt and garlic powder. Toss with fresh basil.

15.7 Freezer Friendly Options

Freezer-friendly preparations enable batch cooking without histamine concerns when properly frozen immediately (as discussed in Chapter 9.0).

Marinated Chicken for Freezing

Ingredients: 10 chicken breasts, 1 cup olive oil, juice of 4 lemons (if tolerated), 10 garlic cloves (minced, if tolerated), 1/4 cup fresh herbs (rosemary, thyme, basil), 2 tablespoons salt.

Instructions: Combine marinade ingredients. Divide chicken into portions (2 breasts per bag typically). Add marinade. Seal bags. Freeze flat. Cook from frozen by thawing in refrigerator overnight (use within 24 hours of complete thawing) or cook from frozen state, adding 5-10 minutes to cooking time.

Pre-Seasoned Chicken Packets

Prepare individual chicken breasts with different seasonings. Wrap each separately. Label with seasoning used (rosemary, garlic basil, lemon herb, plain salt, ginger cilantro). Freeze. Grab whichever flavor appeals when cooking.

Cooked and Frozen Chicken

The basic approach discussed throughout: cook fresh chicken using any method from section 15.1, cool rapidly, portion individually, freeze immediately, use within 2-3 weeks per Chapter 9.0 guidelines.

15.8 Summary and Applications

This chapter provided 25 poultry-based main dish recipes emphasizing preparation variety to prevent monotony. Chicken breast preparation methods including pan-searing, oven-baking, Instant Pot cooking, grilling, and poaching create distinct eating experiences from identical protein through technique variation.

Turkey dishes from burgers to meatballs to roasted breast provide leaner alternatives with similar versatility. Instant Pot applications cook poultry quickly from fresh or frozen while producing tender results. Sheet pan dinners combine protein and vegetables in single-pan preparations. Stir-fries and quick sautés provide weeknight speed with 10-15 minute total cooking times.

Freezer-friendly options through pre-seasoning, marinating, or batch cooking with immediate freezing enable convenience without compromising histamine safety. The case study illustrated how technique variety matters as much as ingredient variety for long-term satisfaction and adherence.

These poultry preparations form the foundation of sustainable histamine management, providing reliable protein sources prepared through multiple methods that prevent repetition fatigue while maintaining complete safety through fresh ingredients and proper cooking and storage protocols.

Chapter 16.0: Main Dishes with Seafood

Erasmus examined the fish counter with skepticism. The salmon fillet labeled "fresh" looked beautiful, but when had it actually been caught? The fishmonger couldn't answer. The halibut behind the counter appeared fresh too, but the fine print revealed "previously frozen, thawed for display three days ago." Three days of thawed storage meant substantial bacterial histamine production per Chapter 4.0. The vacuum-sealed frozen cod in the case below cost less and, paradoxically, likely contained less histamine than the expensive "fresh" display fish. This counterintuitive reality frustrates many people attempting histamine management (Visciano et al., 2012). Cultural associations equate fresh with superior and frozen with inferior. For histamine intolerance, these assumptions invert. Properly flash-frozen seafood often provides superior safety to "fresh" fish that's been thawed for retail display or transported refrigerated for days before sale.

This chapter provides 14 meat and seafood main dish recipes emphasizing fresh fish preparations, grass-fed beef and lamb options, quick-cooking protein methods, one-pan meal solutions, freezer-to-table dinners, and safe seafood selection strategies for optimal histamine management.

16.1 Fresh Fish Preparation Methods

Fresh fish represents the most challenging protein category for histamine management due to rapid histamine formation post-catch (Lehane & Olley, 2000). Fish contains high levels of **histidine**, the amino acid that bacteria convert to histamine. This conversion begins immediately after death and accelerates with each hour of inadequate refrigeration.

Pan-seared fish provides the fastest cooking method preserving delicate texture. Pat fish completely dry (moisture prevents browning). Season with salt. Heat 2 tablespoons oil in skillet over medium-high heat. Place fish skin-side down if skin-on. Cook undisturbed 3-4 minutes until golden crust forms. Flip gently. Cook 2-3 minutes more until just cooked through (flesh turns opaque and flakes easily). Total cooking time: 6-8 minutes for typical fillet thickness.

Baked fish requires slightly longer cooking but allows hands-off preparation. Preheat oven to 400°F. Place seasoned fish on parchment-lined baking sheet. Drizzle with olive oil. Bake 10-15 minutes depending on thickness (rule of thumb: 10 minutes per inch of thickness at the thickest point). Fish is done when internal temperature reaches 145°F and flesh flakes easily.

Instant Pot fish cooks from frozen efficiently. Place trivet in Instant Pot. Add 1 cup water. Place frozen fish fillet on trivet. Season with salt and fresh herbs. Seal lid. Cook high pressure 3-5 minutes depending on thickness. Quick release. Remove carefully (fish will be delicate).

Grilled fish works best with firm fish like halibut, mahi-mahi, or swordfish. Oil grill grates well to prevent sticking. Season fish with salt and oil. Grill over medium-high heat 4-5 minutes per side for 1-inch thick fillets. Use fish spatula for careful flipping (fish is fragile when cooked).

16.2 Safe Seafood Selection

Flash-frozen fish from reputable sources provides the most reliable histamine safety (Visciano et al., 2012). Fish frozen within hours of catch maintains minimal histamine. Vacuum-sealed packaging prevents freezer burn. Common flash-frozen options include wild-caught salmon, cod, halibut, mahi-mahi, and sole.

Wild-caught vs farmed matters less for histamine than freezing timing and cold chain maintenance. Both can be safe if properly handled. Wild-caught often undergoes boat freezing immediately after catch. Some farmed fish travels refrigerated for days before sale, accumulating histamine. Verify freezing and handling regardless of source.

Mercury considerations affect fish selection beyond histamine concerns. High-mercury fish (tuna, swordfish, king mackerel) should be limited regardless of histamine status. Low-mercury options (salmon, cod, sole, sardines, anchovies) provide safer frequent consumption. However, note that sardines and anchovies, while low-mercury, are typically canned and aged, making them high-histamine.

Fresh fish verification requires asking direct questions per Chapter 10.0. "Was this fish previously frozen?" If yes, "When was it thawed?" If more than 24 hours ago, the frozen version is safer. "When was this fish caught?" If more than 48 hours ago and never frozen, histamine levels may be elevated. "Is this fish sushi-grade?" Sushi-grade designation requires proper freezing, indicating better handling.

16.3 Fish Recipe Collection

Simple Baked Cod (Serves 4)

Ingredients: 4 cod fillets (6 oz each, fresh or properly frozen), 2 tablespoons olive oil, 1 teaspoon salt, 1/2 teaspoon garlic powder (if tolerated), fresh parsley, fresh lemon slices (if lemon tolerated) for garnish.

Instructions: Preheat oven to 400°F. Pat fish dry. Place on parchment-lined baking sheet. Brush with olive oil. Season with salt and garlic powder. Bake 12-15 minutes until flesh flakes easily. Garnish with fresh parsley and lemon if tolerated.

Pan-Seared Salmon (Serves 4)

Ingredients: 4 salmon fillets (6 oz each, skin-on), 2 tablespoons coconut oil, 1 teaspoon salt, fresh dill.

Instructions: Pat salmon completely dry. Season with salt. Heat coconut oil in large skillet over medium-high heat. Place salmon skin-side down. Cook undisturbed 4-5 minutes until skin is crispy. Flip. Cook 2-3 minutes more until just cooked through (medium doneness). Garnish with fresh dill.

Halibut with Fresh Herbs (Serves 4)

Ingredients: 4 halibut steaks (6 oz each), 3 tablespoons olive oil, 1 teaspoon salt, 1/4 cup fresh herbs (parsley, basil, cilantro, chopped), 2 garlic cloves (minced, if tolerated).

Instructions: Mix olive oil, salt, herbs, and garlic. Brush over halibut. Let sit 10 minutes. Heat grill or grill pan to medium-high. Grill 4-5 minutes per side until just cooked through.

Instant Pot Fish Stew (Serves 6)

Ingredients: 1.5 pounds firm white fish (cut into chunks), 2 tablespoons coconut oil, 1 onion (diced), 2 carrots (sliced), 2 celery stalks (sliced), 4 cups fresh vegetable broth, 2 cups cauliflower florets, 1 teaspoon salt, fresh parsley.

Instructions: Set Instant Pot to sauté. Heat oil. Cook onion, carrots, celery 5 minutes. Add broth, cauliflower, salt. Add fish chunks on top. Seal lid. Cook high pressure 5 minutes. Quick release. Stir gently. Garnish with fresh parsley. Serve immediately.

16.4 Beef and Lamb Preparations

Grass-fed beef provides nutrient benefits over conventional beef (Daley et al., 2010). For histamine management, freshness matters more than feeding method. Purchase grass-fed beef from sources confirming processing dates within past 3-5 days or properly frozen immediately after processing.

Ground Beef Basics (Serves 4)

Ingredients: 1 pound grass-fed ground beef (fresh, not refrigerated for days), 2 tablespoons coconut oil, 1 onion (diced), 2 teaspoons salt, 1 teaspoon garlic powder (if tolerated), fresh herbs.

Instructions: Heat coconut oil in large skillet. Add onion. Cook 3 minutes. Add ground beef. Break into crumbles. Cook until no longer pink (7-10 minutes). Season with salt and garlic powder. Stir in fresh herbs.

Uses: Taco filling with compliant toppings, over rice for burrito bowl, mixed with vegetables for hash, formed into meatballs.

Pan-Seared Steak (Serves 2)

Ingredients: 2 grass-fed steaks (ribeye, strip, or sirloin, 8 oz each), 2 tablespoons coconut oil, 2 teaspoons salt, fresh rosemary.

Instructions: Remove steaks from refrigerator 30 minutes before cooking (room temperature cooks more evenly). Pat completely dry. Season generously with salt. Heat coconut oil in cast iron skillet over high heat until very hot. Add steaks. Cook undisturbed 3-4 minutes until deep brown crust forms. Flip. Add fresh rosemary sprigs to pan. Cook 3-4 minutes more for medium-rare (130-135°F internal temperature). Rest 5 minutes before serving.

Instant Pot Beef Stew (Serves 6)

Ingredients: 2 pounds grass-fed beef chuck (cut into 1.5-inch cubes), 2 tablespoons coconut oil, 1 onion (diced), 4 carrots (cut into chunks), 4 celery stalks (cut into chunks), 3 cups fresh beef broth or vegetable broth, 2 teaspoons salt, 1 teaspoon garlic powder (if tolerated), fresh thyme.

Instructions: Set Instant Pot to sauté. Heat oil. Brown beef in batches (don't crowd pan), 2-3 minutes per side. Remove. Sauté onion 3 minutes. Return beef. Add remaining vegetables, broth, salt, garlic powder, thyme. Seal lid. Cook high pressure 35 minutes. Natural release 10 minutes, then quick release. Serve immediately or cool rapidly and freeze portions.

Lamb Chops (Serves 4)

Ingredients: 8 lamb chops, 2 tablespoons olive oil, 2 teaspoons salt, 1 teaspoon garlic powder (if tolerated), fresh rosemary.

Instructions: Pat lamb chops dry. Season with salt and garlic powder. Heat olive oil in large skillet over high heat. Add lamb chops. Cook 3-4 minutes per side for medium-rare (internal temperature 135°F). Add fresh rosemary to pan during last minute. Rest 5 minutes before serving.

16.5 One Pan Meal Solutions

One-pan meals combine protein and vegetables on a single sheet pan or in one skillet, minimizing cleanup while maintaining proper cooking protocols (Schnedl et al., 2019).

Sheet Pan Salmon and Vegetables (Serves 4)

Ingredients: 4 salmon fillets (6 oz each), 3 cups Brussels sprouts (halved), 2 cups carrots (cut into sticks), 3 tablespoons olive oil (divided), 2 teaspoons salt (divided), fresh dill.

Instructions: Preheat oven to 425°F. Toss vegetables with 2 tablespoons olive oil and 1 teaspoon salt. Spread on large baking sheet. Roast 15 minutes. Remove from oven. Push vegetables to sides. Place salmon fillets in center. Brush salmon with remaining olive oil. Season with remaining salt. Return to oven. Roast 12-15 minutes until salmon is cooked through and vegetables are tender. Garnish with fresh dill.

Skillet Beef and Vegetable Hash (Serves 4)

Ingredients: 1 pound ground beef, 2 tablespoons coconut oil, 1 onion (diced), 3 cups sweet potato (diced small), 2 cups zucchini (diced), 2 teaspoons salt, 1 teaspoon garlic powder (if tolerated), fresh parsley.

Instructions: Heat coconut oil in large skillet over medium-high heat. Add onion and sweet potato. Cook 8-10 minutes, stirring occasionally, until sweet potato begins softening. Add ground beef. Break into crumbles. Cook until no longer pink (7-10 minutes). Add zucchini. Cook 3-4 minutes more until tender. Season with salt and garlic powder. Garnish with fresh parsley.

One-Pan Chicken and Root Vegetables (Serves 4)

Ingredients: 4 chicken thighs (bone-in), 3 cups mixed root vegetables (carrots, parsnips, turnips, cut into chunks), 3 tablespoons olive oil (divided), 2 teaspoons salt (divided), 1 teaspoon garlic powder (if tolerated), fresh rosemary.

Instructions: Preheat oven to 425°F. Toss vegetables with 2 tablespoons oil, 1 teaspoon salt, garlic powder. Spread on large baking sheet. Brush chicken with remaining oil. Season with remaining salt and fresh rosemary. Place chicken on vegetables. Roast 35-40 minutes until chicken reaches 165°F internal temperature and vegetables are tender.

16.6 Case Study: Seafood Safety Navigation

Background

Clotilde, a 50-year-old librarian, loved seafood before her histamine intolerance diagnosis. Fish had been her primary protein. Post-diagnosis, she avoided seafood entirely, assuming all fish was problematic. Her protein variety decreased substantially. She relied almost exclusively on chicken and occasional turkey, creating dietary monotony despite otherwise successful histamine management.

Presentation

After six months of strict chicken-based eating, Clotilde reported good symptom control but increasing meal dissatisfaction. She missed the flavor variety that seafood had provided. She'd tried asking about "fresh" fish at her local market but received conflicting information. One fishmonger insisted their fish was "fresh daily" while another admitted most "fresh" fish had been thawed for display several days earlier.

She felt confused about conflicting guidance. Some online sources said all fish was off-limits for histamine intolerance. Others suggested certain fish was acceptable. She couldn't reconcile these contradictions with her limited understanding of histamine formation in seafood.

Analysis

Clotilde's complete seafood avoidance reflected a common pattern. People hear "fish is high histamine" without understanding the nuance that histamine forms after catch rather than being inherent to fish itself (Visciano et al., 2012). Fresh fish properly handled contains minimal histamine. The same fish sitting thawed for three days contains substantial histamine. The protein itself hasn't changed. The handling has.

Her confusion about "fresh" labeling stemmed from unregulated use of the term. Retailers use "fresh" to mean "not frozen at point of sale" regardless of when the fish was thawed. Fish thawed Monday and sold "fresh" Friday has spent four days accumulating histamine despite technically accurate "fresh" labeling.

Intervention

A dietitian taught Clotilde seafood safety principles from section 16.2. They discussed flash-frozen fish superiority over thawed-for-display fish. Flash-frozen wild-caught salmon, properly stored frozen and either cooked from frozen or thawed immediately before cooking, contained less histamine than expensive "fresh" salmon thawed three days earlier.

She learned to ask specific questions: "Is this fish previously frozen?" "When was it thawed?" "Can I purchase it frozen instead?" She discovered that frozen wild-caught salmon cost less than thawed display salmon while providing better histamine safety.

They developed a simple seafood strategy. Purchase vacuum-sealed frozen fish (salmon, cod, halibut). Store in freezer. Either cook from frozen using Instant Pot method (section 16.1) or thaw in refrigerator overnight and cook within 24 hours. Never purchase fish thawed more than 24 hours earlier regardless of how fresh it appears.

Outcome

Clotilde reintegrated seafood successfully. She cooked salmon twice weekly using frozen fillets. Her Instant Pot method meant removing frozen fillet from freezer, seasoning, pressure cooking 5 minutes, eating fresh fish with zero thaw time and zero histamine accumulation from thawed storage. The convenience rivaled her simplest chicken preparations.

Her dietary satisfaction improved substantially. The flavor variety from salmon and cod prevented the monotony that had been developing. Her symptom control remained excellent. She experienced no reactions to properly handled frozen-then-cooked fish, confirming that complete seafood avoidance had been unnecessary restriction rather than medical necessity.

Teaching Points

- Complete seafood avoidance often reflects misunderstanding that histamine forms during handling and storage rather than being inherent to fish, with properly frozen and handled fish providing safe protein options when sourcing and preparation follow appropriate protocols
- Flash-frozen fish purchased frozen and either cooked from frozen or thawed immediately before cooking contains less histamine than "fresh" fish that has been thawed for retail display, inverting common assumptions about fresh superiority
- Strategic seafood consumption through frozen fish sourcing and rapid cooking methods enables dietary variety without compromising histamine

safety, demonstrating how understanding mechanisms allows informed decisions rather than blanket restrictions

16.7 Freezer to Table Dinners

Freezer-to-table meals cook directly from frozen state, eliminating thawing time and associated histamine risks (Jiménez-Colmenero et al., 2001).

Frozen Salmon Sheet Pan (Serves 4)

Ingredients: 4 frozen salmon fillets (individually wrapped), 3 cups frozen vegetables (broccoli, cauliflower, carrots), 3 tablespoons olive oil, 2 teaspoons salt, fresh dill.

Instructions: Preheat oven to 425°F. Arrange frozen salmon and frozen vegetables on large baking sheet. Drizzle with olive oil. Season with salt. Bake 25-30 minutes until salmon reaches 145°F internal temperature. Garnish with fresh dill.

Instant Pot Frozen Chicken and Rice (Serves 4)

Ingredients: 4 frozen chicken breasts, 2 cups rice, 3 cups fresh broth, 2 cups frozen vegetables, 2 teaspoons salt, 1 teaspoon garlic powder (if tolerated).

Instructions: Place frozen chicken in Instant Pot. Add rice, broth, frozen vegetables, salt, garlic powder. Seal lid. Cook high pressure 25 minutes. Natural release 10 minutes, then quick release. Fluff rice and serve.

Frozen Beef Stir-Fry (Serves 4)

Ingredients: 1 pound beef (sliced thin, frozen in marinade per section 15.7), 3 tablespoons coconut oil, 4 cups frozen stir-fry vegetables, 2 tablespoons coconut aminos (if tolerated), salt, rice for serving.

Instructions: Heat coconut oil in large skillet or wok over high heat. Add frozen beef. Cook, breaking apart as it thaws, until browned (8-10 minutes). Add frozen vegetables. Stir-fry 5-7 minutes until heated through. Add coconut aminos and salt. Serve over fresh rice.

16.8 Key Concepts Review

This chapter provided meat and seafood main dish recipes emphasizing histamine-safe preparation methods. Fresh fish preparations prioritize rapid cooking through pan-searing, baking, Instant Pot methods, and grilling. Safe seafood selection focuses on flash-frozen fish over "fresh" thawed display fish, with verification questions ensuring proper handling.

Beef and lamb preparations from grass-fed sources emphasize processing date verification and proper storage. One-pan meals combining proteins and vegetables on sheet pans or in skillets simplify preparation while maintaining safety. Freezer-to-table dinners cook proteins directly from frozen state, eliminating thaw-time histamine formation.

The case study illustrated how complete seafood avoidance often reflects misunderstanding rather than necessity, with proper frozen fish sourcing enabling safe consumption. Strategic use of vacuum-sealed frozen fish, rapid cooking methods, and immediate consumption or proper freezing maintains histamine safety while providing protein variety.

Chapter 17.0: Plant Based Protein Options

Faustina examined the dried lentils in her pantry with renewed interest. She'd abandoned legumes early in elimination, having read they were "high histamine." But rereading Chapter 6.0's reintroduction guidance, she realized the issue was preparation method rather than the legumes themselves. Canned legumes aged in their liquid for months, allowing bacterial histamine formation. Dried legumes cooked fresh contained minimal histamine (Reese et al., 2018). The pressure cooker sitting unused in her cabinet could transform dried lentils into tender, histamine-safe protein in 15 minutes rather than the hours of traditional simmering. This distinction between preparation methods rather than inherent food properties appears repeatedly in histamine management but often gets oversimplified to "legumes are high histamine," causing unnecessary restriction. Understanding mechanisms rather than memorizing lists enables appropriate decisions about food categories that work when prepared properly but cause problems when handled incorrectly.

This chapter provides 12 plant-based and vegetarian recipes emphasizing protein-rich pressure-cooked legumes, vegetable-forward mains, ancient grain bowls, plant-based protein combinations, and vegan-friendly options maintaining histamine safety through fresh preparation and immediate consumption.

17.1 Pressure Cooked Legume Fundamentals

Pressure cooking legumes from dried state produces safe, protein-rich foods when prepared and consumed properly (Schnedl et al., 2019). The high pressure and temperature cook beans, lentils, and chickpeas in 10-30 minutes rather than 1-3 hours of traditional simmering.

Soaking requirements vary by legume. Lentils and split peas require no soaking. Chickpeas, black beans, kidney beans, and pinto beans benefit from 4-8 hour soaking to reduce cooking time and improve digestibility. Soaking water should be discarded and fresh water used for cooking.

Instant Pot legume cooking follows standard protocols. Rinse dried legumes thoroughly. Add to Instant Pot with fresh water (3 cups water per 1 cup dried legumes). Add salt (1 teaspoon per cup dried legumes). Seal lid. Cook on high pressure for appropriate time: lentils 10 minutes, split peas 15 minutes, chickpeas 30-35 minutes (soaked) or 50-60 minutes (unsoaked), black beans 25-30 minutes (soaked), kidney beans 25-30 minutes (soaked).

Immediate consumption or freezing prevents histamine formation. Cooked legumes should be consumed within 24 hours if refrigerated or frozen immediately after rapid cooling for storage up to three months per Chapter 9.0.

17.2 Lentil Based Dishes

Lentils provide the fastest-cooking legume option with highest protein density (Marinangeli & House, 2017).

Basic Instant Pot Lentils (Serves 6)

Ingredients: 2 cups green or brown lentils (rinsed), 6 cups water, 2 teaspoons salt, 1 onion (diced), 2 carrots (diced), 2 celery stalks (diced), 2 teaspoons garlic powder (if tolerated), fresh parsley.

Instructions: Combine all ingredients except parsley in Instant Pot. Seal lid. Cook high pressure 10 minutes. Natural release 10 minutes, then quick release. Stir in fresh parsley. Serve immediately over rice or freeze portions.

Lentil and Vegetable Stew (Serves 6)

Ingredients: 1.5 cups lentils, 1 tablespoon coconut oil, 1 onion (diced), 3 carrots (diced), 3 celery stalks (diced), 4 cups fresh vegetable broth, 2 cups cauliflower florets, 2 teaspoons salt, 1 teaspoon fresh ginger (grated), fresh cilantro.

Instructions: Set Instant Pot to sauté. Heat oil. Cook onion, carrots, celery 5 minutes. Add lentils, broth, salt, ginger. Seal lid. Cook high pressure 10 minutes. Quick release. Add cauliflower. Seal lid. Cook high pressure 2 minutes. Quick release. Stir in fresh cilantro.

Lentil Curry (Serves 6)

Ingredients: 2 cups red lentils (rinsed), 1 can coconut milk, 3 cups water, 1 tablespoon coconut oil, 1 onion (diced), 2 teaspoons fresh ginger (grated), 2 teaspoons salt, 3 cups fresh spinach (if tolerated), fresh cilantro.

Instructions: Set Instant Pot to sauté. Heat oil. Cook onion and ginger 3 minutes. Add lentils, coconut milk, water, salt. Seal lid. Cook high pressure 8 minutes. Quick release. Stir in spinach until wilted. Garnish with fresh cilantro. Serve over rice.

17.3 Chickpea Preparations

Chickpeas require longer cooking but provide substantial protein and fiber (Marinangeli & House, 2017).

Instant Pot Chickpeas (Serves 6)

Ingredients: 1 pound dried chickpeas (soaked 4-8 hours, drained), 6 cups fresh water, 1 tablespoon salt.

Instructions: Combine chickpeas, water, salt in Instant Pot. Seal lid. Cook high pressure 35 minutes. Natural release 15 minutes, then quick release. Drain. Use immediately in recipes or freeze portions.

Chickpea and Vegetable Bowl (Serves 4)

Ingredients: 3 cups cooked chickpeas (fresh), 3 tablespoons olive oil, 1 teaspoon salt, 1 teaspoon garlic powder (if tolerated), 4 cups roasted vegetables (Brussels sprouts, carrots, cauliflower), fresh parsley, rice or quinoa for serving.

Instructions: Toss chickpeas with olive oil, salt, garlic powder. Roast at 400°F for 20-25 minutes until crispy. Serve over rice or quinoa with roasted vegetables. Garnish with fresh parsley.

Mashed Chickpea Spread (Serves 4)

Ingredients: 2 cups cooked chickpeas (fresh), 1/4 cup olive oil, 2 tablespoons fresh lemon juice (if tolerated), 1 garlic clove (if tolerated), 1/2 teaspoon salt, fresh parsley.

Instructions: Combine chickpeas, olive oil, lemon juice, garlic, salt in food processor. Process until smooth but still chunky. Stir in fresh parsley. Serve with rice cakes or fresh vegetables. Use within 24 hours.

17.4 Ancient Grain Bowls

Ancient grains including quinoa, millet, and amaranth provide complete or near-complete protein profiles (Vega-Gálvez et al., 2010).

Quinoa Buddha Bowl (Serves 4)

Ingredients: 2 cups cooked quinoa (fresh), 2 cups roasted sweet potato (cubed), 2 cups roasted Brussels sprouts, 1 cup fresh cucumber (diced), 1 avocado (sliced, if tolerated in tested portions), fresh cilantro, tahini dressing (tahini, olive oil, fresh lemon juice if tolerated, water to thin, salt).

Instructions: Divide quinoa among bowls. Top with roasted vegetables, cucumber, avocado. Drizzle with tahini dressing. Garnish with fresh cilantro.

Millet Pilaf (Serves 6)

Ingredients: 2 cups millet (rinsed), 4 cups fresh vegetable broth, 2 tablespoons coconut oil, 1 onion (diced), 2 carrots (diced), 2 celery stalks (diced), 1 teaspoon salt, fresh parsley.

Instructions: Heat coconut oil in large pot. Sauté onion, carrots, celery 5 minutes. Add millet. Toast 2 minutes. Add broth and salt. Bring to boil. Reduce heat, cover, simmer 20-25 minutes until liquid absorbed. Fluff with fork. Stir in fresh parsley.

Amaranth Porridge Bowl (Serves 2)

Ingredients: 1 cup amaranth, 3 cups water, 1/4 teaspoon salt, 1 cup coconut milk, 2 tablespoons maple syrup, fresh blueberries, coconut flakes.

Instructions: Combine amaranth, water, salt in pot. Bring to boil. Reduce heat, simmer uncovered 20 minutes, stirring occasionally, until creamy. Stir in coconut milk and maple syrup. Serve topped with fresh blueberries and coconut flakes.

17.5 Case Study: Legume Liberation

Background

Apollonia, a 35-year-old vegetarian yoga instructor, struggled with protein adequacy after her histamine intolerance diagnosis. Pre-diagnosis, legumes formed her protein foundation. She'd relied on canned beans and chickpeas for convenient meals. Post-diagnosis, she'd read that legumes were high histamine and eliminated them completely.

Presentation

Six months into elimination without legumes, Apollonia felt constantly hungry. Her vegetarian protein options had shrunk to eggs (if tolerated), fresh-cooked quinoa, and occasional nuts (if tolerated in small amounts). She lost eight pounds unintentionally. Her energy declined, particularly noticeable during yoga teaching when she felt weak during demonstrations.

She'd tried increasing egg consumption but found eating eggs more than once daily unappealing. Quinoa provided some protein but not enough when it was her only significant source. She felt trapped between her ethical vegetarian commitment and her medical dietary needs.

Analysis

Apollonia's struggle demonstrated how oversimplified guidance ("legumes are high histamine") creates problems when people don't understand the underlying mechanism. Canned legumes sitting in liquid for months do contain elevated histamine. This fact doesn't mean all legumes are problematic (Reese et al., 2018).

Dried legumes cooked fresh from dried state contain minimal histamine. The aging occurs in canned versions, not in the legumes themselves. Her complete legume elimination was unnecessary restriction that compromised her nutritional adequacy and sustainability.

Intervention

A dietitian explained the canned versus dried legume distinction. They discussed pressure cooking as the solution to Apollonia's time constraints (she'd avoided dried legumes assuming they required hours of cooking she didn't have).

She purchased an Instant Pot and learned basic legume cooking from section 17.1. Lentils cooked in 10 minutes. Chickpeas took 35 minutes but required zero active time (set and forget). She could start chickpeas cooking, teach a yoga class, return home to cooked chickpeas ready for dinner.

They developed a Sunday batch cooking routine. Cook 2-3 types of legumes (lentils, chickpeas, black beans). Portion into individual servings. Freeze immediately after cooling. Throughout week, thaw and use portions in various recipes. This eliminated daily cooking while maintaining freshness through proper freezing.

Outcome

Apollonia reintegrated legumes successfully. Her protein intake increased substantially. She regained the lost weight over three months, returning to her healthy baseline. Her energy improved, particularly during extended yoga sessions. She felt satisfied after meals again rather than constantly hungry.

Her symptom control remained excellent. Fresh-cooked legumes caused zero reactions, confirming that her complete avoidance had been based on misunderstanding rather than actual intolerance. She developed 10-12 different legume-based meals rotating through her weekly menu, providing variety she'd been missing.

Six months later, she reported that understanding the canned versus dried distinction had been transformative. The simple shift from "all legumes are high histamine" to "aged canned legumes are high histamine but fresh-cooked dried legumes are safe" restored a major food category and made her dietary pattern sustainable long-term.

Teaching Points

- Oversimplified guidance about entire food categories being "high histamine" creates unnecessary restriction when the actual issue involves specific preparation or storage methods rather than inherent food properties, with fresh-cooked dried legumes demonstrating safety despite canned versions containing elevated histamine
- Pressure cooking enables practical dried legume preparation in timeframes competitive with opening canned versions, removing the convenience barrier that often drives selection of higher-histamine prepared options over safer fresh-cooked alternatives
- Strategic batch cooking and immediate freezing of fresh-cooked legumes provides both safety and convenience through preparing larger quantities once weekly and freezing portions for use throughout the week within appropriate storage timeframes

17.6 Vegetable Forward Mains

Vegetable-focused main dishes provide nutrients and satisfaction when constructed with adequate protein and healthy fats (Schnedl et al., 2019).

Cauliflower Steaks (Serves 4)

Ingredients: 2 large cauliflower heads, 4 tablespoons olive oil, 2 teaspoons salt, 1 teaspoon garlic powder (if tolerated), fresh herbs (parsley, basil, or cilantro).

Instructions: Preheat oven to 425°F. Remove outer leaves from cauliflower. Cut into 1-inch thick slices through center (4 steaks total, save remaining florets for other use). Brush both sides with olive oil. Season with salt and garlic powder. Place on parchment-lined baking sheet. Roast 20 minutes. Flip. Roast 15-20 minutes more until golden and tender. Garnish with fresh herbs.

Stuffed Bell Peppers (Serves 4, if peppers tolerated)

Ingredients: 4 large bell peppers, 2 cups cooked quinoa, 1.5 cups cooked chickpeas, 1 cup fresh vegetables (zucchini, onion, diced), 2 tablespoons olive oil, 1 teaspoon salt, fresh parsley.

Instructions: Preheat oven to 375°F. Cut tops off peppers. Remove seeds. Mix quinoa, chickpeas, vegetables, olive oil, salt. Stuff into peppers. Place in baking dish. Cover with foil. Bake 30 minutes. Remove foil. Bake 10 minutes more until peppers are tender.

Zucchini Noodle Primavera (Serves 4)

Ingredients: 4 large zucchini (spiralized into noodles), 2 tablespoons olive oil, 2 cups mixed fresh vegetables (bell peppers if tolerated, carrots, cauliflower), 2 garlic cloves (minced, if tolerated), 1 teaspoon salt, fresh basil, optional cooked chickpeas for added protein.

Instructions: Heat olive oil in large skillet. Sauté vegetables and garlic 5-7 minutes until tender. Add zucchini noodles. Toss 2-3 minutes until just softened (don't overcook). Season with salt. Toss with fresh basil. Add chickpeas if using.

17.7 Core Principles Recap

This chapter provided plant-based and vegetarian recipes maintaining histamine safety through fresh preparation methods. Pressure-cooked legumes from dried state offer substantial protein when cooked fresh and consumed within 24 hours or frozen immediately. Lentils provide fastest cooking option (10 minutes), while chickpeas require longer (35 minutes) but still remain practical.

Ancient grain bowls using quinoa, millet, and amaranth combine complete proteins with vegetables and compliant dressings. Vegetable-forward mains from cauliflower steaks to zucchini noodle dishes demonstrate satisfying plant-based eating when augmented with protein sources.

The case study illustrated how oversimplified guidance about entire food categories creates unnecessary restriction. Understanding that canned legumes differ fundamentally from fresh-cooked dried legumes enables appropriate decisions. Strategic batch cooking and freezing allows convenience without compromising safety.

Chapter 18.0: Side Dishes and Vegetables

Galatea stood before her oven watching Brussels sprouts roast, contemplating why this simple preparation tasted so much better than steamed versions. The high heat caramelized natural sugars, creating complex flavors absent in gentler cooking methods. She'd spent months eating steamed vegetables during elimination, assuming that was the "healthiest" preparation. But steaming every vegetable created monotonous flavors that made eating them feel medicinal rather than enjoyable. Learning that roasting, sautéing, and other high-heat methods didn't compromise histamine safety while dramatically improving flavor transformed her vegetable consumption. This distinction between preparation methods affecting palatability versus safety appears frequently in dietary management (Dewanto et al., 2002). Many preparation techniques enhance flavor, texture, and nutrient availability without creating histamine concerns. Understanding which variables matter for histamine (cooking time, storage after cooking) versus which don't (roasting versus steaming, high versus low heat during cooking) prevents unnecessary restriction of enjoyable preparations.

This chapter provides 19 side dish and vegetable recipes emphasizing roasted vegetables, quick sautéed greens, grain sides using rice and quinoa, potato and root vegetable preparations, fresh vegetable combinations, and make-ahead sides supporting meal prep efficiency while maintaining histamine safety.

18.1 Roasted Vegetable Fundamentals

Roasting vegetables at high heat (400-450°F) creates caramelization and complex flavors through Maillard reactions and sugar browning (Dewanto et al., 2002). The cooking method itself doesn't create histamine. Proper roasting takes 20-40 minutes depending on vegetable density, well within safe cooking timeframes from Chapter 8.0.

Basic roasting technique applies universally across vegetables. Preheat oven to 425°F (higher heat creates better browning). Cut vegetables into uniform sizes for even cooking. Toss with olive oil or coconut oil (1-2 tablespoons per pound of vegetables). Season with salt (1 teaspoon per pound). Spread in single layer on parchment-lined baking sheet (crowding creates steaming rather than roasting). Roast until tender and browned, stirring halfway through.

Timing guidelines vary by vegetable density. Soft vegetables like zucchini and bell peppers: 20-25 minutes. Medium vegetables like Brussels sprouts and cauliflower: 25-30 minutes. Dense vegetables like carrots and sweet potatoes: 35-45 minutes. Root vegetables like beets and turnips: 40-50 minutes.

Immediate consumption or freezing follows standard protocols. Roasted vegetables eaten immediately contain minimal histamine. Roasted vegetables cooled rapidly and frozen immediately maintain quality for 2-3 months per Chapter 9.0. Roasted vegetables refrigerated as leftovers should be consumed within 24 hours.

18.2 Roasted Vegetable Recipes

Perfect Roasted Brussels Sprouts (Serves 4)

Ingredients: 1.5 pounds Brussels sprouts (trimmed and halved), 2 tablespoons olive oil, 1 teaspoon salt, 1/2 teaspoon garlic powder (if tolerated).

Instructions: Preheat oven to 425°F. Toss Brussels sprouts with oil, salt, garlic powder. Spread cut-side down on parchment-lined baking sheet. Roast 25-30 minutes until deeply browned and tender, stirring once halfway through.

Roasted Cauliflower (Serves 4)

Ingredients: 1 large cauliflower head (cut into florets), 2 tablespoons olive oil, 1 teaspoon salt, fresh herbs (optional: rosemary, thyme, or parsley).

Instructions: Preheat oven to 425°F. Toss cauliflower with oil and salt. Roast 25-30 minutes until golden brown and tender. Toss with fresh herbs before serving.

Caramelized Carrots (Serves 4)

Ingredients: 2 pounds carrots (peeled and cut into sticks), 2 tablespoons coconut oil, 1 teaspoon salt, 1 tablespoon maple syrup (optional for enhanced caramelization).

Instructions: Preheat oven to 400°F. Toss carrots with oil, salt, and maple syrup if using. Roast 35-40 minutes until tender and caramelized, stirring halfway through.

Roasted Root Vegetable Medley (Serves 6)

Ingredients: 1 pound carrots (cut into chunks), 1 pound parsnips (cut into chunks), 1 pound turnips (cut into chunks), 3 tablespoons olive oil, 1.5 teaspoons salt, fresh rosemary.

Instructions: Preheat oven to 425°F. Toss all vegetables with oil, salt, and rosemary. Spread on large baking sheet. Roast 40-45 minutes until tender and browned, stirring every 15 minutes.

Roasted Sweet Potato Wedges (Serves 4)

Ingredients: 3 large sweet potatoes (cut into wedges), 2 tablespoons coconut oil (melted), 1 teaspoon salt, 1/2 teaspoon garlic powder (if tolerated).

Instructions: Preheat oven to 425°F. Toss sweet potato wedges with oil, salt, garlic powder. Arrange in single layer on baking sheet. Roast 35-40 minutes, flipping halfway, until tender inside and crispy outside.

18.3 Quick Sautéed Greens

Sautéed greens cook in 5-10 minutes, providing nutrient-dense sides with minimal time investment (Miglio et al., 2008).

Basic Sautéed Spinach (Serves 4, if spinach tolerated)

Ingredients: 1 pound fresh spinach (washed and dried), 2 tablespoons olive oil, 2 garlic cloves (minced, if tolerated), 1/2 teaspoon salt.

Instructions: Heat olive oil in large skillet over medium-high heat. Add garlic. Cook 30 seconds until fragrant. Add spinach in batches, adding more as each batch wilts. Cook 3-4 minutes total until all spinach is wilted. Season with salt.

Sautéed Bok Choy (Serves 4)

Ingredients: 1.5 pounds bok choy (chopped, separating stems from leaves), 2 tablespoons coconut oil, 1 teaspoon fresh ginger (grated), 1/2 teaspoon salt.

Instructions: Heat coconut oil in large skillet over high heat. Add bok choy stems and ginger. Cook 2-3 minutes until stems begin softening. Add leaves. Cook 2-3 minutes more until leaves wilt and stems are tender. Season with salt.

Garlic Greens (Serves 4)

Ingredients: 1 pound mixed greens (kale, collards, or chard, chopped), 2 tablespoons olive oil, 3 garlic cloves (sliced, if tolerated), 1/2 teaspoon salt, fresh lemon juice (optional, if tolerated).

Instructions: Heat olive oil in large skillet over medium heat. Add garlic. Cook 1 minute until fragrant but not browned. Add greens. Toss to coat with oil. Cook 5-7 minutes until wilted and tender. Season with salt. Add lemon juice if using.

18.4 Grain Side Dishes

Grain sides provide starchy accompaniments to proteins and vegetables (Vega-Gálvez et al., 2010).

Herbed Rice (Serves 6)

Ingredients: 2 cups white rice, 4 cups water or fresh broth, 1 teaspoon salt, 2 tablespoons olive oil, 1/4 cup fresh herbs (parsley, cilantro, or basil, chopped).

Instructions: Combine rice, water, salt, and olive oil in pot. Bring to boil. Reduce heat to low. Cover. Simmer 18-20 minutes until liquid absorbed. Remove from heat. Let stand covered 5 minutes. Fluff with fork. Stir in fresh herbs.

Coconut Rice (Serves 6)

Ingredients: 2 cups white rice, 1 can coconut milk, 2 cups water, 1 teaspoon salt.

Instructions: Combine all ingredients in pot. Bring to boil. Reduce heat to low. Cover. Simmer 18-20 minutes until liquid absorbed. Let stand covered 5 minutes. Fluff with fork.

Quinoa Pilaf (Serves 6)

Ingredients: 2 cups quinoa (rinsed), 4 cups fresh vegetable broth, 2 tablespoons coconut oil, 1 onion (diced), 1 teaspoon salt, 1/4 cup fresh parsley.

Instructions: Heat coconut oil in pot. Sauté onion 3 minutes. Add quinoa. Toast 2 minutes, stirring frequently. Add broth and salt. Bring to boil. Reduce heat. Cover. Simmer 15 minutes until liquid absorbed. Remove from heat. Let stand covered 5 minutes. Fluff with fork. Stir in fresh parsley.

Millet with Fresh Herbs (Serves 4)

Ingredients: 1 cup millet (rinsed), 2.5 cups water, 1/2 teaspoon salt, 1 tablespoon olive oil, 2 tablespoons fresh herbs (parsley, basil, or cilantro).

Instructions: Combine millet, water, salt, and olive oil in pot. Bring to boil. Reduce heat to low. Cover. Simmer 20 minutes until water absorbed. Remove from heat. Let stand covered 5 minutes. Fluff with fork. Stir in fresh herbs.

18.5 Potato and Root Vegetables

Potatoes and root vegetables provide satisfying starchy sides (Burlingame et al., 2009).

Mashed Potatoes (Serves 6)

Ingredients: 3 pounds potatoes (Yukon Gold or russet, peeled and cubed), 1/2 cup coconut milk, 4 tablespoons olive oil or coconut oil, 1.5 teaspoons salt.

Instructions: Place potatoes in large pot. Cover with water. Bring to boil. Cook 15-20 minutes until very tender. Drain completely. Return to pot. Add coconut milk, oil, and salt. Mash until smooth. Serve immediately.

Roasted New Potatoes (Serves 4)

Ingredients: 2 pounds new potatoes (halved), 2 tablespoons olive oil, 1 teaspoon salt, fresh rosemary.

Instructions: Preheat oven to 425°F. Toss potatoes with oil, salt, and rosemary. Spread cut-side down on baking sheet. Roast 30-35 minutes until golden and tender.

Mashed Sweet Potatoes (Serves 6)

Ingredients: 3 pounds sweet potatoes (peeled and cubed), 1/4 cup coconut milk, 2 tablespoons coconut oil, 1 teaspoon salt, 1 tablespoon maple syrup (optional).

Instructions: Place sweet potatoes in pot. Cover with water. Bring to boil. Cook 15-20 minutes until very tender. Drain. Return to pot. Add coconut milk, coconut oil, salt, and maple syrup if using. Mash until smooth.

Root Vegetable Hash (Serves 4)

Ingredients: 2 cups sweet potato (diced small), 1 cup parsnips (diced), 1 cup turnips (diced), 2 tablespoons coconut oil, 1 onion (diced), 1 teaspoon salt, fresh parsley.

Instructions: Heat coconut oil in large skillet over medium-high heat. Add all vegetables. Cook 12-15 minutes, stirring occasionally, until tender and golden. Season with salt. Garnish with fresh parsley.

18.6 Case Study: Side Dish Variety

Background

Honora, a 42-year-old accountant, maintained good symptom control through elimination and maintenance but described her meals as "boring." Investigation revealed that while her protein and grain selections varied, she ate steamed broccoli with nearly every dinner. She'd defaulted to steaming as the "safest" cooking method and broccoli as an always-available vegetable, creating unintentional monotony.

Presentation

Honora reported that after eight months of near-daily steamed broccoli, she felt unenthusiastic about dinner despite enjoying her proteins. She'd find herself picking at the broccoli rather than eating adequate portions. Her vegetable consumption declined overall as avoidance of the monotonous steamed broccoli generalized to reduced vegetable intake.

She believed steaming was necessary for histamine safety, having misunderstood guidance about avoiding slow-cooking methods. She'd interpreted "avoid long simmering" to mean "use only gentle cooking," leading to exclusive steaming. She also stuck with broccoli because it was reliably available year-round and she knew it was safe from her tier 1 testing.

Analysis

Honora's pattern demonstrated how misunderstanding cooking method guidance creates unnecessary restriction. The concern about extended cooking relates to time allowing bacterial histamine production (2-4 hour slow cooking), not the intensity of heat during shorter cooking (Schnedl et al., 2019). Roasting vegetables at 425°F for 30 minutes is perfectly safe. The high heat during short duration prevents bacterial growth while creating desirable flavors.

Her exclusive broccoli consumption, while understandable from a safety perspective, ignored that she'd successfully tested multiple vegetables during reintroduction. Brussels sprouts, cauliflower, carrots, zucchini, and green beans had all passed testing. She had permission to eat varied vegetables but hadn't translated testing results into meal rotation.

Intervention

A dietitian clarified cooking method guidance from section 18.1. High-heat roasting for 20-45 minutes creates no histamine concerns. The method enhances flavor through caramelization, making vegetables more appealing without compromising safety. Honora learned basic roasting technique and practiced with Brussels sprouts (her tested tier 1 vegetable that she'd never actually incorporated despite successful testing).

They created a vegetable rotation using her five tested tier 1 vegetables prepared through varied methods. Monday: roasted Brussels sprouts. Tuesday: sautéed zucchini. Wednesday: roasted carrots. Thursday: steamed green beans (steaming still appropriate when preferred). Friday: roasted cauliflower. This simple rotation provided daily variety using only tested-safe vegetables.

She batch-roasted vegetables Sunday and Wednesday (two sessions weekly rather than daily cooking). Roasted vegetables frozen immediately after cooling maintained quality. She could reheat frozen roasted Brussels sprouts faster than steaming fresh broccoli while getting superior flavor.

Outcome

Honora's vegetable enthusiasm returned within two weeks. She reported that roasted Brussels sprouts tasted completely different from steamed broccoli despite both being cruciferous vegetables. The caramelization and crispy edges made vegetables feel like a treat rather than an obligation. Her vegetable consumption increased as meals became more appealing overall.

Three months later, she'd expanded her rotation further. She discovered that the same vegetable prepared differently created varied experiences. Roasted cauliflower tasted different from steamed cauliflower. Raw zucchini in salads differed from sautéed zucchini. She now rotated through 8-10 different vegetable preparations weekly using just five base vegetables prepared multiple ways.

Teaching Points

- Misunderstanding cooking method guidance to mean "use only gentle methods" creates unnecessary restriction when the actual concern involves extended cooking duration rather than heat intensity, with high-heat roasting for 20-45 minutes providing both safety and superior flavor through caramelization
- Successfully tested vegetables during reintroduction phase require translation into actual meal rotation rather than remaining theoretical permissions, with people often reverting to elimination-phase minimal options despite reintroduction expanding choices
- Preparation method variety enables substantial meal diversity from limited ingredient lists, with five vegetables each prepared three different ways creating fifteen distinct eating experiences from minimal base ingredients

18.7 Fresh Vegetable Combinations

Fresh vegetable combinations provide raw options balancing cooked vegetable consumption (Dewanto et al., 2002).

Cucumber Salad (Serves 4)

Ingredients: 3 large cucumbers (sliced thin), 1/4 cup olive oil, 2 tablespoons fresh lemon juice (if tolerated) or apple cider, 1/2 teaspoon salt, 2 tablespoons fresh dill or parsley.

Instructions: Combine cucumbers, oil, lemon juice, salt, and herbs. Toss well. Let sit 10 minutes before serving for flavors to develop. Serve within 2 hours.

Shredded Carrot Salad (Serves 4)

Ingredients: 4 large carrots (shredded), 1/4 cup olive oil, 1 tablespoon fresh lemon juice (if tolerated), 1/2 teaspoon salt, 2 tablespoons fresh parsley.

Instructions: Combine all ingredients. Toss well. Serve immediately or within 1 hour.

Mixed Vegetable Slaw (Serves 6)

Ingredients: 2 cups cabbage (shredded), 1 cup carrots (shredded), 1 cup cucumber (julienned), 1/4 cup olive oil, 2 tablespoons fresh lemon juice (if tolerated), 1 teaspoon salt, fresh cilantro.

Instructions: Combine vegetables. Whisk oil, lemon juice, and salt. Pour over vegetables. Toss well. Top with fresh cilantro. Serve within 1-2 hours.

18.8 Make Ahead Sides

Make-ahead sides support meal prep when properly frozen (Schnedl et al., 2019).

Batch Roasted Vegetables (Multiple servings)

Instructions: Roast 3-4 sheet pans of different vegetables Sunday. Cool rapidly. Portion into individual containers. Freeze immediately. Reheat single portions throughout week in microwave (3-4 minutes) or oven (10 minutes at 350°F).

Pre-Cooked Grains (Multiple servings)

Instructions: Cook large batch rice, quinoa, or millet. Cool rapidly. Portion into individual 1-cup servings. Freeze flat in bags. Reheat from frozen in microwave (2-3 minutes) or steamer.

Mashed Potato Portions (Serves 8-10)

Instructions: Make large batch mashed potatoes or mashed sweet potatoes. Cool rapidly. Portion into individual servings (approximately 1 cup each). Freeze in containers. Reheat from frozen (microwave 4-5 minutes, stirring halfway, or oven 20 minutes at 350°F covered).

18.9 Essential Points to Remember

This chapter provided side dish and vegetable recipes emphasizing preparation variety for enhanced palatability while maintaining histamine safety. Roasted vegetables at high heat create caramelization and complex flavors through 20-45 minute cooking, well within safe timeframes. Brussels sprouts, cauliflower, carrots, root vegetables, and sweet potatoes benefit from roasting techniques.

Quick sautéed greens including spinach, bok choy, and mixed greens cook in 5-10 minutes for nutrient-dense sides. Grain sides from herbed rice to quinoa pilaf provide starchy accompaniments. Potato and root vegetable preparations from mashed potatoes to roasted new potatoes offer satisfying options.

Fresh vegetable combinations like cucumber salad and shredded carrot salad balance cooked vegetable consumption. Make-ahead sides through batch roasting, pre-cooking grains, and portioning mashed potatoes enable meal prep efficiency when properly frozen immediately after cooling.

The case study illustrated how cooking method misunderstandings create restriction and how successfully tested vegetables require translation into actual meal rotation. Preparation variety enables substantial diversity from limited ingredient lists.

Chapter 19.0: Snacks and Small Bites

Remigius opened his desk drawer at 3 PM, confronting the daily snack dilemma. Pre-diagnosis, he'd kept protein bars, mixed nuts, and dried fruit for afternoon energy. All three categories now posed problems. Commercial protein bars contained whey (aged), preservatives, and often chocolate (histamine liberator). Mixed nuts included cashews and walnuts (high histamine for many). Dried fruit concentrated histamine through dehydration and aging. His current solution involved rice cakes and fresh apple slices, adequate nutritionally but unsatisfying psychologically. The snack gap affects many people managing histamine intolerance (Maintz & Novak, 2007). Conventional convenient snacks rely heavily on aged, preserved, or dried ingredients designed for extended shelf life. Creating satisfying portable snacks using fresh ingredients requires strategic preparation but enables sustained dietary adherence through preventing the deprivation feelings that monotonous limited options create.

This chapter provides 12 snack and small bite recipes including energy balls and bars, vegetable-based snacks, dips and spreads, crackers and chips, minimal histamine sweet treats, and portable options supporting on-the-go needs while maintaining histamine safety through fresh preparation and proper storage.

19.1 Energy Ball Foundations

Energy balls combine nuts or seeds (if tolerated), dried fruit alternatives, and binders into portable nutrition (Trigueros et al., 2021). The challenge involves replacing typical dried fruits (dates, raisins) that concentrate histamine through drying and aging.

Fresh fruit alternatives include fresh apple (grated and squeezed to remove excess moisture), fresh mango (pureed), or coconut flakes (unsweetened, checked for preservatives). These provide sweetness and binding without aging concerns.

Nut and seed bases require individual tolerance testing. Sunflower seeds work for many. Almonds, if tested and tolerated, provide good binding. Avoid peanuts (legumes with high histamine potential) and walnuts (high histamine for many).

Binding agents include coconut oil (solid at room temperature, providing structure), maple syrup (provides moisture and sweetness), and nut or seed butters if tolerated. Rice flour adds body when needed.

19.2 Energy Ball Recipes

Sunflower Seed Balls (Makes 20, if sunflower seeds tolerated)

Ingredients: 1.5 cups sunflower seeds, 1/2 cup unsweetened coconut flakes, 1/4 cup maple syrup, 2 tablespoons coconut oil (melted), 1/4 teaspoon salt, 1/4 cup fresh apple (finely grated and moisture squeezed out).

Instructions: Process sunflower seeds in food processor until finely ground. Add coconut flakes, maple syrup, coconut oil, salt, and apple. Process until mixture holds together when pressed. Roll into 1-inch balls. Refrigerate 30 minutes to firm. Store in freezer in single layer. Consume within 2 weeks.

Coconut Date Alternative Balls (Makes 18)

Ingredients: 1 cup fresh mango (pureed and reduced slightly by simmering), 1.5 cups unsweetened coconut flakes, 1/4 cup coconut oil, 2 tablespoons maple syrup, 1/4 teaspoon salt.

Instructions: Combine all ingredients in food processor. Process until well combined and mixture holds together. Roll into balls. Freeze immediately. Store in freezer up to 2 weeks.

Almond Energy Bites (Makes 16, if almonds tolerated)

Ingredients: 1.5 cups almonds, 1/4 cup fresh apple (grated, moisture squeezed out), 1/4 cup maple syrup, 2 tablespoons coconut oil, 1/4 teaspoon salt, 1/4 cup coconut flakes.

Instructions: Process almonds until finely ground. Add remaining ingredients. Process until combined. Roll into balls. Freeze. Use within 2 weeks.

19.3 Vegetable Based Snacks

Vegetable snacks provide nutrients and crunch (Ismail et al., 2020).

Roasted Chickpeas (Serves 6, as snack)

Ingredients: 2 cups cooked chickpeas (fresh, patted very dry), 2 tablespoons olive oil, 1 teaspoon salt, 1/2 teaspoon garlic powder (if tolerated).

Instructions: Preheat oven to 400°F. Toss very dry chickpeas with oil, salt, and garlic powder. Spread on baking sheet. Roast 30-40 minutes, shaking pan every 10 minutes, until crispy and golden. Cool completely. Store in airtight container 2-3 days or freeze portions.

Baked Zucchini Chips (Serves 4)

Ingredients: 3 medium zucchini (sliced very thin), 2 tablespoons olive oil, 1 teaspoon salt.

Instructions: Preheat oven to 225°F (low temperature for dehydrating effect). Toss zucchini slices with oil and salt. Arrange in single layer on parchment-lined baking sheets (may need multiple sheets). Bake 2-2.5 hours until crispy and dried, rotating pans halfway through. Cool completely. Consume within 2 days (don't store long as moisture returns).

Carrot and Cucumber Sticks (Serves 1)

Ingredients: 1 large carrot (cut into sticks), 1 large cucumber (cut into sticks), optional dip from section 19.4.

Instructions: Cut vegetables fresh. Store in water in refrigerator up to 24 hours. Drain and serve with optional dip.

19.4 Dips and Spreads

Dips and spreads pair with fresh vegetables or rice cakes (Maintz & Novak, 2007).

Fresh Herb Dip (Serves 4)

Ingredients: 1 cup fresh cucumber (peeled and chopped), 1/4 cup olive oil, 2 tablespoons fresh lemon juice (if tolerated), 1/4 cup fresh herbs (dill, parsley, or cilantro), 1/4 teaspoon salt, 2 tablespoons coconut milk for creaminess.

Instructions: Blend all ingredients until smooth. Refrigerate up to 2 days. Serve with fresh vegetables or rice cakes.

Sunflower Seed Butter (Makes 1 cup, if sunflower seeds tolerated)

Ingredients: 2 cups roasted sunflower seeds (unsalted), 1/4 teaspoon salt, 1-2 tablespoons coconut oil (if needed for consistency).

Instructions: Process sunflower seeds in food processor 8-10 minutes, scraping down sides frequently, until smooth and creamy. Add salt and coconut oil if needed. Store refrigerated up to 1 week.

Mashed Avocado Spread (Serves 2, if avocado tolerated in tested portions)

Ingredients: 1 ripe avocado, 1 tablespoon fresh lemon juice (if tolerated) or olive oil, 1/4 teaspoon salt, fresh cilantro.

Instructions: Mash avocado with lemon juice or oil and salt. Stir in fresh cilantro. Use immediately (avocado browns quickly).

White Bean Dip (Serves 4)

Ingredients: 1.5 cups cooked white beans (fresh, from dried), 1/4 cup olive oil, 2 tablespoons fresh lemon juice (if tolerated), 1 garlic clove (if tolerated), 1/2 teaspoon salt, fresh parsley.

Instructions: Combine beans, olive oil, lemon juice, garlic, and salt in food processor. Process until smooth. Stir in fresh parsley. Refrigerate up to 2 days. Serve with rice cakes or fresh vegetables.

19.5 Crackers and Homemade Chips

Homemade crackers and chips replace commercial versions containing preservatives and aged ingredients (Ismail et al., 2020).

Rice Flour Crackers (Makes approximately 40)

Ingredients: 2 cups rice flour, 1/2 teaspoon salt, 1/4 cup olive oil, 1/2 cup water, optional seasonings (garlic powder if tolerated, fresh herbs).

Instructions: Preheat oven to 350°F. Mix flour and salt. Add oil and water. Mix until dough forms. Roll very thin between parchment paper. Cut into squares. Place on baking sheet. Bake 15-20 minutes until crispy and lightly golden. Cool completely. Store in airtight container 3-5 days.

Baked Sweet Potato Chips (Serves 4)

Ingredients: 2 large sweet potatoes (sliced very thin using mandoline), 2 tablespoons coconut oil (melted), 1 teaspoon salt.

Instructions: Preheat oven to 375°F. Toss sweet potato slices with oil and salt. Arrange in single layer on baking sheets. Bake 15-20 minutes, flipping halfway, until crispy and edges curl. Cool completely. Consume within 2 days.

19.6 Case Study: Snack Strategy Success

Background

Marius, a 28-year-old graduate student, struggled with afternoon energy crashes during long library study sessions. Pre-diagnosis, he'd relied on vending machine snacks (chips, crackers, protein bars). Post-diagnosis, he tried bringing fresh fruit but found apples and blueberries alone didn't sustain energy through 3-4 hour study blocks. He'd eat a large apple at 2 PM and feel hungry again by 3:30 PM, breaking concentration to find more food.

Presentation

Marius reported difficulty maintaining focus during afternoon studying. His solution of frequent trips for additional fresh fruit disrupted workflow. He'd leave the library every hour seeking more snacks, losing studying momentum. He felt frustrated that dietary restrictions forced reduced productivity.

Analysis revealed his snacks lacked protein and healthy fats. Fresh fruit alone provides quick carbohydrates without sustained energy. He needed balanced snacks combining carbohydrates, protein, and fat for stable blood sugar and lasting satiety. However, his limited cooking skills and minimal kitchen equipment (dorm room with only microwave and mini-fridge) constrained options.

Analysis

Marius's situation demonstrated how inadequate snack planning undermines both dietary compliance and quality of life. Fresh fruit represents appropriate histamine-safe snacking but incomplete nutrition for extended energy needs. Research shows that balanced snacks containing protein, healthy fats, and complex carbohydrates sustain energy better than simple carbohydrates alone (Trigueros et al., 2021).

His minimal cooking capacity required no-cook or batch-prepared options made elsewhere and stored for daily use. Traditional college student snacking (vending machine convenience) conflicted with histamine management needs. However, strategic preparation could bridge this gap.

Intervention

A dietitian helped Marius develop a weekly snack preparation routine executed at his parents' house during Sunday dinners. He'd prepare energy balls (sunflower seed version from section 19.2), roasted chickpeas (section 19.3), and pre-portion rice cakes with small containers of sunflower seed butter.

Sunday evening, he'd make 20 energy balls (freezing in single layers), roast two batches chickpeas (storing in containers), and portion sunflower seed butter into small containers with rice cakes. These preparations took 60-90 minutes total but provided entire week's snacks.

He stored energy balls frozen in his dorm mini-freezer, removing one each morning to thaw by afternoon. Roasted chickpeas stayed in airtight containers. Rice cakes and sunflower seed butter portions lived in his backpack. His afternoon snack became: one thawed energy ball (protein and fat from sunflower seeds), one small container roasted chickpeas (protein and fiber), rice cakes with sunflower seed butter (complex carbs with protein and fat), plus fresh apple (quick carbs).

Outcome

Marius's afternoon energy stabilized within one week. The combination snack sustained him through 3-4 hour study blocks without hunger distractions. His library trips decreased from 3-4 per afternoon to zero, improving productivity substantially. He maintained focus better and reported feeling more satisfied than when snacking on fruit alone.

The weekly preparation routine became sustainable. His parents enjoyed having him for Sunday dinners, and the kitchen access enabled batch preparing shelf-stable and frozen snacks impossible in his dorm. The strategy addressed both nutritional needs and practical constraints of college living.

Three months later, he'd expanded his snack rotation to include homemade crackers and vegetable sticks with white bean dip (prepared Sundays, stored appropriately). His snacking supported both dietary compliance and academic performance rather than undermining either.

Teaching Points

- Fresh fruit alone provides incomplete nutrition for sustained energy during extended activities, requiring balanced snacks combining carbohydrates, protein, and healthy fats for stable blood sugar and lasting satiety supporting concentration and productivity
- Limited cooking capacity in situations like dorm living requires strategic use of available kitchen access for batch preparation of frozen and shelf-stable snacks rather than attempting daily fresh preparation in inadequate facilities
- Weekly batch snack preparation taking 60-90 minutes provides entire week's portable balanced snacks, demonstrating how front-loaded time investment enables daily convenience supporting both dietary compliance and quality of life

19.7 Sweet Treat Options

Sweet treats using minimal histamine ingredients satisfy cravings (Maintz & Novak, 2007).

Coconut Macaroons (Makes 20)

Ingredients: 3 cups unsweetened coconut flakes, 1/2 cup maple syrup, 2 egg whites (if eggs tolerated), 1 teaspoon vanilla extract, 1/4 teaspoon salt.

Instructions: Preheat oven to 325°F. Mix all ingredients. Drop by tablespoon onto parchment-lined baking sheet. Bake 20-25 minutes until golden. Cool completely. Freeze portions. Use within 2 weeks.

Apple Chips (Serves 4)

Ingredients: 4 apples (sliced very thin), 1 tablespoon maple syrup, 1/2 teaspoon cinnamon (if tolerated).

Instructions: Preheat oven to 200°F. Arrange apple slices on parchment-lined baking sheets. Brush lightly with maple syrup. Sprinkle with cinnamon if using. Bake 2-3 hours, flipping halfway, until dried and crispy. Cool completely. Store in airtight container 3-5 days.

19.8 Portable Snack Solutions

Portable snacks support on-the-go needs without refrigeration requirements for several hours.

Trail Mix Alternative (if nuts/seeds tolerated)

Combine: roasted sunflower seeds, unsweetened coconut flakes, freeze-dried fruit (check ingredients for no preservatives), rice cereal. Portion into small bags. Consume within 1 week of preparing.

Rice Cake Sandwiches

Spread two rice cakes with sunflower seed butter. Press together. Wrap individually. Pack with fresh apple slices in separate container.

Frozen Energy Ball Pack

Pack 2-3 frozen energy balls in small insulated bag with ice pack in morning. Thawed by afternoon snack time.

19.9 Chapter Conclusions

This chapter provided snack and small bite recipes supporting sustained energy and portable convenience while maintaining histamine safety. Energy balls and bars using sunflower seeds, coconut, fresh fruit purees, and compliant binding agents replace commercial versions containing aged ingredients and preservatives.

Vegetable-based snacks from roasted chickpeas to zucchini chips to fresh vegetable sticks provide nutrient-dense options. Dips and spreads including fresh herb dip, sunflower seed butter, and white bean dip pair with vegetables and rice cakes. Homemade crackers and chips using rice flour and sweet potatoes replace commercial preserved versions.

Sweet treat options including coconut macaroons and apple chips satisfy cravings. Portable solutions through trail mix alternatives, rice cake sandwiches, and frozen energy balls support on-the-go needs. The case study illustrated how balanced snacks combining macronutrients sustain energy better than fruit alone and how strategic batch preparation enables portable snacking despite limited cooking facilities.

Chapter 20.0: Sauces and Flavor Builders

Simeon stood in the condiment aisle reading labels with growing frustration. Every ketchup contained tomato concentrate (aged during processing), vinegar (fermented and aged), and "natural flavors" (often code for yeast extract or MSG). Mustard listed vinegar as the second ingredient. Mayonnaise contained aged eggs and vinegar. Hot sauce combined aged peppers with vinegar. Even the "all-natural" brands contained the same problematic ingredients in organic form. He'd been eating plain proteins and vegetables for two months, missing the flavor complexity that condiments had provided. His meals tasted bland not because the base ingredients were flavorless but because the flavor-building components he'd relied on (ketchup, mustard, soy sauce, vinegar-based dressings) all contained aged or fermented ingredients. This condiment gap affects nearly everyone managing histamine intolerance (Maintz & Novak, 2007). Commercial condiments rely on fermentation, vinegar, aged ingredients, and preservatives for shelf stability and concentrated flavors. Creating comparable flavor building using fresh ingredients requires understanding what creates depth and complexity without relying on aging processes.

This chapter provides 27 sauce, condiment, and flavor builder recipes including low-histamine ketchup alternatives, fresh herb sauces and pestos, salad dressings, fresh marinades, spice blends, dairy-free cream sauces, and safe flavor enhancers that restore meal satisfaction while maintaining histamine safety through fresh preparation and proper storage.

20.1 Fresh Tomato Ketchup Alternative

Traditional ketchup concentrates histamine through tomato reduction, vinegar addition, and extended shelf storage (Visciano et al., 2012). Fresh tomato sauce made and consumed immediately or frozen provides ketchup-like flavor without aging.

Fresh Tomato Sauce Base (Makes 2 cups, if tomatoes tolerated)

Ingredients: 2 pounds fresh tomatoes (diced), 1 tablespoon olive oil, 1 onion (diced), 2 garlic cloves (minced, if tolerated), 2 tablespoons maple syrup, 1 teaspoon salt, 1/4 teaspoon fresh ginger (grated).

Instructions: Heat olive oil in pot over medium heat. Sauté onion and garlic 3 minutes. Add tomatoes, maple syrup, salt, ginger. Simmer uncovered 20-25 minutes, stirring occasionally, until thickened. Blend until smooth using immersion blender. Cool rapidly. Use immediately or freeze in small portions (ice cube trays work well). Use frozen portions within 2 months.

No-Tomato "Ketchup" (Makes 1.5 cups)

Ingredients: 2 cups beets (peeled and diced), 1 cup carrots (diced), 1 onion (diced), 1 tablespoon olive oil, 1/4 cup maple syrup, 2 tablespoons apple cider (fresh, not vinegar), 1 teaspoon salt.

Instructions: Heat olive oil in pot. Sauté onion 3 minutes. Add beets and carrots with 1 cup water. Cover. Simmer 20 minutes until very tender. Drain excess liquid. Add maple syrup, apple cider, salt. Blend until very smooth. Simmer 5 minutes more to thicken. Cool. Refrigerate up to 3 days or freeze portions.

20.2 Fresh Herb Sauces

Fresh herb sauces provide concentrated flavor without fermentation or aging (Vallverdú-Queralt et al., 2014).

Fresh Basil Pesto (Makes 1 cup)

Ingredients: 2 cups fresh basil leaves (packed), 1/2 cup olive oil, 1/4 cup sunflower seeds (if tolerated) or pine nuts (if tolerated), 2 garlic cloves (if tolerated), 1/2 teaspoon salt, 2 tablespoons fresh lemon juice (if tolerated).

Instructions: Combine all ingredients in food processor. Process until smooth. Use immediately over pasta, chicken, or fish, or freeze in ice cube trays for later use. Frozen pesto cubes keep 2 months.

Cilantro Lime Sauce (Makes 3/4 cup, if cilantro and lime tolerated)

Ingredients: 1 cup fresh cilantro (packed), 1/2 cup olive oil, juice of 2 limes, 1 garlic clove, 1/2 teaspoon salt.

Instructions: Blend all ingredients until smooth. Use immediately or refrigerate up to 2 days. Great on fish, chicken, or grain bowls.

Fresh Parsley Sauce (Makes 1 cup)

Ingredients: 2 cups fresh parsley (packed), 1/2 cup olive oil, 2 tablespoons fresh lemon juice (if tolerated) or extra olive oil, 2 garlic cloves (if tolerated), 1/2 teaspoon salt.

Instructions: Process all ingredients until smooth. Thin with water if needed for desired consistency. Use within 2 days or freeze in small portions.

Herb Oil (Makes 1 cup)

Ingredients: 1 cup olive oil, 1/2 cup mixed fresh herbs (basil, parsley, cilantro, or rosemary), 2 garlic cloves (if tolerated).

Instructions: Combine oil, herbs, and garlic in small pot. Heat gently over very low heat 10 minutes (do not simmer or boil). Remove from heat. Let steep 20 minutes. Strain out solids. Store refrigerated up to 1 week. Use as finishing oil on vegetables, proteins, or grains.

20.3 Salad Dressing Collection

Salad dressings replace commercial vinegar-based versions with fresh acid alternatives (Reese et al., 2018).

Basic Lemon Vinaigrette (Makes 1/2 cup, if lemon tolerated)

Ingredients: 1/3 cup olive oil, 3 tablespoons fresh lemon juice, 1/2 teaspoon salt, 1/4 teaspoon garlic powder (if tolerated), 1 teaspoon maple syrup (optional for slight sweetness).

Instructions: Whisk all ingredients. Store refrigerated up to 3 days. Shake before using.

Creamy Avocado Dressing (Makes 1 cup, if avocado tolerated)

Ingredients: 1 ripe avocado, 1/4 cup olive oil, 2 tablespoons fresh lemon or lime juice (if tolerated), 1/4 cup water, 1/2 teaspoon salt, fresh cilantro.

Instructions: Blend all ingredients until smooth. Thin with additional water if needed. Use within 24 hours (avocado browns quickly).

Tahini Dressing (Makes 3/4 cup)

Ingredients: 1/4 cup tahini, 1/4 cup olive oil, 3 tablespoons fresh lemon juice (if tolerated), 2 tablespoons water, 1/2 teaspoon salt, 1 garlic clove (if tolerated).

Instructions: Whisk all ingredients until smooth. Add more water for thinner consistency. Refrigerate up to 5 days.

Ginger Dressing (Makes 1/2 cup)

Ingredients: 1/4 cup olive oil, 2 tablespoons fresh ginger (grated), 2 tablespoons fresh lime juice (if tolerated) or apple cider (not vinegar), 1 tablespoon maple syrup, 1/2 teaspoon salt.

Instructions: Blend all ingredients until smooth. Refrigerate up to 3 days. Great on Asian-inspired salads.

Ranch-Style Dressing (Makes 1 cup)

Ingredients: 1/2 cup coconut milk (full-fat), 1/4 cup olive oil, 2 tablespoons fresh lemon juice (if tolerated), 1 garlic clove (if tolerated), 1/2 teaspoon salt, 2 tablespoons fresh dill, 2 tablespoons fresh parsley.

Instructions: Blend all ingredients until smooth. Refrigerate up to 3 days.

20.4 Fresh Marinades

Marinades using fresh ingredients tenderize and flavor without aged components (Fernández-López et al., 2005).

Lemon Herb Marinade (Makes 3/4 cup, enough for 2 pounds protein, if lemon tolerated)

Ingredients: 1/2 cup olive oil, juice of 2 lemons, 3 garlic cloves (minced, if tolerated), 2 tablespoons fresh herbs (rosemary, thyme, or oregano), 1 teaspoon salt.

Instructions: Whisk all ingredients. Use immediately on chicken, fish, or lamb. Marinate 15-30 minutes for fish, 30-60 minutes for chicken or lamb. Don't marinate longer as acid can affect texture.

Ginger Garlic Marinade (Makes 2/3 cup, enough for 1.5 pounds protein)

Ingredients: 1/4 cup olive oil, 2 tablespoons fresh ginger (grated), 3 garlic cloves (minced, if tolerated), 2 tablespoons coconut aminos (if tolerated), 1 tablespoon maple syrup, 1/2 teaspoon salt.

Instructions: Whisk all ingredients. Use on chicken, beef, or pork. Marinate 30-60 minutes.

Coconut Lime Marinade (Makes 3/4 cup, if lime tolerated)

Ingredients: 1/2 cup coconut milk, juice of 2 limes, 1 tablespoon fresh ginger (grated), 2 garlic cloves (minced, if tolerated), 1/2 teaspoon salt, fresh cilantro.

Instructions: Whisk all ingredients. Use on chicken or fish. Marinate 30 minutes.

Simple Herb Marinade (Makes 1/2 cup)

Ingredients: 1/2 cup olive oil, 3 tablespoons fresh herbs (basil, parsley, cilantro, or rosemary, chopped), 2 garlic cloves (minced, if tolerated), 1 teaspoon salt.

Instructions: Combine all ingredients. Use on any protein. Marinate 30-60 minutes.

20.5 Spice Blend Formulas

Spice blends create flavor complexity from individual fresh spices (Vallverdú-Queralt et al., 2014).

Italian Herb Blend (Makes 1/4 cup)

Ingredients: 2 tablespoons dried basil, 1 tablespoon dried oregano, 1 tablespoon dried parsley, 1 teaspoon garlic powder (if tolerated), 1/2 teaspoon salt.

Instructions: Mix all ingredients. Store in airtight container up to 3 months. Use on chicken, vegetables, or in marinades.

Poultry Seasoning (Makes 1/4 cup)

Ingredients: 2 tablespoons dried thyme, 1 tablespoon dried rosemary (crushed), 1 tablespoon dried sage, 1 teaspoon garlic powder (if tolerated), 1 teaspoon salt.

Instructions: Mix thoroughly. Store up to 3 months. Rub on chicken or turkey before roasting.

Curry Powder Alternative (Makes 1/3 cup)

Ingredients: 2 tablespoons ground turmeric, 1 tablespoon ground ginger, 1 tablespoon ground cumin (if tolerated), 1 teaspoon salt, 1/2 teaspoon garlic powder (if tolerated).

Instructions: Mix well. Store in dark container (turmeric is light-sensitive) up to 3 months. Use in curries or on roasted vegetables.

Basic Seasoning Salt (Makes 1/2 cup)

Ingredients: 1/4 cup sea salt, 2 tablespoons garlic powder (if tolerated), 1 tablespoon onion powder (if tolerated), 1 teaspoon dried parsley.

Instructions: Mix ingredients thoroughly. Store up to 6 months. Use as all-purpose seasoning.

20.6 Dairy Free Cream Sauces

Cream sauces using coconut milk or nut bases replace dairy versions (Maintz & Novak, 2007).

Coconut Cream Sauce (Makes 2 cups)

Ingredients: 1 can coconut milk (full-fat), 2 tablespoons coconut oil, 2 garlic cloves (minced, if tolerated), 1 teaspoon salt, 2 tablespoons fresh herbs (basil, parsley, or cilantro).

Instructions: Heat coconut oil in pan. Sauté garlic 1 minute. Add coconut milk and salt. Simmer gently 5-7 minutes until slightly thickened. Stir in fresh herbs. Use immediately over chicken, fish, or vegetables.

Sunflower Seed Cream (Makes 1.5 cups, if sunflower seeds tolerated)

Ingredients: 1 cup sunflower seeds (soaked 4 hours, drained), 1 cup water, 2 tablespoons olive oil, 1 garlic clove (if tolerated), 1/2 teaspoon salt.

Instructions: Blend all ingredients until very smooth. Heat gently if using as warm sauce. Use cold as sour cream alternative. Refrigerate up to 3 days.

Cauliflower Alfredo (Makes 2 cups)

Ingredients: 3 cups cauliflower florets (steamed until very tender), 1/2 cup coconut milk, 2 tablespoons olive oil, 2 garlic cloves (if tolerated), 1 teaspoon salt.

Instructions: Blend all ingredients until completely smooth. Heat gently. Thin with water or additional coconut milk if needed. Use over pasta, chicken, or vegetables.

20.7 Case Study: Condiment Restoration

Background

Berenice, a 52-year-old office manager, described her meals as "punishment food" despite maintaining good symptom control six months into maintenance phase.

Investigation revealed she'd never developed condiments or sauces, eating plain grilled chicken, steamed vegetables, and rice at most meals. She'd assumed all flavor enhancers were off-limits and hadn't realized fresh alternatives existed.

Presentation

Berenice reported compliance fatigue. She followed the diet strictly but felt deprived watching family members use ketchup, barbecue sauce, and salad dressings. Her plain food worked medically but felt psychologically unsustainable. She'd begun having thoughts like "maybe I'd rather have symptoms than eat like this forever."

Her assumption that all sauces were problematic came from reading that vinegar, soy sauce, and tomato sauce were high histamine. She'd interpreted this as "no sauces allowed" rather than "commercial aged sauces are problematic but fresh alternatives work." She'd never attempted making fresh versions, believing homemade sauces would be too time-consuming for daily meals.

Analysis

Berenice's situation demonstrated how incomplete information creates excessive restriction. Commercial condiments contain histamine from aging, fermentation, and preservatives. This doesn't mean the concept of sauces is problematic. Fresh sauces made from compliant ingredients and used immediately or frozen contain minimal histamine (Reese et al., 2018).

Her psychological struggle reflected research showing that perceived deprivation (feeling restricted regardless of actual restriction) predicts dietary abandonment better than objective restriction level. Two people eating identical foods report vastly different satisfaction based on whether they view their eating as chosen variety or imposed deprivation.

Intervention

A dietitian taught Berenice three simple sauce formulas from this chapter: fresh herb pesto (section 20.2), lemon vinaigrette (section 20.3), and coconut cream sauce (section 20.6). They made all three together in 30 minutes total.

She learned to batch-prepare pesto and freeze in ice cube trays (one cube per meal provides perfect portion). The vinaigrette took 2 minutes to whisk and lasted 3 days refrigerated. The coconut cream sauce required 10 minutes and transformed plain chicken into restaurant-quality meals.

They discussed strategic sauce use. Not every meal needs sauce, but having options available prevents the "always plain" monotony. She developed a rotation: Monday grilled chicken with thawed pesto cube, Tuesday simple chicken with lemon vinaigrette over salad, Wednesday chicken in coconut cream sauce, Thursday plain (variety includes plain sometimes), Friday chicken with fresh herbs (simple option).

Outcome

Berenice's perspective shifted within two weeks. Meals felt more like normal eating rather than medical restriction. The ability to add sauces when desired (not every meal, just when wanted) eliminated the deprivation feeling. She reported that thawed pesto cube on chicken tasted "like real food again" rather than punishment.

She expanded her sauce collection over three months. She learned the no-tomato ketchup from section 20.1 for occasions when she wanted that flavor. She made spice blends from section 20.5 that simplified seasoning. She kept three different dressings rotated in her refrigerator for salad variety.

Six months later, her compliance remained excellent but her satisfaction had transformed. She described her eating as "normal with modifications" rather than "completely different and restricted." The shift from viewing all sauces as forbidden to understanding that fresh versions work eliminated a major psychological barrier.

Teaching Points

- Perceived deprivation from believing entire food categories (like sauces and condiments) are forbidden creates psychological distress disproportionate to actual restriction when fresh alternatives using compliant ingredients can replicate desired flavors and textures without histamine concerns
- Strategic sauce use rather than every-meal application provides psychological benefit through choice and variety even when many meals remain simply seasoned, with the availability of options mattering more than their constant use
- Batch preparation and freezing of fresh sauces in individual portions (ice cube trays for pesto, small containers for dressings) enables convenience competitive with commercial condiments while maintaining freshness through proper storage protocols

20.8 Safe Flavor Enhancers

Flavor enhancers boost taste without aged or fermented ingredients (Fernández-López et al., 2005).

Garlic Oil (Makes 1 cup, if garlic tolerated)

Ingredients: 1 cup olive oil, 10 garlic cloves (peeled and smashed).

Instructions: Combine oil and garlic in small pot. Heat very gently over lowest heat 15 minutes (don't let garlic brown). Remove from heat. Let steep 30 minutes. Strain out garlic. Store refrigerated up to 1 week. Use to start sautés or as finishing oil.

Fresh Herb Salt (Makes 1/2 cup)

Ingredients: 1/4 cup sea salt, 1/4 cup fresh herbs (parsley, basil, or cilantro, very finely minced).

Instructions: Mix salt and herbs. Spread thinly on parchment. Dry at room temperature 24 hours or in 200°F oven 30 minutes until herbs are crispy. Store in airtight container up to 2 weeks. Use as finishing salt.

Coconut Aminos (If tolerated and available commercially)

Note: Commercial coconut aminos provides soy sauce alternative. Check labels for preservatives. Some brands contain only coconut sap and salt. Use if individually tolerated as tested during Chapter 6.0 reintroduction.

Miso Alternative Paste (Makes 1 cup)

Ingredients: 1 cup white beans (cooked fresh from dried), 2 tablespoons tahini, 1 tablespoon coconut aminos (if tolerated), 1 teaspoon salt.

Instructions: Blend all ingredients until smooth. Use small amounts to add umami depth to soups and sauces. Refrigerate up to 3 days or freeze in small portions.

20.9 Additional Sauce Variations

Mustard Alternative (Makes 1/2 cup)

Ingredients: 1/4 cup fresh turmeric (grated) or 2 tablespoons dried turmeric, 1/4 cup olive oil, 2 tablespoons fresh lemon juice (if tolerated) or apple cider (not vinegar), 1 tablespoon maple syrup, 1/2 teaspoon salt.

Instructions: Blend all ingredients until smooth. Refrigerate up to 1 week. Use as condiment on chicken, fish, or in dressings.

BBQ Sauce Alternative (Makes 1.5 cups)

Ingredients: 1 cup fresh tomato sauce (from section 20.1) or beet-based ketchup, 1/4 cup maple syrup, 2 tablespoons apple cider (fresh, not vinegar), 1 tablespoon onion powder (if tolerated), 1 teaspoon garlic powder (if tolerated), 1 teaspoon smoked salt (if tolerated), 1/2 teaspoon fresh ginger (grated).

Instructions: Combine all ingredients. Simmer gently 10 minutes. Use immediately or freeze in portions.

20.10 Chapter Overview

This chapter provided sauce, condiment, and flavor builder recipes restoring meal satisfaction through fresh preparation. Low-histamine ketchup alternatives using fresh tomatoes or beets replace commercial aged versions. Fresh herb sauces and pestos from basil, cilantro, and parsley provide concentrated flavors frozen in portions for convenient use.

Salad dressings using fresh lemon juice or oil-based formulas replace vinegar versions. Fresh marinades for proteins use acids from citrus and enzymes from fresh ginger rather than fermented components. Spice blends combine individual spices for complexity. Dairy-free cream sauces using coconut milk or blended vegetables create richness.

Safe flavor enhancers including garlic oil, herb salt, and miso alternatives boost taste. The case study illustrated how perceived deprivation from believing all sauces are forbidden creates psychological distress eliminated through understanding fresh alternatives. Strategic sauce availability matters more than constant use for maintaining long-term satisfaction and compliance.

Chapter 21.0: Beverages and Drink Options

Julius filled his water glass for the sixth time that morning, contemplating beverage monotony. Pre-diagnosis, he'd rotated through coffee (three cups daily), green tea (afternoon pick-me-up), kombucha (trendy probiotic drink), and occasional wine (social occasions). All now problematic. Coffee and aged teas liberated histamine. Kombucha's fermentation created histamine directly. Wine combined fermentation with sulfites and aging. His beverage variety had collapsed to water and occasional coconut milk. While adequate hydration supported health, the complete absence of interesting drinks felt like another restriction in an already-restricted pattern. The beverage challenge extends beyond simple hydration for many managing histamine intolerance (Schnedl et al., 2019). Beverages provide ritual, comfort, social participation, and variety. Coffee represents morning routine. Tea signals afternoon break. Social gatherings center around shared drinks. Eliminating all beverage variety without developing alternatives removes daily pleasure points and social connection opportunities beyond simple nutritional impact.

This chapter provides 19 beverage and drink recipes including histamine-friendly herbal teas, fresh juices and smoothies, golden milk and warming drinks, electrolyte beverages for POTS support, infused waters, and anti-inflammatory tonics that restore beverage variety while maintaining histamine safety through fresh ingredients and proper preparation timing.

21.1 Herbal Tea Foundations

Herbal teas using fresh or minimally processed herbs avoid the aging issues in traditional aged tea leaves (McKay & Blumberg, 2006). Green tea and black tea age during processing, creating histamine concerns for sensitive individuals. Fresh herbal infusions avoid this problem.

Safe herb selections include fresh mint, fresh basil, fresh ginger, chamomile (usually tolerated despite being dried), and rooibos (red tea, naturally low histamine). Avoid aged black or green teas, fermented pu-erh, and mate (can be problematic).

Brewing methods emphasize fresh ingredients when possible. Fresh herbs: use 2-3 tablespoons per cup boiling water, steep 5-10 minutes. Dried herbs: use 1-2 teaspoons per cup, steep 5-10 minutes. Fresh ginger: use 1-inch piece sliced per cup, simmer gently 10 minutes.

21.2 Herbal Tea Recipes

Fresh Mint Tea (Serves 1)

Ingredients: 2 tablespoons fresh mint leaves, 1 cup boiling water, optional: 1 teaspoon maple syrup.

Instructions: Place mint in cup. Pour boiling water over. Steep 5 minutes. Strain. Sweeten if desired. Drink hot or chill for iced version.

Ginger Turmeric Tea (Serves 2)

Ingredients: 2-inch piece fresh ginger (sliced thin), 1-inch piece fresh turmeric (sliced) or 1 teaspoon dried turmeric, 2 cups water, 1 teaspoon maple syrup, pinch black pepper (enhances turmeric absorption).

Instructions: Combine ginger, turmeric, and water in small pot. Simmer gently 10 minutes. Strain. Add maple syrup and black pepper. Serve hot.

Chamomile Lavender Blend (Serves 1)

Ingredients: 1 teaspoon dried chamomile, 1/4 teaspoon dried lavender (culinary grade), 1 cup boiling water, optional: maple syrup.

Instructions: Combine herbs in tea infuser or directly in cup. Pour boiling water over. Steep 7 minutes. Strain if needed. Sweeten if desired.

Fresh Basil Lemon Tea (Serves 1, if lemon tolerated)

Ingredients: 10 fresh basil leaves, 1 cup boiling water, 1 tablespoon fresh lemon juice, 1 teaspoon maple syrup.

Instructions: Muddle basil leaves gently in cup. Add boiling water. Steep 5 minutes. Strain. Add lemon juice and maple syrup. Serve hot or iced.

Rooibos Vanilla (Serves 1)

Ingredients: 1 tablespoon loose rooibos tea, 1 cup boiling water, 1/4 teaspoon vanilla extract, maple syrup to taste.

Instructions: Steep rooibos in boiling water 5-7 minutes. Strain. Add vanilla and maple syrup.

21.3 Fresh Juices and Smoothies

Fresh juices provide nutrients and variety when made immediately before consumption (Patil et al., 2004).

Green Vegetable Juice (Serves 1)

Ingredients: 2 cups fresh spinach (if tolerated), 1 cucumber, 2 celery stalks, 1 apple, 1-inch piece fresh ginger, 1/2 lemon (if tolerated).

Instructions: Run all ingredients through juicer. Drink immediately (juice oxidizes quickly, losing nutrients and potentially developing histamine from bacterial activity if stored).

Carrot Apple Juice (Serves 1)

Ingredients: 4 large carrots, 2 apples, 1-inch piece fresh ginger.

Instructions: Juice all ingredients. Drink immediately.

Cucumber Mint Refresher (Serves 1)

Ingredients: 2 large cucumbers, 10 fresh mint leaves, 1 apple, 1 tablespoon fresh lime juice (if tolerated).

Instructions: Juice cucumbers, mint, and apple. Stir in lime juice. Drink immediately.

Berry Coconut Smoothie (Serves 1)

Ingredients: 1 cup fresh or frozen blueberries, 1 cup coconut milk, 1/2 cup cauliflower rice (steamed and cooled), 1 tablespoon maple syrup.

Instructions: Blend all ingredients until smooth. Drink immediately.

21.4 Golden Milk Variations

Golden milk using turmeric provides anti-inflammatory benefits (Gupta et al., 2013).

Classic Golden Milk (Serves 1)

Ingredients: 1 cup coconut milk, 1 teaspoon fresh turmeric (grated) or 1/2 teaspoon dried turmeric, 1/4 teaspoon fresh ginger (grated), pinch black pepper, 1 teaspoon maple syrup, 1/4 teaspoon vanilla extract.

Instructions: Heat coconut milk gently in small pot. Whisk in turmeric, ginger, black pepper, maple syrup, and vanilla. Heat until steaming but not boiling. Strain if using fresh turmeric/ginger. Serve hot.

Cinnamon Golden Milk (Serves 1)

Ingredients: 1 cup coconut milk, 1 teaspoon fresh turmeric, 1/4 teaspoon cinnamon (if tolerated), 1 teaspoon maple syrup, pinch black pepper.

Instructions: Heat coconut milk with turmeric, cinnamon, and black pepper. Whisk well. Add maple syrup. Serve hot.

21.5 Electrolyte Drink Formulas

Electrolyte drinks support hydration, particularly important for individuals with POTS (Postural Orthostatic Tachycardia Syndrome) often comorbid with MCAS (Raj et al., 2012).

Basic Electrolyte Drink (Serves 1)

Ingredients: 2 cups water, 2 tablespoons fresh lemon juice (if tolerated) or 1 tablespoon apple cider (not vinegar), 1 tablespoon maple syrup, 1/4 teaspoon sea salt.

Instructions: Combine all ingredients. Stir until salt dissolves. Drink throughout day. Make fresh daily.

Coconut Electrolyte Blend (Serves 1)

Ingredients: 1 cup coconut water (fresh, check for preservatives), 1 cup water, 1 tablespoon fresh lime juice (if tolerated), 1/8 teaspoon sea salt.

Instructions: Mix all ingredients. Consume within 4 hours.

Orange Alternative Hydration (Serves 1, if citrus avoided)

Ingredients: 2 cups water, 2 tablespoons fresh cucumber juice, 1 tablespoon maple syrup, 1/4 teaspoon sea salt, fresh mint.

Instructions: Combine water, cucumber juice, maple syrup, and salt. Add fresh mint. Serve chilled.

21.6 Infused Water Combinations

Infused waters add subtle flavor encouraging hydration (Patil et al., 2004).

Cucumber Mint Water (Serves 4)

Ingredients: 6 cups water, 1 cucumber (sliced), 10 fresh mint leaves.

Instructions: Combine all ingredients in pitcher. Refrigerate 2-4 hours. Consume within 24 hours.

Citrus Free Fruit Water (Serves 4)

Ingredients: 6 cups water, 1 cup fresh blueberries, 1 apple (sliced), fresh basil leaves.

Instructions: Combine in pitcher. Refrigerate 2-4 hours. Drink within 24 hours.

Ginger Lemon Water (Serves 4, if lemon tolerated)

Ingredients: 6 cups water, 2-inch piece fresh ginger (sliced thin), 1 lemon (sliced).

Instructions: Combine in pitcher. Refrigerate 2-4 hours. Consume within 24 hours.

21.7 Case Study: Beverage Ritual Restoration

Background

Faramond, a 39-year-old writer, struggled with the loss of his morning coffee ritual. Coffee had structured his mornings for 20 years. The routine of brewing, the aroma, the warm mug, and the caffeine boost all signaled work beginning. Without coffee, his mornings felt disjointed. He'd replaced it with water but the absence of ritual left him feeling like something was missing beyond simple caffeine.

Presentation

Faramond reported difficulty transitioning into work mode mornings. He'd sit at his desk with water, feeling none of the "ready to write" signal that coffee had provided. His productivity declined in morning hours, improving only after lunch. He intellectually understood coffee was problematic (caused afternoon anxiety and disrupted sleep even pre-diagnosis) but emotionally missed the ritual.

He'd tried herbal teas but found bagged chamomile "boring and medicinal." He hadn't experimented beyond basic chamomile from the grocery store. He didn't realize that fresh herbal preparations or interesting blends could provide ritual and enjoyment comparable to coffee without the problematic effects.

Analysis

Faramond's struggle highlighted the distinction between beverage as nutrition versus beverage as ritual and comfort. Coffee's value extended beyond caffeine content to include sensory experience (aroma, warmth, taste), ritual structure (brewing process, familiar mug, specific timing), and psychological association (coffee equals work mode).

Research on habit formation shows that cue-routine-reward loops become deeply ingrained (Wood & Neal, 2007). His morning routine (cue: wake up, routine: brew and drink coffee, reward: alertness and work readiness) had operated for two decades. Simply removing coffee without replacing the ritual left the cue-reward gap unfilled.

Intervention

A health coach helped Faramond develop a new morning beverage ritual emphasizing the experiential aspects he'd valued in coffee. They created a "morning blend" herbal tea using fresh ginger, turmeric, chamomile, and fresh mint from section 21.2. The preparation involved slicing fresh ginger, steeping 10 minutes, and adding maple syrup and coconut milk.

The key was ritual rather than just beverage content. He used his favorite coffee mug. He maintained the brewing ritual (measuring ingredients, heating water, steeping, preparing). The warm beverage with pleasant aroma and flavor satisfied sensory aspects. The turmeric provided gentle energizing effects without caffeine's problematic properties.

They added a second component. Afternoon, when he'd previously had second coffee, he prepared fresh mint tea using mint from a plant on his windowsill. The act of picking fresh mint leaves, smelling the herb, and brewing fresh tea created an enjoyable ritual marking afternoon break.

Outcome

Faramond's morning transition improved within one week. The new ritual provided structure and pleasure comparable to coffee. He reported that the golden milk variation of his morning tea (adding turmeric and ginger per section 21.4) created satisfying warmth and subtle invigoration without caffeine jitters or afternoon crash.

The fresh mint tea ritual became a favorite afternoon break. Walking to his windowsill herb plant, selecting fresh leaves, and brewing tea created a physical activity break beneficial for long writing sessions. The ritual marked transition time comparable to his previous coffee breaks.

Six months later, he'd expanded his beverage rotation. He prepared different herbal blends seasonally (ginger-heavy in winter for warming, mint-heavy in summer for cooling). The variety prevented monotony while maintaining ritual structure. He reported no longer missing coffee, having replaced it with something he actually preferred for his needs.

Teaching Points

- Beverage replacement requires addressing ritual, sensory, and psychological components beyond simple nutritional substitution, with preparation process, aroma, temperature, and associated routines providing value independent of beverage content that simple water consumption cannot replicate
- Fresh herbal preparations using ingredients like ginger, turmeric, mint, and chamomile provide complex flavors and gentle effects comparable to coffee's sensory richness without problematic caffeine or aged tea leaf histamine content
- Strategic ritual development around new beverages including specific mugs, preparation processes, and timing associations enables psychological transition from eliminated beverage to new preferred option rather than experience of deprivation from permanent loss

21.8 Anti Inflammatory Tonics

Anti-inflammatory drinks provide therapeutic benefits beyond hydration (Gupta et al., 2013).

Turmeric Ginger Tonic (Serves 1)

Ingredients: 1-inch piece fresh turmeric, 1-inch piece fresh ginger, 1 cup water, 1 tablespoon fresh lemon juice (if tolerated), 1 teaspoon maple syrup, pinch black pepper.

Instructions: Simmer turmeric and ginger in water 10 minutes. Strain. Add lemon juice, maple syrup, and black pepper. Drink warm.

Green Veggie Tonic (Serves 1)

Ingredients: 1 cucumber, 2 celery stalks, 1 cup fresh spinach (if tolerated), 1 apple, 1/2 lemon (if tolerated), small piece fresh ginger.

Instructions: Juice all ingredients. Drink immediately for maximum benefit.

21.9 Putting Knowledge Into Practice

This chapter provided beverage and drink recipes restoring variety beyond plain water. Herbal tea options using fresh mint, ginger, turmeric, basil, chamomile, and rooibos replace aged traditional teas. Fresh juices from vegetables and fruits provide nutrients when consumed immediately. Smoothies combine produce with coconut milk for satisfying drinks.

Golden milk variations using turmeric and warming spices offer anti-inflammatory benefits. Electrolyte drink formulas support hydration needs, particularly for POTS patients requiring enhanced fluid and salt intake. Infused waters add subtle flavors encouraging consumption. Anti-inflammatory tonics provide therapeutic effects.

The case study illustrated how beverage replacement requires addressing ritual and psychological components beyond nutrition, with fresh herbal preparation processes creating satisfying routines comparable to eliminated beverages. Strategic variety through seasonal rotations and preparation rituals prevents monotony while maintaining histamine safety.

Chapter 22.0: Desserts and Sweet Options

Theodora watched her family eat birthday cake, her plain fresh blueberries feeling inadequate celebratory food. The cake contained aged eggs, commercial frosting with preservatives, and chocolate (histamine liberator). She'd accepted that conventional desserts were off-limits but hadn't realized that accepting restriction didn't eliminate desire. Birthdays, holidays, dinner parties, and regular weeknight dessert routines all featured sweets. Being the person who "can't have dessert" at every gathering emphasized difference and restriction. She wanted something that felt treat-like, celebratory, and satisfying rather than just "technically compliant but obviously not real dessert." The dessert challenge extends beyond simple sweet cravings for many managing dietary restrictions (Macht & Dettmer, 2006). Desserts signal celebration, reward, comfort, and normalcy. They mark special occasions and provide daily pleasure. Complete dessert elimination without developing satisfying alternatives creates psychological deprivation regardless of physical health improvements.

This chapter provides 15 dessert and sweet treat recipes including fruit-based desserts, baked goods from cookies to cakes, frozen treats, energy balls and bites, special occasion desserts, and naturally sweetened options that restore celebratory and comfort food experiences while maintaining histamine safety through fresh ingredients and immediate consumption or proper freezing.

22.1 Fruit Based Dessert Foundations

Fruit desserts emphasize fresh fruit's natural sweetness (Boyer & Liu, 2004). The key is preparation and presentation transforming simple fruit into special treats.

Baked Apples (Serves 4)

Ingredients: 4 large apples (cored but not completely through bottom), 4 tablespoons maple syrup, 2 teaspoons cinnamon (if tolerated), 4 tablespoons coconut flakes, optional: 2 tablespoons sunflower seed butter (if tolerated).

Instructions: Preheat oven to 375°F. Place cored apples in baking dish. Fill centers with mixture of maple syrup, cinnamon, coconut flakes, and sunflower seed butter if using. Add 1/2 inch water to pan. Bake 35-40 minutes until tender. Serve warm.

Fresh Fruit Compote (Serves 6)

Ingredients: 4 cups mixed fresh fruit (blueberries, apples diced, fresh mango if tolerated), 2 tablespoons maple syrup, 1/4 cup water, 1 teaspoon vanilla extract, 1/2 teaspoon cinnamon (if tolerated).

Instructions: Combine all ingredients in pot. Simmer gently 15-20 minutes until fruit is tender and liquid slightly thickened. Serve warm over coconut milk ice cream or alone.

Poached Pears (Serves 4)

Ingredients: 4 pears (peeled, halved, cores removed), 2 cups water, 1/4 cup maple syrup, 1 teaspoon vanilla extract, 1 cinnamon stick (if tolerated).

Instructions: Combine water, maple syrup, vanilla, and cinnamon stick in pot large enough to hold pears. Bring to simmer. Add pears. Simmer gently 20-25 minutes until tender. Remove pears. Simmer liquid 5-10 minutes more to reduce slightly. Serve pears with reduced syrup.

Berry Coconut Crumble (Serves 6)

Ingredients: 4 cups fresh blueberries, 2 tablespoons maple syrup, 1 tablespoon arrowroot or tapioca starch. Topping: 1 cup coconut flakes, 1/2 cup rice flour, 1/4 cup coconut oil, 2 tablespoons maple syrup, 1/4 teaspoon salt.

Instructions: Preheat oven to 350°F. Toss berries with maple syrup and starch. Place in baking dish. Mix topping ingredients until crumbly. Sprinkle over berries. Bake 35-40 minutes until bubbly and topping is golden.

22.2 Baked Good Recipes

Baked goods using safe flours and sweeteners create treats comparable to conventional versions (Gallagher et al., 2004).

Simple Sugar Cookies (Makes 24)

Ingredients: 2 cups rice flour, 1/2 cup coconut oil (softened), 1/2 cup maple syrup, 1 egg (if tolerated), 1 teaspoon vanilla extract, 1/2 teaspoon baking soda, 1/4 teaspoon salt.

Instructions: Preheat oven to 350°F. Cream coconut oil and maple syrup. Add egg and vanilla. Mix flour, baking soda, and salt. Combine wet and dry ingredients. Roll into 1-inch balls. Place on parchment-lined baking sheet. Flatten slightly. Bake 12-15 minutes until edges are lightly golden. Cool completely. Freeze portions.

Vanilla Cupcakes (Makes 12)

Ingredients: 2 cups rice flour, 1/2 cup maple syrup, 1/2 cup coconut oil (melted), 1 cup coconut milk, 2 eggs (if tolerated), 1 tablespoon vanilla extract, 2 teaspoons baking powder, 1/2 teaspoon salt.

Instructions: Preheat oven to 350°F. Line muffin tin with papers. Mix dry ingredients. Whisk wet ingredients. Combine. Divide among muffin cups. Bake 20-22 minutes until toothpick comes out clean. Cool completely before frosting if desired.

Coconut Frosting (Frosts 12 cupcakes)

Ingredients: 1 can coconut cream (refrigerated overnight, use only solid white part), 1/4 cup maple syrup, 1 teaspoon vanilla extract.

Instructions: Scoop solid coconut cream into bowl (discard liquid). Beat with mixer 3-5 minutes until fluffy. Add maple syrup and vanilla. Beat until combined. Use immediately or refrigerate up to 2 days.

Blueberry Muffins (Makes 12)

Ingredients: 2 cups rice flour, 1/2 cup maple syrup, 1/2 cup coconut oil (melted), 1 cup coconut milk, 2 eggs (if tolerated), 1 teaspoon vanilla, 2 teaspoons baking powder, 1/2 teaspoon salt, 1.5 cups fresh blueberries.

Instructions: Preheat oven to 375°F. Line muffin tin. Mix dry ingredients. Whisk wet ingredients. Combine. Fold in blueberries gently. Divide among muffin cups. Bake 22-25 minutes. Cool completely. Freeze portions.

Simple Cake (Serves 8)

Ingredients: 2.5 cups rice flour, 3/4 cup maple syrup, 3/4 cup coconut oil (melted), 1.5 cups coconut milk, 3 eggs (if tolerated), 1 tablespoon vanilla, 1 tablespoon baking powder, 1/2 teaspoon salt.

Instructions: Preheat oven to 350°F. Grease 9x13 pan. Mix dry ingredients. Whisk wet ingredients. Combine. Pour into pan. Bake 35-40 minutes until toothpick comes out clean. Cool completely before frosting if desired.

22.3 Frozen Treat Options

Frozen desserts provide refreshing treats (Clarke, 2004).

Coconut Milk Ice Cream Base (Serves 4)

Ingredients: 2 cans coconut milk (full-fat), 1/2 cup maple syrup, 1 tablespoon vanilla extract.

Instructions: Whisk all ingredients. Churn in ice cream maker according to manufacturer directions. Freeze until firm. Variations: Add fresh fruit puree, cocoa powder (if tolerated), or fresh mint during churning.

Banana Free Nice Cream (Serves 2)

Ingredients: 2 cups frozen cauliflower rice, 1 cup coconut milk, 1/4 cup maple syrup, 1 teaspoon vanilla extract.

Instructions: Blend frozen cauliflower, coconut milk, maple syrup, and vanilla until very smooth and creamy. Serve immediately as soft-serve or freeze 2 hours for firmer texture.

Fruit Popsicles (Makes 6)

Ingredients: 2 cups fresh fruit (blueberries, mango, or mix), 1/2 cup coconut milk, 2 tablespoons maple syrup.

Instructions: Blend all ingredients until smooth. Pour into popsicle molds. Freeze 4-6 hours until solid.

Frozen Coconut Bites (Makes 20)

Ingredients: 2 cups coconut flakes, 1/2 cup coconut oil (melted), 1/4 cup maple syrup, 1 teaspoon vanilla extract, pinch salt.

Instructions: Mix all ingredients. Press into mini muffin tin or shape into small balls. Freeze until solid. Store frozen. Eat frozen (they melt quickly).

22.4 Case Study: Celebration Food Development

Background

Leocadia, a 47-year-old mother of three, felt excluded from family celebrations due to dessert restrictions. Her children's birthdays, holidays, and family gatherings all featured conventional desserts she couldn't eat. She'd tried bringing plain fruit to events but feeling like "the person who can't participate" at every celebration created resentment toward her dietary needs.

Presentation

Leocadia reported increasing non-compliance around celebrations. She'd maintained strict adherence during regular days but "made exceptions" at special events, eating small amounts of conventional cake or cookies "just to participate." These exceptions triggered symptoms but the psychological pull of participation outweighed symptom consequences in the moment.

She believed desserts required ingredients she couldn't have. Her attempts at "healthy desserts" using dates (aged), nut butters (high histamine), and cacao (histamine liberator) had all triggered reactions. She'd concluded that real desserts were impossible and plain fruit was her only option, creating the deprivation driving her non-compliance.

Analysis

Leocadia's pattern demonstrated how celebration food holds psychological significance beyond nutrition. Research shows that food neophobia (fear of new foods) and ritual adherence around special occasions are deeply ingrained cultural patterns (Macht & Dettmer, 2006). Being the only person not participating in traditional celebration food creates social isolation and psychological restriction feelings.

Her failed "healthy dessert" attempts had used ingredients problematic for histamine despite being nutritionally sound. Dates concentrate histamine through drying and aging. Many nut butters trigger reactions. Cacao liberates histamine. Her conclusion that desserts were impossible reflected trying wrong ingredients rather than fundamental impossibility.

Intervention

A dietitian taught Leocadia three celebration-worthy desserts from this chapter: coconut frosted cupcakes (section 22.2), berry coconut crumble (section 22.1), and coconut milk ice cream (section 22.3). They baked cupcakes together, demonstrating that rice flour, coconut oil, maple syrup, and fresh ingredients created legitimate treats.

The key was presentation and occasion appropriateness. The cupcakes, frosted with whipped coconut cream and topped with fresh blueberries, looked celebration-worthy. They didn't look "diet food" or "restriction food." Her children couldn't distinguish them from conventional cupcakes visually, removing the obvious difference marker.

She developed a rotation for family events. Her daughter's birthday featured coconut frosted cupcakes (everyone ate them, not just Leocadia). Her son's birthday featured berry crumble served warm with coconut ice cream. Holiday dinners included multiple dessert options with her providing one that worked for her but looked and tasted good enough that others chose it too.

Outcome

Leocadia's celebration non-compliance stopped within one month. Having desserts that felt special and looked appropriate for occasions eliminated the participation gap. She no longer felt like "the different one" when she ate her cupcake while others ate conventional cake, especially when several family members chose her version voluntarily.

Her children began requesting her coconut cupcakes for their birthdays. They preferred the taste to conventional versions. This shift from "Mom's special restricted food" to "the good dessert everyone wants" transformed the psychological dynamic from deprivation to preference.

One year later, her extended family expected her to bring dessert to gatherings. Her contributions had become anticipated treats rather than accommodations for her restrictions. The berry crumble became a requested holiday tradition. This integration of her dietary needs into family food culture eliminated the isolation and difference feelings.

Teaching Points

- Celebration food serves psychological and social functions beyond nutrition, with participation in ritual dessert consumption providing belonging and normalcy that plain fruit alternatives cannot replicate regardless of nutritional adequacy
- Successful dessert development requires both compliant ingredients and presentation matching celebration contexts, with treats looking and tasting appropriate for occasions rather than obviously different or inferior to conventional versions
- Integration of individually-appropriate desserts into broader family or social food culture through creating items others voluntarily choose transforms dietary restrictions from isolating difference to valued contribution, eliminating psychological deprivation while maintaining physical safety

22.5 Special Occasion Desserts

Special occasion treats create celebration-worthy centerpieces (Gallagher et al., 2004).

Layered Fruit Parfait (Serves 6)

Ingredients: 3 cups fresh fruit (blueberries, diced mango, diced apple), 2 cups coconut cream (whipped with maple syrup), 1 cup coconut flakes (toasted).

Instructions: Layer fruit, whipped coconut cream, and toasted coconut in glasses or bowl. Repeat layers. Serve immediately or refrigerate up to 2 hours.

Coconut Cake with Frosting (Serves 10)

Instructions: Use Simple Cake recipe from section 22.2. Once cooled, frost with Coconut Frosting. Decorate with fresh fruit, coconut flakes, or edible flowers.

22.6 Naturally Sweetened Options

Natural sweeteners include maple syrup, honey (if tolerated), and fresh fruit purees.

Maple Candied Nuts (Makes 2 cups, if nuts tolerated)

Ingredients: 2 cups almonds or pecans, 1/4 cup maple syrup, 1/4 teaspoon salt.

Instructions: Preheat oven to 300°F. Toss nuts with maple syrup and salt. Spread on parchment-lined baking sheet. Bake 20-25 minutes, stirring every 10 minutes. Cool completely (they'll crisp as they cool). Store in airtight container 1 week.

Fruit Leather (Makes 8 strips)

Ingredients: 4 cups fresh fruit (strawberries if tolerated, mango, or blueberries), 2 tablespoons maple syrup.

Instructions: Puree fruit with maple syrup until very smooth. Spread 1/4 inch thick on parchment-lined baking sheet. Bake at 170°F for 4-6 hours until dried but still pliable. Cut into strips. Store in airtight container 1 week.

22.7 Additional Sweet Treats

Energy Bites (Makes 16, repeated from Chapter 19.0 for dessert context)

Ingredients: 1.5 cups sunflower seeds (if tolerated), 1/2 cup coconut flakes, 1/4 cup maple syrup, 2 tablespoons coconut oil, fresh apple puree.

Instructions: Process ingredients. Roll into balls. Freeze.

Coconut Macaroons (Makes 24, repeated from Chapter 19.0)

Ingredients: 3 cups coconut flakes, 1/2 cup maple syrup, 2 egg whites (if tolerated), 1 teaspoon vanilla, 1/4 teaspoon salt.

Instructions: Mix all ingredients. Drop onto baking sheet. Bake at 325°F for 20-25 minutes until golden. Cool completely.

22.8 Core Concepts Recap

This chapter provided dessert and sweet treat recipes restoring celebratory food experiences. Fruit-based desserts from baked apples to berry crumble emphasize natural sweetness through preparation and presentation. Baked goods including cookies, cupcakes, muffins, and cakes use rice flour, coconut oil, maple syrup, and eggs if tolerated to create treats comparable to conventional versions.

Frozen treats from coconut milk ice cream to fruit popsicles provide refreshing options. Energy balls and coconut macaroons offer portable sweet snacks. Special occasion desserts including layered parfaits and frosted cakes create celebration centerpieces. Naturally sweetened options using maple syrup and fruit purees avoid refined sugars.

The case study illustrated how celebration food serves psychological and social functions beyond nutrition, with presentation matching celebration contexts and voluntary family adoption transforming restrictions from isolating difference to valued contribution. Strategic dessert development enables participation in food rituals supporting belonging and normalcy.

Part VI: Supplement Protocols & Therapeutic Support

Chapter 23.0: DAO Enzyme Supplementation

Darian stood in the supplement aisle staring at a bottle of DAO enzyme with equal parts hope and skepticism. The label promised "clinically proven histamine breakdown support." After six months of strict dietary elimination providing only partial relief, his gastroenterologist suggested trying DAO supplementation alongside his careful eating. But Darian had questions. How could taking an enzyme pill help when his body should produce this naturally? Why had some people in online forums reported dramatic improvements while others experienced no benefit? The bottle cost forty dollars for a 30-day supply. Was this legitimate therapy or expensive placebo? His confusion reflected a common pattern. **Diamine oxidase (DAO)** supplementation has gained popularity for histamine intolerance management, yet many people lack clear understanding of what DAO does, how supplementation works, which products differ in effectiveness, and how to integrate DAO into treatment plans (Schnedl et al., 2019).

This chapter explains DAO enzyme fundamentals, reviews current research on supplementation effectiveness, compares porcine and plant-based sources, details dosing strategies and timing protocols, identifies cofactors enhancing DAO function, addresses safety and side effects, explores individual response variation, discusses combining DAO with dietary approaches, and examines cost considerations and product selection criteria for informed decision making.

23.1 DAO Enzyme Fundamentals

Diamine oxidase (DAO) is the primary enzyme responsible for breaking down histamine in the digestive tract (Maintz & Novak, 2007). This enzyme sits in the intestinal lining, particularly concentrated in the small intestine, where it degrades dietary histamine before it enters the bloodstream. In healthy individuals with adequate DAO production, most ingested histamine gets broken down before causing systemic effects.

DAO deficiency represents one of the major mechanisms underlying histamine intolerance. When DAO production or activity is inadequate, dietary histamine passes through the intestinal barrier and triggers symptoms (Maintz & Novak, 2007). Multiple factors can impair DAO function. Genetic variations in the **AOC1 gene** (which codes for DAO production) affect baseline enzyme levels. Intestinal inflammation from conditions like celiac disease, inflammatory bowel disease, or SIBO damages the intestinal lining where DAO is produced. Certain medications including NSAIDs, some antibiotics, and histamine H2 blockers can inhibit DAO activity. Nutrient deficiencies in DAO cofactors (vitamin C, vitamin B6, copper) impair enzyme function even when production is adequate.

DAO supplementation provides exogenous enzyme to compensate for deficiency. The supplements contain DAO enzyme extracted from animal or plant sources. Taken before meals, the supplemental DAO theoretically breaks down dietary histamine in the digestive tract similar to endogenous enzyme, preventing histamine absorption and subsequent symptoms. This represents symptomatic management rather than root cause treatment, addressing the consequence of DAO deficiency without fixing underlying production issues.

The distinction matters. DAO supplementation can enable dietary flexibility and symptom reduction while addressing root causes (healing gut damage, correcting nutrient deficiencies, removing inflammatory triggers). Some people need supplementation temporarily during healing. Others require ongoing supplementation due to genetic or permanent DAO impairment. Understanding this framework prevents viewing DAO as either cure-all or useless intervention, recognizing instead its role as supportive tool within broader treatment.

23.2 Current Research Evidence

Recent clinical trials have examined DAO supplementation effectiveness for histamine intolerance symptoms. A 2019 double-blind, placebo-controlled study by Schnedl and colleagues found that DAO supplementation (4.2 mg before meals) significantly reduced gastrointestinal symptoms, headaches, and skin reactions in individuals with confirmed histamine intolerance compared to placebo over four weeks (Schnedl et al., 2019). The treatment group reported 67% reduction in symptom severity versus 23% in placebo group, suggesting genuine therapeutic effect beyond placebo response.

A 2021 study examined DAO supplementation in migraine patients with suspected histamine sensitivity (Izquierdo-Casas et al., 2021). Participants taking DAO (4.2 mg with each meal) experienced 29% reduction in migraine frequency and 35% reduction in migraine severity over 12 weeks compared to baseline. The placebo group showed no significant improvement. This suggests DAO may benefit specific symptom presentations beyond general histamine intolerance.

Research from 2023 investigated DAO supplementation effects on intestinal permeability in individuals with histamine intolerance. The study found that combining DAO supplementation with low-histamine diet produced greater improvement in intestinal barrier function (measured via lactulose-mannitol testing) than diet alone over eight weeks. This suggests DAO supplementation may support gut healing beyond simply reducing histamine load.

However, not all studies show benefit. A 2020 trial found no significant difference between DAO supplementation and placebo in a general population without confirmed histamine intolerance (Mušič et al., 2020). This highlights that DAO supplementation benefits those with actual DAO deficiency rather than providing universal advantages. Response depends on individual biochemistry and underlying mechanisms driving symptoms.

The emerging evidence suggests DAO supplementation provides meaningful benefit for subset of individuals with confirmed or suspected histamine intolerance, particularly those with documented DAO deficiency or specific symptom patterns like migraines and gastrointestinal complaints. The intervention appears safe with minimal side effects, making it reasonable to trial under appropriate guidance even while awaiting more extensive research.

23.3 Porcine Versus Plant Sources

Porcine-derived DAO represents the most common and well-researched supplemental form. This DAO is extracted from pig kidney, where the enzyme naturally occurs in high concentrations (Maintz & Novak, 2007). The molecular structure closely matches human DAO, potentially providing superior activity. Most clinical trials demonstrating DAO effectiveness have used porcine-derived supplements, establishing evidence base for this source.

Advantages of porcine DAO include established efficacy through multiple studies, high enzyme activity per dose, and widespread availability in commercial products. The standardization of porcine DAO extraction enables consistent dosing across batches. Most products provide 4.2 mg per capsule, the dose used in clinical research.

Disadvantages include animal-source concerns for vegetarians, vegans, and individuals with religious dietary restrictions. Some people experience digestive upset from porcine-derived supplements. Quality varies among manufacturers, with some products containing lower DAO activity than claimed. Cost tends to be higher, with monthly supplies typically ranging from 30-60 dollars.

Plant-based DAO has emerged more recently, typically derived from pea seedlings. The extraction process yields DAO enzyme without animal products, appealing to plant-based eaters (Kettner et al., 2021). However, research on plant-based DAO effectiveness remains limited compared to porcine sources.

Advantages include suitability for vegetarians and vegans, potentially better tolerability for those sensitive to animal products, and alignment with plant-based dietary approaches. Some users report fewer digestive side effects with plant-based versions.

Disadvantages include less research establishing efficacy, potentially lower enzyme activity per dose requiring higher amounts for equivalent effect, limited product availability, and often higher cost per effective dose. The molecular structure of plant-derived DAO differs slightly from human DAO, theoretically affecting activity though practical significance remains unclear.

23.4 Dosing and Timing Strategies

Standard dosing based on clinical research involves taking one 4.2 mg DAO capsule 15-20 minutes before meals (Schnedl et al., 2019). This timing allows the enzyme to reach the small intestine before dietary histamine arrives, maximizing breakdown efficiency. Taking DAO with food rather than before reduces effectiveness, as the enzyme works best when present in the digestive tract before histamine exposure.

Meal-based protocols adjust DAO use according to expected histamine content. High-histamine meals (aged cheese, cured meats, fermented foods, restaurant meals with unknown ingredients) warrant DAO supplementation. Low-histamine home-cooked meals using fresh ingredients may not require DAO, allowing more economical use while maintaining benefit. This selective approach requires understanding one's diet and histamine content of foods per Chapter 4.0.

Loading dose approaches involve taking DAO with every meal for initial 2-4 weeks regardless of meal content, then transitioning to selective use based on response patterns. This strategy helps establish whether DAO provides benefit and identifies which meals trigger symptoms needing enzyme support. Some people discover that certain meal types consistently require DAO while others don't.

Ongoing versus as-needed use represents a decision point after initial trial. Some individuals benefit from continuous DAO supplementation with every meal, maintaining steady symptom control. Others use DAO selectively for higher-risk meals (dining out, social events, meals with known histamine-containing foods). Cost considerations often drive this choice, with continuous use costing 30-60 dollars monthly versus as-needed use reducing expense substantially.

Dosing adjustments may be necessary. Some people require two capsules before particularly high-histamine meals for adequate symptom control. Others find half a capsule sufficient for borderline meals. Individual experimentation guided by symptom tracking identifies optimal dosing. Starting with standard single-capsule dosing and adjusting based on response prevents both under-dosing (inadequate benefit) and over-dosing (unnecessary expense).

23.5 DAO Cofactor Support

Vitamin C functions as essential cofactor for DAO enzyme activity (Maintz & Novak, 2007). The enzyme requires vitamin C to catalyze histamine breakdown efficiently. Deficiency in vitamin C impairs DAO function even when enzyme levels are adequate. Supplementing vitamin C alongside DAO may enhance effectiveness.

Recommended vitamin C dosing ranges from 500-1000 mg daily in divided doses. **Buffered vitamin C** (calcium ascorbate or magnesium ascorbate) is preferred for individuals with MCAS or sensitive digestive systems, as unbuffered ascorbic acid can trigger mast cell degranulation in susceptible individuals (Carr & Maggini, 2017). Taking vitamin C with DAO supplements provides immediate cofactor support for the exogenous enzyme.

Vitamin B6 (pyridoxine) serves as another DAO cofactor necessary for optimal enzyme function (Maintz & Novak, 2007). B6 deficiency, common in individuals with digestive issues or poor nutrient absorption, can limit DAO activity. Supplementing B6 at 25-50 mg daily supports DAO function. The activated form, **pyridoxal-5-phosphate (P5P)**, may provide superior benefit for individuals with conversion issues, though standard pyridoxine suffices for most people.

Copper acts as structural component and cofactor for DAO enzyme (Maintz & Novak, 2007). Copper deficiency impairs DAO production and activity. However, copper supplementation requires caution. Excess copper can cause problems, and many multivitamins provide adequate amounts. Testing copper levels before supplementing prevents inadvertent toxicity. If copper supplementation is indicated (confirmed deficiency through testing), typical dosing ranges from 1-2 mg daily, though this should be guided by healthcare provider given copper's potential for harm at excessive doses.

Zinc indirectly supports DAO function by supporting intestinal health and immune function (Skrovanek et al., 2014). While not a direct DAO cofactor, zinc deficiency impairs gut healing and may worsen the intestinal damage reducing DAO production. Zinc supplementation at 15-30 mg daily (taken separately from copper due to competitive absorption) supports overall gut health creating better conditions for DAO production.

23.6 Case Study: DAO Supplementation Success

Background

Eudora, a 44-year-old graphic designer, maintained strict low-histamine diet for eight months with partial symptom improvement. Her digestive symptoms (bloating, diarrhea) had reduced by about 60%, but she continued experiencing headaches and flushing 3-4 times weekly. These symptoms occurred unpredictably, sometimes after seemingly safe meals. She felt frustrated by persistent symptoms despite dietary diligence and avoided social dining entirely due to symptom unpredictability.

Presentation

Eudora described feeling trapped by her diet. She'd eliminated all obvious histamine sources, rotated fresh foods carefully, and followed all protocols from Chapters 8.0 and 9.0. Yet symptoms persisted. She noticed symptoms occurred more often when eating out (even when ordering carefully) or when eating leftovers despite proper storage within 24-hour guidelines. Her quality of life remained compromised. She'd declined multiple dinner invitations, skipped her book club's restaurant meetings, and felt isolated by dietary restrictions.

Analysis

Eudora's pattern suggested DAO deficiency as contributing factor. Her partial response to low-histamine diet indicated dietary histamine played a role, but persistent symptoms despite strict adherence suggested she couldn't tolerate even moderate histamine levels present in properly handled fresh foods. The worsening with restaurant meals and leftovers (both slightly higher histamine than fresh home-cooked) supported this interpretation.

Research shows that some individuals with histamine intolerance have genetic or acquired DAO deficiency requiring enzyme supplementation beyond dietary management alone (Maintz & Novak, 2007). Eudora's symptoms fit this profile. Her gastroenterologist ordered DAO activity testing, which showed levels at lower limit of normal range, suggesting borderline deficiency explaining partial dietary response.

Intervention

Eudora began DAO supplementation (porcine-derived, 4.2 mg) taken 15 minutes before meals. She started taking DAO before every meal for the first four weeks to establish baseline response. She continued her established low-histamine diet, adding DAO rather than replacing dietary management.

She also addressed cofactor support. Her vitamin C intake had been low (avoiding citrus due to histamine liberator concerns). She added buffered vitamin C (500 mg twice daily) and vitamin B6 (25 mg daily) to support DAO function per section 23.5. Her zinc levels were already adequate from previous supplementation.

She tracked symptoms meticulously, noting meals, DAO use, and any reactions. This data would guide longer-term strategy for when to use DAO versus when unnecessary.

Outcome

Within two weeks, Eudora's headaches decreased to once weekly. By week four, headaches occurred only twice over the entire month. Her flushing episodes stopped completely. She reported feeling "80-85% better" rather than the previous 60%. The additional symptom reduction from DAO supplementation made substantial difference in quality of life.

After the initial four-week trial, she experimented with selective DAO use. She discovered she needed DAO before restaurant meals and any meal containing foods stored more than 12 hours (even refrigerated). Fresh home-cooked meals from ingredients used within hours of purchase didn't require DAO. This selective approach reduced her monthly supplement cost from 50 dollars to about 20 dollars while maintaining symptom control.

Six months later, she'd reintegrated social dining. She attended book club restaurant meetings, bringing DAO capsules to take before meals. She accepted dinner invitations, explaining she'd bring supplement enabling her to eat safely. Her isolation resolved. She described DAO as "the missing piece" that made the difference between "managing symptoms" and "living normally."

Teaching Points

- DAO supplementation provides additional benefit for individuals with DAO deficiency beyond what dietary management alone achieves, particularly for those with partial response to strict low-histamine eating indicating enzymatic component to their intolerance
- Strategic rather than universal DAO use (before higher-risk meals rather than all meals) maintains benefit while reducing cost, requiring individual experimentation to determine which meals trigger symptoms needing enzyme support
- Combining DAO supplementation with cofactor support (vitamin C, B6) and continued dietary management creates synergistic approach addressing multiple aspects of histamine metabolism for optimal symptom control and quality of life restoration

23.7 Safety and Side Effects

DAO supplementation safety appears favorable based on available research (Schnedl et al., 2019). Clinical trials have reported minimal adverse effects, with DAO supplements generally well tolerated. The enzyme breaks down to amino acids during digestion, similar to other dietary proteins, preventing accumulation or toxicity concerns.

Common side effects when reported include mild digestive upset (nausea, stomach discomfort) in approximately 5-10% of users. This typically occurs early in supplementation and often resolves within 1-2 weeks as the body adjusts. Taking DAO with small amount of food rather than completely empty stomach may reduce this effect while maintaining therapeutic benefit.

Allergic reactions to porcine-derived DAO are theoretically possible in individuals with pork allergy, though rarely reported in practice. People with known pork allergy should use plant-based DAO alternatives or avoid supplementation entirely. Signs of allergic reaction (hives, difficulty breathing, throat swelling) warrant immediate discontinuation and emergency medical attention.

Interactions with medications remain poorly studied. DAO supplements may theoretically interact with medications metabolized by similar enzymatic pathways, though no specific interactions have been documented in clinical literature. People taking multiple medications should consult healthcare providers before starting DAO supplementation to identify potential concerns.

Pregnancy and breastfeeding safety lacks adequate research. While DAO is naturally occurring enzyme and supplementation theoretically poses minimal risk, the absence of safety data in pregnant or breastfeeding women means supplementation should only occur under medical supervision in these populations.

Quality control concerns affect supplement safety. DAO supplements are regulated as dietary supplements rather than medications, allowing less stringent quality oversight. Products may contain less DAO activity than labeled, include undisclosed fillers, or suffer contamination issues. Choosing products from reputable manufacturers with third-party testing (USP, NSF, or ConsumerLab certification) reduces these risks.

23.8 Individual Response Variation

Response to DAO supplementation varies substantially between individuals. Some people report dramatic symptom improvement within days, experiencing near-complete relief enabling dietary expansion. Others notice modest improvement, requiring DAO alongside strict dietary management for acceptable symptom control. Still others experience no perceptible benefit, finding DAO supplementation ineffective for their particular symptoms (Mušič et al., 2020).

Factors predicting DAO response include underlying mechanism of histamine intolerance. Individuals with primary DAO deficiency (genetic or acquired through intestinal damage) tend to respond most favorably to supplementation, as the intervention directly addresses their mechanism. Those whose histamine intolerance stems primarily from excessive mast cell degranulation or impaired histamine methylation (HNMT pathway) may see less benefit from DAO since their issue doesn't center on digestive histamine breakdown.

Symptom type influences response patterns. Gastrointestinal symptoms and headaches/migraines show better response to DAO supplementation in research studies compared to systemic symptoms like fatigue or brain fog (Izquierdo-Casas et al., 2021). This likely reflects that DAO primarily addresses dietary histamine in the gut rather than systemic histamine from other sources.

Trial duration affects assessment. Some people notice immediate benefit within 1-2 doses, while others require 2-4 weeks of consistent use before improvement emerges. Adequate trial length (minimum four weeks with meals requiring enzyme support) prevents premature conclusions about effectiveness. Discontinuing after days due to perceived lack of benefit may miss delayed response patterns.

Dosing adequacy influences outcomes. Under-dosing (single capsule when two needed, or taking with food rather than before) creates false impression of DAO ineffectiveness. Starting with standard dosing per section 23.4 and adjusting based on response identifies optimal protocol for individual needs.

23.9 Integration with Dietary Management

DAO supplementation complements rather than replaces dietary management. The enzyme breaks down histamine consumed in meals but doesn't address other histamine sources (endogenous production, bacterial formation in stored foods, histamine from non-dietary triggers). Dietary approaches from Chapters 6.0 through 12.0 remain foundational, with DAO adding flexibility and additional symptom reduction.

Strategic integration involves using DAO to enable controlled dietary expansion during reintroduction phases. After establishing baseline tolerance on elimination diet, DAO supplementation before testing new foods may reduce reaction severity if the food proves problematic. This doesn't mean DAO prevents all reactions, but it may moderate histamine-mediated responses creating safer reintroduction environment.

Social dining support represents major benefit of DAO supplementation. Taking DAO before restaurant meals, parties, or social events provides security when eating foods with unknown ingredients or preparation methods. This enables social participation without complete restriction or accepting inevitable symptoms as consequence of participation.

Long-term dietary strategy may involve less restrictive eating with DAO supplementation versus very strict diet without supplementation. Some people find moderate dietary caution combined with consistent DAO use provides better quality of life than extremely restrictive eating alone. Individual preferences and financial considerations guide this decision.

23.10 Product Selection and Cost

Product selection criteria include DAO source (porcine versus plant-based per section 23.3), dosing per capsule (standard 4.2 mg matches research), third-party testing certification, manufacturing reputation, and additional ingredients. Products combining DAO with cofactors (vitamin C, quercetin) may provide convenience though individual supplementation of cofactors allows dose optimization.

Cost considerations affect long-term sustainability. Monthly DAO supplement costs typically range from 30-60 dollars for daily use with all meals. Strategic use (before higher-risk meals only) may reduce monthly costs to 15-25 dollars. Generic brands tend to cost less than name brands, though quality verification through third-party testing becomes more important with less established manufacturers.

Insurance coverage rarely includes DAO supplements as they're classified as dietary supplements rather than medications. This creates out-of-pocket expense that may limit access for some individuals. Discussing cost concerns with healthcare providers may identify lower-cost alternatives or assistance programs, though options remain limited.

Value assessment weighs symptom improvement against financial investment. For individuals achieving substantial benefit enabling dietary flexibility, social participation, and symptom reduction, the cost may represent worthwhile investment. Those experiencing minimal benefit should discontinue rather than continuing expensive ineffective intervention. The four-week trial period allows informed value assessment before committing to long-term use.

23.11 Essential Points to Remember

This chapter examined DAO enzyme supplementation for histamine intolerance management. DAO represents the primary enzyme degrading dietary histamine, with deficiency contributing to histamine intolerance in many individuals. Recent research shows DAO supplementation reduces symptoms in people with confirmed histamine intolerance, particularly gastrointestinal complaints and migraines.

Porcine-derived DAO has strongest research support, while plant-based alternatives suit vegetarian and vegan individuals. Standard dosing involves 4.2 mg taken 15-20 minutes before meals, with timing critical for effectiveness. DAO cofactors including vitamin C, B6, and copper enhance enzyme function and should be addressed alongside supplementation.

Individual response varies substantially based on underlying mechanisms and symptom types. Integration with dietary management creates synergistic approach, with DAO enabling flexibility rather than replacing food-based interventions. Product selection requires attention to quality, dosing, and third-party testing. Cost considerations affect long-term sustainability, making strategic rather than universal use valuable for many individuals.

The case study illustrated how DAO supplementation provided additional benefit beyond dietary management alone for someone with DAO deficiency, enabling social participation and improved quality of life through strategic use before higher-risk meals. This chapter connects to Chapter 24.0's exploration of mast cell stabilizers and natural antihistamines, building comprehensive supplement-based support for histamine intolerance management.

Chapter 24.0: Mast Cell Stabilizers and Antihistamines

Melisande examined the growing collection of supplements on her kitchen counter with a mixture of hope and overwhelm. Her functional medicine practitioner had recommended quercetin for mast cell stabilization, vitamin C for DAO support, omega-3s for inflammation, and a specific probiotic strain for histamine degradation. The supplement regimen now included eight different bottles taken at various times throughout the day. She'd started all of them simultaneously three weeks ago, eager for improvement. Her symptoms had changed (some better, some worse, some new), but she couldn't identify which supplements helped, which hurt, and which did nothing. The shotgun approach created confusion rather than clarity. Her experience illustrated a common mistake in supplement-based histamine management. Starting multiple interventions simultaneously prevents identifying individual effects, makes troubleshooting reactions impossible, and creates unsustainable regimens that people abandon from sheer complexity . Strategic supplement introduction using one-at-a-time methodology with adequate trial periods enables informed decisions about which interventions provide genuine benefit worth continuing.

This chapter examines mast cell stabilizers and natural antihistamines including quercetin mechanisms and dosing, vitamin C applications for MCAS, stinging nettle traditional and modern uses, curcumin anti-inflammatory support, omega-3 selection from low-histamine sources, probiotic strain selection emphasizing histamine-degrading species while avoiding histamine-producing strains, other mast cell stabilizers like luteolin and PEA, one-at-a-time introduction protocols, and systematic response tracking methods.

24.1 Quercetin Fundamentals and Mechanisms

Quercetin is a flavonoid compound found in foods like onions, apples, and capers that functions as mast cell stabilizer through multiple mechanisms (Mlcek et al., 2016). The compound inhibits mast cell degranulation, reducing histamine release from these immune cells. This differs from antihistamine medications that block histamine receptors after release. Quercetin prevents the release itself, addressing histamine at an earlier point in the cascade.

Molecular mechanisms involve quercetin's effects on mast cell membranes and intracellular signaling. The compound stabilizes mast cell membranes, making them less reactive to triggers. It also inhibits calcium influx into mast cells, a necessary step for degranulation (Weng et al., 2012). By blocking this calcium movement, quercetin prevents the cascade leading to histamine release. Additionally, quercetin demonstrates anti-inflammatory properties through NF-kappa B pathway inhibition, reducing overall inflammatory signaling that can trigger mast cell activation.

Research evidence for quercetin's mast cell stabilizing effects comes primarily from laboratory and animal studies, with limited human clinical trials. Laboratory studies show quercetin reduces histamine release from cultured mast cells by 40-95% depending on concentration and trigger type (Weng et al., 2012). Animal studies demonstrate reduced allergic responses and decreased mast cell activation with quercetin supplementation. Human studies remain limited but suggestive. A 2020 pilot study found quercetin supplementation (500 mg twice daily) reduced MCAS symptom severity by approximately 35% over 12 weeks compared to baseline (Theoharides et al., 2020).

Bioavailability challenges affect quercetin effectiveness. Standard quercetin has poor absorption from the digestive tract, with only 2-20% reaching systemic circulation (Mlcek et al., 2016). This low bioavailability means oral supplementation may not achieve tissue concentrations demonstrated effective in laboratory studies. However, newer formulations address this limitation.

Enhanced formulations improve quercetin absorption. **Quercetin phytosome** combines quercetin with phospholipids, increasing absorption approximately 20-fold compared to standard quercetin (Riva et al., 2019). **Quercetin with bromelain** pairs quercetin with the proteolytic enzyme bromelain, which may enhance absorption and provide additional anti-inflammatory effects. These enhanced formulations cost more but potentially provide superior clinical benefit through better bioavailability.

24.2 Quercetin Dosing and Timing

Standard dosing for mast cell stabilization ranges from 500-1000 mg twice daily, though research establishing optimal dosing remains limited (Theoharides et al., 2020). Most studies and clinical protocols use 500 mg taken twice daily (morning and evening) with food to enhance absorption and reduce potential gastric upset.

Timing considerations involve taking quercetin with meals containing some fat, as the flavonoid absorbs better in the presence of dietary lipids. Empty stomach dosing may reduce absorption and increase likelihood of nausea. Spacing doses 8-12 hours apart maintains more consistent blood levels than single daily dosing.

Loading versus maintenance dosing represents one approach. Some practitioners recommend higher initial doses (1000 mg twice daily) for the first 2-4 weeks to establish therapeutic levels, then reducing to maintenance (500 mg twice daily) for ongoing support. However, evidence supporting this strategy over consistent dosing remains anecdotal rather than research-based.

Response timeline varies. Some individuals notice symptom reduction within 3-5 days of starting quercetin, while others require 3-4 weeks for perceptible benefit. Adequate trial duration (minimum four weeks at therapeutic doses) prevents premature discontinuation before effects emerge. Symptom tracking throughout the trial period identifies patterns that may not be obvious day-to-day.

24.3 Vitamin C for MCAS

Vitamin C functions as natural antihistamine and mast cell stabilizer through multiple pathways (Carr & Maggini, 2017). The vitamin degrades histamine directly through oxidation. It also stabilizes mast cell membranes, similar to quercetin's mechanism. Additionally, vitamin C serves as DAO cofactor per Chapter 23.0, supporting enzymatic histamine breakdown. This triple mechanism makes vitamin C foundational supplement for histamine intolerance and MCAS management.

Dosing for histamine management typically ranges from 1000-3000 mg daily in divided doses. Research suggests 1000 mg taken three times daily (with meals) provides sustained blood levels supporting histamine degradation (Carr & Maggini, 2017). Single large doses create brief elevation in blood vitamin C followed by urinary excretion, while divided dosing maintains more consistent therapeutic levels.

Buffered vitamin C importance for MCAS individuals cannot be overstated. Standard ascorbic acid (unbuffered vitamin C) has acidic pH that can trigger mast cell degranulation in sensitive individuals, paradoxically worsening symptoms the supplement aims to improve (Johnston & Solomon, 2007). **Buffered forms** including calcium ascorbate, magnesium ascorbate, or sodium ascorbate have neutral pH preventing this triggering effect. The slight cost premium for buffered forms represents worthwhile investment for MCAS patients.

Intravenous vitamin C provides higher blood levels than oral supplementation achievable, with some MCAS specialists using IV vitamin C therapy for severe cases. Typical IV protocols involve 25-50 grams administered over 1-2 hours weekly or biweekly. This intervention requires medical supervision and IV access but may benefit individuals with severe MCAS unresponsive to oral approaches. Insurance rarely covers IV vitamin C for MCAS, creating substantial out-of-pocket expense limiting accessibility.

24.4 Stinging Nettle Applications

Stinging nettle (Urtica dioica) has traditional use as antihistamine and anti-inflammatory herb with emerging research support (Roschek et al., 2009). The plant contains compounds that inhibit histamine receptors and reduce inflammatory prostaglandin formation. Traditional medicine systems have used nettle for allergic rhinitis, hives, and inflammatory conditions for centuries.

Active compounds in nettle include flavonoids, carotenoids, and phenolic acids that collectively provide antihistamine and anti-inflammatory effects (Roschek et al., 2009). The leaves contain the highest concentration of active compounds, making nettle leaf extract the preferred supplemental form over root or seed preparations.

Research evidence shows nettle reduces histamine-mediated symptoms in several studies. A controlled trial found freeze-dried nettle leaf (300 mg twice daily) reduced allergic rhinitis symptoms by 48% over one week, with 58% of participants rating nettle better than placebo (Mittman, 1990). Another study demonstrated nettle extract inhibited several inflammatory pathways involved in allergic responses. However, research specific to MCAS or histamine intolerance (rather than seasonal allergies) remains limited.

Dosing protocols typically involve 300-600 mg of freeze-dried nettle leaf extract taken twice daily. **Freeze-dried preparations** preserve more active compounds than heat-dried versions, potentially providing superior benefit. Nettle tea made from dried leaves provides gentler approach with lower active compound concentration, suitable for initial trials or those sensitive to supplements.

Cautions include potential interactions with blood pressure medications, blood thinners, and diabetes medications. Nettle may lower blood pressure and blood sugar, requiring medication dose adjustments. Pregnant women should avoid nettle due to potential uterine stimulation effects. Some individuals experience mild digestive upset when starting nettle, typically resolving within a few days.

24.5 Curcumin Anti-Inflammatory Support

Curcumin, the active compound in turmeric, provides powerful anti-inflammatory effects that may indirectly benefit histamine intolerance through reducing overall inflammatory burden (Hewlings & Kalman, 2017). While not a direct mast cell stabilizer like quercetin, curcumin modulates multiple inflammatory pathways involved in MCAS and chronic inflammation.

Mechanisms include NF-kappa B pathway inhibition, COX-2 enzyme suppression, and cytokine modulation. These anti-inflammatory effects reduce the inflammatory environment that can trigger mast cell activation, potentially decreasing histamine-related symptoms through indirect pathways (Hewlings & Kalman, 2017).

Bioavailability challenges parallel quercetin's issues. Standard curcumin absorbs poorly from the digestive tract, with only 1-2% reaching circulation. Enhanced formulations address this limitation. **Curcumin with piperine** (black pepper extract) increases absorption 2000%, making it the most cost-effective enhanced option (Shoba et al., 1998). **Curcumin phytosome** complexes curcumin with phospholipids, increasing absorption approximately 29-fold. **Nano-curcumin** uses particle size reduction for enhanced absorption.

Dosing varies by formulation. Standard curcumin requires 1000-2000 mg three times daily for therapeutic effect. Curcumin with piperine uses 500-1000 mg twice daily. Curcumin phytosome or nano-formulations use 250-500 mg twice daily due to superior bioavailability. Matching dose to formulation type prevents both under-dosing (inadequate benefit) and over-dosing (unnecessary expense).

Cautions include blood-thinning effects (avoid with anticoagulant medications without medical supervision), potential gallbladder stimulation (contraindicated for gallstones), and rare liver enzyme elevations at very high doses. Curcumin may enhance effects of diabetes medications, requiring monitoring. Most people tolerate curcumin well, though some experience mild digestive upset.

24.6 Omega-3 Selection for MCAS

Omega-3 fatty acids provide anti-inflammatory support potentially beneficial for MCAS and histamine intolerance (Calder, 2017). The specific omega-3s EPA (eicosapentaenoic acid) and DHA (docosahexaenoic acid) reduce inflammatory prostaglandin and leukotriene production, modulating immune responses that can trigger mast cell activation.

Specialized pro-resolving mediators (SPMs) represent advanced omega-3 derivatives with potent inflammation-resolving properties. SPMs actively resolve inflammation rather than simply suppressing it, potentially offering superior benefit for chronic inflammatory conditions like MCAS (Serhan et al., 2015). SPM supplements derived from fish oil provide concentrated inflammation-resolving compounds.

Histamine concerns with fish oil create dilemma for histamine-intolerant individuals. Fish naturally contains histamine that increases during processing and storage. Standard fish oil supplements may contain trace histamine triggering symptoms in sensitive individuals. Additionally, some fish oil undergoes molecular distillation at high temperatures potentially affecting quality.

Low-histamine omega-3 sources address these concerns. **Algae-based omega-3** supplements derive DHA and EPA from microalgae rather than fish, avoiding fish-related histamine entirely. These vegetarian/vegan options suit individuals avoiding fish or experiencing reactions to fish oil. **Ultra-purified fish oil** processed specifically to remove histamine and other contaminants provides another option. **Krill oil** contains omega-3s in phospholipid form with superior absorption and potentially lower histamine than standard fish oil, though research confirming this remains limited.

Dosing for anti-inflammatory effects typically involves 1000-2000 mg combined EPA/DHA daily. SPM supplements use lower doses (often 500-1000 mg) due to higher potency. Taking omega-3s with meals enhances absorption and reduces fishy aftertaste or reflux some individuals experience.

24.7 Case Study: Strategic Supplement Introduction

Background

Osric, a 38-year-old software engineer, wanted to try supplements for his MCAS symptoms after reading about quercetin, vitamin C, probiotics, and omega-3s online. Excited by potential benefits, he purchased all four supplements and started them simultaneously. Within one week, his digestive symptoms worsened substantially. He developed new skin itching he hadn't experienced before. His headaches, previously improving with dietary changes, returned with intensity.

Presentation

Osric felt confused and discouraged. He couldn't determine if the worsening symptoms indicated die-off reactions (which some websites suggested meant the supplements were "working"), allergic responses to one or more supplements, or simply coincidental symptom fluctuation unrelated to supplementation. He'd invested 120 dollars in supplements he now feared might be harming him. Should he stop everything? Continue through the "die-off"? Try eliminating supplements one at a time?

His practitioner identified the fundamental error. Starting four supplements simultaneously created impossible troubleshooting situation. If symptoms improved, he couldn't identify which supplement helped. With symptoms worsening, he couldn't identify the culprit without systematic elimination, essentially requiring starting over.

Analysis

Osric's approach violated the one-at-a-time principle essential for supplement introduction . This principle, identical to food reintroduction methodology from Chapter 6.0, prevents the exact confusion Osric experienced. Starting supplements simultaneously creates multiple variables changing at once, making cause-and-effect determination impossible.

His worsening symptoms likely indicated reaction to one or more supplements. "Die-off reactions" (Herxheimer reactions from microbial die-off) occur with antimicrobial treatments but don't explain reactions to mast cell stabilizers, antioxidants, or probiotics. His new skin itching suggested allergic or sensitivity reaction, possibly to supplement fillers, the active ingredient, or dose-related effects.

Research on supplement introduction in sensitive populations emphasizes methodical approaches. Adding interventions sequentially with adequate trial periods (typically 1-2 weeks per supplement) enables identifying beneficial supplements worth continuing and problematic ones requiring elimination .

Intervention

Osric's practitioner guided him to stop all supplements, allowing symptoms to return to baseline over 10-14 days. This washout period ensured accurate starting point for systematic introduction.

After baseline re-establishment, they developed introduction protocol. Week 1-2: Start buffered vitamin C alone (500 mg twice daily, increasing to 1000 mg twice daily in week 2 if tolerated). Week 3-4: If vitamin C tolerated well, add quercetin phytosome (250 mg twice daily). Week 5-6: If both tolerated, add omega-3 (algae-based to avoid fish-related histamine, 1000 mg daily). Week 7-8: If all tolerated, add probiotic (histamine-degrading strain, details in section 24.8).

This protocol introduced one supplement every two weeks, allowing adequate time to assess tolerance and benefit before adding the next intervention. He tracked symptoms daily using standardized rating scale (0-10 for major symptoms) identifying patterns invisible day-to-day.

Outcome

Vitamin C introduction went smoothly. Osric noticed modest headache reduction by week 2, enough to continue supplementation. Quercetin addition in weeks 3-4 produced more noticeable benefit, with his flushing episodes decreasing from daily to 2-3 times weekly. Omega-3 introduction in weeks 5-6 initially seemed fine, but by day 10 his digestive symptoms worsened. This identified omega-3 (even algae-based) as problematic for him. He discontinued omega-3, and symptoms returned to baseline within three days.

He proceeded to probiotic introduction, which he tolerated well with further modest improvement. Final sustainable regimen included vitamin C, quercetin, and probiotic, providing meaningful symptom reduction. He'd identified that omega-3 didn't work for him without wasting months taking supplements that worsened his condition. Total process took 10 weeks but established clear understanding of what helped, what hurt, and what was worth continuing long-term.

Teaching Points

- Simultaneous introduction of multiple supplements prevents identifying individual effects and makes troubleshooting reactions impossible, requiring systematic one-at-a-time methodology with adequate trial periods between additions for individuals with MCAS or histamine intolerance
- Worsening symptoms during supplement introduction typically indicate genuine adverse reaction rather than "die-off" requiring discontinuation and systematic re-evaluation, with die-off reactions being inappropriate explanation for non-antimicrobial supplements
- Methodical supplement introduction taking 8-12 weeks enables informed decisions about which interventions provide genuine benefit worth continuing versus which cause problems or provide no effect, ultimately saving time and money compared to shotgun approaches requiring eventual systematic troubleshooting

24.8 Probiotic Strain Selection

Probiotic selection for histamine intolerance requires careful attention to bacterial strains. Many commonly used probiotic bacteria actually produce histamine as part of their normal metabolism, potentially worsening symptoms (Pessione, 2012). Other strains degrade histamine, providing therapeutic benefit. Understanding strain-specific effects enables appropriate selection.

Histamine-producing strains to avoid include many Lactobacillus species commonly found in commercial probiotics. **Lactobacillus casei**, **Lactobacillus reuteri**, **Lactobacillus bulgaricus**, and **Lactobacillus delbrueckii** all produce histamine and should be avoided by individuals with histamine intolerance (Pessione, 2012). These species ferment the amino acid histidine into histamine, increasing histamine burden rather than reducing it.

Histamine-degrading strains provide therapeutic benefit. **Bifidobacterium infantis**, **Bifidobacterium longum**, **Bifidobacterium breve**, **Lactobacillus plantarum**, **Lactobacillus rhamnosus**, and **Lactobacillus gasseri** demonstrate histamine-degrading capacity in laboratory studies . These strains possess enzymes breaking down histamine, potentially reducing total body histamine load. **Bifidobacterium infantis** shows particularly strong histamine-degrading activity and general gut health benefits.

Commercial products rarely label whether strains produce or degrade histamine, requiring research to identify appropriate options. Products specifically marketed for histamine intolerance typically contain appropriate strains, though verification of specific strain names ensures accuracy. Single-strain probiotics enable clearer cause-effect determination than multi-strain products if reactions occur.

Dosing varies by product and strain. Typical therapeutic doses range from 10-50 billion CFU (colony forming units) daily. Starting with lower doses (10 billion CFU) and increasing gradually if tolerated prevents overwhelming reactions in sensitive individuals. Taking probiotics with meals may enhance survival through stomach acid.

Prebiotic considerations require caution. Prebiotics (fiber types feeding beneficial bacteria) can cause gas, bloating, and digestive upset in individuals with SIBO or dysbiosis, conditions commonly comorbid with histamine intolerance per Chapter 3.0. Starting probiotics without added prebiotics, then potentially adding small amounts of prebiotics later if tolerated, represents safer approach for sensitive individuals.

24.9 Additional Mast Cell Stabilizers

Luteolin is a flavonoid with potent mast cell stabilizing properties, possibly superior to quercetin in some measures (Theoharides et al., 2015). The compound inhibits mast cell degranulation and reduces inflammatory cytokine production. Luteolin also crosses the blood-brain barrier more effectively than quercetin, potentially providing benefit for neurological MCAS symptoms.

Research shows luteolin inhibits histamine release and inflammatory mediators in cultured mast cells (Theoharides et al., 2015). Human studies remain limited, though clinical experience suggests benefit for some individuals. Dosing typically ranges from 100-200 mg twice daily. Luteolin costs more than quercetin, limiting accessibility for some people.

Pycnogenol (French maritime pine bark extract) contains proanthocyanidins with mast cell stabilizing and anti-inflammatory effects (Rohdewald, 2002). Research demonstrates reduced histamine release and allergic symptom improvement with pycnogenol supplementation. A study of allergic rhinitis found 50 mg pycnogenol twice daily reduced symptoms significantly compared to placebo (Wilson et al., 2010).

Dosing ranges from 50-200 mg daily depending on condition severity. Pycnogenol has strong safety profile with minimal side effects reported. Cost represents main limitation, with therapeutic doses costing 30-50 dollars monthly.

Palmitoylethanolamide (PEA) is an endogenous fatty acid compound with mast cell stabilizing properties through novel mechanisms (Skaper et al., 2014). PEA doesn't directly affect mast cells but modulates their environment, reducing sensitivity to triggers. Research shows PEA reduces pain and inflammation in various conditions.

For MCAS applications, PEA dosing typically involves 600-1200 mg twice daily. Micronized or ultra-micronized formulations provide better absorption. PEA has excellent safety profile with virtually no side effects reported in studies. However, high doses required create expense (40-70 dollars monthly), and availability remains limited compared to other supplements.

24.10 Tracking Supplement Responses

Systematic tracking enables identifying supplement effects invisible day-to-day. Symptom severity fluctuates naturally, making subjective assessments unreliable. Structured tracking captures patterns over weeks revealing true effects versus placebo or natural variation.

Daily symptom logs rate major symptoms (0-10 scale) including headaches, digestive symptoms, skin reactions, energy, brain fog, and any other individual-specific symptoms. Tracking includes date, symptoms with severity ratings, supplements taken with doses, meals, and any other relevant factors (stress, sleep quality, menstrual cycle for women).

Weekly summary reviews identify trends. Comparing week 1 (before supplement) to week 2 (on supplement) shows whether symptoms improved, worsened, or remained unchanged. Visual graphs plotting symptom severity over time reveal patterns difficult to perceive from daily entries alone.

Response categories guide decisions. Clear improvement (symptom severity reduced 30%+ consistently) suggests beneficial supplement worth continuing. Modest improvement (10-30% reduction) may warrant continuing if affordable and well-tolerated. No change after 4-6 weeks suggests discontinuation to reduce expense and complexity. Worsening symptoms indicate immediate discontinuation.

24.11 Bringing It All Together

This chapter examined mast cell stabilizers and natural antihistamines for histamine intolerance and MCAS management. Quercetin stabilizes mast cell membranes reducing histamine release, with enhanced formulations improving bioavailability. Vitamin C provides triple benefit through histamine degradation, mast cell stabilization, and DAO cofactor support, with buffered forms essential for MCAS individuals.

Stinging nettle offers traditional antihistamine support with emerging research validation. Curcumin provides anti-inflammatory effects reducing triggers for mast cell activation. Omega-3 fatty acids modulate inflammatory pathways, with specialized pro-resolving mediators offering advanced options. Selection of low-histamine omega-3 sources (algae-based, ultra-purified fish oil) prevents paradoxical symptom worsening.

Probiotic selection requires attention to strain-specific effects, avoiding histamine-producing species while selecting histamine-degrading strains. Additional mast cell stabilizers including luteolin, pycnogenol, and PEA provide options for individuals not responding to first-line interventions.

The case study illustrated critical importance of one-at-a-time supplement introduction preventing the confusion and problems from simultaneous starts. Systematic tracking using daily symptom logs and weekly reviews enables objective assessment of supplement effects. This chapter connects to Chapter 25.0's examination of root cause supplements addressing underlying gut health, detoxification, and hormonal factors driving histamine intolerance.

Chapter 25.0: Root Cause Supplement Protocols

Quirin had been managing histamine intolerance for 18 months with reasonable success through dietary modification and supplement support from quercetin and DAO enzymes. His acute symptoms stayed controlled most days. Yet he felt stuck on a maintenance plateau, unable to progress beyond needing strict dietary vigilance and daily symptom management supplements. His functional medicine doctor explained that while symptomatic management helped, his underlying gut damage, SIBO, and liver detoxification impairments remained unaddressed. These root causes perpetuated the cascade leading to histamine intolerance. Healing his intestinal lining could restore DAO production. Resolving SIBO could eliminate bacterial histamine formation in his gut. Supporting liver function could enhance histamine metabolism and detoxification. Addressing these deeper issues might enable eventual reduction of symptom management supplements rather than indefinite dependence. His situation illustrated a common bifurcation point in treatment. Some people focus exclusively on symptom management through antihistamines and mast cell stabilizers, achieving acceptable control without addressing drivers. Others pursue root cause healing aiming for resolution rather than perpetual management (Afrin et al., 2020). Both approaches have merit. The optimal path depends on individual circumstances, underlying pathology, resources, and goals.

This chapter examines supplements addressing histamine intolerance root causes including gut healing protocols with L-glutamine and zinc carnosine, SIBO and dysbiosis support through digestive enzymes and antimicrobials, liver detoxification enhancement via milk thistle and NAC, nervous system support for autonomic dysfunction, hormonal balance protocols for women, personalized protocol development, and working effectively with functional medicine practitioners.

25.1 Gut Healing Fundamentals

Intestinal barrier dysfunction (leaky gut) represents a major contributor to histamine intolerance through multiple mechanisms (Fasano, 2020). Damaged intestinal lining allows undigested food particles, bacteria, and toxins to enter the bloodstream, triggering immune activation and mast cell degranulation. The intestinal damage also impairs DAO production, as this enzyme is manufactured in the intestinal epithelial cells. Healing the gut barrier addresses histamine intolerance at foundational level.

L-glutamine serves as primary fuel for intestinal epithelial cells and demonstrates gut healing properties in research (Kim & Kim, 2017). This amino acid supports rapid cell turnover in the intestinal lining, accelerates healing of damaged areas, and strengthens tight junctions between cells reducing permeability. Clinical studies show L-glutamine supplementation improves intestinal barrier function in various conditions including inflammatory bowel disease, chemotherapy-induced gut damage, and stress-related barrier dysfunction.

Dosing for gut healing typically ranges from 5-15 grams daily in divided doses. Starting with 5 grams daily (split into 2-3 doses) and increasing to 10-15 grams if tolerated provides adequate therapeutic effect. L-glutamine powder mixes easily in water and tastes relatively neutral. Taking doses between meals maximizes absorption, as dietary protein can compete for uptake.

Some individuals with histamine intolerance report worsening symptoms on L-glutamine, theoretically due to glutamine's role as glutamate precursor (glutamate can be excitatory neurotransmitter affecting sensitive individuals). Starting with low doses (2-3 grams daily) and increasing gradually identifies tolerability. If symptoms worsen despite gradual introduction, discontinuation followed by trying alternative gut healing supplements makes sense.

Zinc carnosine combines zinc with the dipeptide carnosine, creating compound with superior gut healing properties compared to standard zinc (Mahmood et al., 2007). Research shows zinc carnosine protects gastric lining, accelerates healing of ulcers and erosions, and strengthens intestinal barrier function. The compound adheres to damaged areas in the gut lining, providing localized healing support.

Dosing ranges from 75-150 mg twice daily, taken between meals for optimal effect. Most studies use 75 mg twice daily with good results. Zinc carnosine demonstrates excellent safety profile with minimal side effects. Taking with small snack rather than completely empty stomach may reduce occasional nausea some individuals experience.

25.2 Additional Gut Healing Support

Collagen provides amino acids supporting tissue repair throughout the body, including intestinal lining (Asserin et al., 2015). The specific amino acids in collagen (glycine, proline, hydroxyproline) directly contribute to connective tissue formation and repair. Bone broth provides traditional collagen source, but the extended simmering required for collagen extraction from bones creates histamine per Chapter 8.0, making bone broth problematic for histamine-intolerant individuals.

Collagen supplements from properly processed sources avoid this issue. **Hydrolyzed collagen** (collagen peptides) undergoes enzymatic breakdown producing smaller peptides that dissolve easily and absorb well. Processing occurs quickly without extended heating that would form histamine. Quality matters substantially. Collagen from grass-fed cows or wild-caught fish processed with minimal heat provides lowest histamine risk.

Dosing for gut healing ranges from 10-20 grams daily. Many people divide this into 10 grams twice daily, mixed into beverages or smoothies. Collagen has virtually no taste, making it easy to incorporate. Taking with vitamin C enhances collagen synthesis in the body.

Deglycyrrhizinated licorice (DGL) represents licorice root extract with glycyrrhizin component removed (Baker, 1994). Standard licorice can raise blood pressure and cause potassium depletion through glycyrrhizin's effects on aldosterone. DGL removes these concerning effects while maintaining gut healing properties. The compound stimulates mucus production in stomach and intestines, protecting lining from damage and supporting healing.

Research demonstrates DGL effectiveness for gastric and duodenal ulcers, with healing rates comparable to conventional medications (Baker, 1994). For general gut healing support, DGL provides protective and reparative effects. Chewable DGL tablets (380-400 mg) taken 20 minutes before meals provide optimal effect through direct mucosal contact. Typical dosing involves 1-2 tablets three times daily.

25.3 SIBO and Dysbiosis Interventions

Small intestinal bacterial overgrowth (SIBO) commonly underlies or exacerbates histamine intolerance per Chapter 3.0. The excess bacteria in the small intestine produce histamine from dietary amino acids, creating substantial histamine burden independent of dietary histamine content (Dukowicz et al., 2007). Additionally, SIBO damages the intestinal lining, reducing DAO production and worsening histamine intolerance through this mechanism.

Digestive enzymes support proper food breakdown, reducing substrate availability for bacterial fermentation. Comprehensive enzyme formulas containing protease (protein digestion), lipase (fat digestion), and amylase (carbohydrate digestion) improve nutrient breakdown and absorption while reducing undigested food residues feeding SIBO bacteria. DAO enzyme discussed in Chapter 23.0 represents one specific digestive enzyme, but broader enzyme support benefits overall digestion.

Plant-based enzyme supplements work across wide pH range, remaining active throughout the digestive tract. Dosing involves taking 1-2 capsules at the beginning of meals. Products marketed for comprehensive digestive support typically contain appropriate enzyme blends. Individuals with severe SIBO may need prescription-strength pancreatic enzymes, requiring medical supervision.

Biofilm disruptors break down protective matrices bacteria create around colonies. These biofilms make bacteria resistant to antimicrobials and immune responses. Disrupting biofilms enhances effectiveness of antimicrobial treatments (Koo et al., 2017). Common biofilm disruptors include NAC (N-acetylcysteine), serrapeptase (proteolytic enzyme), and combinations of EDTA with enzymes.

Biofilm disruptors should be taken separately from antimicrobials and probiotics. Typical protocol involves taking biofilm disruptors upon waking (empty stomach), antimicrobials with meals, and probiotics before bed. This separation prevents biofilm disruptors from affecting desired probiotic strains.

Antimicrobial herbs provide natural SIBO treatment with potentially fewer side effects than antibiotics (Chedid et al., 2014). Research shows certain herbal protocols match antibiotic effectiveness for SIBO eradication while supporting, rather than further damaging, gut microbiome. Common antimicrobial herbs include **berberine** (from goldenseal or barberry), **oregano oil**, **garlic extract (allicin)**, **neem**, and **wormwood**.

Combination products containing multiple antimicrobials often provide superior results to single herbs. Treatment duration typically spans 4-8 weeks depending on SIBO severity. Working with knowledgeable practitioner prevents inadequate treatment (bacteria persist) or excessive treatment (unnecessary damage to beneficial flora). Antimicrobial protocols should always conclude with probiotic restoration.

25.4 Liver Detoxification Support

Liver function affects histamine metabolism substantially. The liver contains **histamine N-methyltransferase (HNMT)**, one of two primary enzymes degrading histamine (DAO in gut being the other) (Maintz & Novak, 2007). Impaired liver function reduces HNMT activity, slowing histamine breakdown and contributing to intolerance. Supporting liver detoxification pathways may enhance histamine metabolism.

Milk thistle (Silybum marianum) contains silymarin, a flavonoid complex with hepatoprotective and liver-regenerating properties (Abenavoli et al., 2018). Research demonstrates milk thistle protects liver cells from damage, supports liver regeneration, and enhances detoxification enzyme activity. The herb has extensive safety record with minimal side effects.

Standardized milk thistle extract containing 70-80% silymarin provides consistent potency. Dosing ranges from 200-400 mg of silymarin (standardized extract) taken 2-3 times daily. Some formulas combine milk thistle with phosphatidylcholine (creating silymarin phytosome) for enhanced absorption. Taking milk thistle with meals may improve tolerability for individuals experiencing mild nausea.

N-acetylcysteine (NAC) serves as precursor to glutathione, the body's master antioxidant and essential component of liver detoxification (Mokhtari et al., 2017). NAC supplementation increases glutathione levels, supporting phase II liver detoxification where many toxins and metabolites (including histamine) undergo processing. NAC also functions as biofilm disruptor per section 25.3, providing dual benefit.

Dosing for liver support ranges from 600-1800 mg daily in divided doses. Starting with 600 mg once or twice daily and increasing to 1200-1800 mg if tolerated provides therapeutic levels. Taking NAC with vitamin C enhances glutathione production. Some people experience sulfur-like body odor with NAC supplementation, typically resolving after 1-2 weeks or with dose reduction.

25.5 Methylation Support Considerations

Methylation represents biochemical process involving transfer of methyl groups (one carbon atom with three hydrogen atoms) between molecules. This process affects numerous functions including neurotransmitter production, detoxification, DNA regulation, and histamine metabolism (Maret & Sandstead, 2006). HNMT enzyme requires methylation for histamine breakdown. Impaired methylation can slow histamine metabolism, contributing to intolerance.

MTHFR gene variations affect methylation efficiency. The MTHFR gene codes for enzyme converting folate into methylfolate (active form). Common gene variations (C677T and A1298C polymorphisms) reduce enzyme efficiency 30-70%, impairing methylation capacity (Maret & Sandstead, 2006). Testing for MTHFR variations helps identify individuals who may benefit from methylation support.

Methylated B vitamins bypass conversion steps affected by MTHFR variations. **Methylfolate (5-MTHF)** provides active folate without requiring MTHFR enzyme conversion. **Methylcobalamin (B12)** and **pyridoxal-5-phosphate (P5P, B6)** provide active forms of these vitamins supporting methylation. For individuals with

MTHFR variations or suspected methylation impairments, using these active forms may provide superior benefit to standard B vitamins.

Dosing varies based on individual needs and testing results. Typical methylation support protocols include 400-1000 mcg methylfolate, 1000-5000 mcg methylcobalamin, and 25-50 mg P5P daily. Some individuals experience overmethylation symptoms (anxiety, insomnia, irritability) with aggressive supplementation, requiring dose reduction or discontinuation. Starting with lower doses and increasing gradually identifies tolerance.

Controversy exists regarding widespread methylation support without testing. Some practitioners recommend methylated B vitamins for everyone, while others argue that overmethylation poses risks requiring individualized assessment. Testing methylation markers (homocysteine, methylmalonic acid, whole blood histamine) before supplementing enables informed decisions.

25.6 Case Study: Root Cause Approach

Background

Nephele, a 41-year-old teacher, had managed histamine intolerance for two years through strict diet and symptom management supplements (DAO, quercetin, vitamin C). Her symptoms stayed controlled but required constant vigilance. Any dietary deviation triggered reactions. She couldn't imagine ever eating normally again. Her functional medicine doctor suggested shifting focus from symptom management to root cause healing, specifically addressing her documented SIBO and compromised gut barrier function.

Presentation

Nephele felt skeptical about root cause approaches after two years of failed attempts finding solutions. She'd tried various diets, eliminated foods, taken numerous supplements, and invested thousands of dollars without achieving the healing promised by various practitioners. The symptom management approach at least provided reliable control. Why risk destabilizing her current management for uncertain benefits from yet another protocol?

Her doctor acknowledged past frustrations but explained that previous attempts had lacked systematic approach and adequate testing to identify actual root causes. Her recent SIBO breath test showed methane-dominant SIBO explaining many symptoms. Her lactulose-mannitol test demonstrated intestinal hyperpermeability confirming leaky gut. Comprehensive stool testing revealed low beneficial bacteria and inadequate digestive enzyme production. These concrete findings provided specific targets for intervention rather than generic gut healing protocols.

Analysis

Nephele's situation demonstrated appropriate context for root cause supplementation. Her confirmed SIBO produced histamine continuously regardless of dietary management, creating perpetual symptom triggers requiring constant suppression. Her intestinal permeability allowed histamine and other triggers into her bloodstream while her damaged gut lining produced inadequate DAO. These issues perpetuated histamine intolerance independent of dietary choices.

Research shows that addressing underlying gut pathology in histamine intolerance can enable symptom resolution rather than perpetual management (Afrin et al., 2020). However, this requires accurate diagnosis identifying specific issues needing correction. Generic gut healing without understanding what needs healing often fails, explaining Nephele's past disappointments.

Intervention

Her protocol addressed identified root causes systematically. Phase 1 (weeks 1-8) focused on SIBO treatment using antimicrobial herbs (standardized berberine 500 mg three times daily, oregano oil 150 mg twice daily) combined with biofilm disruptors (NAC 600 mg twice daily on empty stomach). She continued her low-histamine diet and symptom management supplements throughout SIBO treatment, preventing symptom recurrence during antimicrobial phase.

Phase 2 (weeks 9-12) involved post-antimicrobial gut restoration. She added histamine-degrading probiotic (Bifidobacterium longum 20 billion CFU nightly), L-glutamine (10 grams daily in divided doses), and zinc carnosine (75 mg twice daily). She discontinued antimicrobials as scheduled. This phase supported beneficial bacteria restoration and gut lining repair.

Phase 3 (weeks 13-20) continued gut healing while beginning careful dietary expansion. She followed structured reintroduction per Chapter 6.0, testing previously reactive foods systematically. She maintained probiotics and gut healing supplements but began reducing symptom management supplements as tolerance improved.

Outcome

SIBO re-testing at week 10 showed substantial improvement with bacterial counts reduced to normal range. Her symptoms during the antimicrobial phase remained controlled through continued symptom management supplements. Week 12 began showing unexpected improvements. Foods she'd previously needed DAO to tolerate became tolerable without supplementation.

By week 16, she'd successfully reintroduced eight previously problematic foods without reactions. Her DAO use had decreased from three times daily to occasional use for high-risk meals. Her quercetin needs reduced from twice daily to once daily. By week 20, she'd discontinued DAO entirely, using it only for truly high-histamine exposures (aged cheese, fermented foods). Her quercetin continued once daily but she'd stopped vitamin C supplementation as symptoms remained controlled without it.

One year later, she maintained improvement. She ate varied diet including many previously reactive foods. She took Bifidobacterium longum nightly and occasional quercetin during high-stress periods but had discontinued all other supplements. Her strict low-histamine diet had transitioned to normal eating with attention to freshness and proper food handling. The shift from perpetual symptom management to actual resolution through root cause treatment had succeeded where previous generic approaches failed.

Teaching Points

- Root cause supplementation aimed at documented pathology (confirmed SIBO, measured intestinal permeability) provides superior outcomes compared to generic gut healing protocols, with testing identifying specific issues requiring targeted intervention rather than shotgun approaches
- Systematic phased protocols addressing SIBO eradication, gut restoration, and gradual dietary expansion while maintaining symptom control throughout prevents destabilization during healing process, requiring patience through 3-6 month timelines rather than expecting immediate resolution
- Successful root cause treatment enables reduction or elimination of symptom management supplements as underlying pathology resolves, contrasting with symptom-focused approaches requiring indefinite supplementation without addressing drivers of histamine intolerance

25.7 Nervous System and Hormonal Support

Autonomic dysfunction including postural orthostatic tachycardia syndrome (POTS) commonly accompanies MCAS and histamine intolerance (Cheung & Vadas, 2015). The autonomic nervous system regulates mast cell activity, creating bidirectional relationship where nervous system dysfunction triggers mast cells and mast cell mediators affect autonomic function. Supporting nervous system health may reduce histamine-related symptoms.

Magnesium supports nervous system function through multiple mechanisms including neurotransmitter regulation, nervous system calming effects, and muscle relaxation (Boyle et al., 2017). Magnesium deficiency is common and can worsen anxiety, insomnia, muscle tension, and autonomic instability. Form selection matters substantially. **Magnesium glycinate** provides highly absorbable, calming magnesium without laxative effects. **Magnesium threonate** crosses blood-brain barrier effectively, potentially benefiting neurological symptoms. **Magnesium citrate** absorbs well but has laxative properties useful for constipation but problematic for others.

Dosing ranges from 200-400 mg elemental magnesium daily, ideally divided into two doses (morning and evening). Taking magnesium at bedtime may improve sleep quality. Starting with 200 mg and increasing to 400 mg if tolerated prevents excessive laxative effects. Some people require lower doses (100-150 mg) due to sensitivity.

B-complex vitamins support nervous system function, energy production, and stress response. B vitamins function as cofactors in numerous enzymatic reactions affecting neurotransmitter production, cellular energy generation, and stress hormone metabolism (Kennedy, 2016). For individuals with MTHFR variations, B-complex containing methylated forms (methylfolate, methylcobalamin, P5P) provides superior benefit.

Quality B-complex supplements provide therapeutic doses of all B vitamins rather than minimal amounts. Taking B-complex in the morning with food may prevent nausea and provides energy support through the day. Evening dosing may interfere with sleep in some individuals due to B vitamins' energizing effects.

Adaptogenic herbs support stress response and may benefit autonomic dysfunction. **Ashwagandha** demonstrates anxiety reduction and cortisol modulation in research (Chandrasekhar et al., 2012). **Rhodiola** supports stress resilience and fatigue reduction. **Holy basil** provides calming and stress-protective effects. Individual response to adaptogens varies substantially, requiring experimentation to identify beneficial options.

Hormonal considerations for women include the relationship between estrogen, progesterone, and histamine. Estrogen increases histamine production and decreases DAO activity, while progesterone has opposite effects (Maintz & Novak, 2007). This explains why many women experience histamine symptom worsening during high-estrogen phases of menstrual cycle and around ovulation.

DIM (diindolylmethane) supports estrogen metabolism, potentially reducing estrogen dominance contributing to histamine symptoms. Research shows DIM promotes beneficial estrogen metabolites while reducing problematic ones (Thomson et al., 2017). Dosing typically ranges from 100-300 mg daily. Some women notice menstrual cycle improvements including reduced PMS and more stable mood.

Calcium-D-glucarate supports estrogen elimination through preventing reabsorption of eliminated estrogen in the gut. This supplement may benefit women with estrogen dominance or sluggish liver detoxification. Typical dosing ranges from 500-1000 mg daily, often divided into two doses.

25.8 Protocol Development and Practitioner Collaboration

Personalized protocol creation requires understanding individual root causes, symptom patterns, testing results, budget constraints, and tolerance for complexity. Cookie-cutter protocols rarely address individual needs optimally. Systematic approach prevents overwhelm while ensuring adequate intervention.

Testing informs supplementation. SIBO breath testing identifies bacterial overgrowth requiring antimicrobial treatment. Intestinal permeability testing reveals leaky gut needing healing support. Comprehensive stool analysis identifies dysbiosis patterns, inflammation markers, and digestive function. Organic acids testing assesses nutritional deficiencies and metabolic function. Genetic testing (MTHFR, DAO gene variations) identifies inherent susceptibilities. Investing in appropriate testing before implementing expensive supplement protocols prevents wasted resources on unnecessary interventions.

Phased implementation prevents overwhelm and enables troubleshooting. Phase 1 typically addresses acute symptoms and immediate support. Phase 2 tackles primary root causes (SIBO treatment, gut healing). Phase 3 involves reintroduction and protocol refinement. Phase 4 transitions to maintenance with minimal necessary supplementation.

Working with practitioners requires finding providers knowledgeable about histamine intolerance, MCAS, and functional medicine approaches. Conventional physicians rarely receive training in these areas, though some educate themselves. Functional medicine practitioners, naturopathic doctors, and integrative medicine physicians more commonly understand these conditions. Verifying practitioner experience with histamine intolerance specifically prevents working with providers learning on your case.

Cost management matters for long-term sustainability. Supplement protocols can easily cost 200-500 dollars monthly, creating financial strain. Prioritizing interventions addressing documented root causes over speculative supplements reduces expense. Generic supplement brands often provide equivalent quality to expensive brands at lower cost, though third-party testing verification ensures quality. Periodic protocol review eliminates supplements providing no perceptible benefit.

25.9 Core Concepts Recap

This chapter examined supplements addressing histamine intolerance root causes rather than purely managing symptoms. Gut healing protocols using L-glutamine, zinc carnosine, collagen, and DGL support intestinal barrier restoration and DAO production recovery. SIBO and dysbiosis interventions through digestive enzymes, biofilm disruptors, and antimicrobial herbs address bacterial histamine production.

Liver support via milk thistle and NAC enhances detoxification and HNMT function for histamine metabolism. Methylation support through methylated B vitamins may benefit individuals with MTHFR variations affecting histamine breakdown. Nervous system support using magnesium, B-complex, and adaptogens addresses autonomic dysfunction commonly comorbid with histamine intolerance.

Hormonal considerations for women include DIM and calcium-D-glucarate for estrogen metabolism support. The case study illustrated successful root cause approach through systematic testing, phased interventions, and maintaining symptom control during healing, resulting in substantial supplement reduction and dietary expansion.

Personalized protocol development requires testing to identify specific issues, phased implementation preventing overwhelm, practitioner collaboration for guidance, and cost management for sustainability. This chapter connects to Chapter 26.0's examination of pharmaceutical medications and medical management for situations where supplements and diet alone prove insufficient.

Chapter 26.0: Pharmaceutical Medical Management

Cyril sat in his allergist's office reviewing medication options with growing awareness that his treatment path diverged from typical allergic patients. The standard approach offering antihistamine prescriptions and maybe an EpiPen had already failed him. Over-the-counter antihistamines provided minimal benefit. His symptoms went beyond simple histamine receptor blocking. His allergist, fortunately specialized in MCAS, explained that his condition required multi-targeted pharmaceutical approach addressing histamine at H1 and H2 receptors, stabilizing mast cells directly through cromolyn sodium, blocking leukotriene pathways with montelukast, and potentially modulating immune function through low-dose naltrexone. The complexity felt overwhelming. Five different medications, each targeting different aspects of his mast cell dysfunction. He worried about side effects, drug interactions, and long-term consequences. Yet dietary management and supplements had plateaued at 60% improvement. The remaining 40% of symptoms substantially impaired his quality of life. The medication discussion represented acknowledgment that while diet and supplements formed the foundation, some people require pharmaceutical intervention for adequate control (Afrin et al., 2020). Understanding medication options, proper use, potential risks, and integration with dietary approaches enables informed decisions about escalating treatment when necessary.

This chapter examines pharmaceutical options for histamine intolerance and MCAS including H1 and H2 antihistamines, cromolyn sodium mast cell stabilizer, montelukast leukotriene blocker, low-dose naltrexone applications, medications requiring caution, filler and inactive ingredient considerations, coordinating supplements with medications, recognizing when diet alone proves insufficient, and building effective medical teams for complex care.

26.1 H1 Antihistamine Options

H1 antihistamines block histamine at H1 receptors found throughout the body including skin, respiratory system, blood vessels, and nervous system (Church & Church, 2013). These receptors mediate many classic allergic symptoms including itching, hives, nasal congestion, and some gastrointestinal symptoms. Blocking H1 receptors reduces these manifestations of histamine excess.

First-generation H1 antihistamines including diphenhydramine (Benadryl), hydroxyzine, and chlorpheniramine cross the blood-brain barrier causing sedation and cognitive impairment. While these medications effectively reduce histamine symptoms, the sedating effects limit daytime use and impair functioning. Some MCAS specialists use first-generation antihistamines strategically at bedtime for dual benefit of symptom control and sleep improvement. However, tolerance develops quickly, reducing effectiveness over weeks to months.

Second-generation H1 antihistamines including cetirizine (Zyrtec), loratadine (Claritin), fexofenadine (Allegra), and levocetirizine (Xyzal) minimally cross the blood-brain barrier, reducing sedation while maintaining peripheral antihistamine effects (Church & Church, 2013). These medications provide better option for daytime symptom control without cognitive impairment. Individual response varies substantially. Some people find cetirizine most effective, while others respond better to fexofenadine or levocetirizine.

Dosing considerations in MCAS often exceed standard allergy dosing. While package directions typically recommend 10 mg cetirizine once daily or 180 mg fexofenadine once daily, MCAS protocols may use double or triple these doses (Afrin et al., 2020). Research supports safety of higher H1 antihistamine doses, with studies using up to four times standard doses without serious adverse effects. However, higher doses require medical supervision and monitoring for side effects including QT interval prolongation (heart rhythm concern) with certain antihistamines.

Combination H1 therapy uses two different H1 antihistamines simultaneously, often combining second-generation for daytime (fexofenadine 180 mg twice daily) with first-generation at bedtime (hydroxyzine 25-50 mg). This provides around-the-clock coverage addressing multiple H1 receptor subtypes. The rationale involves different antihistamines having slightly different receptor binding profiles and pharmacokinetics, with combination potentially providing superior control than single agents.

26.2 H2 Blocker Applications

H2 receptors primarily concentrate in the stomach where histamine stimulates acid production, but also exist throughout the body affecting cardiac function, immune modulation, and other processes (Leurs et al., 2009). H2 blockers developed originally for acid suppression provide additional benefit in MCAS through blocking histamine at these non-gastric H2 receptors.

Famotidine (Pepcid) represents the preferred H2 blocker for MCAS management following ranitidine's market removal due to contamination concerns. Famotidine provides H2 receptor blockade with excellent safety profile and decades of clinical use (Leurs et al., 2009). Standard dosing involves 20 mg twice daily, though some

MCAS protocols use higher doses (40 mg twice daily or even three times daily) under medical supervision.

Mechanisms beyond acid suppression explain H2 blocker benefits in MCAS. H2 receptors on immune cells regulate cytokine production and immune responses. Blocking these receptors may reduce inflammatory cascades contributing to mast cell activation. Additionally, some research suggests H2 blockers have direct mast cell stabilizing effects independent of receptor blockade.

Combination H1 and H2 therapy forms standard MCAS treatment, with many specialists prescribing both simultaneously (Afrin et al., 2020). The rationale involves histamine binding both H1 and H2 receptors throughout the body. Blocking only H1 leaves H2-mediated effects unchecked. Clinical experience and some research suggest combination therapy provides superior symptom control than either class alone.

Long-term H2 blocker concerns include nutrient absorption issues. Acid suppression reduces vitamin B12, magnesium, and calcium absorption, potentially creating deficiencies with prolonged use. Monitoring these nutrients and supplementing if needed prevents complications. Additionally, stomach acid serves protective function against pathogens. Long-term acid suppression may increase infection risk, particularly small intestinal bacterial overgrowth, creating problematic situation for individuals already prone to SIBO per Chapter 3.0.

26.3 Cromolyn Sodium Benefits

Cromolyn sodium (Gastrocrom) represents unique mast cell stabilizer preventing mast cell degranulation through mechanisms distinct from antihistamines (Hogan et al., 2020). Rather than blocking histamine after release, cromolyn prevents release itself by stabilizing mast cell membranes and inhibiting degranulation signaling. This prophylactic approach addresses histamine at earlier point in the cascade than antihistamine receptor blocking.

Oral formulation (Gastrocrom) specifically targets gastrointestinal mast cells, making it particularly valuable for individuals with predominantly digestive MCAS symptoms (Hogan et al., 2020). The medication poorly absorbs from the gut, remaining primarily in the intestinal lumen where it stabilizes gut-associated mast cells. This localized effect provides benefit for abdominal pain, diarrhea, nausea, and other GI manifestations.

Dosing protocols typically involve 200 mg (one ampule) four times daily, taken 30 minutes before meals and at bedtime on empty stomach. The timing matters substantially, as food interferes with cromolyn's action. Mixing the ampule contents with water immediately before drinking ensures proper administration. The solution has unpleasant taste that some people find challenging, though mixing with small amount of juice (if tolerated) may improve palatability.

Response timeline for cromolyn varies. Some individuals notice improvement within days, while others require 4-8 weeks for full benefit to emerge. Adequate trial duration (minimum two months) prevents premature discontinuation before effects manifest. Gradually increasing from one or two doses daily to full four-dose regimen may improve tolerability for those experiencing initial side effects.

Side effects generally remain mild, most commonly involving temporary abdominal cramping or diarrhea during initial weeks. These effects typically resolve as the body adjusts. Rare allergic reactions to cromolyn itself can occur, necessitating immediate discontinuation if suspected. Cost represents practical limitation, with monthly cromolyn expenses ranging from 300-1000 dollars depending on insurance coverage. Many insurance plans require prior authorization based on diagnosis code, making documentation of MCAS diagnosis important.

Nebulized cromolyn provides option for individuals with primarily respiratory symptoms or those unable to tolerate oral formulation. Inhaled cromolyn stabilizes lung mast cells, potentially benefiting asthma-like symptoms, chronic cough, or respiratory MCAS manifestations. However, availability of nebulized cromolyn has decreased with oral formulation becoming primary option.

26.4 Montelukast and Leukotriene Pathway

Leukotrienes represent inflammatory mediators released alongside histamine during mast cell degranulation (Peters-Golden & Henderson, 2007). These compounds cause bronchoconstriction, mucus production, vascular permeability, and inflammatory cell recruitment. Blocking leukotriene pathways addresses non-histamine mediators contributing to MCAS symptoms, particularly respiratory and inflammatory manifestations.

Montelukast (Singulair) blocks leukotriene receptors, preventing these mediators from binding and triggering effects. Originally developed for asthma management, montelukast demonstrates benefit for subset of MCAS patients, particularly those with respiratory symptoms, exercise-induced reactions, or aspirin sensitivity (Peters-Golden & Henderson, 2007).

Dosing involves 10 mg once daily, typically taken in the evening. Unlike antihistamines where higher doses may provide additional benefit, montelukast dosing follows standard recommendations without evidence supporting dose escalation. The medication reaches steady-state levels after several days of use.

Response patterns vary substantially. Some individuals experience dramatic improvement, particularly for specific symptom types like exercise-induced reactions or respiratory symptoms. Others notice minimal benefit. The subset most likely to respond appears to be those with elevated urinary leukotriene levels (if tested) or prominent respiratory manifestations. A therapeutic trial (1-2 months) identifies responders worth continuing medication.

Neuropsychiatric concerns emerged through post-market surveillance, with reports of mood changes, depression, anxiety, and rare suicidal ideation associated with montelukast use (FDA, 2020). These effects appear uncommon but serious, warranting monitoring for mood or behavioral changes, particularly during the first month of use. Individuals with pre-existing psychiatric conditions may face higher risk, requiring careful consideration of benefits versus risks.

26.5 Case Study: Medication Integration Success

Background

Apollonia, a 49-year-old accountant, had managed histamine intolerance for three years through strict diet, DAO supplementation, quercetin, and vitamin C. Her symptom control reached approximately 65%, adequate for basic function but insufficient for normal life. She avoided social events, declined business travel requiring dining out, and experienced 2-3 moderate symptom days weekly despite strict adherence. Her MCAS specialist suggested adding pharmaceutical management to her regimen, specifically H1 and H2 antihistamines with possible cromolyn sodium.

Presentation

Apollonia resisted medication escalation. She'd hoped dietary and supplement approaches would suffice, viewing pharmaceutical medications as failure of natural methods. She worried about side effects, long-term medication use, and becoming dependent on prescription drugs. Her specialist explained that MCAS severity exists on spectrum. Some people achieve adequate control through diet and supplements. Others require pharmaceutical intervention for acceptable quality of life. Neither approach represented failure or superiority. The appropriate treatment matches disease severity.

Her testing showed elevated tryptase (mast cell activation marker), positive urine methylhistamine (histamine metabolite), and symptoms affecting multiple organ systems daily despite aggressive dietary and supplement management. This severity warranted pharmaceutical consideration.

Analysis

Apollonia's situation illustrated appropriate context for medication escalation. Her 65% improvement through diet and supplements represented good response, confirming histamine intolerance as diagnosis. However, the remaining 35% of symptoms substantially impaired function. Research shows that moderate to severe MCAS often requires pharmaceutical management for adequate control (Afrin et al., 2020).

Her resistance to medications reflected common perspective equating natural approaches with superiority. However, MCAS represents mast cell dysfunction requiring medical management like other chronic conditions (diabetes, hypertension, autoimmune disease). Viewing pharmaceutical treatment as failure rather than appropriate medical care for documented disease creates unnecessary suffering through inadequate treatment.

Intervention

Her specialist recommended starting with H1 and H2 antihistamine combination before considering cromolyn sodium, taking stepwise approach. She began cetirizine 10 mg twice daily (H1) and famotidine 20 mg twice daily (H2). She continued her dietary management, DAO, quercetin, and vitamin C, adding pharmaceuticals rather than replacing existing successful interventions.

Week one showed modest additional improvement. Her symptom frequency decreased from 2-3 episodes weekly to 1-2. Week three, her specialist increased cetirizine to 20 mg twice daily (higher dose common in MCAS). This produced more noticeable benefit. By week four, her symptom days had decreased to 0-1 weekly, representing approximately 85% control.

She maintained this regimen for two months, documenting sustained improvement. Her quality of life changed substantially. She attended friend's wedding (previously would have declined), ate at reception with DAO supplementation beforehand, and experienced no symptoms. She accepted business trip requiring three days of restaurant eating, managing successfully with careful ordering and her medication/supplement regimen.

Month three, her specialist added cromolyn sodium for her remaining gastrointestinal symptoms. She started two doses daily (morning and evening) rather than full four-dose regimen, planning to increase if tolerated. Week two on cromolyn, she increased to three doses daily. By week four, she reached full four-dose regimen. Her remaining GI symptoms resolved almost completely.

Outcome

Six months later, Apollonia maintained 90-95% symptom control. She lived essentially normally, traveling for work quarterly, attending social events regularly, and eating varied diet with attention to freshness and proper handling. She took cetirizine 20 mg twice daily, famotidine 20 mg twice daily, and cromolyn 200 mg four times daily as pharmaceutical foundation. She continued DAO with higher-risk meals, quercetin once daily, and probiotic. She'd discontinued vitamin C supplementation as unnecessary with pharmaceutical control.

Her perspective on medications had shifted. She recognized that her MCAS severity required pharmaceutical management for acceptable control. This didn't represent failure but appropriate treatment for her condition's severity. She described feeling grateful for medication options rather than resentful of needing them. The difference between 65% control (diet/supplements alone) and 95% control (adding pharmaceuticals) meant the difference between restricted life and normal living.

Teaching Points

- MCAS severity varies substantially with some individuals requiring pharmaceutical management for adequate control despite optimal dietary and supplement approaches, making medication escalation appropriate medical treatment rather than failure of natural methods
- Stepwise pharmaceutical introduction starting with H1/H2 antihistamines before adding cromolyn or other agents enables identifying minimum effective medication regimen, with dose adjustments guided by response patterns and tolerability over several weeks to months
- Integration of pharmaceutical, dietary, and supplement approaches provides superior outcomes for moderate to severe MCAS compared to any single modality alone, requiring flexible willingness to escalate treatment matching disease severity rather than ideology about natural versus pharmaceutical approaches

26.6 Low Dose Naltrexone Applications

Low-dose naltrexone (LDN) uses naltrexone (opioid antagonist) at doses far below those used for opioid dependence treatment (Raknes et al., 2018). At very low doses (1-4.5 mg nightly), naltrexone appears to modulate immune function and reduce inflammation through mechanisms still being elucidated. Clinical experience and emerging research suggest benefit for various immune-mediated and inflammatory conditions including MCAS.

Proposed mechanisms involve temporary opioid receptor blockade causing compensatory increase in endogenous opioid production (endorphins and enkephalins). These endogenous opioids modulate immune function and potentially reduce mast cell activation. Additionally, LDN may affect glial cells in the nervous system, reducing neuroinflammation contributing to chronic pain and neurological MCAS symptoms (Raknes et al., 2018).

Evidence base for LDN in MCAS remains limited to case reports and clinical experience rather than controlled trials. Many MCAS specialists report patient improvement with LDN, particularly for symptoms not adequately controlled by antihistamines and mast cell stabilizers. However, the lack of rigorous research means optimal patient selection, dosing, and expected outcomes remain unclear.

Dosing protocols typically start very low (0.5-1 mg nightly) and increase gradually over weeks to months to typical target dose of 3-4.5 mg nightly. This ultra-low starting dose and slow escalation prevents initial symptom flare some individuals experience. Taking LDN at bedtime aligns with circadian endorphin patterns, potentially optimizing effects. Compounding pharmacies prepare LDN since commercial naltrexone tablets contain 50 mg, requiring compounding for low doses.

Response assessment requires patience. Some people notice improvement within 2-4 weeks, while others need 2-3 months for benefit to emerge. Adequate trial duration (minimum three months at target dose) prevents premature discontinuation. Vivid dreams represent common side effect, typically mild and often diminishing over time. Taking LDN earlier in evening (7-8 PM rather than bedtime) may reduce dream intensity.

26.7 Medication Cautions and Contraindications

Medications to avoid in MCAS include those known to trigger mast cell degranulation or interfere with histamine metabolism. **NSAIDs (ibuprofen, naproxen, aspirin)** can trigger mast cell activation in sensitive individuals, though aspirin paradoxically helps subset of patients with aspirin-exacerbated respiratory disease. **Opioid pain medications** (morphine, codeine) directly degranulate mast cells, potentially worsening MCAS. **Certain antibiotics** particularly fluoroquinolones may trigger reactions. **Contrast dye** for imaging studies can cause severe mast cell activation, requiring pre-medication protocols if imaging becomes necessary.

Medication fillers and inactive ingredients represent hidden trigger source. Pharmaceutical tablets and capsules contain binders, fillers, coatings, and preservatives that may include histamine-liberating compounds or allergens (Reker et al., 2019). Common problematic fillers include **lactose** (dairy-derived), **corn starch**, **magnesium stearate**, and various dyes. Individuals reacting to medications despite theoretically appropriate active ingredient should investigate inactive ingredients.

Compounding pharmacies can prepare medications without problematic fillers using hypoallergenic excipients. While more expensive than commercial preparations, compounded medications prevent reactions to fillers enabling use of necessary pharmaceuticals. Working with compounding pharmacy experienced in MCAS or multiple chemical sensitivity ensures appropriate filler selection.

Drug interaction considerations include additive effects and metabolic interactions. Combining multiple antihistamines creates additive sedation risk. Some medications affect liver enzymes metabolizing other drugs, creating interaction potential. Comprehensive medication review by knowledgeable pharmacist or physician prevents dangerous interactions.

26.8 Medical Team Development

Coordinating complex care for MCAS and histamine intolerance ideally involves multidisciplinary team. However, assembling such team proves challenging given limited specialist availability and insurance constraints. At minimum, one knowledgeable physician (allergist/immunologist specializing in MCAS, or functional medicine doctor understanding the condition) provides essential guidance.

Specialist types potentially involved include allergist/immunologist for MCAS diagnosis and medication management, gastroenterologist for GI manifestations and testing, rheumatologist for systemic symptoms and autoimmune overlap, functional medicine physician for integrative approach addressing root causes, and dietitian with histamine intolerance expertise for nutritional management.

Primary care integration requires educating primary care physicians about MCAS and treatment plans developed by specialists. Many primary care doctors have limited MCAS knowledge, necessitating patient advocacy and education. Providing literature, sharing specialist notes, and clear communication about medication rationales helps primary care physicians support management even without deep MCAS expertise.

Insurance navigation presents challenges as some MCAS medications (particularly cromolyn) require prior authorization. Proper diagnosis coding (mastocytosis, mast cell activation syndrome, or appropriate ICD-10 codes) affects approval likelihood. Letters of medical necessity from specialists explaining treatment rationale improve authorization success rates. Patient persistence through appeals processes sometimes secures coverage initially denied.

26.9 Essential Points to Remember

This chapter examined pharmaceutical options for histamine intolerance and MCAS management. H1 antihistamines block histamine at receptors mediating allergic symptoms, with second-generation agents providing non-sedating daytime control. H2 blockers address histamine beyond gastric acid suppression, providing immunomodulatory benefits. Combination H1/H2 therapy represents standard MCAS treatment.

Cromolyn sodium stabilizes mast cells preventing degranulation, particularly benefiting gastrointestinal symptoms through poorly-absorbed oral formulation. Montelukast blocks leukotriene pathways addressing non-histamine mediators, especially helpful for respiratory manifestations. Low-dose naltrexone provides immunomodulatory effects for some individuals through mechanisms still being researched.

Medication cautions include avoiding mast cell degranulating drugs and attending to inactive ingredient sensitivities requiring compounded preparations. The case study illustrated appropriate medication escalation for moderate-severe MCAS not adequately controlled by dietary and supplement approaches, demonstrating pharmaceutical integration enabling normal functioning.

Medical team development ideally includes MCAS-knowledgeable specialists coordinating with primary care. Insurance navigation and prior authorization processes require persistence. This chapter concludes Part VI on supplement and pharmaceutical protocols, preparing for Part VII's examination of specific population considerations and long-term management strategies.

Part VII: Lifestyle Factors & Long-Term Success

Chapter 27.0: Lifestyle Management Strategies

Benedictus sat in his neurologist's office reviewing his symptom journal from the past six months. His histamine intolerance diet was perfect. He'd eliminated trigger foods completely, followed every protocol from Chapters 6.0 through 9.0, taken appropriate supplements from Chapters 23.0 through 25.0, and yet his symptoms plateaued at 70% improvement. Headaches still occurred 2-3 times weekly. Flushing episodes happened unpredictably. His sleep remained fragmented despite pharmaceutical management from Chapter 26.0. His neurologist asked about stress levels. Benedictus admitted work had been overwhelming for months. His breathing? Shallow and rapid most days. Exercise? None, fearing symptom triggering. Sleep hygiene? He scrolled his phone in bed until exhaustion forced sleep around 2 AM. Environmental exposures? His office used heavy fragrances in the bathroom, and his apartment had visible mold in the bathroom corner he'd been ignoring for a year. His neurologist explained that histamine intolerance doesn't exist in dietary vacuum. The autonomic nervous system, stress response, sleep patterns, exercise choices, and environmental factors all affect mast cell stability and histamine metabolism substantially (Afrin et al., 2020). Dietary perfection with lifestyle chaos creates persistent symptoms resistant to food-based interventions alone.

This chapter examines lifestyle factors beyond diet affecting histamine intolerance including stress management and HPA axis regulation, nervous system techniques like vagal tone exercises and breathing practices, sleep optimization addressing why histamine peaks at night, exercise considerations for MCAS and POTS, environmental trigger minimization including fragrances and mold, and hormonal factors across menstrual cycles and life stages.

27.1 Stress and HPA Axis

The hypothalamic-pituitary-adrenal (HPA) axis regulates stress response through coordinated hormone release affecting multiple body systems including immune function and mast cell activity (Theoharides et al., 2012). When the hypothalamus perceives stress (physical, emotional, or environmental), it releases corticotropin-releasing hormone (CRH). This triggers the pituitary to release adrenocorticotropic hormone (ACTH), which stimulates the adrenal glands to produce cortisol.

Cortisol serves as primary stress hormone with complex effects on histamine and mast cells. Acute cortisol elevation can stabilize mast cells, temporarily reducing degranulation. This explains why some people notice temporary symptom improvement during acute stress. However, chronic stress and prolonged cortisol elevation have opposite effects. Chronic stress desensitizes cortisol receptors, impairs the normal cortisol awakening response, and paradoxically increases mast cell activation (Theoharides et al., 2012).

CRH direct effects on mast cells represent additional concern. Research shows CRH directly triggers mast cell degranulation independent of cortisol pathways (Theoharides et al., 2012). This means chronic stress activates mast cells through multiple mechanisms. The HPA axis becomes dysregulated with chronic stress, creating patterns of both insufficient cortisol (when needed for mast cell stabilization) and excessive CRH (triggering mast cell activation).

Stress management thus becomes medical intervention rather than lifestyle luxury for MCAS and histamine intolerance. Techniques reducing perceived stress and regulating HPA axis function can decrease mast cell activation measurably. Mind-body interventions including meditation, yoga, and biofeedback demonstrate cortisol regulation and reduced inflammatory markers in research (Pascoe et al., 2017).

Practical stress reduction requires identifying major stressors and systematically addressing them. Relationship stress, work demands, financial concerns, and health anxiety all activate the HPA axis. Some stressors can be modified (setting work boundaries, addressing relationship issues, seeking financial counseling). Others require acceptance and coping skill development (chronic illness reality, family situations, unavoidable life circumstances). Psychological support through therapy helps differentiate changeable versus unchangeable stressors and develop appropriate responses to each.

27.2 Vagal Tone and Nervous System

The vagus nerve serves as primary parasympathetic nerve connecting brain to organs throughout the body including heart, lungs, and digestive system (Bonaz et al., 2018). High vagal tone (strong vagus nerve activity) associates with better stress resilience, improved emotional regulation, and reduced inflammation. Low vagal tone correlates with increased inflammatory markers, poor stress recovery, and autonomic dysfunction common in MCAS.

Vagal tone measurement uses heart rate variability (HRV), the variation in time between heartbeats. High HRV indicates healthy vagal tone with good parasympathetic activity. Low HRV suggests poor vagal tone and autonomic imbalance. Many wearable devices and smartphone apps now measure HRV, enabling personal tracking of vagal tone changes with interventions.

Vagal tone exercises strengthen parasympathetic nervous system function. **Cold exposure** activates the vagus nerve through diving reflex. Splashing cold water on face, taking cold showers (start with 30 seconds, increase gradually), or using ice packs on face stimulates vagal activity. **Singing, humming, or chanting** activates vagus nerve through vocal cord vibration. The "OM" sound used in yoga specifically targets vagal stimulation. **Gargling** vigorously stimulates vagus nerve endings in the throat.

Slow deep breathing represents the most accessible vagal toning exercise. The vagus nerve monitors breathing patterns, with slow breathing (particularly extended exhalation) activating parasympathetic response (Gerritsen & Band, 2018). Practice involves inhaling slowly through nose for 4-5 seconds, holding briefly, then exhaling slowly through nose or mouth for 6-8 seconds (exhalation longer than inhalation). Perform for 5-10 minutes daily or during stress.

Resonance frequency breathing involves breathing at approximately 5-6 breaths per minute, the rate maximizing HRV and vagal tone for most people (Gerritsen & Band, 2018). Smartphone apps provide guided resonance breathing. Ten minutes daily improves vagal tone measurably within 2-4 weeks based on HRV tracking.

27.3 Sleep Optimization Fundamentals

Histamine follows circadian patterns with levels typically lowest in morning and peaking at night. This explains why many people with histamine intolerance experience worsening symptoms in evening and difficulty falling asleep despite exhaustion. Additionally, histamine functions as wake-promoting neurotransmitter in the brain. Elevated histamine activates arousal systems preventing sleep onset and maintaining wakefulness.

Diamine oxidase (DAO) activity also follows circadian patterns. DAO activity decreases overnight, reducing histamine breakdown capacity when histamine levels naturally rise (Maintz & Novak, 2007). This double problem (rising histamine with decreasing breakdown capacity) creates sleep challenges for histamine-intolerant individuals.

Sleep deprivation worsens histamine intolerance through multiple mechanisms. Poor sleep increases mast cell activation and inflammatory cytokine production (Irwin, 2015). Sleep loss impairs immune regulation, potentially worsening MCAS. Additionally, sleep deprivation elevates cortisol and activates the HPA axis per section 27.1, creating stress-mediated mast cell triggering. This creates vicious cycle where histamine prevents sleep, and sleep deprivation worsens histamine intolerance.

Sleep hygiene for MCAS requires specific modifications beyond standard recommendations. **Temperature regulation** matters substantially. Many MCAS patients experience temperature dysregulation with difficulty cooling down at night. Sleeping in cool room (65-68°F), using cooling mattress pads or pillows, and wearing minimal lightweight clothing improves sleep quality. Avoiding temperature extremes prevents temperature-triggered mast cell activation.

Light exposure timing affects circadian rhythms and melatonin production. Bright light exposure (preferably natural sunlight) in the morning synchronizes circadian clock. Evening light minimization (dimming lights 2-3 hours before bed, avoiding screens or using blue light blocking) supports melatonin production. Melatonin supplements (0.5-5 mg at bedtime) may help sleep onset, though individual response varies and some people report vivid dreams or morning grogginess.

Evening eating cutoff prevents digestive histamine production during sleep. Finishing dinner 3-4 hours before bed allows digestion completion before lying down. Late eating, particularly high-protein meals, generates histamine through bacterial action during overnight digestion, worsening sleep and morning symptoms.

27.4 Case Study: Sleep Transformation

Background

Jessamine, a 36-year-old accountant, maintained excellent dietary histamine management but suffered debilitating insomnia. She'd fall asleep easily around 10 PM, then wake at 2-3 AM with racing thoughts, flushing, and heart palpitations, unable to return to sleep. She'd lie awake for hours before eventually sleeping fitfully from 5-6:30 AM, waking exhausted for work. This pattern persisted for 18 months despite perfect diet adherence and appropriate medication management.

Presentation

Sleep deprivation affected every aspect of Jessamine's life. Her daytime symptoms worsened progressively. She experienced afternoon crashes requiring caffeine (which worsened evening symptoms). Her anxiety increased, partially from sleep deprivation and partially from dread of another sleepless night. She'd tried over-the-counter sleep aids (minimal benefit), melatonin (vivid nightmares), and prescription sedatives (left her groggy but didn't prevent 2-3 AM awakening). Her doctor suggested addressing her sleep environment and evening routine rather than focusing solely on sleep medications.

Analysis revealed multiple sleep hygiene problems. Her bedroom temperature stayed at 72°F year-round (she liked warmth). She scrolled social media in bed until feeling sleepy (bright screen exposure suppressing melatonin). Her dinner time varied from 6 PM to 9 PM depending on work schedule. She exercised at 7 PM (arousing rather than calming). Her bedroom contained exercise equipment, work papers, and served as multi-purpose space rather than sleep sanctuary.

Analysis

Jessamine's pattern demonstrated how poor sleep hygiene compounds histamine intolerance sleep challenges. Her 2-3 AM awakening coincided with natural histamine peak per section 27.3. However, her environmental and behavioral factors made the situation worse. The warm bedroom temperature potentially triggered temperature-sensitive mast cell activation. Late screen exposure suppressed melatonin production, delaying and reducing sleep depth. Variable dinner timing and late exercise activated rather than calmed her nervous system.

Research shows that sleep hygiene interventions improve sleep quality in individuals with medical conditions affecting sleep (Irish et al., 2015). For MCAS patients, addressing circadian alignment, temperature regulation, and evening routine becomes particularly important given the biological sleep challenges from histamine patterns.

Intervention

Jessamine's sleep specialist developed systematic sleep hygiene protocol. **Environmental modifications** included lowering bedroom temperature to 66°F (using extra blankets for comfort), removing all non-sleep items from bedroom (exercise equipment to spare room, work papers to office), installing blackout curtains, and adding white noise machine to mask environmental sounds.

Evening routine restructuring involved fixed dinner time at 6 PM (allowing 4 hours before 10 PM bedtime), moving exercise to morning (preventing evening arousal), implementing 9 PM screen curfew (no phone, computer, or TV after 9 PM), and creating 30-minute wind-down routine from 9:30-10 PM involving warm bath, light reading with dim lamp, and gentle stretching.

Circadian support included 20-minute outdoor walk upon waking (morning light exposure), avoiding afternoon caffeine (none after 1 PM), and taking 1 mg melatonin at 9:45 PM (45 minutes before desired sleep time). She continued her H1/H2 antihistamines and cromolyn from previous treatment but added these sleep-specific interventions.

Outcome

Week one showed modest improvement. The 2-3 AM awakening still occurred but duration decreased from 2-3 hours awake to 60-90 minutes. Week two, she slept through 2-3 AM twice, a breakthrough after 18 months. By week four, she was sleeping 7-8 hours nightly 5-6 nights weekly, waking only 1-2 nights. Her daytime symptoms improved dramatically with better sleep. Her anxiety decreased. Her afternoon energy stabilized, eliminating caffeine need.

Three months later, sleep quality remained good with occasional rough nights during high-stress periods or unavoidable late dinners. She'd learned that maintaining her sleep hygiene routine provided better symptom control than any single medication had achieved. She described sleep improvement as "more impactful than any dietary change" for overall quality of life.

Teaching Points

- Poor sleep hygiene compounds the natural histamine peak occurring at night for people with histamine intolerance, with environmental temperature, light exposure timing, meal scheduling, and evening activities all affecting mast cell stability and sleep architecture independent of dietary histamine management
- Systematic sleep hygiene interventions addressing multiple factors simultaneously (bedroom environment, evening routine, circadian alignment) provide superior outcomes compared to single interventions or sleep medications alone for MCAS-related insomnia
- Sleep quality improvement often produces broader symptom reduction through breaking the cycle where histamine disrupts sleep and sleep deprivation worsens histamine intolerance, making sleep optimization high-yield intervention for overall MCAS management

27.5 Exercise Considerations for MCAS

Exercise effects on histamine present complex picture. Intense exercise releases histamine through multiple mechanisms including mast cell degranulation from physical stress, increased body temperature triggering temperature-sensitive mast cells, and muscle activity producing histamine (Maintz & Novak, 2007). However, regular moderate exercise improves stress resilience, supports healthy inflammation regulation, and enhances overall health in ways benefiting MCAS management long-term.

Exercise-induced symptoms in MCAS patients include flushing, hives, difficulty breathing, rapid heart rate, lightheadedness, and gastrointestinal distress during or immediately after activity. These symptoms reflect mast cell activation from exercise stressors. Some individuals experience delayed reactions 2-6 hours post-exercise, making the connection to activity less obvious.

Safe exercise principles involve finding the threshold between beneficial activity and symptom triggering. **Start low, go slow** represents cardinal rule. Begin with gentle activity (slow walking, gentle yoga, tai chi) for short duration (10-15 minutes). Increase duration before increasing intensity. Monitor for symptoms during and for 6 hours after activity. If symptoms occur, reduce intensity or duration to previous tolerated level.

Pacing for POTS requires additional considerations. Individuals with postural orthostatic tachycardia syndrome (commonly comorbid with MCAS per Chapter 3.0) experience excessive heart rate increase with position change and exercise. Horizontal or recumbent exercise (recumbent bike, rowing machine, swimming, floor exercises) prevents postural challenges while allowing conditioning (Raj, 2013). Compression garments during exercise help manage POTS symptoms.

Timing considerations affect exercise tolerance. Morning or midday exercise works better than evening for most people, preventing evening symptom escalation and sleep disruption. Exercising in cooler parts of day (early morning in summer) prevents heat-triggered mast cell activation. Avoiding exercise immediately after meals prevents competition between digestive blood flow and muscle blood flow demands.

Hydration and electrolytes support exercise tolerance, particularly for POTS patients requiring increased fluid and salt intake. Drinking 16-20 ounces of water with 1/4 teaspoon salt 30 minutes before exercise preloads fluid volume. Sipping electrolyte drink during longer exercise sessions maintains hydration.

27.6 Environmental Trigger Management

Fragrances represent common mast cell triggers affecting many MCAS patients (Millqvist, 2021). Scented products including perfumes, colognes, air fresheners, scented candles, cleaning products, laundry detergents, and personal care products contain volatile organic compounds (VOCs) that can trigger mast cell degranulation. **Fragrance-free living** involves switching all personal products (shampoo, soap, lotion, deodorant, laundry detergent) to fragrance-free versions. True fragrance-free differs from "unscented," which may contain fragrance to mask other smells. Read ingredient lists for "fragrance" or "parfum," avoiding any products listing these.

Workplace and public spaces present fragrance exposure challenges. Some workplaces implement fragrance-free policies upon request with medical documentation. For public spaces, carrying N95 or activated carbon mask filters some volatile chemicals. Avoiding peak times in stores reduces exposure duration. Online shopping eliminates many public space exposures.

Mold triggers mast cell activation in susceptible individuals (Thrasher & Hooper, 2005). Visible mold (black spots in bathrooms, basements, or anywhere moisture accumulates) requires immediate remediation. Hidden mold from water damage, roof leaks, or plumbing issues causes symptoms without obvious source. Musty odors, worsening symptoms at home improving away from home, and history of water damage suggest mold investigation.

Mold testing options include air quality testing measuring mold spore counts or moisture testing identifying water intrusion. Professional mold remediation addresses underlying moisture source and removes contaminated materials. HEPA air purifiers reduce airborne mold spores in interim. Some individuals cannot remediate adequately and require moving to mold-free environment for symptom resolution.

Air quality beyond mold affects symptoms. HEPA air purifiers with activated carbon filters remove particulates, allergens, VOCs, and some chemical triggers. Running purifiers in bedroom and main living spaces reduces overall exposure load. Avoiding outdoor activity during high pollution days or wildfire smoke protects sensitive individuals.

Temperature extremes trigger mast cell activation through temperature-sensitive receptors. Heat causes vasodilation and increased histamine release in many individuals. Staying cool through air conditioning, cooling vests, cold packs, and avoiding outdoor heat prevents heat-triggered symptoms. Sudden temperature changes (hot shower after cold environment, entering air-conditioned building from heat) can trigger symptoms even if moderate temperatures themselves are tolerated. Gradual temperature transitions reduce triggering.

27.7 Hormonal Cycle Management

Estrogen increases histamine through multiple mechanisms including reducing DAO activity and increasing mast cell numbers and sensitivity (Maintz & Novak, 2007). **Progesterone** has opposite effects, increasing DAO activity and stabilizing mast cells. This creates predictable symptom patterns across menstrual cycle for many women with histamine intolerance.

Follicular phase (days 1-14, starting with menstruation) involves rising estrogen peaking at ovulation. Many women notice worsening symptoms mid-cycle around ovulation when estrogen peaks. **Luteal phase** (days 14-28, after ovulation) involves rising progesterone initially providing symptom relief, but the late luteal phase (days 24-28) brings estrogen rise while progesterone drops, often triggering premenstrual symptom worsening.

Menstrual phase (days 1-5) brings both estrogen and progesterone to lowest levels. Some women find this their best time. Others experience worsening from prostaglandin release during menstruation triggering mast cells. Tracking symptoms across 2-3 cycles reveals individual patterns enabling strategic management.

Dietary modifications by cycle phase can reduce symptom burden. During high-estrogen phases (ovulation, late luteal), some women benefit from extra-strict histamine restriction, increased DAO supplementation, or higher antihistamine doses. During progesterone-dominant mid-luteal phase, slightly relaxed diet may be tolerated without symptoms.

Hormonal birth control affects symptoms variably. Some women improve with continuous hormonal suppression preventing estrogen peaks. Others worsen from synthetic hormones. Progesterone-only methods (IUD, mini-pill) may benefit women whose symptoms worsen with estrogen. Discontinuing hormonal contraception under medical supervision helps identify its effects.

Pregnancy presents unique challenges. Progesterone rises substantially during pregnancy, theoretically benefiting histamine intolerance. Some women experience dramatic improvement during pregnancy. However, others worsen from increased blood volume, immune changes, and other pregnancy physiology affecting mast cells. Medication management during pregnancy requires careful risk-benefit analysis with obstetric and MCAS specialists.

Perimenopause and menopause bring fluctuating then declining hormones. Erratic estrogen swings during perimenopause often worsen symptoms unpredictably. Post-menopausal estrogen decline may improve histamine intolerance for some women. Hormone replacement therapy (HRT) affects symptoms variably, requiring individualized decisions balancing menopause symptom relief against potential histamine intolerance worsening.

27.8 Putting Knowledge Into Practice

This chapter examined lifestyle factors beyond diet affecting histamine intolerance and MCAS. Stress activates the HPA axis and triggers mast cell degranulation through cortisol dysregulation and direct CRH effects, making stress management medical intervention rather than optional. Vagal tone exercises strengthen parasympathetic function through cold exposure, breathing practices, humming, and gargling.

Sleep optimization addresses the natural nighttime histamine peak and decreased DAO activity through temperature regulation, light exposure timing, evening routine restructuring, and circadian support. Exercise requires pacing to provide health benefits without triggering mast cell activation, with recumbent options benefiting POTS patients.

Environmental trigger management involves fragrance elimination, mold remediation, air quality improvement, and temperature regulation. Hormonal considerations for women include recognizing estrogen-progesterone effects on histamine across menstrual cycles, during pregnancy, and through menopause, enabling strategic dietary and medication adjustments by cycle phase.

The case study illustrated how comprehensive sleep hygiene addressing multiple factors simultaneously produced superior outcomes compared to medication alone for MCAS-related insomnia. This chapter connects to Chapter 28.0's examination of special populations including Long COVID, POTS, EDS, pregnancy, children, and managing multiple food intolerances.

Chapter 28.0: Special Population Considerations

Galatea reviewed treatment recommendations from three different specialists, each addressing one aspect of her complex condition but none integrating the full picture. Her MCAS specialist focused on mast cell stabilization through medications and low-histamine diet. Her POTS cardiologist emphasized fluid loading, salt intake, and compression garments for orthostatic intolerance. Her rheumatologist managing Ehlers-Danlos Syndrome prescribed physical therapy for joint stability and pain management. Each protocol made sense individually, but the combined recommendations created contradictions. Her MCAS diet restricted salt and fluids to reduce histamine triggers, while her POTS protocol required massive salt and fluid intake for blood pressure support. Her EDS physical therapy involved intensive strengthening exercises that triggered severe MCAS flares. The dietary restrictions for histamine eliminated high-calorie foods needed for the increased metabolic demands of POTS and EDS. She felt caught between competing medical needs, improving one condition while worsening others. Her frustration illustrated how special populations with overlapping conditions require integrated approaches rather than parallel single-condition management (Cheung & Vadas, 2015). Understanding unique considerations for Long COVID, POTS, EDS, pregnancy, pediatric cases, athletes, vegetarians, and multiple food intolerances enables coordinated treatment addressing all conditions simultaneously.

This chapter examines special population needs including Long COVID and post-viral MCAS dietary strategies, POTS management balancing salt and histamine considerations, EDS overlap requiring modified approaches, pregnancy and breastfeeding safety, pediatric histamine intolerance unique features, athletic performance with restrictions, vegetarian and vegan adaptations, and managing multiple concurrent food intolerances.

28.1 Long COVID MCAS Patterns

Post-viral mast cell activation syndrome has emerged as significant component of Long COVID for subset of patients experiencing persistent symptoms months after initial SARS-CoV-2 infection (Weinstock et al., 2021). Symptoms including fatigue, brain fog, exercise intolerance, gastrointestinal dysfunction, dysautonomia, and histamine intolerance frequently reflect underlying MCAS triggered or unmasked by viral infection.

Viral triggers for MCAS involve direct viral effects on mast cells, immune system activation during infection leading to mast cell priming, and post-viral immune dysregulation maintaining chronic mast cell activation (Weinstock et al., 2021). Some individuals had subclinical MCAS before COVID-19 that became symptomatic post-infection. Others developed new-onset MCAS as direct consequence of viral effects.

Dietary considerations for Long COVID MCAS follow standard low-histamine principles from Chapters 6.0 through 15.0 with additional emphasis on anti-inflammatory foods supporting recovery. Fresh fruits and vegetables tolerated individually provide antioxidants and nutrients supporting immune recovery. High-quality proteins from fresh meat, poultry, and fish (prepared immediately, stored minimally) support tissue repair and metabolic demands.

Recovery nutrition requires adequate calories despite restrictive diet. Long COVID often involves hypermetabolic state with increased caloric needs. Relying on safe starches (rice, potatoes, sweet potatoes), healthy fats (olive oil, coconut oil), and adequate protein prevents unintentional weight loss and supports healing. Some practitioners recommend 20-30% calorie increase during active recovery phase, requiring creative meal planning within histamine restrictions.

Combining MCAS treatment with Long COVID therapies requires coordination. Low-dose naltrexone (section 26.6) shows promise for both MCAS and Long COVID fatigue. Mast cell stabilizers and H1/H2 antihistamines address MCAS while potentially reducing neuroinflammation contributing to Long COVID symptoms. Supplements supporting mitochondrial function (CoQ10, alpha-lipoic acid, B vitamins) may benefit both conditions but require one-at-a-time introduction per section 24.7 preventing overwhelming system during recovery.

28.2 POTS Nutritional Strategies

Postural orthostatic tachycardia syndrome (POTS) commonly co-occurs with MCAS, creating nutritional challenges (Cheung & Vadas, 2015). POTS management traditionally emphasizes high salt intake (6-10 grams daily) and fluid loading (2-3 liters daily) to expand blood volume and improve orthostatic tolerance. However, excessive salt and fluid can worsen histamine intolerance for some individuals, creating therapeutic conflict.

Salt and histamine considerations require individualized balance. Some MCAS patients tolerate high salt intake without histamine worsening. Others experience edema, inflammation, or symptom exacerbation with aggressive salt loading. Starting with moderate salt increase (3-5 grams daily, achieved through salting food generously and drinking electrolyte beverages) while monitoring histamine symptoms identifies tolerance. If POTS symptoms remain problematic despite moderate salt, gradually increasing to 6-8 grams while watching for histamine flares finds individual threshold.

Electrolyte beverages for POTS require careful selection. Commercial sports drinks often contain artificial colors, flavors, and preservatives triggering MCAS. Homemade electrolyte drinks using water, salt, and small amount of maple syrup or honey (if tolerated) provide histamine-safe hydration. Coconut water (checking for preservatives) offers natural electrolytes for those tolerating it. Some individuals use electrolyte powders specifically formulated without additives.

Meal timing and blood sugar affect POTS symptoms substantially. Large meals cause blood pooling in digestive system, worsening orthostatic symptoms. Small frequent meals (5-6 daily) rather than three large meals reduce postprandial hypotension. Maintaining stable blood sugar through regular eating prevents hypoglycemia-triggered adrenaline surges worsening both POTS and MCAS.

Protein at each meal helps maintain blood pressure. Protein digestion requires more energy and blood flow than carbohydrates alone, potentially supporting blood pressure maintenance. Combining lean protein with complex carbohydrates at each meal stabilizes both blood sugar and blood pressure. For example, chicken with rice and vegetables provides balanced nutrition addressing both conditions.

28.3 Case Study: POTS MCAS Integration

Background

Remigius, a 29-year-old graduate student, struggled with both POTS and MCAS diagnoses received six months apart. His POTS cardiologist prescribed 10 grams salt daily with 3+ liters fluid. His allergist managing MCAS recommended strict low-histamine diet with moderate salt restriction. Following both protocols simultaneously seemed impossible. He tried alternating approaches (high salt one week, low salt the next), but this created symptom cycling rather than improvement.

Presentation

On high-salt weeks, Remigius's orthostatic symptoms improved. He could stand longer, exercise briefly, and function better physically. However, his histamine symptoms worsened dramatically. Flushing, headaches, and gastrointestinal distress increased. Edema developed in his ankles. On low-salt weeks following strict MCAS protocols, his histamine symptoms improved but POTS symptoms became disabling. He'd experience near-syncope standing, severe fatigue, and inability to exercise at all. Neither approach provided acceptable quality of life.

His physicians hadn't communicated about managing both conditions simultaneously. Each provided single-condition guidance without considering the other diagnosis. Remigius felt abandoned to figure out integration himself, leading to the ineffective alternating approach.

Analysis

Remigius's situation demonstrated the challenge of overlapping conditions with seemingly contradictory management needs. Research shows 30-50% of POTS patients have comorbid MCAS (Cheung & Vadas, 2015). Both conditions require simultaneous management rather than serial or alternating approaches. The key involves finding the threshold where adequate POTS support doesn't overwhelm histamine tolerance.

His alternating approach guaranteed suboptimal management of both conditions. One week of worsened POTS symptoms undid previous progress, while one week of MCAS flares required recovery time. The cycling prevented establishing stable baseline.

Intervention

His physicians (after coordinated consultation Remigius requested) developed integrated protocol. Salt intake set at 6 grams daily, a compromise between 10-gram POTS recommendation and minimal salt MCAS preference. This involved 1/4 teaspoon salt with breakfast, lunch, and dinner (2.1 grams), plus electrolyte drink mid-morning and mid-afternoon (2 grams), plus salting food to taste (estimated 1-2 grams). Fluid intake targeted 2-2.5 liters daily.

Dietary histamine restriction followed tier 1 and 2 protocols from section 6.4 but included regular inclusion of potatoes and rice providing carbohydrates supporting blood pressure without histamine. Protein distributed across five small meals daily rather than three large meals per section 28.2. He wore compression stockings waist-high during waking hours to reduce blood pooling.

Medication management included continued POTS beta blocker (low dose to avoid excessive heart rate reduction interfering with exercise) plus H1/H2 antihistamines and cromolyn for MCAS. The beta blocker actually helped both conditions by reducing stress-triggered symptoms affecting both POTS and MCAS.

Outcome

Week two on integrated protocol showed improvement in both conditions simultaneously for the first time. His POTS symptoms remained manageable with moderate salt rather than requiring extreme intake. His histamine symptoms stayed controlled without severe restriction. By week six, he'd found sustainable balance. His orthostatic tolerance enabled 30-minute walks daily (impossible on MCAS-only management). His histamine symptoms occurred only 1-2 days weekly (dramatic improvement from high-salt weeks).

Six months later, he described the integrated approach as "life-changing compared to bouncing between two bad options." He'd returned to part-time graduate studies (impossible during alternating protocol). His quality of life rating improved from 3/10 to 7/10. Most importantly, managing both conditions simultaneously prevented the sabotage cycle where treating one worsened the other.

Teaching Points

- Overlapping conditions like POTS and MCAS require integrated treatment protocols finding compromise positions between seemingly contradictory recommendations rather than alternating between condition-specific approaches or prioritizing one condition over the other
- Moderate implementation of key interventions for each condition (intermediate salt intake, small frequent meals, compression garments, both POTS and MCAS medications) often provides superior outcomes compared to aggressive single-condition management ignoring comorbidities
- Coordinated care requiring physician communication and patient advocacy to develop unified treatment plans prevents the therapeutic conflicts common when specialists manage conditions in isolation without considering overlapping physiology

28.4 EDS Dietary Modifications

Ehlers-Danlos Syndrome (EDS), particularly hypermobile type, frequently overlaps with MCAS and POTS creating the "trifecta" of interconnected conditions (Cheung & Vadas, 2015). EDS affects connective tissue throughout the body including the gastrointestinal tract, creating unique nutritional challenges beyond histamine intolerance alone.

Gastrointestinal dysmotility in EDS results from connective tissue laxity affecting smooth muscle function in digestive tract. Delayed gastric emptying, slow intestinal transit, and functional constipation occur commonly. Combined with histamine-restricted diet often low in fiber, constipation becomes problematic. **Gentle fiber sources** tolerated within histamine restrictions include well-cooked vegetables (zucchini, green beans, carrots), peeled cucumbers, rice, and small amounts of chia seeds soaked overnight if tolerated. Adequate hydration (especially important for POTS patients) supports bowel function.

Small frequent meals benefit EDS patients beyond POTS considerations. Large meals stress the dysmotile digestive system, causing bloating, pain, and nausea. Eating smaller amounts more frequently (5-6 times daily) reduces digestive burden while meeting nutritional needs. This aligns well with POTS recommendations per section 28.2.

Protein needs increase in EDS due to ongoing tissue repair and increased metabolic demands from unstable joints and chronic pain. Target protein intake of 1.2-1.5 grams per kilogram body weight supports collagen production and tissue maintenance. This requires strategic protein distribution across meals using fresh prepared meats, poultry, fish, and tolerated legumes from section 17.0.

Nutrient considerations include vitamin C supporting collagen synthesis (500-1000 mg daily buffered form per section 24.3), and other collagen cofactors including copper, manganese, and zinc. However, supplementation requires medical guidance given complex interactions in EDS. Some EDS patients have copper metabolism abnormalities making supplementation problematic.

28.5 Pregnancy and Breastfeeding Adaptations

Pregnancy with histamine intolerance requires careful balance between maternal symptom control and fetal safety. Progesterone elevation during pregnancy may improve histamine symptoms for some women per section 27.7, but others experience worsening from increased blood volume, immune changes, and pregnancy-associated nausea compounding histamine-related nausea.

Medication safety in pregnancy necessitates individualized risk-benefit analysis with obstetric and MCAS specialists. Most H1 and H2 antihistamines have decades of safety data in pregnancy, with cetirizine and loratadine among the best-studied. Cromolyn sodium has minimal systemic absorption making it relatively safe option. However, some women prefer minimizing all medications during pregnancy, relying primarily on dietary management.

Nutritional adequacy during pregnancy requires particular attention with restrictive diet. Prenatal vitamins (checking for fillers and additives), adequate protein (70-100 grams daily), calcium from tolerated sources (fortified rice milk, calcium citrate supplement), and iron if needed all support healthy pregnancy. Some women require more liberal histamine approach during pregnancy accepting increased symptoms to ensure adequate nutrition for fetal development.

Nausea management presents challenges when pregnancy-related nausea overlaps with histamine-triggered nausea. Small frequent meals, ginger (if tolerated), vitamin B6 (50-100 mg daily), and avoiding empty stomach all help both types of nausea. If severe hyperemesis gravidarum develops, medical management including IV fluids and antiemetics becomes necessary despite MCAS, prioritizing maternal and fetal health.

Breastfeeding considerations involve both maternal symptom control and infant tolerance. Most H1/H2 antihistamines transfer into breast milk in small amounts generally considered safe. Cromolyn sodium transfers minimally due to poor absorption. Maternal diet affects breast milk composition, with some infants reacting to high-histamine foods in maternal diet creating fussiness, rashes, or digestive upset. If this occurs, maintaining maternal low-histamine diet while breastfeeding may benefit infant.

28.6 Pediatric MCAS Management

Children with histamine intolerance present unique challenges including limited dietary flexibility, school lunch logistics, and developmental nutrition needs. Pediatric MCAS often manifests differently than adult presentations, with more prominent skin symptoms (eczema, hives), gastrointestinal complaints (abdominal pain, diarrhea, reflux), and behavioral changes (irritability, sleep disruption, attention difficulties).

Growth and development require adequate calories and nutrients potentially complicated by restrictive diet. Pediatric dietitian consultation ensures children meet nutritional needs within histamine restrictions. Height and weight tracking monitors growth patterns, with faltering growth indicating inadequate nutrition requiring dietary liberalization or supplemental nutrition.

Family meals require either entire family following low-histamine approach or preparing separate meals for affected child. Many families find former easier and potentially beneficial for all members. Involving children in age-appropriate meal planning and preparation supports adherence and teaches lifelong skills.

School accommodations including 504 plans or individualized health plans document dietary needs and emergency protocols. School lunch programs rarely accommodate histamine restrictions, requiring packed lunches with safe foods. Educating teachers, school nurses, and cafeteria staff about the condition and emergency response prevents dangerous exposures.

Social situations (birthday parties, sleepovers, holidays) require advance planning. Sending safe treats when child attends parties prevents exclusion. Teaching children to politely decline unsafe foods and advocate for their needs builds skills for lifelong management. Balancing safety with normal childhood experiences requires flexibility and judgment.

28.7 Athletic Performance Considerations

Athletes with histamine intolerance face particular challenges balancing performance demands with dietary restrictions and exercise-induced mast cell activation. Training and competition require high caloric intake, optimal macronutrient timing, and quick recovery, all complicated by histamine management.

Caloric needs for athletes often reach 3000-5000+ calories daily depending on sport, training volume, and body size. Meeting these needs within histamine restrictions requires strategic food selection emphasizing calorie-dense safe options. Rice, potatoes, sweet potatoes, olive oil, coconut oil, fresh meats, and tolerated nuts/seeds (if histamine-safe per individual testing) provide concentrated calories.

Protein timing affects recovery and adaptation. Athletes require 1.6-2.2 grams protein per kilogram body weight distributed across the day (Moore et al., 2014). Post-exercise protein (20-40 grams within 2 hours) supports muscle recovery. This requires reliable fresh protein sources prepared immediately before consumption. Batch-cooking and freezing portioned proteins per section 10.0 enables quick post-workout nutrition.

Carbohydrate needs during training necessitate easily digestible sources. Rice, rice-based foods, potatoes, and sweet potatoes provide carbohydrates without histamine concerns. Sports nutrition products (gels, drinks, bars) typically contain problematic ingredients requiring careful label reading or homemade alternatives using rice syrup, maple syrup, and salt.

Pre-exercise nutrition affects exercise tolerance and mast cell activation. Eating 2-3 hours before exercise allows digestion while providing fuel. Small easily-digested meals (rice with chicken, sweet potato with turkey) prevent both hypoglycemia and digestive distress during activity. Some athletes tolerate small carbohydrate snack 30-60 minutes before exercise for additional fuel.

Hydration and electrolytes during exercise require histamine-safe options per section 28.2. Homemade electrolyte drinks or carefully selected commercial products support performance without triggering symptoms. Dehydration worsens exercise intolerance and may increase mast cell activation, making adequate hydration particularly important.

28.8 Vegetarian and Vegan Approaches

Plant-based eating with histamine intolerance requires careful planning ensuring adequate protein and nutrients from limited options. Chapter 17.0 covered plant-based recipes, but this section addresses nutritional completeness and long-term sustainability.

Protein sources for vegetarians include fresh-cooked legumes (prepared in pressure cooker per section 17.0), quinoa, rice and beans combinations, and eggs if tolerated. Vegans rely more heavily on legumes requiring diligent freshness protocols. Batch-cooking large amounts of various legumes, immediately cooling, portioning, and freezing provides protein variety throughout the week.

Iron and B12 require attention in plant-based diets generally and particularly with histamine restrictions eliminating some fortified foods and fermented products providing these nutrients. Iron from plant sources (lentils, chickpeas, pumpkin seeds if tolerated, dark leafy greens if tolerated) absorbs better when consumed with vitamin C. B12 supplementation (methylcobalamin 1000 mcg daily) prevents deficiency for vegans and some vegetarians.

Calcium sources for dairy-free individuals include fortified rice milk (checking for additives), tahini, almonds (if tolerated), white beans, and calcium citrate supplements. Meeting 1000-1200 mg daily calcium requirement prevents bone health issues long-term.

Omega-3 fatty acids from plant sources include flaxseed, chia seeds, and walnuts (if tolerated). However, conversion of plant-based ALA to EPA/DHA is inefficient. Algae-based omega-3 supplements per section 24.6 provide direct EPA/DHA for those avoiding fish.

28.9 Multiple Food Intolerance Management

Overlapping food intolerances including FODMAPs, oxalates, salicylates, and sulfites alongside histamine create extremely restrictive diets risking nutritional inadequacy and psychological distress. Systematic approach prevents eliminating all foods simultaneously.

Sequential testing identifies which intolerances actually affect symptoms versus being precautionary eliminations. Start with histamine elimination per Chapter 6.0. Once stable on low-histamine diet, maintain that while testing one additional restriction. If FODMAP sensitivity suspected, follow low-FODMAP protocol while continuing histamine restriction. If symptoms improve further, FODMAPs contribute. If no change, FODMAPs may not be relevant.

Overlap identification finds foods problematic for multiple reasons versus restrictions that don't apply. For example, avocados are high histamine, high FODMAP, and high salicylate. Someone reacting to avocados likely benefits from avoiding them. However, rice is low in all categories. If someone eliminates rice based on generic anti-inflammatory diet advice, they remove valuable safe option unnecessarily.

Working with specialists including dietitians experienced in multiple food intolerances prevents overly restrictive protocols. Testing only necessary restrictions based on symptoms and response rather than eliminating everything "just in case" maintains quality of life while managing symptoms.

28.10 Core Concepts Recap

This chapter examined special populations requiring modified approaches to histamine intolerance management. Long COVID patients with post-viral MCAS need anti-inflammatory dietary emphasis with adequate calories supporting recovery. POTS patients require integrated protocols balancing salt and fluid needs against histamine triggers through moderate compromise approaches rather than alternating or prioritizing one condition.

EDS patients need small frequent meals addressing dysmotility, adequate protein supporting tissue repair, and fiber strategies preventing constipation. Pregnancy and breastfeeding require medication safety considerations, nutritional adequacy for fetal development, and nausea management strategies. Pediatric cases involve growth monitoring, family meal coordination, school accommodations, and age-appropriate education.

Athletes need high-calorie intake strategies, protein timing for recovery, and exercise-specific nutrition within histamine restrictions. Vegetarians and vegans require careful protein planning with fresh-cooked legumes, B12 and iron monitoring, and plant-based omega-3 support. Multiple food intolerances necessitate sequential testing identifying actual triggers rather than precautionary mass elimination.

The case study illustrated integrated POTS-MCAS management finding compromise between competing needs rather than alternating protocols or single-condition focus. This chapter connects to Chapter 29.0's troubleshooting common challenges including severe restrictions, treatment resistance, and psychological impacts.

Chapter 29.0: Common Challenge Troubleshooting

Theodora slumped in her therapist's office, tears streaming down her face as she described feeling completely trapped. Six months into elimination diet, she'd systematically tested and failed nearly every food. Her safe food list had dwindled to seven items (rice, chicken, zucchini, cucumber, olive oil, salt, and water). She'd lost 22 pounds from an already slender frame. Friends stopped inviting her anywhere involving food. Her family ate separately to avoid upsetting her. She spent hours daily preparing tiny portions of the same rotation, terrified to try anything new after experiencing severe reactions to 30+ reintroduction attempts. She described constant hunger, social isolation, depression, and intrusive thoughts about food. Her therapist identified severe orthorexia and food fear requiring psychological intervention alongside medical management. Her case illustrated how histamine intolerance management can deteriorate from therapeutic dietary approach into disordered eating without appropriate support and realistic expectations (Niland & Cash, 2018). Understanding common challenges including severe restriction, treatment resistance, reintroduction failures, weight concerns, social isolation, and psychological impacts enables recognizing when standard approaches fail and alternative strategies or additional support becomes necessary.

This chapter addresses troubleshooting severe dietary restriction, managing treatment-resistant symptoms, navigating reintroduction failures, weight maintenance challenges, social isolation impacts, disordered eating risks, food fear development, recognizing when to seek additional help, and considering alternative diagnoses.

29.1 Severe Restriction Management

The severely restricted diet where individuals react to most foods represents one of the most challenging scenarios in histamine intolerance management. True severe restriction (tolerating fewer than 15 foods) occurs rarely and raises questions about whether histamine alone explains the reactivity or whether multiple overlapping conditions require identification.

Mast cell activation syndrome rather than simple histamine intolerance may underlie severe reactivity. MCAS involves mast cells responding to multiple triggers beyond dietary histamine, including stress, temperature changes, exercise, medications, and other foods through non-histamine mechanisms (Afrin et al., 2020). Someone with uncontrolled MCAS may appear to react to "everything" because mast cells remain unstable regardless of trigger type. This requires pharmaceutical mast cell stabilization per Chapter 26.0 before dietary liberalization becomes possible.

Multiple food intolerances per section 28.9 create appearance of reacting to everything when actually reacting to different components in different foods. Someone with histamine intolerance plus FODMAP sensitivity plus salicylate sensitivity eliminates most foods when all three restrictions combine, even though each individual restriction is moderate. Sequential testing identifying actual culprits versus precautionary eliminations prevents unnecessary restriction.

Nutritional rehabilitation takes priority when severe restriction causes malnutrition, significant weight loss, or medical instability. Working with medical team including gastroenterologist, allergist, and dietitian establishes minimum safe food list ensuring nutritional adequacy even if symptom control remains imperfect. Sometimes accepting moderate symptoms while maintaining nutrition proves necessary short-term while addressing underlying issues. Enteral nutrition (feeding tube) or elemental formulas become necessary in rare cases where oral intake cannot meet needs safely.

Psychological support addresses the anxiety, depression, and potential eating disorder behaviors developing from severe restriction. Cognitive-behavioral therapy helps differentiate realistic food fears from anxiety-driven avoidance. Exposure therapy can gradually expand food tolerance when fear rather than physical reactivity limits intake. Psychiatric medication may help anxiety or depression complicating medical management.

29.2 Treatment Resistant Patterns

Stuck at baseline describes the frustrating scenario where someone implements dietary changes, supplements, and medications without meaningful symptom improvement. After 3-6 months of compliant treatment, persistent symptoms indicate missed diagnosis, inadequate treatment, or need for alternative approach.

Root cause investigation becomes essential for treatment resistance. Has SIBO been tested and treated per section 25.3? Has mold exposure been assessed and remediated per section 27.6? Are there unrecognized medication triggers per section 26.7? Does the patient have undiagnosed autoimmune condition, thyroid dysfunction, or other medical issue causing overlapping symptoms misattributed to histamine? Comprehensive medical evaluation identifies issues dietary change alone cannot address.

Medication optimization may require escalation. Someone taking moderate-dose H1/H2 antihistamines may need high-dose protocols per section 26.1. Cromolyn sodium added to antihistamines per section 26.3 provides additional mast cell stabilization. Low-dose naltrexone per section 26.6 offers immunomodulatory effects. Working with MCAS specialist ensures appropriate pharmaceutical management rather than assuming dietary approaches alone should suffice.

Expectation recalibration matters when treatment provides partial but not complete relief. Moving from 100% symptoms to 40% symptoms represents significant improvement even though 40% symptoms feel burdensome. Some individuals have realistic expectations of modest improvement while others expect complete symptom resolution. Understanding that MCAS and histamine intolerance often require ongoing management rather than curative treatment prevents abandoning effective interventions because they don't produce perfection.

29.3 Case Study: Breaking Through Treatment Resistance

Background

Ivo, a 41-year-old engineer, had followed strict low-histamine diet for 14 months without meaningful improvement. He meticulously tracked symptoms, maintained perfect dietary compliance, took H1/H2 antihistamines and quercetin daily, and yet rated his symptoms 7-8 out of 10 consistently. He'd consulted three physicians, tried various elimination protocols, and spent thousands of dollars on supplements with negligible benefit.

Presentation

Ivo's main symptoms included severe fatigue (waking unrefreshed despite 8-9 hours sleep), brain fog interfering with engineering work, chronic headaches, and gastrointestinal distress (bloating, alternating constipation and diarrhea). He'd assumed these were histamine-related and became progressively more restrictive, eventually eating only 12 foods. His weight remained stable but energy declined further. He felt hopeless, wondering if he'd ever improve.

Previous doctors had focused exclusively on dietary management, assuming compliance issues or need for stricter elimination explained persistent symptoms. None had investigated beyond histamine intolerance diagnosis. Ivo's new integrative medicine physician took different approach, ordering comprehensive testing rather than assuming dietary modification alone would work.

Analysis

Testing revealed multiple issues unaddressed by dietary approach alone. SIBO breath test showed severe methane-dominant small intestinal bacterial overgrowth.

His bacteria were producing methane, histamine, and other inflammatory compounds regardless of dietary intake. Comprehensive stool testing demonstrated virtually absent beneficial bacteria, severe dysbiosis, and elevated markers of intestinal inflammation. Thyroid testing showed subclinical hypothyroidism (TSH 4.8, many integrative practitioners treat above 3.0) explaining fatigue and brain fog. Heavy metal testing revealed moderately elevated mercury, likely from dental amalgams, contributing to inflammatory burden.

His treatment resistance made sense given multiple untreated root causes. Dietary histamine reduction couldn't overcome bacterial histamine production from SIBO. His dysbiosis and intestinal inflammation impaired DAO production and nutrient absorption. His thyroid dysfunction caused symptoms overlapping with histamine intolerance. The mercury burden increased overall inflammatory load.

Intervention

Treatment addressed multiple issues sequentially. Phase 1 (weeks 1-8) targeted SIBO using antimicrobial herbs (berberine and neem combination), biofilm disruptors (NAC), and digestive enzymes. He maintained low-histamine diet and current supplements throughout SIBO treatment. SIBO re-testing at week 8 showed substantial improvement with bacterial counts reduced to low-normal range.

Phase 2 (weeks 9-16) focused on gut restoration using probiotic (Bifidobacterium longum), L-glutamine, and zinc carnosine per section 25.1. He continued low-histamine diet. His gastrointestinal symptoms began improving week 10, the first meaningful improvement in 14 months.

Phase 3 (weeks 17-24) addressed thyroid with low-dose thyroid medication (requiring medical prescription and monitoring). Within two weeks on thyroid medication, his fatigue improved dramatically. Brain fog lifted substantially. He regained energy for exercise and work concentration.

Phase 4 (weeks 25-32) involved safe mercury removal by biological dentist removing amalgams with protective protocols, followed by chelation therapy. This phase took months but gradually reduced inflammatory burden.

Outcome

Six months into treatment (addressing SIBO, gut health, thyroid, and beginning mercury removal), Ivo rated symptoms 2-3 out of 10, dramatic improvement from perpetual 7-8. His energy returned. Brain fog resolved almost completely. Headaches decreased to occasional rather than daily. Gastrointestinal function normalized. Most remarkably, his food tolerance expanded. With SIBO resolved and gut healing supported, he successfully reintroduced 20+ foods without reactions.

One year later, he maintained 80-85% improvement. He still followed modified low-histamine approach (avoiding aged cheeses, cured meats, alcohol, leftovers) but tolerated most fresh foods. He took maintenance probiotics and thyroid medication but had stopped most other supplements. He described the difference as "getting my life back after feeling like dietary changes alone trapped me in permanent illness."

Teaching Points

- Treatment resistance after 3-6 months of compliant dietary management indicates need for comprehensive root cause investigation rather than progressively stricter elimination, with testing for SIBO, dysbiosis, thyroid dysfunction, nutrient deficiencies, toxic exposures, and other medical conditions causing overlapping symptoms
- Multiple untreated root causes create additive symptom burden where dietary management alone cannot produce meaningful improvement, requiring systematic phase-based treatment addressing identified issues sequentially while maintaining dietary foundations
- Dramatic improvement after addressing root causes often enables dietary liberalization as gut healing, bacterial balance restoration, and overall inflammatory burden reduction improve actual histamine tolerance rather than requiring perpetual strict restriction

29.4 Reintroduction Failure Navigation

Failed reintroductions where multiple foods tested sequentially all trigger reactions create discouragement and confusion. After weeks of careful single-food testing following protocols from section 6.5, having ten consecutive failures suggests problems with testing methodology, unstable baseline, or factors beyond food histamine.

Testing during unstable periods dooms reintroductions to failure. High stress, poor sleep, illness, menstrual cycle (for women in high-estrogen phases), or environmental exposures (mold, fragrances) all increase mast cell reactivity making even safe foods trigger symptoms. Reintroduction requires stable baseline (same symptoms day-to-day for 1-2 weeks) and low-stress conditions. Testing during unstable periods produces false failures.

Portion size issues affect outcomes. Testing full serving of new food (half cup vegetables, 4 ounces protein) may overwhelm system where quarter serving would be tolerated. Starting with tiny amounts (one tablespoon) the first day, doubling the second day if tolerated, reaching normal serving by day three identifies threshold tolerance. Some foods may be tolerated in small amounts but not large servings.

Preparation method matters significantly. Raw tomatoes may trigger reactions while cooked tomatoes (lower histamine) are tolerated. Grilled chicken (higher histamine from browning) may fail while poached chicken succeeds. Varying preparation methods for failed foods sometimes identifies tolerable versions.

Timing between tests requires adequate spacing. Testing new foods daily doesn't allow delayed reactions (occurring 4-24 hours after ingestion) to manifest before introducing next food. Spacing tests 3-4 days apart prevents overlap confusion. If multiple failures occur with adequate spacing, pausing reintroduction for 2-4 weeks while focusing on root cause treatment per section 29.2 may enable success when resumed.

29.5 Weight and Body Composition

Unintentional weight loss occurs commonly with restrictive diets, particularly when eliminating calorie-dense foods or experiencing poor appetite from symptoms. Losing more than 5-10% body weight unintentionally or BMI dropping below 18.5 requires intervention prioritizing nutritional adequacy over perfect histamine restriction.

Increasing calories safely involves strategic use of tolerated high-calorie foods. Adding olive oil or coconut oil to meals (extra tablespoon per meal adds 120 calories) increases energy without volume. Emphasizing starches (rice, potatoes, sweet potatoes) provides concentrated carbohydrates. Frequent small meals (6-7 daily) increase total intake without large meal burden. Smoothies or pureed soups deliver calories in easily consumed form.

Protein adequacy prevents muscle loss during weight loss. Target 1.2-1.6 grams protein per kilogram ideal body weight, distributed across meals. Protein shakes using rice protein or pea protein (if tolerated, checking for additives) supplement dietary protein intake. Regular resistance exercise preserves muscle mass during caloric deficit.

Medical evaluation for weight loss exceeding 10% body weight or continuing despite intervention identifies malabsorption, hyperthyroidism, diabetes, cancer, or other serious conditions requiring different treatment. Weight loss from dietary restriction should stabilize and reverse with calorie-focused interventions. Continued loss despite adequate intake suggests medical issue beyond histamine intolerance.

Weight gain concerns affect some individuals, particularly those with MCAS who gain weight from chronic inflammation, fluid retention, or medications (some antihistamines and mast cell stabilizers may cause weight gain). Inflammatory weight differs from fat accumulation, often appearing as edema, bloating, and fluid shifts rather than adipose tissue.

Anti-inflammatory approaches address inflammatory weight through mast cell stabilization, stress reduction, sleep optimization, and gentle exercise rather than caloric restriction potentially worsening symptoms. Some individuals lose inflammatory weight as MCAS control improves without intentional weight loss efforts. Focusing on symptom management and health markers (energy, sleep, symptom frequency) rather than scale weight prevents unhealthy restriction for weight control.

29.6 Social Isolation and Relationships

Social withdrawal develops gradually as individuals decline invitations involving food, feel embarrassed explaining dietary needs, or experience anxiety about symptom unpredictability in public. Over months, social connections atrophy as participation becomes rare. Research shows chronic illness-related social isolation increases depression, anxiety, and worsens health outcomes (Leigh-Hunt et al., 2017).

Relationship strain occurs when partners, family, or friends don't understand the condition, view dietary needs as excessive or attention-seeking, or feel burdened by accommodation requirements. Dining becomes source of conflict rather than connection. Well-meaning loved ones may pressure eating restricted foods ("just this once won't hurt") or dismiss symptoms as psychosomatic.

Communication strategies help relationships survive dietary restrictions. Clearly explaining the condition using accessible language (avoiding medical jargon), sharing reputable educational resources, and demonstrating willingness to accommodate others while maintaining boundaries supports understanding. For example, bringing own food to gatherings, eating beforehand then attending for socializing, or hosting events at home enables participation without requiring others to cater.

Finding community through online support groups, local MCAS/histamine intolerance meetups, or chronic illness communities reduces isolation. Connecting with others who understand lived experience provides validation and practical tips while reducing feeling of being alone in restrictions. Some people develop closest friendships through shared health challenges.

Maintaining participation in non-food social activities (exercise groups, book clubs, hobby groups, religious communities) sustains connections without food-centered pressure. Suggesting alternative activities when friends propose restaurants (walking, movies, museums) enables socializing on accessible terms.

29.7 Disordered Eating Recognition

Orthorexia represents unhealthy obsession with eating only "pure" or "healthy" foods, developing into disordered eating pattern (Niland & Cash, 2018). While medical elimination diets are necessary for some conditions, orthorexia involves rigid food rules, extreme anxiety about food quality, social isolation around eating, and self-worth tied to dietary adherence beyond medical necessity.

Warning signs of progression from therapeutic restriction to disordered eating include spending excessive time planning/preparing food (3+ hours daily), severe anxiety when safe foods unavailable, eliminating foods beyond medical necessity "just to be safe," progressive restriction despite adequate symptom control, social withdrawal solely due to food anxiety, and thoughts about food dominating waking hours.

Food fear versus food intolerance requires differentiation. Food intolerance produces physical reactions (hives, flushing, gastrointestinal distress) from specific foods reliably. Food fear produces anxiety-driven avoidance without physical reactions, or physical symptoms from anxiety rather than food itself. Panic attacks triggered by eating previously "unsafe" food now deemed safe through testing represents food fear rather than intolerance.

Body image concerns develop when weight loss from restriction creates distorted relationship with weight and food. Some individuals continue restricting despite adequate symptom control because they fear weight regain. Others develop compensatory behaviors (excessive exercise, purging) addressing weight fears rather than symptoms.

Professional support from therapists specializing in eating disorders and medical conditions helps differentiate necessary restriction from disordered patterns. Cognitive-behavioral therapy, exposure therapy for food fears, and nutritional counseling reestablish healthy relationship with food while maintaining medical management. Psychiatric medication may help anxiety or obsessive-compulsive features driving rigid food rules.

29.8 When Additional Help Needed

Recognizing limitations of self-management prevents prolonged suffering when professional help would accelerate improvement. Situations warranting additional support include symptoms persisting despite 6+ months compliant treatment, progressive restriction beyond medical necessity, significant weight loss or malnutrition, severe anxiety or depression, suicidal ideation, or inability to maintain employment or relationships due to symptoms.

Building medical team per section 26.8 provides coordinated care. Allergist or immunologist for MCAS diagnosis and medication management, gastroenterologist for GI workup and SIBO testing, functional medicine physician for root cause investigation, registered dietitian for nutritional adequacy and meal planning, and therapist for psychological support create comprehensive team addressing all aspects.

Second opinions help when current treatment produces no improvement or when diagnosis uncertainty exists. Seeking evaluation at MCAS specialty center or academic medical center with expertise provides access to current research and treatment approaches. Some people require multiple consultations before finding providers who understand and effectively treat their condition.

Alternative diagnoses require consideration when histamine intolerance treatment fails. Conditions with overlapping symptoms include celiac disease, inflammatory bowel disease, eosinophilic esophagitis, small intestinal fungal overgrowth (SIFO), bile acid malabsorption, endometriosis, interstitial cystitis, and various autoimmune conditions. Appropriate testing rules out alternative explanations for symptoms.

29.9 Chapter Conclusions

This chapter addressed common challenges complicating histamine intolerance management. Severe restriction affecting fewer than 15 foods requires investigating MCAS rather than simple histamine intolerance, identifying multiple overlapping food intolerances, prioritizing nutrition, and providing psychological support preventing disordered eating development.

Treatment resistance after compliant management necessitates root cause investigation through SIBO testing, mold assessment, medication review, and comprehensive medical evaluation. Medication optimization, expectation recalibration, and systematic root cause treatment enables breakthrough for stuck cases.

Reintroduction failures reflect unstable baseline testing, inadequate spacing between tests, or preparation method issues more than food intolerance requiring permanent elimination. Weight concerns involve both unintentional loss requiring calorie-focused intervention and inflammatory gain addressed through mast cell stabilization rather than restriction.

Social isolation and relationship strain develop from chronic dietary restriction requiring communication strategies, community building, and non-food social participation. Disordered eating risk includes orthorexia development, food fear, and body image distortion necessitating professional mental health support.

The case study illustrated how treatment resistance from multiple untreated root causes (SIBO, dysbiosis, hypothyroidism, toxic exposure) prevented dietary management success until systematic investigation and phase-based treatment addressed identified issues. This chapter connects to Chapter 30.0's examination of progress tracking, goal setting, and long-term success strategies.

Chapter 30.0: Progress Tracking and Success

Aurelian opened his symptom journal from 18 months earlier, barely recognizing the person described in those desperate pages. Early entries documented daily migraines, constant digestive distress, debilitating fatigue, and reactions to nearly every food attempted. His life had revolved around symptoms, medical appointments, and frantic internet searching for answers. The later pages told different story. Gradual symptom reduction, expanding safe food lists, returning energy, and resumed activities appeared in increasingly optimistic entries. The final entry, written yesterday, described hiking three miles with friends, eating lunch at a restaurant (carefully selected menu items), and experiencing zero symptoms for the entire day. He'd reached a milestone unimaginable 18 months ago yet almost unnoticed in the gradual progress. Reviewing his journal reminded him how far he'd come and reinforced the value of systematic tracking enabling objective progress assessment (Bebb et al., 2007). Without written documentation, the slow incremental improvements would have felt insignificant day-to-day. The journal proved what memory couldn't capture. He'd transformed from severely restricted and symptomatic to living mostly normally with minimal dietary modifications. His journey illustrated that histamine intolerance management produces gradual rather than dramatic change, requiring patient consistency and comprehensive tracking revealing progress invisible to daily perception.

This chapter examines progress tracking tools and methods, symptom diary templates, supplement tracking systems, medical appointment preparation, realistic goal setting, celebrating non-scale victories, building resilience, creating personalized protocols, maintenance strategies, and the path forward.

30.1 Comprehensive Symptom Tracking

Symptom tracking provides objective data revealing patterns invisible to memory and perception. Daily symptom ratings using consistent scales (0-10 where 0 equals no symptoms, 10 equals worst imaginable) enable comparison across weeks and months. Without tracking, people forget baseline severity when improvement occurs gradually, leading to discouragement despite actual progress.

Digital versus paper tracking both work well depending on personal preference. Smartphone apps designed for symptom tracking offer convenience, reminders, and automatic graphing. Paper journals provide tactile engagement some people prefer and don't require devices. Spreadsheets on computer enable detailed tracking with custom categories and analysis. The best system is whichever you'll actually use consistently.

Essential tracking elements include date, symptom types and severity (digestive, headaches, skin reactions, fatigue, brain fog, etc.), food intake with timing, supplements and medications, sleep quality and duration, stress level, menstrual cycle day for women, exercise, and any environmental exposures or unusual events. This comprehensive view identifies triggers and patterns beyond food alone per Chapter 27.0.

Frequency matters more than perfection. Daily entries provide most detail but require commitment. Some people track daily during elimination and reintroduction phases, then shift to weekly check-ins during maintenance. Minimum useful frequency involves tracking 3-4 days weekly, ensuring variety across weekdays and weekends capturing different routine patterns.

Pattern identification emerges after 2-4 weeks of consistent tracking. Reviewing entries weekly identifies correlations between foods and symptoms, stress and flares, sleep quality and symptom severity, or hormonal patterns. These insights guide treatment adjustments impossible to identify from memory alone.

30.2 Food and Symptom Templates

Food diary structure documents everything consumed with portions and timing. Include all foods, beverages, supplements, and medications. Note preparation methods (raw, cooked, grilled, etc.) as this affects histamine content per Chapter 8.0. Record timing relative to symptoms, as delayed reactions occurring 4-24 hours after ingestion require temporal tracking for identification.

Sample daily entry format might include:

Date: January 15, 2026 Symptoms (0-10 scale): Headache: 3, Digestive: 2, Fatigue: 4, Skin: 0 Overall symptom rating: 3/10

Breakfast (8:00 AM): Rice with coconut milk, blueberries, maple syrup. 1 cup coffee. Snacks (10:30 AM): Rice cakes with sunflower seed butter Lunch (12:30 PM): Grilled chicken breast, steamed broccoli, baked sweet potato, olive oil Snacks (3:00 PM): Apple slices Dinner (6:00 PM): Baked cod, rice, sautéed zucchini Evening: Chamomile tea

Supplements: AM: H1 antihistamine, H2 blocker, quercetin 500mg, vitamin C 1000mg PM: H2 blocker, quercetin 500mg, probiotic

Sleep: 7 hours, woke twice, overall quality 6/10 Exercise: 20-minute walk Stress: 5/10 (work deadline) Notes: Mild headache afternoon may relate to work stress or need more water

Correlation tracking over time reveals whether specific foods consistently associate with symptoms or if stress, sleep, and hormones play larger roles. Someone noticing symptoms every Thursday might discover work stress pattern rather than food trigger. Women tracking menstrual cycles often identify hormonal symptom patterns per section 27.7.

30.3 Supplement and Medication Logs

Supplement tracking documents what you're taking, doses, timing, and effects. Given the one-at-a-time introduction protocol from section 24.7, detailed records prevent confusion about which supplements helped, which did nothing, and which caused problems.

Template format:

Supplement: Quercetin phytosome Start date: January 1, 2026 Dose: 250mg twice daily Timing: Morning and evening with food Week 1 observations: Mild nausea first 2 days, resolved Week 2 observations: Headaches decreased from 5-6/week to 2-3/week Week 4 decision: Continue, appears beneficial for headaches Cost: $35/month

Medication tracking similarly documents prescription medications including H1/H2 antihistamines, cromolyn sodium, or other MCAS medications from Chapter 26.0. Include prescribing physician, start date, dose changes, side effects, and effectiveness ratings. This information helps medical appointments per section 30.4.

Interaction monitoring involves noting if new supplements or medications change effects of existing interventions. Adding curcumin (blood-thinning properties) while taking aspirin requires medical awareness. Tracking enables identifying these interactions early.

30.4 Medical Appointment Preparation

Pre-appointment organization maximizes limited physician time. Most appointments last 15-20 minutes, insufficient for unorganized symptom description. Bringing prepared summary enables focused productive discussion.

Appointment preparation checklist includes:

- One-page symptom summary (current symptoms with severity, improvement/worsening since last visit)

- Food diary highlights (patterns identified, successful reintroductions, problem foods)
- Supplement/medication list (everything currently taking with doses)
- Question list (3-5 priority questions, most important first)
- Test results (if obtained from other providers or labs)
- Treatment goals (what you hope to achieve in coming months)

Question prioritization ensures most important issues get addressed. Physicians may not reach question 10 on your list. Putting critical questions first (medication adjustment requests, concerning new symptoms, test result discussion) before minor issues (supplement recommendations, general nutrition questions) prevents leaving with major concerns unaddressed.

Follow-up scheduling at appointment end books next visit ensuring continuity. For stable patients, 3-6 month follow-ups monitor long-term progress. For complex cases or medication titration, monthly visits may be appropriate. Scheduling before leaving prevents appointment gaps where problems arise without physician access.

30.5 Case Study: Tracking Enabled Success

Background

Salome, a 33-year-old teacher, struggled with inconsistent symptom patterns she couldn't explain. Some days she felt nearly normal. Others brought severe symptoms despite eating the same foods. After six months of elimination diet producing modest improvement, she felt discouraged by unpredictability preventing her from identifying reliable triggers or successful interventions.

Presentation

Salome described feeling like she was "guessing randomly" about what helped. She'd try new supplements, feel better for a few days, then symptoms would return. She'd eliminate foods, improve briefly, then worsen again. She couldn't identify patterns because she relied on memory rather than systematic tracking. Her physician suggested comprehensive symptom diary before making treatment changes.

She reluctantly agreed, skeptical that writing things down would reveal anything. She'd tried occasional tracking before but never maintained it beyond a few days. Her physician emphasized consistency mattering more than perfection, suggesting tracking 5 days weekly minimum for one month before drawing conclusions.

Analysis

Week three of tracking revealed eye-opening patterns Salome never recognized. Her symptoms worsened dramatically every month days 12-14 and days 24-28, corresponding precisely to ovulation and premenstrual phase when estrogen peaks per section 27.7. The tracking showed foods she'd blamed for reactions (chicken, rice, cucumbers) actually caused no symptoms. Her symptom days aligned with hormonal patterns regardless of food intake.

Second pattern involved stress. Her worst symptom days occurred Wednesdays and Thursdays (midweek work stress peak) and Sundays (anticipatory anxiety about upcoming week). Food remained identical but stress level correlated with symptoms more than any dietary factor.

Third pattern revealed sleep quality. Days following poor sleep (noted as 4-5/10 quality) consistently showed elevated symptoms. Days after excellent sleep (8-9/10 quality) brought minimal symptoms even during high-estrogen cycle phases.

Intervention

Understanding actual triggers enabled targeted intervention. For hormonal patterns, Salome increased H1/H2 antihistamine doses during ovulation and late luteal phases rather than maintaining constant dosing. She added quercetin 500mg three times daily during high-estrogen weeks instead of twice daily year-round. This strategic dose adjustment cost less than constant high-dose while providing support when needed.

For stress management, she implemented Wednesday and Thursday evening yoga classes (stress reduction during peak stress days). She started Sunday evening relaxing ritual (bath, light reading, early bedtime) preventing anticipatory anxiety sleep disruption. She added brief meditation practice daily per section 27.2.

For sleep optimization, she applied protocols from section 27.3 including temperature reduction, screen curfew, and fixed sleep schedule. She prioritized sleep on nights before known high-stress days (Tuesday and Wednesday nights).

Outcome

Three months of tracking and targeted intervention produced dramatic improvement. Her symptom frequency decreased from 4-5 days weekly to 1-2 days weekly. Symptoms occurred predictably during late luteal phase (manageable with dose adjustment) rather than randomly. She reintroduced 15 foods successfully after recognizing previous "reactions" coincided with hormonal or stress patterns rather than food triggers.

Most importantly, tracking empowered her. Instead of feeling victimized by unpredictable symptoms, she understood her patterns and proactively managed them. She continued tracking 3 days weekly long-term, maintaining insight enabling early intervention when patterns shifted.

Teaching Points

- Comprehensive symptom tracking revealing correlations between symptoms and hormonal cycles, stress patterns, sleep quality, and other non-food factors prevents misattribution of symptoms to dietary triggers when actual drivers involve lifestyle and physiological patterns
- Consistent tracking for minimum 3-4 weeks enables pattern identification invisible to memory alone, with daily memory bias toward recent dramatic events rather than actual statistical patterns across weeks requiring objective documentation
- Targeted interventions addressing identified patterns (strategic supplement dosing by cycle phase, stress management during high-stress periods, sleep optimization) produce superior outcomes compared to static protocols ignoring individual pattern variation

30.6 Realistic Goals and Timelines

Goal setting requires balancing ambition with realism. Complete symptom elimination may not be achievable for everyone, particularly those with genetic DAO deficiency or severe MCAS. Setting goal of 80-90% symptom reduction rather than 100% prevents feeling like failure when modest symptoms persist despite excellent management.

SMART goals (Specific, Measurable, Achievable, Relevant, Time-bound) create actionable targets. Instead of "feel better," try "reduce headaches from daily to 2-3 times weekly within 3 months through elimination diet and cromolyn sodium." This provides clear outcome measurement and timeline.

Dietary goals might include "successfully reintroduce 10 tier 1 foods within 4 months" or "expand safe food list from 12 to 25 items by end of year." These create tangible markers of progress beyond symptom reduction alone.

Lifestyle goals from Chapter 27.0 include "practice vagal tone exercises 10 minutes daily 5 days weekly" or "achieve 7-8 hours sleep nightly 5 nights weekly within 2 months." These lifestyle changes support overall health beyond histamine management.

Timeline expectations prevent discouragement. Elimination diet shows initial results 2-4 weeks. Root cause treatments (SIBO protocol, gut healing) require 3-6 months. Supplement protocols need 1-3 months for full effects. Complex cases with multiple issues may require 12-18 months for substantial improvement. Understanding typical timelines prevents abandoning effective treatments prematurely.

30.7 Non-Scale Victories Recognition

Quality of life improvements often precede complete symptom resolution. Celebrating these victories maintains motivation during gradual progress. Non-scale victories include increased energy enabling normal activities, improved sleep quality, better concentration at work, reduced medication needs, expanding food variety, resuming exercise or hobbies, and decreasing anxiety about symptoms.

Social victories matter tremendously. Attending events previously avoided, eating out successfully, traveling, hosting dinner parties, and maintaining relationships despite dietary needs all represent significant achievements. These social reconnections improve mental health and life satisfaction independent of physical symptom severity.

Psychological victories include reduced food fear, decreased health anxiety, improved body image, and better stress management. Developing self-efficacy (confidence in managing the condition) represents major success even if some symptoms persist. Transitioning from feeling victimized by illness to feeling empowered managing it fundamentally changes experience.

Independence victories involve reduced medical dependency as you develop expertise managing your condition. Knowing how to adjust protocols during flares, troubleshoot new symptoms, research unfamiliar situations, and make informed decisions about treatment creates autonomy. Working collaboratively with physicians rather than dependently improves long-term outcomes.

30.8 Building Resilience and Flexibility

Resilience involves adapting to challenges, recovering from setbacks, and maintaining function despite difficulties (Southwick et al., 2014). Chronic illness management requires resilience as perfect control proves impossible. Developing resilience enables navigating inevitable challenges (accidental exposures, stressful periods, treatment plateaus) without complete derailment.

Resilience strategies include maintaining social connections per section 29.6, engaging in meaningful activities beyond illness management, practicing acceptance of things beyond control while actively managing modifiable factors, developing problem-solving skills through troubleshooting challenges, and building self-compassion rather than self-criticism when setbacks occur.

Flexibility prevents rigid thinking sabotaging long-term management. Recognizing that one dietary lapse doesn't ruin all progress, treatment adjustments represent adaptation rather than failure, and good-enough management beats perfect restriction enables sustainable approaches. Perfectionism creates vulnerability to giving up entirely when perfection proves unattainable.

Growth mindset views challenges as learning opportunities rather than proof of failure (Dweck, 2006). Someone with growth mindset experiencing supplement reaction thinks "I learned that supplement doesn't work for me, now I can try alternatives." Fixed mindset thinks "I can't tolerate any supplements, I'll never improve." Growth mindset enables persistence through difficulties.

30.9 Personalized Protocol Development

Your unique protocol emerges through systematic testing, tracking, and refinement over months. The protocols in this book provide frameworks, but individual variation means your optimal approach will differ from others' protocols. Documenting what works specifically for you creates personalized management plan.

Protocol elements include:

- Safe food lists (tier 1, tier 2, tier 3 from section 6.4 adapted to your testing results)
- Meal planning strategies (batch cooking schedule, emergency meals, eating out protocols)
- Supplement regimen (which supplements, what doses, timing, when to adjust)
- Medication management (current prescriptions, PRN medications for flares, emergency protocols)
- Lifestyle practices (stress management techniques, sleep hygiene routine, exercise approach)
- Trigger management (environmental controls, hormonal adjustments, seasonal variations)
- Healthcare team (physician contacts, appointment schedules, emergency contacts)

Protocol documentation creates reference preventing forgetting successful strategies when symptoms stabilize. Written protocols help family members understand your needs and support management. They facilitate medical appointments by providing clear current management summary.

Regular review and refinement keeps protocols current. Quarterly protocol review assesses what's working, what's outdated, and what needs modification. As your condition improves, protocols may simplify (fewer medications, less restriction). If setbacks occur, protocols may temporarily intensify (stricter diet, increased supplements) before re-liberalizing.

30.10 Maintenance Phase Strategies

Maintenance begins when symptoms achieve stable acceptable level with consistent management. This typically occurs 6-12 months into treatment after completing elimination, reintroduction, and root cause addressing. Maintenance differs from active treatment through less frequent monitoring and greater automation of successful practices.

Dietary maintenance involves rotating through established safe foods without constant vigilance, occasional controlled exposures to tier 3 foods during low-stress periods, and maintaining core histamine principles (fresh food, proper storage, avoiding aged items) without obsessive restriction. Most people find 80-90% compliance with low-histamine principles adequate for symptom control during maintenance, allowing 10-20% flexibility for special occasions.

Supplement maintenance often simplifies from active treatment phase. Many supplements introduced during healing (L-glutamine, zinc carnosine, high-dose vitamin C) may taper or discontinue once gut healing completes. Core supplements providing ongoing benefit (DAO with meals, daily quercetin, probiotic) continue long-term. Regular reassessment (stopping supplements individually to assess ongoing necessity) prevents taking unnecessary interventions.

Medication maintenance maintains baseline control while allowing adjustments for predictable patterns (hormonal cycling, seasonal changes, stress periods). Some people require constant medication for stability. Others use medications PRN during flares while maintaining dietary and lifestyle management. Individual patterns identified through tracking inform maintenance medication approaches.

Lifestyle maintenance involves incorporating stress management, sleep hygiene, exercise, and environmental controls as permanent habits rather than temporary interventions. These practices support overall health beyond histamine management, benefiting long-term wellness even as dietary restrictions potentially liberalize.

Monitoring frequency decreases during stable maintenance. Monthly detailed tracking shifts to weekly brief check-ins. Quarterly physician visits replace monthly appointments. This reduced intensity prevents burnout while maintaining enough monitoring to catch early warning signs of decline requiring intervention adjustment.

30.11 Your Path Forward

This final chapter examined tools and strategies for successful long-term histamine intolerance management. Comprehensive symptom tracking using consistent scales and methods reveals patterns invisible to memory, enabling targeted interventions addressing actual triggers. Food diaries, supplement logs, and medical appointment preparation create organized approach maximizing treatment effectiveness.

Realistic goal setting with appropriate timelines prevents discouragement, while celebrating non-scale victories maintains motivation during gradual improvement. Building resilience through social connection, meaningful activities, problem-solving skills, and self-compassion enables navigating inevitable challenges without derailment.

Personalized protocol development creates individualized management plans based on your unique testing results, tracking insights, and response patterns. Maintenance phase strategies simplify successful active treatment protocols into sustainable long-term approaches balancing symptom control with quality of life.

The case study illustrated how comprehensive tracking revealed hormonal, stress, and sleep patterns driving symptoms previously misattributed to foods, enabling targeted interventions producing dramatic improvement. This demonstrates that progress often comes from understanding your individual patterns rather than following generic protocols.

Your journey with histamine intolerance represents learning process requiring patience, consistency, and willingness to adjust approaches based on results. The path forward involves continuing practices that work, modifying those that don't, and maintaining hope that gradual improvement, though not always linear, is achievable for most people with appropriate comprehensive management.

Appendix A: Comprehensive Food Lists

This appendix provides detailed food categorization for histamine intolerance management. Use these lists alongside the elimination and reintroduction protocols from Chapters 6.0 and 7.0. Individual tolerance varies substantially, so these lists serve as starting points requiring personal testing per section 6.5.

A.1 Complete Low Histamine Foods

Fresh Meats and Poultry (prepared and consumed within 24 hours of purchase or defrosting)

- Chicken (all cuts, fresh or frozen immediately after slaughter)
- Turkey (fresh breast, thighs, ground)
- Duck (fresh)
- Lamb (fresh chops, leg, ground)
- Beef (fresh steaks, roasts, ground beef)
- Bison (fresh cuts)
- Venison (fresh, properly handled)
- Rabbit (fresh)
- Quail (fresh)

Fresh Fish (flash-frozen within hours of catch, or purchased frozen and cooked immediately after thawing)

- Cod (frozen or very fresh)
- Haddock (frozen)
- Sole (frozen)
- Halibut (frozen)
- Pollock (frozen)
- Tilapia (frozen, farm-raised)
- Trout (fresh, eaten same day as caught or purchased frozen)
- Salmon (frozen immediately after catch, not previously thawed display fish)

Eggs (individual tolerance varies)

- Chicken eggs (fresh, properly stored)
- Duck eggs (fresh)
- Quail eggs (fresh)

Note: Some people tolerate eggs well, others react. Test during reintroduction phase per section 6.5.

Fresh Vegetables (tier 1, generally well tolerated)

- Zucchini (cooked or raw)
- Cucumber (peeled if wax coating present)
- Carrots (raw or cooked)
- Sweet potatoes (all preparations)
- White potatoes (all preparations except fried in old oil)
- Butternut squash (cooked)
- Acorn squash (cooked)
- Spaghetti squash (cooked)
- Summer squash (yellow, cooked or raw)
- Green beans (fresh, cooked)
- Broccoli (fresh, cooked, some people tolerate)
- Cauliflower (fresh, cooked)
- Brussels sprouts (fresh, cooked)
- Asparagus (fresh, cooked)
- Beets (fresh, cooked)
- Parsnips (cooked)
- Turnips (cooked)
- Rutabaga (cooked)
- Celery (raw or cooked)
- Bell peppers (fresh, all colors except green which may be less tolerated)
- Lettuce (butter, romaine, red leaf, green leaf)
- Bok choy (cooked)
- Cabbage (green, red, savoy, cooked or raw in small amounts)
- Fresh herbs (basil, cilantro, parsley, dill, mint, chives, oregano, thyme, rosemary, sage)

Fresh Fruits (tier 1 and some tier 2)

- Apples (fresh, not aged or mealy)
- Blueberries (fresh or frozen without additives)
- Mango (fresh, ripe)
- Melon (cantaloupe, honeydew, watermelon, fresh and ripe)
- Peaches (fresh, ripe, some people tolerate)
- Cherries (fresh, sweet varieties, some people tolerate)
- Grapes (fresh, seedless varieties)
- Pears (fresh, ripe)
- Apricots (fresh, very ripe, some people tolerate)
- Figs (fresh, not dried, some people tolerate)
- Dragon fruit (fresh)
- Lychee (fresh)
- Rambutan (fresh)

- Persimmon (fresh, ripe)

Grains and Starches

- White rice (all varieties, jasmine, basmati, arborio, sushi)
- Brown rice (if tolerated, some find it more triggering)
- Rice noodles (check for additives)
- Rice pasta (check for additives)
- Rice crackers (plain, check ingredients)
- Rice cakes (plain)
- Quinoa (well-rinsed before cooking)
- Millet
- Amaranth
- Oats (gluten-free, some people tolerate)
- Tapioca (flour and pearls)
- Arrowroot (flour)
- Potato starch

Legumes (fresh cooked from dried, consumed within 24 hours or frozen immediately)

- Lentils (red, green, brown, black, cooked fresh)
- Chickpeas (cooked fresh from dried, not canned)
- White beans (navy, cannellini, great northern, cooked fresh)
- Black beans (cooked fresh from dried)
- Kidney beans (cooked fresh from dried)
- Pinto beans (cooked fresh from dried)
- Mung beans (cooked fresh)
- Split peas (green or yellow, cooked fresh)

Oils and Fats

- Olive oil (extra virgin, cold-pressed)
- Coconut oil (virgin, unrefined)
- Avocado oil (if avocados tolerated)
- Ghee (clarified butter, if dairy tolerated)
- Butter (fresh, if dairy tolerated, organic grass-fed preferred)

Dairy Alternatives

- Rice milk (plain, unsweetened, check for additives)
- Coconut milk (canned, full-fat, no guar gum if sensitive)
- Oat milk (if oats tolerated, check ingredients)

- Coconut cream (for cooking)
- Coconut yogurt (plain, check for live cultures and additives)

Sweeteners

- Maple syrup (pure, grade A or B)
- Honey (raw, local, if tolerated by individual, some react)
- Coconut sugar (granulated)
- Date sugar (ground dried dates, may not be tolerated if dates problematic)

Beverages

- Water (filtered)
- Herbal teas (chamomile, rooibos, fresh mint, fresh ginger)
- Coconut water (fresh or packaged without preservatives, check tolerance)

A.2 High Histamine Foods to Avoid

Aged, Cured, or Fermented Meats

- All cured meats (salami, pepperoni, prosciutto, ham, bacon)
- Aged sausages
- Hot dogs (processed)
- Deli meats (turkey, roast beef, chicken lunch meat)
- Smoked meats (smoked salmon, smoked turkey, smoked beef)
- Dried meats (beef jerky, biltong)
- Canned meats (tuna, salmon, sardines, anchovies)
- Meat spreads and pates

Fish and Seafood (especially if not flash-frozen immediately after catch)

- All fish purchased "fresh" from seafood counter (unless verified caught that day)
- Tuna (especially canned)
- Mackerel (especially canned or smoked)
- Sardines (canned)
- Anchovies (canned or preserved)
- Herring (pickled or smoked)
- Shellfish (shrimp, crab, lobster, clams, mussels, oysters, scallops)
- Smoked fish (lox, smoked salmon, smoked trout)
- Fish sauce
- Oyster sauce

Fermented and Aged Dairy

- All aged cheeses (cheddar, gouda, parmesan, blue cheese, swiss, brie, camembert)
- Yogurt (commercial with multiple bacterial strains)
- Kefir
- Buttermilk
- Sour cream (aged)
- Cottage cheese (check tolerance, some do better with fresh)
- Cream cheese (check tolerance)

Fermented Vegetables and Products

- Sauerkraut
- Kimchi
- Pickles (fermented, not fresh refrigerated)
- Pickled vegetables (all types)
- Miso
- Tempeh
- Natto
- Soy sauce
- Tamari
- Worcestershire sauce
- Fish sauce
- All vinegars (except fresh apple cider vinegar may be tolerated by some)

Alcoholic Beverages

- Wine (red and white, high histamine)
- Beer (fermented, high histamine)
- Champagne (fermented)
- Hard cider (fermented)
- Spirits (whiskey, bourbon, rum, vodka, gin, all contain or trigger histamine)

Certain Vegetables

- Tomatoes (fresh and especially cooked, canned, sauce, paste, ketchup)
- Eggplant (contains histamine)
- Spinach (high histamine, especially cooked or wilted)
- Pumpkin (some people tolerate, others don't)
- Avocado (histamine liberator, though some tolerate)

Certain Fruits

- Strawberries (histamine liberator)
- Citrus fruits (oranges, lemons, limes, grapefruit, histamine liberators)
- Bananas (especially overripe, histamine liberator)
- Papaya (histamine liberator)
- Pineapple (histamine liberator)
- Kiwi (histamine liberator)
- Dried fruits (raisins, dates, prunes, apricots, figs, all concentrated histamine)

Nuts and Seeds (aged or rancid)

- Peanuts (high histamine)
- Cashews (high histamine)
- Walnuts (high histamine)
- Pecans (check tolerance)
- Brazil nuts (check tolerance)
- Almonds (check tolerance, some do okay with fresh)

Processed and Packaged Foods

- Instant meals (frozen dinners, microwave meals)
- Canned soups (high histamine from aging)
- Bouillon cubes (unless fresh, low-histamine variety)
- Flavor packets and seasoning mixes
- Processed snack foods (chips, crackers with additives)
- Candy (especially with artificial colors and flavors)
- Commercial baked goods (additives, preservatives)

Leftovers

- Any food stored more than 24 hours after cooking (bacterial histamine formation)
- Previously frozen meat that was thawed and refrozen
- Restaurant leftovers (unknown storage time before serving)

A.3 Histamine Liberators

Histamine liberators trigger mast cells to release histamine without containing high histamine themselves. Individual tolerance varies significantly. Test these during tier 2 or tier 3 reintroduction per section 6.4.

Fruits Known as Histamine Liberators

- Strawberries

- Citrus (oranges, lemons, limes, grapefruit, tangerines, clementines)
- Bananas (especially overripe)
- Papaya
- Pineapple
- Kiwi
- Raspberries (some people tolerate)

Vegetables as Histamine Liberators

- Tomatoes (also contain histamine)
- Avocado (also moderately high histamine)
- Eggplant (also contains histamine)

Other Histamine Liberators

- Cocoa and chocolate (all forms, dark and milk chocolate)
- Alcohol (all types, also inhibits DAO enzyme)
- Shellfish (also often high histamine from handling)
- Egg whites (some people, individual variation)
- Nuts (cashews, walnuts, peanuts especially)
- Additives (artificial colors, preservatives, benzoates, sulfites)
- Licorice root
- Some spices (cinnamon, cloves, anise, nutmeg in large amounts)

A.4 DAO Blocking Medications and Substances

DAO enzyme activity can be inhibited by certain medications and substances, worsening histamine intolerance even with perfect diet. Review medications with physician if taking any of these per Chapter 26.0.

Common DAO Blocking Medications

- NSAIDs (ibuprofen, naproxen, aspirin, indomethacin)
- Antidepressants (certain tricyclics, SSRIs may affect some individuals)
- Antiarrhythmics (propafenone, metoprolol in some studies)
- Antihypertensives (verapamil, dihydralazine)
- Muscle relaxants (certain types)
- H2 blockers (paradoxically, ranitidine and cimetidine block DAO, though famotidine less so)
- Antibiotics (isoniazid, clavulanic acid, chloroquine)
- Mucolytics (acetylcysteine in some studies)

Substances That Block DAO

- Alcohol (significantly impairs DAO function)
- Black tea (contains compounds inhibiting DAO)
- Green tea (less than black but still inhibitory)
- Energy drinks (various ingredients may affect DAO)
- Mate tea

Note: Never discontinue prescribed medications without physician guidance. Discuss alternatives if medications contribute to symptoms.

A.5 Other Biogenic Amines

Biogenic amines besides histamine can cause similar symptoms through competing for degradation enzymes. Foods high in other amines may worsen symptoms even if histamine content is low.

Tyramine (degraded by MAO enzyme, similar to histamine effects)

- Aged cheeses (especially high)
- Cured and processed meats
- Fermented foods (sauerkraut, kimchi, soy sauce)
- Overripe fruits (bananas especially)
- Nuts (especially peanuts, walnuts)
- Chocolate
- Alcoholic beverages (wine, beer, spirits)
- Smoked fish
- Yeast extracts

Putrescine and Cadaverine

- Aged meats
- Fermented sausages
- Some fish (especially if not fresh)
- Citrus fruits
- Some vegetables (tomatoes)

Spermine and Spermidine

- Aged cheeses
- Certain fermented products
- Shellfish
- Some fruits

Phenylethylamine

- Chocolate and cocoa
- Certain cheeses
- Red wine
- Some fermented foods

Clinical Significance: People with histamine intolerance often have impaired degradation of other biogenic amines. Avoiding high-tyramine foods alongside high-histamine foods often produces better symptom control than histamine restriction alone.

A.6 SIGHI List Interpretation Guide

The Swiss Interest Group Histamine Intolerance (SIGHI) maintains compatibility lists rating foods from 0 (well tolerated) to 3 (poorly tolerated). Understanding how to interpret and apply these ratings helps practical food selection.

SIGHI Rating System

- 0 (Green): Well tolerated by most people with histamine intolerance
- 1 (Yellow/Light Orange): Moderately tolerated, test during reintroduction
- 2 (Orange): Poorly tolerated by many, avoid during elimination
- 3 (Red): Very poorly tolerated, high histamine or histamine liberator

Interpreting SIGHI Ratings

The SIGHI list provides general guidance based on compiled research and patient reports. However, individual tolerance varies substantially. Use ratings as starting framework, not absolute rules.

Rating 0 Foods: Safe for most people during elimination phase per section 6.3. Start with these foods building baseline symptom control.

Rating 1 Foods: Test individually during tier 2 reintroduction per section 6.4. Many people tolerate some rating 1 foods while reacting to others. Individual testing identifies personal tolerance.

Rating 2 Foods: Approach cautiously, testing only after successful tier 1 and tier 2 reintroductions establish good symptom control and tolerance pattern understanding.

Rating 3 Foods: Avoid during elimination and early reintroduction. These foods consistently trigger symptoms in most people with histamine intolerance. Some people never tolerate rating 3 foods, others may tolerate small amounts occasionally after achieving stable long-term symptom control.

SIGHI List Limitations

The list reflects generalizations across many individuals. Your personal tolerance pattern will differ. Some rating 1 foods may be completely safe for you, while some rating 0 foods may trigger symptoms. Use the list as starting point, then customize through systematic testing.

Freshness Considerations: SIGHI ratings assume proper food handling and freshness. Even rating 0 foods become high histamine if stored improperly or aged. Freshness protocols from Chapter 9.0 apply regardless of SIGHI rating.

Combination Effects: Some people tolerate individual rating 1 foods but react when combining multiple rating 1 foods in single meal. Start with single rating 1 foods during testing before combining.

Accessing SIGHI Lists: The SIGHI organization maintains updated compatibility lists available through their website. Lists are available in multiple languages and regularly updated based on new research and patient feedback. Cross-reference SIGHI ratings with personal testing results for optimal individualization.

Appendix B: Product Resources and Tools

Product recommendations change frequently as brands reformulate, new products emerge, and availability varies by region. These resources provide starting points for identifying appropriate products, with emphasis on verification strategies rather than specific brand endorsements.

B.1 DAO Supplement Comparison

Selection Criteria (evaluating DAO supplements)

Source Verification

- Porcine-derived: Most researched, standardized 4.2 mg dose used in clinical trials
- Plant-based: Newer option, suitable for vegetarians/vegans, less research

Quality Markers

- Third-party testing (USP, NSF, or ConsumerLab certification)
- GMP (Good Manufacturing Practices) facility production
- Explicit DAO content per capsule (not proprietary blends hiding amounts)
- Minimal inactive ingredients (avoid unnecessary fillers, colors, additives)

Dosing Considerations

- Standard clinical dose: 4.2 mg DAO per capsule
- Some products provide lower doses requiring multiple capsules
- Calculate cost per mg DAO for value comparison

Cost Analysis Framework

Example calculation:

- Product A: 60 capsules, 4.2 mg each, \$45 → \$0.75 per capsule, \$0.18 per mg DAO
- Product B: 90 capsules, 2 mg each, \$35 → \$0.39 per capsule, \$0.19 per mg DAO

Product B appears cheaper per capsule but costs more per mg DAO and requires taking more capsules daily.

What to Avoid

- Products without listed DAO content
- Supplements combining DAO with many other ingredients (difficult to assess individual effects)
- Unusually cheap products (may indicate low quality or minimal active ingredient)
- Products with extensive filler ingredients (check for personal triggers)

B.2 Recommended Supplement Brands

Quercetin Products (mast cell stabilization)

Standard Quercetin

- Look for: 500 mg capsules, minimal additives
- Avoid: Proprietary blends, excessive fillers
- Price range: $15-30 for 120 capsules

Quercetin Phytosome (enhanced absorption)

- Look for: Quercetin bound to phospholipids
- Dose: 250-500 mg (bioequivalent to higher standard doses)
- Price range: $25-40 for 60 capsules

Quercetin with Bromelain

- Look for: Listed amounts of each ingredient
- Typical ratio: 500 mg quercetin with 50-100 mg bromelain
- Price range: $20-35 for 120 capsules

Vitamin C Options (buffered preferred for MCAS)

Buffered Vitamin C

- Types: Calcium ascorbate, magnesium ascorbate, sodium ascorbate
- Look for: 500-1000 mg per capsule, explicitly labeled "buffered"
- Avoid: Ascorbic acid (unbuffered) if MCAS triggers occur
- Price range: $15-25 for 250 capsules

Liposomal Vitamin C (enhanced absorption)

- Look for: True liposomal encapsulation (not just "liposomal" in name)
- Dose: 500-1000 mg
- Price range: $25-40 for 60 servings

Probiotic Selection (histamine-degrading strains)

Single-Strain Products (easier troubleshooting)

- Bifidobacterium longum
- Bifidobacterium infantis
- Lactobacillus plantarum

Multi-Strain Formulas (after establishing tolerance to single strains)

- Verify all strains are histamine-degrading (avoid L. casei, L. reuteri, L. bulgaricus)
- Look for: 10-50 billion CFU
- Refrigerated versus shelf-stable (both work if properly manufactured)
- Price range: $25-50 for 30-60 day supply

What to Avoid in Probiotics

- Products containing histamine-producing strains
- Probiotics with prebiotics if SIBO or FODMAP sensitive
- Dairy-based probiotics if dairy avoided
- Products with extensive filler ingredients

B.3 Low-Histamine Kitchen Equipment

Food Storage Solutions

Glass Containers

- Borosilicate glass (heat-resistant for freezer-to-oven)
- Airtight snap lids
- Various sizes (single serving to family size)
- Square shapes stack more efficiently than round
- Estimated cost: $30-60 for starter set

Vacuum Sealer

- Removes air preventing oxidation in freezer
- Extends safe frozen storage time
- Look for: External vacuum sealers (under $100) for most home use
- Bags: BPA-free, food-safe
- Estimated cost: $50-150 for sealer, $15-25 for bag rolls

Silicone Storage

- Ice cube trays for pesto, sauce portions
- Flexible silicone bags for freezing
- Muffin pans for portioning
- Estimated cost: $10-30 for assorted items

Cooking Equipment Priorities

Instant Pot (or electric pressure cooker)

- Essential for: Dried legumes (10-60 minutes), frozen-to-table proteins, quick grain cooking
- Size: 6-quart sufficient for most households, 8-quart for large families or batch cooking
- Features needed: Pressure cook, sauté, slow cook functions
- Estimated cost: $80-150

Rice Cooker

- Perfect rice without attention
- Keeps warm safely for several hours
- Size: 3-cup minimum, 5-cup for families
- Features needed: White rice and brown rice settings
- Estimated cost: $30-100

High-Speed Blender

- Smoothies, pureed soups, sauces, energy ball mixtures
- Power: 1000+ watts for whole food processing
- Features: Variable speeds, pulse function
- Estimated cost: $100-400 (budget to high-end)

Food Processor

- Quick vegetable prep, pesto, energy balls
- Size: 7-cup minimum for efficient batch cooking

- Features: Multiple blade options, pulse function
- Estimated cost: $50-200

B.4 Safe Personal Care Products

Fragrance-Free Verification (avoiding mast cell triggers per section 27.6)

Label Reading

- "Fragrance-free" superior to "unscented" (which may contain masking fragrance)
- Check ingredients for: "fragrance," "parfum," "perfume"
- Some natural scents okay for some people (essential oils) but test individually

Common Personal Care Categories

Shampoo and Conditioner

- Look for: Fragrance-free, minimal ingredients
- Avoid: Sulfates (if sensitive), synthetic fragrances, dyes
- Test small amounts first (scalp reactions possible)

Body Wash and Soap

- Look for: Fragrance-free, gentle formulas
- Options: Castile soap (pure olive oil-based), fragrance-free body washes
- Avoid: Heavily fragranced products, antibacterial additives (triclosan)

Lotion and Moisturizer

- Look for: Fragrance-free, minimal ingredient lists
- Common safe options: Petroleum jelly (pure), mineral oil-based, simple formulations
- Avoid: Added fragrances, extensive botanical extracts (individual reactions vary)

Deodorant

- Look for: Fragrance-free, aluminum-free if sensitive
- Options: Crystal deodorant, baking soda-based (if tolerated), fragrance-free commercial
- Expect trial and error finding tolerable option

Laundry Products

- Look for: Fragrance-free detergent, "free and clear" varieties
- Avoid: Fabric softeners, dryer sheets (heavily fragranced, unnecessary)
- Alternatives: Wool dryer balls, vinegar in rinse cycle (if vinegar tolerated)

Cleaning Products

- Look for: Fragrance-free, simple formulations
- Basic options: White vinegar (if tolerated), baking soda, castile soap
- Commercial: "Free and clear" varieties from mainstream brands
- Avoid: Air fresheners, scented candles, plug-in fragrances (major triggers)

B.5 Online Food Sources

Specialty Histamine-Friendly Products

Flash-Frozen Proteins

- Wild-caught fish frozen at sea
- Look for: "flash-frozen," "individually quick frozen (IQF)"
- Verify: Frozen immediately after catch, not previously thawed then refrozen
- Online sources: Specialty seafood companies shipping frozen

Vacuum-Sealed Meats

- Grass-fed beef, pastured chicken frozen immediately after processing
- Look for: Small family farms with flash-freezing capability
- Avoid: Products thawed then refrozen, aged meats

Organic Produce Delivery

- Fresh produce delivered within days of harvest
- Look for: Local or regional services for maximum freshness
- Timing: Order for delivery day you'll prep/freeze

Specialty Items

- DAO supplements (if not available locally)
- Specific probiotics with histamine-degrading strains
- Buffered vitamin C and other supplements
- Verify: Company reputation, third-party testing, customer reviews

Verification Strategies (avoiding poor quality or misrepresented products)

Company Research

- How long in business (established companies more reliable)
- Customer reviews on independent platforms
- Return and quality guarantee policies
- Transparency about sourcing and processing

Product Verification

- Detailed ingredient lists available
- Clear labeling of processing and freeze dates
- Responsive customer service for questions
- Third-party testing when relevant (supplements)

B.6 Apps and Digital Tracking

Symptom Tracking Apps

Features to Look For

- Customizable symptom categories
- 0-10 severity rating scales
- Food and meal logging
- Supplement and medication tracking
- Export capability (for sharing with providers)
- Graphing and trend analysis

Types of Apps

- General symptom trackers (customizable for histamine intolerance)
- Food-specific trackers with built-in food databases
- Specialized histamine intolerance apps (if available in your region)

Evaluation Criteria

- User-friendly interface (will you actually use it daily?)
- Privacy and data security
- Cost (free, one-time purchase, or subscription)
- Offline functionality (for areas without connectivity)

Food Database Apps

Histamine Content Databases

- Some apps include SIGHI compatibility ratings
- Cross-reference multiple sources (one app may have gaps)
- Verify information against reliable sources
- Remember individual variation (apps provide guidelines not absolutes)

General Food Tracking

- Nutritional information (ensuring adequate macro and micronutrients)
- Barcode scanning (checking packaged food ingredients)
- Custom food entry (for homemade items)

Recipe and Meal Planning Apps

Features to Look For

- Custom recipe creation and storage
- Ingredient substitution suggestions
- Nutritional analysis of recipes
- Meal planning with shopping list generation
- Sharing capability (family members accessing meal plans)

Meditation and Stress Management Apps

Relevant Features (for stress management per section 27.1)

- Guided meditation (various lengths for schedule flexibility)
- Breathing exercises (resonance frequency breathing)
- Sleep support (bedtime routines, sleep meditations)
- Progress tracking (consistency monitoring)
- Free options available (many have free versions with core features)

HRV and Vagal Tone Tracking

Heart Rate Variability Monitors

- Many fitness trackers include HRV
- Specialized HRV apps paired with chest strap monitors
- Morning HRV tracking shows stress resilience trends
- Use for monitoring vagal tone exercise effects per section 27.2

Selection Considerations

- Accuracy (chest strap monitors most accurate)
- Ease of use (will you check it daily?)
- Integration with other health data
- Cost (wide range from free apps to $200+ devices)

Reference

Abenavoli, L., Capasso, R., Milic, N., & Capasso, F. (2018). Milk thistle in liver diseases: Past, present, future. Phytotherapy Research, 24(10), 1423-1432.

Afrin, L. B., Ackerley, M. B., Bluestein, L. S., Brewer, J. H., Brook, J. B., Buchanan, A. D., Cuni, L. J., Davey, W. P., Dempsey, T. T., Dorff, S. R., Dubravec, V. A., Dwyer, D. F., Ehlers, G. G., Goldin, L. R., Hagglund, K. H., Harrington, B. J., Kaufman, H. S., Kilgore, E. W., Kovalszki, A., ... Weinstock, L. B. (2020). Diagnosis of mast cell activation syndrome: A global consensus-2. Diagnosis, 8(2), 137-152.

Afrin, L. B., Ackerley, M. B., Bluestein, L. S., Brewer, J. H., Brook, J. B., Buchanan, A. D., ... & Mulloy, A. L. (2016). Diagnosis of mast cell activation syndrome: a global "consensus-2". Diagnosis, 4(3), 137-152.

Afrin, L. B., Weinstock, L. B., & Molderings, G. J. (2021). COVID-19 hyperinflammation and post-COVID-19 illness may be rooted in mast cell activation syndrome. International Journal of Infectious Diseases, 100, 327-332.

Akin, C., Valent, P., & Metcalfe, D. D. (2010). Mast cell activation syndrome: Proposed diagnostic criteria. Journal of Allergy and Clinical Immunology, 126(6), 1099-1104.

Arvanitoyannis, I. S., & Bosnea, L. (2004). Migration of substances from food packaging materials to foods. Critical Reviews in Food Science and Nutrition, 44(2), 63-76.

Asserin, J., Lati, E., Shioya, T., & Prawitt, J. (2015). The effect of oral collagen peptide supplementation on skin moisture and the dermal collagen network. Journal of Cosmetic Dermatology, 14(4), 291-301.

Baker, M. E. (1994). Licorice and enzymes other than 11 beta-hydroxysteroid dehydrogenase. Steroids, 59(2), 136-141.

Bebb, C., Kendrick, D., Coupland, C., Madeley, R., Stewart, J., Brown, K., Burden, T., Sturrock, N., & Heneghan, C. **(2007)**. Patient self-monitoring of chronic illness in primary care. British Journal of General Practice, 57(539), 449-456.

Bodmer, S., Imark, C., & Kneubühl, M. (1999). Biogenic amines in foods: Histamine and food processing. Inflammation Research, 48(6), 296-300.

Bonaz, B., Bazin, T., & Pellissier, S. **(2018)**. The vagus nerve at the interface of the microbiota-gut-brain axis. Frontiers in Neuroscience, 12, 49.

Boyer, J., & Liu, R. H. (2004). Apple phytochemicals and their health benefits. Nutrition Journal, 3, 5.

Boyle, N. B., Lawton, C., & Dye, L. (2017). The effects of magnesium supplementation on subjective anxiety and stress. Nutrients, 9(5), 429.

Burlingame, B., Mouillé, B., & Charrondière, R. (2009). Nutrients, bioactive non-nutrients and anti-nutrients in potatoes. Journal of Food Composition and Analysis, 22(6), 494-502.

Calder, P. C. (2017). Omega-3 fatty acids and inflammatory processes. Nutrients, 9(11), 1205.

Carr, A. C., & Maggini, S. (2017). Vitamin C and immune function. Nutrients, 9(11), 1211.

Castells, M. (2017). Diagnosis and management of anaphylaxis in precision medicine. Journal of Allergy and Clinical Immunology, 140(2), 321-333.

Chandrasekhar, K., Kapoor, J., & Anishetty, S. (2012). A prospective, randomized double-blind, placebo-controlled study of safety and efficacy of a high-concentration full-spectrum extract of ashwagandha root in reducing stress and anxiety in adults. Indian Journal of Psychological Medicine, 34(3), 255-262.

Chedid, V., Dhalla, S., Clarke, J. O., Roland, B. C., Dunbar, K. B., Koh, J., Justino, E., Tomakin, E., & Mullin, G. E. (2014). Herbal therapy is equivalent to rifaximin for the treatment of small intestinal bacterial overgrowth. Global Advances in Health and Medicine, 3(3), 16-24.

Cheung, I., & Vadas, P. (2015). A new disease cluster: Mast cell activation syndrome, postural orthostatic tachycardia syndrome, and Ehlers-Danlos syndrome. Journal of Allergy and Clinical Immunology, 135(2), AB65.

Church, M. K., & Church, D. S. (2013). Pharmacology of antihistamines. Indian Journal of Dermatology, 58(3), 219-224.

Clarke, C. (2004). The science of ice cream. Royal Society of Chemistry.

Comas-Basté, O., Sánchez-Pérez, S., Veciana-Nogués, M. T., Latorre-Moratalla, M., & Vidal-Carou, M. C. (2020). Histamine intolerance: The current state of the art. Biomolecules, 10(8), 1181.

Daley, C. A., Abbott, A., Doyle, P. S., Nader, G. A., & Larson, S. (2010). A review of fatty acid profiles and antioxidant content in grass-fed and grain-fed beef. Nutrition Journal, 9(1), 10.

Dani, M., Dirksen, A., Taraborrelli, P., Torocastro, M., Panagopoulos, D., Sutton, R., & Lim, P. B. (2021). Autonomic dysfunction in 'long COVID': rationale, physiology and management strategies. Clinical Medicine, 21(1), e63-e67.

Dewanto, V., Wu, X., Adom, K. K., & Liu, R. H. (2002). Thermal processing enhances the nutritional value of tomatoes by increasing total antioxidant activity. Journal of Agricultural and Food Chemistry, 50(10), 3010-3014.

Dukowicz, A. C., Lacy, B. E., & Levine, G. M. (2007). Small intestinal bacterial overgrowth. Gastroenterology & Hepatology, 3(2), 112-122.

Dweck, C. S. (2006). Mindset: The new psychology of success. Random House.

Fasano, A. (2020). All disease begins in the (leaky) gut: role of zonulin-mediated gut permeability in the pathogenesis of some chronic inflammatory diseases. F1000Research, 9, 69.

FDA. (2020). FDA requires boxed warning about serious mental health side effects for asthma and allergy drug montelukast. FDA Drug Safety Communication.

Food and Drug Administration. (2021). Food product dating.

Freed, D. L. (1999). Do dietary lectins cause disease? BMJ, 318(7190), 1023-1024.

Gallagher, E., Gormley, T. R., & Arendt, E. K. (2004). Recent advances in the formulation of gluten-free cereal-based products. Trends in Food Science & Technology, 15(3-4), 143-152.

García-Martín, E., Ayuso, P., Martínez, C., Blanca, M., & Agúndez, J. A. (2007). Histamine pharmacogenomics. Pharmacogenomics, 8(6), 693-703.

Gerritsen, R. J. S., & Band, G. P. H. (2018). Breath of life: The respiratory vagal stimulation model of contemplative activity. Frontiers in Human Neuroscience, 12, 397.

Gupta, S. C., Patchva, S., & Aggarwal, B. B. (2013). Therapeutic roles of curcumin: Lessons learned from clinical trials. The AAPS Journal, 15(1), 195-218.

Haas, H. L., Sergeeva, O. A., & Selbach, O. (2008). Histamine in the nervous system. Physiological Reviews, 88(3), 1183-1241.

Hagel, A. F., Layritz, C. M., Hagel, W. H., Hagel, H. J., Hagel, E., Dauth, W., ... & Neurath, M. F. (2013). Intravenous infusion of ascorbic acid decreases serum histamine concentrations in patients with allergic and non-allergic diseases. Naunyn-Schmiedeberg's Archives of Pharmacology, 386(9), 789-793.

Hartmann, C., Dohle, S., & Siegrist, M. (2013). Importance of cooking skills for balanced food choices. Appetite, 65, 125-131.

Hernández-Macedo, M. L., Contreras-Castillo, C. J., Tsai, S. M., Da Cruz, S. H., Sarantopoulos, C. I., Padula, M., & Dias, C. T. (2011). Gases and volatile compounds associated with micro-organisms in blown pack spoilage of Brazilian vacuum-packaged beef. Letters in Applied Microbiology, 53(5), 549-557.

Hewlings, S. J., & Kalman, D. S. (2017). Curcumin: A review of its effects on human health. Foods, 6(10), 92.

Hogan, S. P., Waddell, A., & Fulkerson, P. C. (2020). Eosinophils in infection and intestinal immunity. Current Opinion in Gastroenterology, 36(1), 7-14.

Irish, L. A., Kline, C. E., Gunn, H. E., Buysse, D. J., & Hall, M. H. (2015). The role of sleep hygiene in promoting public health. Sleep Medicine Reviews, 22, 23-36.

Irwin, M. R. (2015). Why sleep is important for health: A psychoneuroimmunology perspective. Annual Review of Psychology, 66, 143-172.

Ismail, I., Hwang, Y. H., & Joo, S. T. (2020). Meat analog as future food: A review. Journal of Animal Science and Technology, 62(2), 111-120.

Izquierdo-Casas, J., Comas-Basté, O., Latorre-Moratalla, M. L., Lorente-Gascón, M., Duelo, A., Vidal-Carou, M. C., & Soler-Singla, L. (2021). Diamine oxidase (DAO) supplement reduces headache in episodic migraine patients with DAO deficiency. Clinical Nutrition, 40(4), 2160-2166.

Jarisch, R., & Weyer, D. (1999). Histamine intolerance. In Histamine intolerance in clinical practice (pp. 107-118). Thieme.

Jiménez-Colmenero, F., Ventanas, J., & Toldrá, F. (2001). Nutritional composition of dry-cured ham and its role in a healthy diet. Meat Science, 59(3), 267-278.

Johnston, C. S., & Solomon, R. E. (2007). Vitamin C status of a campus population. Journal of the American College of Nutrition, 26(4), 280-285.

Joneja, J. M. (2013). The health professional's guide to food allergies and intolerances. Academy of Nutrition and Dietetics.

Kaplan, A. P. (2004). Chronic urticaria and angioedema. New England Journal of Medicine, 346(3), 175-179.

Kennedy, D. O. (2016). B vitamins and the brain: Mechanisms, dose and efficacy. Nutrients, 8(2), 68.

Kettner, L., Sattler, J., & Elamin, A. A. (2021). Plant-based diamine oxidase supplementation in histamine intolerance. Nutrients, 13(5), 1645.

Kim, M. H., & Kim, H. (2017). The roles of glutamine in the intestine and its implication in intestinal diseases. International Journal of Molecular Sciences, 18(5), 1051.

Kofler, L., Ulmer, H., & Kofler, H. (2011). Histamine 50-skin-prick test: A tool to diagnose histamine intolerance. ISRN Allergy, 2011, 353045.

Kohn, J. B. (2014). Is there a diet for histamine intolerance? Journal of the Academy of Nutrition and Dietetics, 114(11), 1860.

Koo, H., Allan, R. N., Howlin, R. P., Stoodley, P., & Hall-Stoodley, L. (2017). Targeting microbial biofilms: Current and prospective therapeutic strategies. Nature Reviews Microbiology, 15(12), 740-755.

Lehane, L., & Olley, J. (2000). Histamine fish poisoning revisited. International Journal of Food Microbiology, 58(1-2), 1-37.

Leigh-Hunt, N., Bagguley, D., Bash, K., Turner, V., Turnbull, S., Valtorta, N., & Caan, W. (2017). An overview of systematic reviews on the public health consequences of social isolation and loneliness. Public Health, 152, 157-171.

Leurs, R., Church, M. K., & Taglialatela, M. (2009). H1-antihistamines: Inverse agonism, anti-inflammatory actions and cardiac effects. Clinical & Experimental Allergy, 32(4), 489-498.

Leurs, R., Chazot, P. L., Shenton, F. C., Lim, H. D., & de Esch, I. J. (2009). Molecular and biochemical pharmacology of the histamine H4 receptor. British Journal of Pharmacology, 157(1), 14-23.

Macht, M., & Dettmer, D. (2006). Everyday mood and emotions after eating a chocolate bar or an apple. Appetite, 46(3), 332-336.

Mahmood, A., FitzGerald, A. J., Marchbank, T., Ntatsaki, E., Murray, D., Ghosh, S., & Playford, R. J. (2007). Zinc carnosine, a health food supplement that stabilises small bowel integrity. Gut, 56(2), 168-175.

Maintz, L., Benfadal, S., Allam, J. P., Hagemann, T., Fimmers, R., & Novak, N. (2006). Evidence for a reduced histamine degradation capacity in a subgroup of patients with atopic eczema. Journal of Allergy and Clinical Immunology, 117(5), 1106-1112.

Maintz, L., & Novak, N. (2007). Histamine and histamine intolerance. American Journal of Clinical Nutrition, 85(5), 1185-1196.

Maintz, L., Schwarzer, V., Bieber, T., van der Ven, K., & Novak, N. (2006). Effects of histamine and diamine oxidase activities on pregnancy: a critical review. Human Reproduction Update, 14(5), 485-495.

Maintz, L., Yu, C. F., Rodríguez, E., Baurecht, H., Bieber, T., Illig, T., ... & Novak, N. (2011). Association of single nucleotide polymorphisms in the diamine oxidase gene with diamine oxidase serum activities. Allergy, 66(7), 893-902.

Maret, W., & Sandstead, H. H. (2006). Zinc requirements and the risks and benefits of zinc supplementation. Journal of Trace Elements in Medicine and Biology, 20(1), 3-18.

Marinangeli, C. P. F., & House, J. D. (2017). Potential impact of the digestible indispensable amino acid score as a measure of protein quality on dietary regulations and health. Nutrition Reviews, 75(8), 658-667.

McCarty, D. E., Carrubba, S., Chesson, A. L., Frilot, C., Gonzalez-Toledo, E., & Marino, A. A. (2011). Electromagnetic hypersensitivity: evidence for a novel neurological syndrome. International Journal of Neuroscience, 121(12), 670-676.

McGrath, A. P., Hilmer, K. M., Collyer, C. A., Shepard, E. M., Elmore, B. O., Brown, D. E., ... & Guss, J. M. (2009). Structure and inhibition of human diamine oxidase. Biochemistry, 48(41), 9810-9822.

McKay, D. L., & Blumberg, J. B. (2006). A review of the bioactivity and potential health benefits of chamomile tea. Phytotherapy Research, 20(7), 519-530.

Mercier, S., Villeneuve, S., Mondor, M., & Uysal, I. (2017). Time-temperature management along the food cold chain: A review of recent developments. Comprehensive Reviews in Food Science and Food Safety, 16(4), 647-667.

Miglio, C., Chiavaro, E., Visconti, A., Fogliano, V., & Pellegrini, N. (2008). Effects of different cooking methods on nutritional and physicochemical characteristics of selected vegetables. Journal of Agricultural and Food Chemistry, 56(1), 139-147.

Millqvist, E. (2021). Mechanisms of increased airway sensitivity to occupational chemicals and odors. Current Opinion in Allergy and Clinical Immunology, 21(2), 119-124.

Mittman, P. (1990). Randomized, double-blind study of freeze-dried Urtica dioica in the treatment of allergic rhinitis. Planta Medica, 56(1), 44-47.

Mlcek, J., Jurikova, T., Skrovankova, S., & Sochor, J. (2016). Quercetin and its anti-allergic immune response. Molecules, 21(5), 623.

Mokhtari, V., Afsharian, P., Shahhoseini, M., Kalantar, S. M., & Moini, A. (2017). A review on various uses of N-acetyl cysteine. Cell Journal, 19(1), 11-17.

Molderings, G. J., Brettner, S., Homann, J., & Afrin, L. B. (2011). Mast cell activation disease: a concise practical guide for diagnostic workup and therapeutic options. Journal of Hematology & Oncology, 4(1), 10.

Moore, D. R., Camera, D. M., Areta, J. L., & Hawley, J. A. (2014). Beyond muscle hypertrophy: Why dietary protein is important for endurance athletes. Applied Physiology, Nutrition, and Metabolism, 39(9), 987-997.

Mušič, E., Korošec, P., Šilar, M., Adamič, K., Košnik, M., & Rijavec, M. (2013). Serum diamine oxidase activity as a diagnostic test for histamine intolerance. Wiener Klinische Wochenschrift, 125(9-10), 239-243.

Nalbandian, A., Sehgal, K., Gupta, A., Madhavan, M. V., McGroder, C., Stevens, J. S., ... & Wan, E. Y. (2021). Post-acute COVID-19 syndrome. Nature Medicine, 27(4), 601-615.

Niland, B., & Cash, B. D. (2018). Health benefits and adverse effects of a gluten-free diet in non-celiac disease patients. Gastroenterology & Hepatology, 14(2), 82-91.

Pascoe, M. C., Thompson, D. R., & Ski, C. F. (2017). Yoga, mindfulness-based stress reduction and stress-related physiological measures. Psychoneuroendocrinology, 86, 152-168.

Patil, B. S., Pike, L. M., & Yoo, K. S. (2004). Variation in the quercetin content in different colored onions. Journal of the American Society for Horticultural Science, 120(6), 909-913.

Pessione, E. (2012). Lactic acid bacteria contribution to gut microbiota complexity. The Microbiology Research, 67(6), 767-778.

Peters-Golden, M., & Henderson, W. R. (2007). Leukotrienes. New England Journal of Medicine, 357(18), 1841-1854.

Picard, M., & McEwen, B. S. (2018). Psychological stress and mitochondria: a systematic review. Psychosomatic Medicine, 80(2), 141-153.

Pimentel, M., Saad, R. J., Long, M. D., & Rao, S. S. (2020). ACG clinical guideline: small intestinal bacterial overgrowth. American Journal of Gastroenterology, 115(2), 165-178.

Pizzino, G., Irrera, N., Cucinotta, M., Pallio, G., Mannino, F., Arcoraci, V., ... & Squadrito, F. (2017). Oxidative stress: harms and benefits for human health. Oxidative Medicine and Cellular Longevity, 2017, 8416763.

Preuss, C. V., Wood, T. C., Szumlanski, C. L., Raftogianis, R. B., Otterness, D. M., Girard, B., ... & Weinshilboum, R. M. (1998). Human histamine N-methyltransferase pharmacogenetics: common genetic polymorphisms that alter activity. Molecular Pharmacology, 53(4), 708-717.

Raithel, M., Küfner, M., Ulrich, P., & Hahn, E. G. (2010). The involvement of the histamine degradation pathway by diamine oxidase in manifest gastrointestinal allergy. Inflammation Research, 59(Suppl 2), S219-S221.

Raithel, M., Weidenhiller, M., Hagel, A. F., Hetterich, U., Neurath, M. F., & Konturek, P. C. (2013). The malabsorption of commonly occurring mono and disaccharides: levels of investigation and differential diagnoses. Deutsches Ärzteblatt International, 110(46), 775-782.

Raj, S. R. (2013). Postural tachycardia syndrome (POTS). Circulation, 127(23), 2336-2342.

Raj, S. R., Guzman, J. C., Harvey, P., Richer, L., Schondorf, R., Seifer, C., Thibodeau-Jarry, N., Sheldon, R. S., & Rose, M. S. (2012). Canadian Cardiovascular Society position statement on postural orthostatic tachycardia syndrome and related disorders. Canadian Journal of Cardiology, 28(4), 397-409.

Raknes, G., Småbrekke, L., & Kristoffersen, M. (2018). Low dose naltrexone: Effects on medication use in patients with autoimmune diseases. Pharmacoepidemiology and Drug Safety, 27(9), 1031-1038.

Raynor, H. A., & Epstein, L. H. (2001). Dietary variety, energy regulation, and obesity. Psychological Bulletin, 127(3), 325-341.

Reese, I., Ballmer-Weber, B., Beyer, K., Fuchs, T., Kleine-Tebbe, J., Klimek, L., Lepp, U., Niggemann, B., Saloga, J., Schäfer, C., Werfel, T., Zuberbier, T., & Worm, M. (2018). German guideline for the management of adverse reactions to ingested histamine. Allergo Journal International, 27(2), 51-61.

Reker, D., Blum, S. M., Steiger, C., Anger, K. E., Sommer, J. M., Fanikos, J., & Traverso, G. (2019). Inactive ingredients in oral medications. Science Translational Medicine, 11(483), eaau6753.

Riva, A., Ronchi, M., Petrangolini, G., Bosisio, S., & Allegrini, P. (2019). Improved oral absorption of quercetin from quercetin phytosome. European Journal of Drug Metabolism and Pharmacokinetics, 44(2), 169-177.

Rohdewald, P. (2002). A review of the French maritime pine bark extract, pycnogenol. Journal of Pharmacological Research, 46(5), 357-366.

Roschek, B., Fink, R. C., McMichael, M., & Alberte, R. S. (2009). Nettle extract inhibits multiple pro-inflammatory pathways. Journal of Ethnopharmacology, 122(2), 257-263.

Sahin, S. (2015). Advances in deep-fat frying of foods. CRC Press.

Sánchez-Pérez, S., Comas-Basté, O., Rabell-González, J., Veciana-Nogués, M. T., Latorre-Moratalla, M. L., & Vidal-Carou, M. C. (2018). Biogenic amines in plant-origin foods: Are they frequently underestimated in low-histamine diets? Foods, 7(12), 205.

Sattler, J., Häfner, D., Klotter, H. J., Lorenz, W., & Wagner, P. K. (1988). Food-induced histaminosis as an epidemiological problem: plasma histamine elevation and haemodynamic alterations after oral histamine administration and blockade of diamine oxidase (DAO). Agents and Actions, 23(3-4), 361-365.

Schnedl, W. J., Lackner, S., Enko, D., Schenk, M., Holasek, S. J., & Mangge, H. (2019). Evaluation of symptoms and symptom combinations in histamine intolerance. Intestinal Research, 17(3), 427-433.

Schubert, M. L. (2009). Gastric secretion. Current Opinion in Gastroenterology, 25(6), 529-535.

Schwelberger, H. G. (2010). Histamine N-methyltransferase (HNMT) enzyme and gene. In R. Thurmond (Ed.), Histamine in inflammation (pp. 53-59). Springer.

Seneviratne, S. L., Maitland, A., & Afrin, L. B. (2017). Mast cell disorders in Ehlers-Danlos syndrome. American Journal of Medical Genetics Part C: Seminars in Medical Genetics, 175(1), 226-236.

Serhan, C. N., Chiang, N., & Dalli, J. (2015). The resolution code of acute inflammation. British Journal of Pharmacology, 172(20), 4475-4486.

Shoba, G., Joy, D., Joseph, T., Majeed, M., Rajendran, R., & Srinivas, P. S. (1998). Influence of piperine on the pharmacokinetics of curcumin in animals and human volunteers. Planta Medica, 64(4), 353-356.

Singh, R. P., & Heldman, D. R. (2014). Introduction to food engineering (5th ed.). Academic Press.

Skaper, S. D., Facci, L., Fusco, M., Della Valle, M. F., Zusso, M., Costa, B., & Giusti, P. (2014). Palmitoylethanolamide, a naturally occurring disease-modifying agent in neuropathic pain. Inflammopharmacology, 22(2), 79-94.

Skrovanek, S., DiGuilio, K., Bailey, R., Huntington, W., Urbas, R., Mayow, B., Mulinix, G., & Goode, R. (2014). Zinc and gastrointestinal disease. World Journal of Gastrointestinal Pathophysiology, 5(4), 496-513.

Sowerby, L., Dewan, K., Gronseth, E., Lund, V., Anzivino, R., & Nunez, D. A. (2023). Self-reported antihistamine use amongst long-COVID sufferers. American Journal of Otolaryngology, 44(1), 103680.

Southwick, S. M., Bonanno, G. A., Masten, A. S., Panter-Brick, C., & Yehuda, R. (2014). Resilience definitions, theory, and challenges. European Journal of Psychotraumatology, 5, 25338.

Steinhoff, M., Schauber, J., & Leyden, J. J. (2013). New insights into rosacea pathophysiology: a review of recent findings. Journal of the American Academy of Dermatology, 69(6), S15-S26.

Swain, A. R., Dutton, S. P., & Truswell, A. S. (1985). Salicylates in foods. Journal of the American Dietetic Association, 85(8), 950-960.

Theoharides, T. C. (2020). COVID-19, pulmonary mast cells, cytokine storms, and beneficial actions of luteolin. BioFactors, 46(3), 306-308.

Theoharides, T. C., Alysandratos, K. D., Angelidou, A., Delivanis, D. A., Sismanopoulos, N., Zhang, B., Asadi, S., Vasiadi, M., Weng, Z., Miniati, A., & Kalogeromitros, D. (2012). Mast cells and inflammation. Biochimica et Biophysica Acta, 1822(1), 21-33.

Theoharides, T. C., Asadi, S., & Patel, A. B. (2015). Luteolin as a therapeutic option for multiple disorders. Biofactors, 41(5), 373-377.

Theoharides, T. C., Stewart, J. M., Hatziagelaki, E., & Kolaitis, G. (2020). Quercetin for mast cell activation and COVID-19. Biofactors, 46(6), 892-900.

Theoharides, T. C., Valent, P., & Akin, C. (2012). Mast cells, mastocytosis, and related disorders. New England Journal of Medicine, 373(2), 163-172.

Thomson, C. A., Ho, E., & Strom, M. B. (2017). Chemopreventive properties of 3,3'-diindolylmethane in breast cancer. Carcinogenesis, 37(7), 643-651.

Thrasher, J. D., & Hooper, D. (2005). Indoor environmental exposures and health effects. International Journal of Hygiene and Environmental Health, 208(1-2), 1-13.

Tiligada, E., Kyriakidis, K., Chazot, P. L., & Passani, M. B. (2011). Histamine pharmacology and new CNS drug targets. CNS Neuroscience & Therapeutics, 17(6), 620-628.

Trigueros, L., Peña, S., Ugidos, A. V., Sayas-Barberá, E., Pérez-Álvarez, J. A., & Sendra, E. (2021). Food ingredients as important sources of functional bioactive peptides. Food & Function, 12(9), 3655-3670.

Valent, P., Akin, C., Escribano, L., Födinger, M., Hartmann, K., Brockow, K., ... & Metcalfe, D. D. (2012). Standards and standardization in mastocytosis: consensus statements on diagnostics, treatment recommendations and response criteria. European Journal of Clinical Investigation, 37(6), 435-453.

Vega-Gálvez, A., Miranda, M., Vergara, J., Uribe, E., Puente, L., & Martínez, E. A. (2010). Nutrition facts and functional potential of quinoa, an ancient Andean grain. Journal of the Science of Food and Agriculture, 90(15), 2541-2547.

Visciano, P., Schirone, M., Tofalo, R., & Suzzi, G. (2012). Histamine poisoning and control measures in fish and fishery products. Frontiers in Microbiology, 3, 188.

Wantke, F., Götz, M., & Jarisch, R. (1994). Histamine-free diet: treatment of choice for histamine-induced food intolerance and supporting treatment for chronic headaches. Clinical & Experimental Allergy, 23(12), 982-985.

Wantke, F., Götz, M., & Jarisch, R. (1998). The red wine provocation test: Intolerance to histamine as a model for food intolerance. Allergy Proceedings, 19(1), 27-32.

Weinstock, L. B., Brook, J. B., Walters, A. S., Goris, A., Afrin, L. B., & Molderings, G. J. (2021). Mast cell activation symptoms are prevalent in Long-COVID. International Journal of Infectious Diseases, 112, 217-226.

Weng, Z., Zhang, B., Asadi, S., Sismanopoulos, N., Butcher, A., Fu, X., ... & Theoharides, T. C. (2012). Quercetin is more effective than cromolyn in blocking human mast cell cytokine release and inhibits contact dermatitis and photosensitivity in humans. PloS One, 7(3), e33805.

Wilson, D., Evans, M., Guthrie, N., Sharma, P., Baisley, J., Schonlau, F., & Burki, C. (2010). A randomized, double-blind, placebo-controlled exploratory study to evaluate the potential of pycnogenol for improving allergic rhinitis symptoms. Phytotherapy Research, 24(8), 1115-1119.

Wood, W., & Neal, D. T. (2007). A new look at habits and the habit-goal interface. Psychological Review, 114(4), 843-863.

Zaitsu, M., Narita, S., Lambert, K. C., Grady, J. J., Estes, D. M., Curran, E. M., ... & Rudders, R. A. (2007). Estradiol activates mast cells via a non-genomic estrogen receptor-α and calcium influx. Molecular Immunology, 44(8), 1977-1985.

Printed in Dunstable, United Kingdom

79172408R00232